BETRAYAL

★ ★ ★ ★ ★ ★ ★ ★ ★

at LITTLE GIBRALTAR

A German Fortress, a Treacherous

American General, and

the Battle to End World War I

WILLIAM WALKER

SCRIBNER

New York   London   Toronto   Sydney   New Delhi

30772 21/8

R

SCRIBNER

An Imprint of Simon & Schuster, Inc.
1230 Avenue of the Americas
New York, NY 10020

First Scribner hardcover edition May 2016

SCRIBNER and design are registered trademarks of The Gale Group, Inc.,
used under license by Simon & Schuster, Inc., the publisher of this work.

For information about special discounts for bulk purchases, please contact
Simon & Schuster Special Sales at 1-866-506-1949 or business@simonandschuster.com.

The Simon & Schuster Speakers Bureau can bring authors to your live event.
For more information or to book an event, contact the Simon & Schuster
Speakers Bureau at 1-866-248-3049 or visit our website at www.simonspeakers.com.

Interior design by Kyle Kabel

Manufactured in the United States of America

1   3   5   7   9   10   8   6   4   2

Library of Congress Cataloging-in-Publication Data

Names: Walker, William T., Jr., author.
Title: Betrayal at Little Gibraltar : a German fortress, a treacherous
American general, and the battle to end World War I / William T. Walker.
Description: First Scribner hardcover edition. | New York : Scribner, 2016.
Includes bibliographical references and index.
Identifiers: LCCN 2015044665
Subjects: LCSH: Argonne, Battle of the, France, 1918. | World War,
1914–1918—Campaigns—Meuse River Valley. | Montfaucon (Meuse, France)—
History, Military—20th century. | United States. Army. Infantry Division, 79th—
History—World War, 1914–1918. | Bullard, Robert Lee, 1861–1947—Military
leadership.
Classification: LCC D545.A63 W35 2016 | DDC 940.4/36—dc23
LC record available at http://lccn.loc.gov/2015044665

ISBN 978-1-5011-1789-3
ISBN 978-1-5011-1792-3 (ebook)

Some material in chapters 18, 19, and 20 appeared previously in my essay "The
Chance of a Miracle at Montfaucon," in Edward Lengel's *A Companion to the
Meuse-Argonne Campaign*, with permission of the publisher, John Wiley & Sons, Inc.

For my wife, Jan; my daughter, Lara; and in memory of my great-uncle, Corporal Richard J. Dickson, 30th Division, USA, killed in action at Bellicourt, France, September 29, 1918

The first casualty when war comes is truth.

—Hiram W. Johnson,
US senator, 1917

Propaganda and Censorship, indispensable if rather ghastly, created a popular version of what happened that was sometimes simply a fable agreed on.

—Thomas Johnson,
World War I correspondent, 1928

Truth is the daughter of time, not of authority.

—Sir Francis Bacon,
English statesman, ca. 1620

CONTENTS

Yanks from "Baltimore's Own" Regiment discovered that advancing over open ground against German fortifications was a dangerous proposition. More than 122,000 Yanks were wounded or killed in the Meuse-Argonne Offensive, making it the bloodiest battle in American history.

PROLOGUE Words Tongued with Fire   xi

PART I
THE STAKES

CHAPTER 1 "Horrors from the Abyss"   3

               Major Harry Parkin's Affidavit   15

CHAPTER 2 Little Gibraltar of the Western Front   19

CHAPTER 3 "Do You Wish to Take Part in the Battle?"   37

CHAPTER 4 "This Appalling Proposition"   57

CHAPTER 5 "Feeling Like Crusaders"   73

CHAPTER 6 Training for Disaster   89

CHAPTER 7 "An Ominous, Dread-Inspiring Place"   107

PART II

BATTLE AND BETRAYAL

CHAPTER 8 Toward Montfaucon and into a Trap 129

CHAPTER 9 "The 79th Is Holding Up the Entire
First Army" 147

CHAPTER 10 "Bayonet and Rifle Butt, Pistol
and Trench Knife" 163

CHAPTER 11 "All America Is Behind Us" 187

CHAPTER 12 "Regardless of Cost" 201

CHAPTER 13 The Cost of "Regardless" 215

CHAPTER 14 Relief and Disgrace 229

CHAPTER 15 Into the Cyclone . . . Once Again 243

CHAPTER 16 Redemption on Corn Willy Hill 265

CHAPTER 17 Making Good . . . at Last 285

PART III

THE WAR AFTER THE WAR

CHAPTER 18 Controlling the Narrative 305

CHAPTER 19 Bullard, Bjornstad, and Booth 323

CHAPTER 20 Betrayal at Little Gibraltar 343

CHAPTER 21 *Denkmal*: Remembering the Doughboys 365

EPILOGUE "Some Could, Some Could Not,
Shake Off Misery" 379

Appendix 389
Acknowledgments 391
Notes 395
Bibliography 417
Photograph Credits 431
Index 433

WORDS TONGUED WITH FIRE

W inters are seldom kind in central Pennsylvania. Around Thanksgiving, snow surges out of the Alleghenies to cover the battlefields of Gettysburg. The landscape, full and lush in other seasons, assumes a pallor befitting the deaths that hallowed the fields surrounding the town and Gettysburg College.

On such a bleak winter's day in 1993, I entered the college library and first encountered the marginalia that would change my life. Searching for information about my great-uncle who had been killed in World War I, I picked up an old book entitled *The American Army in France, 1917–1919*, by General James Harbord.[1] After blowing dust from the cover and leafing through the volume, I began to notice marginalia inscribed and signed by the book's late owner, Major Harry D. Parkin. The veteran was a member of the US 79th Division that had fought to bring the war to an end in the Meuse-Argonne Offensive. The major had helped lead the assault to capture the butte of Montfaucon, site of a top-secret German observatory protected by an underground fortress. In several places, Parkin's marginalia took issue with the book's conclusions about the attack, and he challenged readers to turn to the back of the volume to learn the truth.

On two empty pages in the rear, Parkin wrote that Robert L. Bullard—one of John J. Pershing's senior generals—failed to support the attack on Montfaucon, a deliberate act that caused the deaths of many American soldiers. For an instant, I felt like the innocent passerby accosted by Coleridge's Ancient Mariner. Just like the poem's compulsive raconteur, Harry Parkin had grabbed my arm and revealed a harrowing tale.

For the next few weeks, I tried to push the story from my mind. As a student of military history, I knew full well the misleading lore of old soldiers, men whose lives had often reached a zenith in battle and who thereafter embroidered their tales with extra measures of meaning. I also understood that the "fog of war"— the profound confusion of combat—often distorts judgment. The psychological murk creates ideal conditions for imputed motives, ungenerous characterizations, ignoble conclusions. Surely, I reasoned, Parkin was mistaken: No American general would refuse to assist his fellow soldiers. I was skeptical of Parkin's charge.

As interesting as the matter was, I resisted delving into it for several months, but I was finally forced to acknowledge that the story intrigued me. To disprove Parkin's charge so that I could put aside the issue, I set a demanding test. I would look into Pershing's memoir to see if the incident was mentioned. The American commander was notoriously reticent to acknowledge problems, and if he discussed the incident, the marginalia might warrant further investigation.

Searching Pershing's *My Experiences in the World War*, I found a brief description of the attack on Montfaucon, a fortress known as the Little Gibraltar of the Western Front in honor of the impregnable British citadel guarding the Mediterranean Sea. To my astonishment, Pershing wrote that a "misinterpretation of orders" had resulted in the failure to capture the Mount of the Falcon on the critical first day of battle. For Pershing—who had pledged not to cast blame in his memoir—the gentle reproof was telling. I was hooked.

In the twenty years since my discovery of Parkin's marginalia, I pursued the tale with all the vigor I could muster. I became acquainted with the dust of archives; haunted old bookstores in search of critical volumes; interviewed sons and grandsons of soldiers killed in France; stood in the trenches of the Hindenburg Line; and even descended into the dank bunkers of Montfaucon where light never shines. Seldom did I encounter a blind alley.

On the few occasions when my search seemed stalled, the timely discovery of new evidence propelled my investigation forward.

Eventually these discoveries enabled me to determine the truth about the 79th Division, to solve the mystery of Montfaucon, and to demonstrate that long-forgotten marginalia can prove T. S. Eliot's proposition that "The communication / Of the dead is tongued with fire beyond the language of the living."[2]

—William Walker
Staunton, Virginia, 2016

On the first anniversary of the US declaration of war—April 6, 1918—raw recruits of the 79th Division paraded in front of President Woodrow Wilson and enthusiastic crowds in Baltimore, as pictured in the *New York Times*. Five short months later, the inexperienced men were ordered to capture the most formidable enemy position in France, the Little Gibraltar of the Western Front.

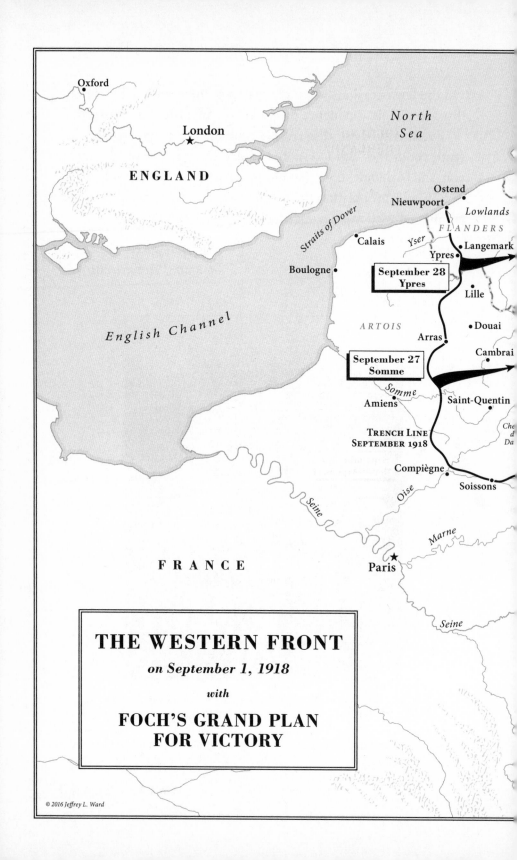

Oxford

North
Sea

London

ENGLAND

Ostend
Nieuwpoort
Lowlands
FLANDERS
Calais   *Yser*   Langemark
Ypres
Boulogne

**September 28
Ypres**

Straits of Dover

Lille

English Channel

ARTOIS   Douai
Arras
Cambrai

**September 27
Somme**

Somme
Amiens   Saint-Quentin

*Che
d
Da*

TRENCH LINE
SEPTEMBER 1918

Compiègne
Oise   Soissons

Seine

Marne

FRANCE   ★ Paris

Seine

THE WESTERN FRONT

on September 1, 1918

with

FOCH'S GRAND PLAN
FOR VICTORY

© 2016 Jeffrey L. Ward

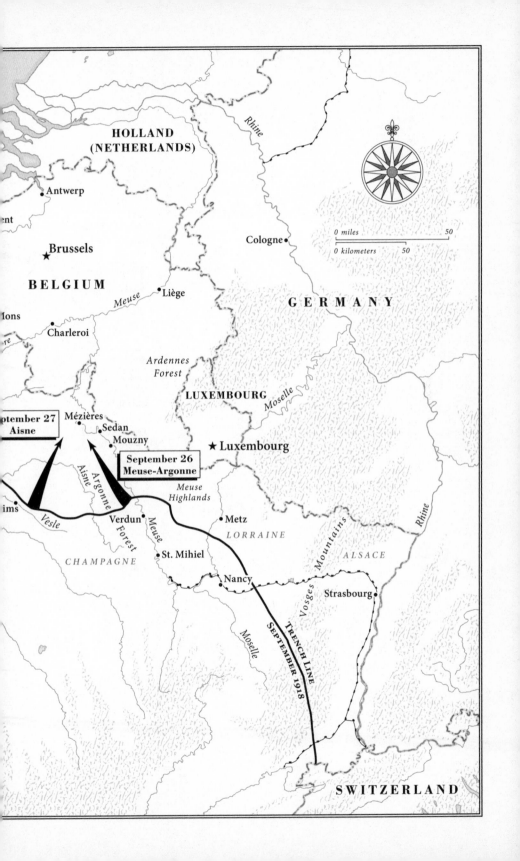

PART I

THE STAKES

The ruins of the French hilltop village of Montfaucon created an impregnable fortress dubbed the Little Gibraltar of the Western Front. Yet the least experienced division in General Pershing's army would be assigned the demanding task of capturing the butte and its top-secret observatory.

CHAPTER I

"HORRORS FROM THE ABYSS"

Among a group of fellow veterans, retired Major Harry Parkin (in uniform) was honored in 1924 by Secretary of War John Weeks with the Distinguished Service Cross for valor atop the French mount that the Americans dubbed "Corn Willy Hill." Parkin's battalion was the first to reach the crest of the shell-torn ridge after a vicious fight. He would be haunted by his war experiences for the rest of his life.

★   ★   ★

I'm back again from hell
With loathsome thoughts to sell;
Secrets of death to tell;
And horrors from the abyss.

—Captain Siegfried Sassoon,
Royal Army, 1917[1]

N o one knew the cause of Harry Parkin's black moods. There was speculation, of course, that the retired major's memories of the trenches were the source. Friends supposed that the stimulus could be something as innocuous as an automobile backfire, a whiff of pungent Burgundy, a newspaper article about a long-forgotten battle, or a face on a street resembling that of a dead comrade.

Whatever the cause, the result was invariable. Harry would ride the streetcar to downtown Los Angeles, take the Angels Flight tram railway down Bunker Hill, ascend to his office high in the Fay Building, and close the door. The grand view of the metropolitan building boom could be captivating, but it soon became apparent that the land developer did not pass his days sighting plots for new homes. Instead, his mind was plumbing a battlefield abyss. Up welled images of a young soldier clutching his eyeball in a muddy palm, a German shell atomizing an officer into a red mist, and ghostly phosgene gas insinuating its way along a winding trench. And always accompanying the scenes was the staccato clatter of Maxim machine guns echoing from Montfaucon.

Whatever shape war's horror assumed, it gnawed deep into Harry's brain, a fierce bite of angst that tightened as years wore on. For a time, Parkin was able to blot out the disturbing visions by retreating to his home study and downing enough Scotch to induce stuporous sleep. But well into the 1930s, as battlefield memories faded to obscurity for most war veterans, Harry's family noted that he was drinking more heavily. It was clear that the former infantry officer had become a living member of the lost generation.

When two or three nights of alcohol failed to muzzle the "black dog," Harry would pack a bag, grab a book, and catch the Red Car interurban from Los Angeles down to the seaside town of Balboa. Business success had accompanied the stocky, ruddy-faced Parkin as he pursued the geographic cure from his native Pittsburgh to Southern California. Leaving the sooty Steel City for the land of perpetual sunlight lifted Harry's mood for a time, especially as his dream of real estate development prospered. Parkin quickly made enough money to purchase a spacious house in an upscale neighborhood just south of the Hollywood Hills, and he and his wife, Alice, also took a modest bungalow in Balboa as a retreat. The house was near the ocean, and waves drowned the murmurs of memory. For a time, Harry appeared to forget about France. But in 1935 when Parkin attended a regimental reunion back East, a heightened sense of dread dogged him back to the coast. Harry's family reluctantly concluded that he would never again enjoy a good day.[2]

Once the site of gatherings filled with laughter, the Balboa house became a solitary retreat where Harry wrestled his demons. That's the way it was on September 14, 1936, as the late summer sun lifted the temperature to a perfect 72 degrees. The weather was ideal, but the major's mood was grim. It was nearing the eighteenth anniversary of his leap into no-man's-land, and the anger of Harry's memories had been stoked by misleading remarks in the memoir of General James G. Harbord, a close friend of American Expeditionary Forces Commander in Chief John J. Pershing. The book, *The American Army in France, 1917–1919*, was one of a large collection that Parkin had mustered in an attempt to understand his battlefield experience. Harbord's analysis of the AEF provided an interesting diversion for Parkin until he read a discussion of the plan for the Meuse-Argonne Offensive, an operation the Allies hoped would end the Great War. The retired major had helped lead the massive campaign as a battalion commander of the 79th Division, a unit that suffered heavy casualties in the first days of combat.

Although the 79th was inexperienced in fighting and filled with undertrained draftees, the division had been assigned the most difficult task of the attack, capturing the hilltop fortress of Montfaucon. Widely known as the Little Gibraltar of the Western Front, the limestone butte in northeastern France disguised a secret German observation post that could direct artillery fire on American soldiers anywhere across the twenty-four-mile-wide battlefront. To protect this valuable asset, the enemy had fortified the hill with hundreds of machine-gun nests and artillery emplacements connected by a network of tunnels. To eliminate the hostile observation directing German guns, AEF planners deemed it imperative that Montfaucon be captured on the first day of battle.

As Harry continued reading about preparations for the offensive, his eyes fell on an exceptionally inflammatory passage. General Harbord described in matter-of-fact terms the logic— actually, the *illogic*—used to assign the nine American assault divisions to their respective sectors of the front.

"The battle order was not based on any particular fitness of a division for the duty expected of it. Each took its turn," wrote Harbord. "The most distant and perhaps most difficult objective in this attack was given the 79th, which had never been under fire. But such things had to be."[3]

The excuse that "such things had to be" infuriated Parkin. The passivity of the statement was anathema to any competent military officer. Every commander knew that on a battlefield, nothing, absolutely *nothing*, "had to be." In Officers Training School, each candidate learned that he was responsible for detecting and correcting defects of a plan, anticipating the unexpected, and meeting every circumstance. When midcareer officers attended the US Army Staff College in Fort Leavenworth, Kansas, they were taught to analyze plans and orders thoroughly, identify weaknesses, and develop alternatives for consideration by senior officers. At any level of military command, an excuse as flimsy as "such things had to be" would be greeted with derision; coming from a senior general like Harbord, the remark was inexcusable.

After reading the offending sentence, Parkin could stomach no more. He picked up a pen and dashed off a refutation of Harbord's excuse in the margin of the page: "This was poor staff work. Veteran 4th Division should have done this job."[4] The 4th Division had arrived in France months before the 79th and earned battle ribbons reversing the desperate German spring offensives of 1918. Its veterans had developed reputations as skilled, resourceful soldiers who could defeat the kaiser's toughest men, even the feared *Stosstruppen*—storm troopers. By contrast, the 79th had arrived in France only two months before the Meuse-Argonne Offensive was to begin on September 26, and had completed less than six weeks of the prescribed twelve weeks of combat training. Fifty percent of the 79th's men had been in the army less than four months; some had never even fired their rifles before landing in France.

Surely the battle-tested 4th, thought Parkin, had been better prepared to lead the dangerous attack on Montfaucon. For some reason, however, the veteran unit was assigned a much easier sector just to the right of the staunchly defended zone faced by the 79th. In an arrangement that complicated cooperation between the two divisions, the 4th was part of another army corps, III Corps, commanded by General Robert L. Bullard. As Parkin read the name of the tough Alabama general in the book, it brought to mind a disturbing story he had heard at the recent regimental reunion.

The story came from an unimpeachable source: Lieutenant Samuel O. Wright, who had been the chaplain of Parkin's regiment. Nearly two decades after the war, he still had the gaunt look of a soldier who had spent too much time at the front. Tall and thin, Wright was a counterpoint to Parkin, who had gained some postwar pounds. Despite their disparate appearances, the two officers "had seen the days," as the Irish say: they were brothers grappling with a common battlefield experience.

The compulsion to talk with like-minded comrades drew many

veterans to reunions, which were usually laborious affairs. After the final speeches touting sacrifice and glory, after endless toasts to declining leaders and dead heroes, after men with wives had drifted off to bed, serious comrades like Parkin and Wright huddled in small groups to exhume painful memories—in hopes of burying them forever. For the retired major, the most disturbing was the bloody assault on Montfaucon. Everything seemed to go wrong for the 79th Division, which had come up short. Despite years of searching, Parkin had discovered no reasonable explanation for his division's failure to capture the butte and its key observatory on the first day of battle. He rejected the notion that the fault lay in his soldiers' lack of aggressiveness, nor could he accept the conclusion of some experts that the officers lacked proper leadership skills. Above all, he grieved the loss of hundreds of his men.

Parkin's guilt must have been palpable to the veteran minister, who offered solace in the form of a story. Wright had stayed in the army after the Armistice, and he had met a colonel who had served in the 4th Division during the attack on Little Gibraltar. The colonel told the chaplain that on the first day of battle, his unit surged well beyond Montfaucon, but he grew concerned about the 79th when he heard the sound of heavy fighting in front of the butte. Because the 4th Division had suffered few casualties advancing in its easy sector, the officer proposed assisting the 79th by sending some of his troops to take Montfaucon from the rear. To do so, however, the colonel was required to secure the permission of his corps commander, General Robert L. Bullard. Bullard angrily replied that he was not going to help General George H. Cameron, the 79th's corps commander, "win any battle laurels."[5] Because of the rivalry between two generals, Wright concluded, the 4th Division charged ahead, leaving soldiers of the 79th to be slaughtered in an unsupported attack against Montfaucon.

Parkin was enraged by the betrayal at the heart of the chaplain's tale. After some reflection, however, he came to understand that the story offered a certain degree of comfort—if not absolution.

It explained the difficulty the 79th had encountered and reassured him that there had been factors at play beyond his control. Above all, the story exposed a villain. From his reading, Parkin knew that Bullard was well suited to the role. The stern West Pointer had established a reputation as a tough taskmaster, who drove his troops without regard for comfort or safety. As a result of his hard charging, Bullard's corps had advanced farther than any other American unit on the first day of the Meuse-Argonne Offensive, a standard of military success trumpeted by front pages across America. Subsequently, Pershing promoted Bullard to lead the Second US Army, a command carrying the three stars of a lieutenant general. He was one of only two officers to earn that rank during the war, and returned home in triumph. The commander of Parkin's V Corps, General Cameron, was demoted and shipped back to the States on a slow boat to disgrace.

On Parkin's train trip home from the reunion, he concluded that Wright's narrative had the ring of truth. Harry was convinced of the chaplain's honesty, and the anonymous colonel from the 4th Division who related the story to Wright had no incentive to lie. In fact, just the opposite. Most officers wanted to protect the reputations of the units in which they had served, but the colonel's story seemed to expose the 4th's culpability. As one who had studied law at Harvard, Parkin realized that eighteen years after the event, it would be difficult to prove Bullard's treachery. But he burned to do so.

At home in Los Angeles, the retired major had only one volume in his extensive library that mentioned the incident Wright described. It was the wartime memoir of Pershing, who after the Armistice had grown reticent to criticize any American comrade-in-arms. But in discussing the initial day of the Meuse-Argonne Offensive, the commanding general noted that the 4th Division had moved quickly forward, and "its left [flank] was more than a mile beyond Montfaucon, but through some misinterpretation of the orders by the III Corps [Bullard's command] the opportunity to capture Montfaucon that day was lost."[6]

The former AEF commander softened this rare rebuke by omitting the name of the officer who had "misinterpreted" the orders. But Pershing's language conveyed the clear implication that the 4th Division *had* been ordered to assist the capture of Little Gibraltar. This tantalizing hint spurred Harry to pursue the matter, but AEF records were still classified. As a retired officer, Parkin had no recourse, and once again, he tried to push the haunting event from his mind. His family noted, however, that when Bullard's name came up in conversation, there was a palpable but silent anger emanating from Harry. The family learned to change the topic quickly to restore equanimity to dinner-table discussions.[7]

As Harry read Harbord's book on that late summer day in Balboa, however, his anger flashed anew. After dashing off marginalia to refute the author's comments on planning, Parkin decided that he had waited long enough. He felt compelled to record his views in full. Near a section describing the plan of attack, he scribbled, "Jealousy between corps commanders prevented this plan from being carried out. *See Page 632* of this book for explanation."[8]

Harry turned to blank pages at the end of the volume, where he inscribed an affidavit—more precisely, an indictment. [See pages 15 to 17.] Using legal standards he had learned at Harvard University, the major related Chaplain Wright's story in detail, complete with a sketch illustrating where the 79th and 4th Divisions were during the battle and how the veteran unit was well positioned to help capture the butte from the rear. In keeping with forensic style, most of Parkin's narrative is direct and dispassionate. But toward the end of the two-page note, his rage flares up: "Bullard received all the high military decorations of America, France, England and Belgium. What he deserved was a long term in military prison for deliberately murdering hundreds of American soldiers."[9] Harry then signed, dated, and recorded the city in which his affidavit was composed, exactly as his legal training dictated.

Although Chaplain Wright had intended his story to be a palliative, it became the toxic touchstone of Parkin's life. Harry recognized that there was scant evidence to prove the accusation of the colonel who had related the incident to Chaplain Wright. And aside from the oblique passage in Pershing's memoir, the tale was based entirely on hearsay inadmissible in any court. But that did not keep the major from turning over the facts obsessively, again and again. As alcohol became Harry's sole companion, he devoted the remaining years of his life to a fruitless quest to solve the mystery of Montfaucon.

Sequestered in his study, Harry Parkin would have been astounded to learn that less than a mile away in Los Angeles, another retired army officer was wrestling with the same dark issue. Unlike Parkin, Major General Ewing E. Booth thought he knew who had caused the debacle at Little Gibraltar. And he had spent much of the last decade and a half assembling evidence to prove that the incident involved deliberate disobedience to orders, as well as a refusal to help American soldiers in danger on the battlefield.

Although the retired general had enjoyed an impressive military career, his slight build and quiet manner did not automatically confer on him what the army calls "command presence": the charismatic attributes of a confident and assertive leader. During the war, most soldiers towered over Booth's slim frame and stooped shoulders, but the wiry, plainspoken officer had a mental toughness that attracted the attention of superiors and inspired the respect of subordinates. As an unassuming brigade commander in the 4th Division, Booth won numerous citations, a full complement of decorations, and the bright stars of a brigadier general. He was a man who pursued each objective with dogged determination, never, however, to the detriment of his men.

Booth's affinity for common soldiers had been acquired the hard way. As a young man from a poor family, he lacked the resources to attend college and the political connections for appointment to West Point. Seeking another course of advancement, he enlisted as a private in the Colorado National Guard in 1893; outstanding performance earned him a second lieutenant's commission just three years later.[10] Months of sleeping on the ground gave Booth the indelible perspective of an enlisted man, along with valuable insights that served him well in the Spanish-American War, Mexican border fighting, and World War I. Of all Pershing's commanders, he most merited the sobriquet of "a soldier's general."

Like many other officers, Booth reassumed his lower permanent rank after the Armistice. As a colonel, he was assigned to the prestigious Staff College. Helping teach the next generation of senior army officers was an enjoyable task, and Booth began to put the war behind him. But one day in the fall of 1920, the colonel got wind of a disturbing statement made by General Hugh Drum, a widely respected officer who headed the college. Discussing the Meuse-Argonne Offensive, the general had declared that "had the Third Corps [Bullard's command] assisted the Fifth Corps [Cameron's command] by turning Montfaucon the results of the battle would have been a much more glorious victory for the American Army."[11] That frank judgment sent reverberations through an already shaky army establishment. In the early 1920s, cutting military budgets was capital sport on Capitol Hill, as congressmen clamored to eliminate unpopular war taxes and return the country to "normalcy." As Pershing battled Congress for every dollar, negative publicity about battlefield disputes was the last thing the army chief of staff wanted.

So Pershing quietly quashed the nascent Montfaucon controversy, just as he had other unsettling issues. The matter quickly was swept under the army's ample carpet to protect the pride of participants and the budget of the service. Worried parties were assured that no one's reputation would be tarnished.[12] Booth, however, was wise enough to realize that such a superficial resolution would not end the affair. Official histories of the war were then being written, and self-serving memoirs were in preparation; both were likely to enflame the controversy. The farsighted colonel understood that the honor of the 4th and the 79th Divisions, their respective commanders, and their soldiers lay entangled around the rocky butte in northeastern France.

Among the numerous ambiguities of World War I, the attack on Montfaucon has received scant attention, due to Pershing's success in dampening internal debate about the matter during the 1920s. The stakes to military reputations were high, because the failure to capture the enemy observation post had almost doomed the Meuse-Argonne Offensive. The one-day delay gave the Germans just enough time to rush reinforcements to the area, fight the offensive to a standstill, and preclude any possibility of a breakthrough that could have ended the war. During the next month, more than seventy-five thousand US casualties were required to jump-start the stalled campaign, losses that helped make the Meuse-Argonne Offensive the bloodiest battle in US Army history.[13] That sad record endures to this day.

Booth knew that most of the blame for the debacle had fallen on the 79th Division and George Cameron's V Corps, but from his personal experience on the battlefield, he was certain that a substantial portion of the responsibility belonged elsewhere. What the colonel knew and what he could prove, however, were entirely different things. But blame was seeping toward the 4th Division. To shield the reputation of his old unit—which he believed spotless—Booth launched a determined effort to collect evidence about the events surrounding the failed assault on Little Gibraltar. During the 1920s and well into the 1930s, he wrote letters to senior officers who had served with him in France, asking for their recollections about the planning and execution of the attack. While Parkin was consumed by a burning anger about Montfaucon and Bullard, Booth pursued a more reasoned, step-by-step approach. The objective of both men, however, was the same.

Although Booth had powerful friends, he had much to lose

by launching his informal investigation. His probing letters and pointed questions carried considerable risk, because they were bound to provoke the ire of those who might be discredited were the truth disclosed. The greatly reduced peacetime army was a close-knit community, and word of Booth's discomfiting inquiries spread quickly.

The colonel's exposure increased substantially when several generals sent discreet signals that he could better spend his time documenting AEF successes. Many of the same officers would sit on promotion boards that would determine the trajectory of Booth's postwar military career; like every other colonel who had once held flag rank, he longed to recapture the stars that graced his shoulders in France.

Every night after completing his official duties, Booth sat at his desk typing letters, following new leads, and assembling a thick file of statements that were increasingly incriminating. For years, he pursued the task with such dedication that many fellow officers began to worry that he was obsessed. To one friend who urged him to drop the matter, Booth replied forcefully, "I am going to push this thing to a solution now while we are all alive and remember the instances. I don't want our grandchildren to cuss us out for being responsible for the failure of the 3rd and 5th Corps to reach the army objective, Sept. 26th, as we cuss out our ancestors for apparently similar features in the Civil War."[14] As the retired major general sat in his Los Angeles home during the dark year of 1936, he became increasingly confident that the end of his quest for the truth was in sight. A clear picture of the events of September 26, 1918, was emerging. Booth believed he would soon be able to demonstrate what and—more importantly—*who* was responsible for the failure to capture Little Gibraltar. As Germany rushed to rearm, and Europe drifted toward the abyss of a new war, the retired officer pondered the documents he had collected to solve a mystery from a different war, indeed, from a different world.

632 INDEX

Woëvre, The, 421.
Wood, Gen. Leonard, 22, 26, 28, 34, 46, 193, 195, 260.
Wright, Col. John W., 470.
Wright, Gen. William M., 422, 435, 450.

YOUNG, COL. HUGH H., 73.

Young Men's Christian Association, 137, 370, 474–477.
Young Women's Christian Association, 476.
Ypres, 447.
Yssonge Farm, 283.

ZEPPELINS, 156.

Chaplain Wright of my regiment, the 316th of the 79th Division, which captured Montfaucon, that is the 79th Division did, remained in the regular army after the war. He told me, after the war, that he had served with the Colonel, also after the war, who had commanded the left regiment of the 4th Division during the Argonne battle. This regiment was in touch with the right regiment of the 79th Division (Ours) all during our bloody frontal attack on the high and stoutly defended town of Montfaucon. It was the 313th Inf which captured this town, the 316th, my regiment, was in close support.

This Colonel told Chaplain Wright that his regiment got beyond Montfaucon on the first day of the battle, and realized that we were having a very hard time in front of Montfaucon, and were losing heavily. He said he could easily have sent a battalion to attack the town in the rear, and have helped us to take it, if the germans had not vacated it upon their approach, as they most certainly would have done. But the Colonel dared not do this without authority as he would be going out of the sector of his division, the 4th. The matter was referred back to Brigade headquarters and to division headquarters, and finally corps headquarters, where general Bullard said he would not help general Cameron, our corps commander, win any battle laurels, so on account of this nasty jealousy between high officers, the help was not sent to us, and the 4th Division went ahead into its much easier advance, and left us to be slaughtered by hundreds in making a frontal attack against machine guns in Montfaucon.

Bullard received all the high military decorations of America, France, England and Belgium. What he deserved was a long term in military prison for deliberately murdering hundreds of American soldiers.

Signed
H. D. Parkin
Ex Major 316th Inf
79th Division

Balboa. Calif. 9/14/36

I am entirely convinced that chaplain Wright was telling the absolute truth in telling me this story. H.D.P.

Left regt of
4th Division
commanded by Col. who told this story

Mont-
faucon

313th Inf

316 Inf

79th Div

The Affidavit

Chaplain Wright of my regiment, the 316th of the 79th Division, which captured Montfaucon, that is the 79th Division did, remained in the regular army after the war. He told me, after the war, that he had served with the colonel, also after the war, who had commanded the left regiment of the 4th Division during the Argonne battle. This regiment was in touch with the right regiment of the 79th Division (ours) all during our bloody frontal attack on the high and stoutly defended town of Montfaucon. It was the 313th Infantry which captured this town, the 316th, my regiment, was in close support.

This colonel told Chaplain Wright that his regiment got beyond Montfaucon on the first day of the battle, and realized that we were having a very hard time in front of Montfaucon, and were losing heavily. He said he could easily have sent a battalion to attack the town in the rear, and have helped us take it, if the Germans had not vacated it upon their approach, as they most certainly would have done. But the colonel dared not do this without authority as he would be going out of the sector of his division, the 4th. The matter was referred back to brigade headquarters and to division headquarters, and finally to corps headquarters, where General Bullard said that he would not help General Cameron, our corps commander, win any battle laurels, so on account of this nasty jealousy between high officers, the help was not sent to us, and the 4th Division went ahead with its much easier advance, and left us to be slaughtered by hundreds in a frontal attack against the machine guns in Montfaucon.

Bullard received all the high military decorations of America, France, England and Belgium. What he deserved was a long term in military prison for deliberately murdering hundreds of American soldiers.

H. D. Parkin (signed)
Ex Major, 316th Infantry, 79th Division
Balboa, Calif. 9/14/36

CHAPTER 2

LITTLE GIBRALTAR OF THE WESTERN FRONT

Two miles behind Montfaucon, Crown Prince Wilhelm of Germany
addressed the troops who assaulted Verdun in 1916.
Willie, as the prince was called, constructed a high-tech observatory
on the butte so that he could direct the horrific battle.

★　　★　　★

The net result of more than six months of continuous attacks was in the main a failure, but a failure
relieved by countless deeds of heroism and great
achievements. The blood of brave men had flowed
in rivers.

—Crown Prince Wilhelm of Germany[1]

Years after World War I, German crown prince Wilhelm still recalled vividly his first sight of Montfaucon. It came on September 3, 1914, little more than two months after the assassination of Austrian archduke Franz Ferdinand in the Bosnian capital of Sarajevo, and just two days after Germany had opened hostilities by invading Belgium and France. Leading ten divisions composing the German Fifth Army, Wilhelm crashed through the French border north of Metz and swept west in an attempt to encircle the vital fortress town of Verdun.

As the thirty-two-year-old general topped a ridge on the west side of the Meuse River, he spied "the proud conical peak" of Montfaucon, defended by troops from France's African colonies.[2] Wilhelm immediately perceived the military significance of the towering butte. Perched on a humpback ridge among the rolling hills and deep ravines of northern France, Montfaucon was a vantage point from which the Germans could observe the entire area around Verdun. The crag would give the invaders a strategic advantage in their campaign to surround and capture the fortifications of the city that formed the critical hinge of what would soon be called the Western Front.

Wilhelm quickly ordered his renowned Metz Corps into action, and its soldiers stormed the steep limestone bluff protecting the butte's eastern flank. Inspired by the belief that the peak was impregnable, the colonial troops fought back strongly. But Germans in spiked helmets pushed the French troops off the height and into the ravines, fields, and woods that lay beyond. Elated by the victory, the crown prince rejected his staff's warnings and spurred his horse toward the mount. He recalled later: "I drove past the transport columns and the battery positions and, amid general cheers and the waving of helmets, went right up to the fighting troops. There, amid all the din of battle and the hurtling enemy shells, I had that glorious feeling of victory which only the fighting line experiences, and from an ideal central position was able to observe the movements of my whole army."[3] Wilhelm galloped on across the flat top of the butte past a church with a distinctive steeple, the only remnant of a medieval monastery that had once graced the promontory until it was destroyed by anticlerical mobs during the French Revolution. Many of the village houses were on fire from the victor's artillery. Wafting from an open window of one wrecked home came the incongruous sound of a popular song played on a piano by a German soldier. *"Puppchen, du bist mein Augenstern!"* ("Darling, you are the apple of my eye!") went the lyrics that brought a smile to the face of Kaiser Wilhelm II's oldest son, rumored to have a keen eye for the ladies.[4] Imperially thin and endowed with an exceptional shock of bright blond hair, the prince was the very picture of the Germanic general, with one major exception: his chin was tragically weak, an unfortunate feature accentuated by a large, drooping mustache. But the younger Wilhelm carried off his leading role by comporting himself in accordance with the army's strict code of discipline and, more importantly, by rigorously following the advice of a seasoned chief of staff appointed by Berlin, General Schmidt von Knobelsdorf.[5]

When the prince reached the far side of the hill, he dismounted to view the sweeping panorama. Standing in an apple orchard covering the gentle slope, he could easily see west to the town of Varennes, where his troops were driving the French army beyond the Aire River. Farther through the smoke of battle, he glimpsed the dark Argonne Forest, where his enemies paused to catch their breath before resuming a precipitous retreat toward Reims. To the south, beyond the Bois de Montfaucon and the villages of Malancourt and Haucourt, Wilhelm spied a low spine of ridges broken by ravines filled with trees and brush. A staff officer pointed out the highest ridge and cited its ominous name: Le Mort Homme (Dead Man). At the east end of this ridgeline lay several of the forts protecting Verdun. Just beyond, the twin belfries of the city cathedral pierced the smoke of battle lying thick in the Meuse River Valley. The prince had little time to enjoy the sight, as he hurried from the butte to catch up with his surging troops. It was clear, however, that the shining moment of victory had made Montfaucon the apple of Wilhelm's eye.

Over the next week, the Germans drove the French lines more than twenty miles south in hopes of rendezvousing with the other wing of the prince's army closing in from east of the Meuse. Together they nearly encircled and isolated Verdun's fortifications. Had they succeeded, Wilhelm would have cut off the city's supplies and reinforcements, leaving France's eastern defenses powerless to stem the German army's westward flow toward the nation's capital.

Simultaneously, a larger mass of German troops had slashed through neutral Luxembourg and Belgium and was driving to take Paris in accordance with a plan credited to Count Alfred von Schlieffen, late chief of the German General Staff. Although recent scholarship has questioned the origin of the strategy, military historian John Keegan called the plan "the most important document of the last hundred years."[6] Whatever the Schlieffen Plan's genesis, its twin concepts guided Germany in two world wars: first, moving through neutral countries to avoid French fortifications, the Germans would defeat France immediately; second, the Germans would then send troops east by rail to attack Russia, which was incapable of mobilizing as quickly as France. Schlieffen envisioned taking Paris in a few weeks—much as Prussia had captured the French capital in the War of 1870, a conflict that led to the loss of the Gallic provinces of Alsace and Lorraine and to the emergence of Germany as a great power.

The kaiser's generals neglected Schlieffen's "deathbed" advice,

most likely apocryphal, to "strengthen the right wing" of the encirclement. As a result, the Germans swung too far east to envelop
Paris.[7] In addition, long logistical lines began to break down, the
kaiser's troops were wearied by days of ceaseless fighting, and the
French regained their composure under the firm leadership of
General Joseph Joffre. Momentum shifted. Inspired by victory
at Mondemont, the French drove back the hated Boche—a con-
temptuous nickname blending the French words for "German
blockhead" with a derisive sneer about the enemy's favorite veg-
etable, cabbage. The German retreat exposed the western flank of
Wilhelm's Fifth Army to French attack, and the crown prince was
ordered to withdraw northward. Wilhelm was furious, because he
was ceding valuable territory that his troops had just captured. Yet
orders were orders, and in the German army, even the kaiser's son
was bound to obey.

As Wilhelm and his staff began to search for a strong line
of defense that could halt the resurgent French, some officers
proposed that the Fifth Army occupy the low line of ridges dominated by Le Mort Homme. Remembering the defensive heights
of Montfaucon, however, the prince chose to anchor his main
line on the craggy butte.[8] Wilhelm's decision insured that in the
years ahead the promontory would become the centerpiece of the
German defensive position and remain closely associated with
the crown prince's disastrous legacy.

In 1915 Montfaucon presided over a series of violent but limited actions that surged north toward the German-held heights,
and then south toward the line of low ridges held by the French.
Then, each side began to trade the hope of regaining mobility for
the safety afforded by hastily constructed trenches. At first, the
fortifications were merely crude ditches in which infantrymen
crouched to avoid rifle fire. Afterward the troops constructed simple dugouts covered by tree trunks and earth to protect against flying shrapnel. As the Western Front solidified into a 450-mile scar
meandering across France, both sides deployed combat engineers

to build bunkers strong enough to resist all but the largest artillery shells. Some of these subterranean structures, which the Germans called *stollen*, were reinforced with concrete and steel and could shelter up to a thousand soldiers, who periodically charged upstairs to man the trenches or assault the enemy.

Because the tactics of offensive warfare had not kept pace with the spectacular development of defensive weapons, the invariable result of frontal assaults on fixed emplacements was disaster for the attackers. Machine guns that fired 500 rounds per minute, *minenwerfers* that heaved explosive canisters weighing up to 840 pounds, and artillery shells with their deadly shrapnel tore the attackers to bits or suffocated them with poison gas. As the battles surged forward and backward across the valley between Montfaucon and Le Mort Homme, both sides suffered heavy losses. Soon, the combatants settled into established lines, and the war became a deadly stalemate, with Western Front manpower "wastage rates" amounting to an average of 2,250 dead and 5,000 wounded per day, even during periods of relative quiet.[9] The Germans, of course, held a natural advantage, because they were firmly entrenched on French soil, with some 20 percent of their enemy's landmass occupied. Strategically, the French and their British allies would be forced to emerge from their trenches and assume the dangerous attackers' role just to regain the status quo ante. Secure in their superb fortifications, the Germans awaited the assaults when they could exact staggering losses on attackers.

As the Meuse-Argonne sector settled into an uneasy stalemate, Montfaucon became increasingly well known. In 1915, new German units replaced those that had previously manned the trenches, and each group insisted on securing evidence that it had served on the commanding hill famously captured by the crown prince. Professional photographers from German towns just across the border made a great living by snapping shots of grinning soldiers amid the ruins. In mobile labs, the photographers printed postcards that were inscribed by troops and sent to relatives in cities and villages across the fatherland. Many German homes shared in Wilhelm's victory by posting on their mantels images of their sons and brothers celebrating in Montfaucon's ruins.

On the butte, the Germans took steps to insure the comfort as well as the safety of their troops. A noncommissioned officers' club in a repaired structure on the back slope was regularly supplied with large barrels of beer, and a swine slaughterhouse operated around the clock to provide bratwurst.[10] Officers enjoyed a luxurious club in nearby Nantillois, where a manicured lawn with comfortable chairs was available for relaxing with fine French champagne. When fall gave way to winter and the holidays arrived, the Germans decorated their underground quarters with greenery and held a traditional Christmas Eve ceremony in the church, which to that point had sustained little damage. The sentimental notes of "Stille Nacht" soared through the building, as high-ranking officers arrayed themselves around the decorated altar to welcome the Prince of Peace.[11]

In wartime, a Christmas lull is often followed by a New Year's frenzy. And 1916 was destined to be a year full of frenzy. The German high command had become increasingly concerned about the toxic effects of stalemate. The war against the Russians was dragging on with no apparent end, and in the Atlantic, German sinkings of merchant ships were beginning to rouse the sleeping American giant. In Berlin, there were fears that the Yanks might shake off their lethargy and enter the war on the Allied side. More worrisome was the impact that the static situation was having on once-aggressive German troops. Trench warfare, complained the impatient crown prince, "had a soporific effect upon the men. That was, indeed, the most serious danger of the whole war of position, that it so easily tended to encourage the placing of one of the strongest sides of human nature, the instinct for self-protection, before duty."[12]

Wilhelm's fears about low troop morale and its effect on the military cohesion of Germany's principalities were confirmed by a flurry of disturbing incidents that occurred as the kaiser's birthday approached in January 1916. Across one snowy trench line, for instance, gray-clad troops yelled to their enemy, "We are Saxons, and after the twenty-ninth, you can have our trenches and the f—— Kaiser too!"[13]

Miles behind the front lines, however, the Germanic warrior ethos burned with undiminished intensity. In a warm chateau near Spa, Belgium, General Erich von Falkenhayn, chief of the Imperial General Staff, was planning a major offensive designed to capture Verdun and break through the surrounding fortifications. In the area, France had invested nothing less than its vast national ego, and if it were to fall, morale would sink precipitously. More importantly, the offensive was aimed directly at the hinge of the Western Front, where the lines shifted from a predominantly east-west direction to a north-south orientation. If the Germans could break this hinge, they would cleave France in two. To underscore this decisive purpose, the army chief of staff named his scheme *Wirkung Gericht*, meaning "a tribunal, or judgment, or . . . an execution place," like Golgotha, the place where Christ was put to death.

The huge offensive required extensive preparation. The German General Staff allocated ten divisions to reinforce Wilhelm's Fifth Army, along with more than 1,200 artillery pieces and 2.5 million shells to launch the *first* phase of the battle. To penetrate the thick walls of French forts, the Germans dispatched seventeen howitzers 380mm (fourteen inches) in diameter and fourteen mortars of the larger 420mm (sixteen-inch) size.[14] Because these guns weighed as much as 315,000 pounds, ten railcars and hundreds of men were needed to transport each one and to build concrete platforms to which their steel carriages were bolted.[15] The mortars were well worth the trouble, because they could propel a 1,826-pound armored shell eight miles.[16] Because the famed German siege artillery was destined to play a premier role in the offensive, Montfaucon would soon rebound into military prominence.

During lulls in fighting, the butte had become the target of bored French artillerists, who sometimes fired a salvo or two at the German-occupied hill towering above them. The desultory barrages slowly took their toll on the remaining houses, and the church also received its share of hits, so that postcards mailed home by Germans document the building's slow-motion destruction.[17]

As damaging as some of the shots were, they failed to diminish the butte's military usefulness. Montfaucon stood well above the surrounding countryside, providing splendid views of Verdun in the east, Le Mort Homme to the south, and the Argonne Forest in the west. As the Germans prepared for the apocalyptic battle, Wilhelm was determined to take full advantage of the view. Knowing that his massive artillery pieces would be more effective against French targets if they were precisely aimed, the crown prince secretly ordered the preparation of an advanced observation post on the mount of the falcon.

On the east side of the butte, about a hundred yards north of the church, stood a chateau, once the home of a wealthy family. It was a two-story structure with a tall attic and deep basement. Although the windows and doors had been blown out, and portions of the roof were destroyed, it took German engineers little time to convert the former home into a command observatory. Using the surrounding walls for camouflage and protection, the kaiser's troops constructed a thirty-five-foot-tall tower on bedrock in the basement, extending through the first and second floors, and terminating about six feet into the twelve-foot attic. The tower was constructed of steel-reinforced concrete walls three feet thick, with a four-foot slab of concrete covering the top.[18] In the tower's hollow middle, the engineers assembled a periscope topped by the most powerful telescope Zeiss opticians could devise. When the device was complete, it penetrated an opening in the protective slab in the attic and on through the highest part of the roof, where it was disguised by two lightning rods.

Access to the telescopic periscope was afforded by eyepieces located on each level of the house. In the attic, the Germans developed a chart room with a detailed map precisely oriented to compass points on the 360-degree sweep of the periscope. In addition to providing stations for observers on the first and second floors, the Germans constructed the device so that in the midst of strong artillery barrages, observers could continue their work from the basement.

To enhance the accuracy of the observatory's targeting data, the Germans constructed a secondary observation post in a ruined pier of the church. By comparing the relative headings from the two sites and factoring in the distance between, German artillery experts could fix their targets precisely. The vital data was relayed to batteries by field telephone and telegraph, or if the lines were broken by shell fire, by complex signal lights on the backside of the butte. Located in deep valleys east of the Meuse River and in the depths of the northern Argonne Forest, German long-range artillery could quickly destroy French targets by precise gunnery adjusted in concert with supplementary information relayed from forward observers near the front lines. Field artillery batteries closer to the front also received sighting information from the butte.

The crown prince's observatory was one of Germany's most closely held secrets. Before the dominance of airpower, Montfaucon's telescopic periscope was the equivalent of today's spy satellites, providing timely, precise information that could help destroy any target within a twenty-mile radius. Because of the position's value, the crown prince was determined to provide his technological masterpiece all the protection he could muster. To construct new fortifications on and around the butte, the Germans employed thousands of Russian prisoners of war shipped from the Eastern Front.

Around the margins of Montfaucon's flat top, the prisoners built fifteen additional observation posts to warn of imminent threats and to provide supplementary data for sighting artillery. Two-story stone-and-concrete structures, these posts were often disguised in the ruins of homes or barns. Machine-gun nests were similarly camouflaged with debris from blasted buildings, and trenches surrounded the front and sides of the hill, from top to bottom.

The bulk of construction, however, took place out of sight, beneath the butte's cratered surface. In the rock, German mining engineers laid out a labyrinth of tunnels and facilities. Included were several large *stollen* that housed and fed hundreds of troops. Tunnels led from the larger galleries to observation posts, machine-gun nests, and even artillery emplacements on the back slope, so that the soldiers would not be exposed to shelling as they moved to battle stations. Lighting for the entire complex was provided by a large gasoline engine driving a dynamo, buried at the rear of the hill. To make things homey, the garrison papered gallery walls, organized musical programs, constructed a café with an ample wine list, and assembled a large library of silent films for use in an underground theater.[19]

The Germans were not content, however, to fortify just the hill and its slopes. In addition to strengthening the forward trenches running along the north side of Forges Brook three miles south of the butte, they constructed a strong intermediate line of fortifications along the crest of a low ridge that ran between the front lines and the mount. To bolster the defense-in-depth strategy, German engineers incorporated two strong field fortifications. On the ridge north of the ruined village of Malancourt, they constructed the Oeuvre du Demon, or "Work of the Demon." Respectfully named by French troops who had the misfortune to attack it, the work was an interconnected complex of earthen fortifications, a concrete blockhouse, and large *stollen* with multiple machine guns shielded from direct fire. Together the weapons could deliver a steel deluge on anyone approaching through the valley running northward from Malancourt.

Farther west, the Redoute du Golfe provided similar protection in a large clearing, or *golfe*, between the Bois de Montfaucon and the Bois de Cuisy. Designed to be self-contained, the redoubt was surrounded by dense barbed wire and featured broad fields of fire that could exact an awful price on attackers. The redoubt and the Work of the Demon, as well as the observatory, tunnels, and additional defenses, converted the butte into an underground fortress capable of repelling any conceivable attack. At this point, the French dubbed the butte impregnable, and the underground fortress earned its title, Little Gibraltar of the Western Front, just in time to participate in the largest battle of world history.

On the clear morning of February 21, 1916, a massive German barrage directed by the Montfaucon observatory announced the arrival of the day of judgment for Verdun. The brick-and-concrete walls of Fort Douaumont and its sisters were blasted repeatedly by direct hits from the nearly one-ton shells of Germany's largest mortars. Shortly thereafter, the fort's stunned and disoriented garrison surrendered to a single German sergeant who crawled through a shell hole and bluffed the French soldiers into believing that he was the first of a much larger force.[20] The fort had been designed to hold out for months; its fall only four days after the start of the battle shattered the confidence of Verdun's defenders.

There was panic in the city, as the French mined the critical bridges across the Meuse in preparation for abandoning the river's east bank. As the Montfaucon-sighted artillery blasted away, however, the French appointed hard-fighting General Henri Philippe Pétain, who issued the famous order: "They shall not pass!" Through force of will, the crusty Pétain calmed his troops, who clung to steep ridges and huddled in bunkers north and east of Verdun. Although the Germans initially pushed within four miles of the city center, the French dug in their heels and conceded no more ground. To regain momentum, Wilhelm redoubled his artillery barrages, infantry attacks, and poison gas, and introduced a new weapon: panic-inducing flamethrowers. All these elements combined to create what the crown prince called the "mill on the Meuse [that] ground to powder the hearts as well as the bodies of the troops."[21]

No amount of Sturm und Drang could disguise the fact that the Germans were losing almost as many men as the French, and the attackers' morale began to wane. As spring neared, Falkenhayn and Wilhelm met to review alternatives, and their eyes turned toward the rolling hills west of the Meuse River. Together they decided to attack the line of French-held ridges south of Montfaucon in hopes of installing artillery in the hills to cut the vital flow of enemy supplies along the French railroad from Reims and on the La Voie Sacrée road from Bar-le-Duc. In early March, Le Mort Homme and its sister ridge, Côte 304 (named for its height in meters), became the targets of particularly violent German artillery bombardments called *trommelfeuer* (drumfire), for the unbroken roar of shells that sounded like the rolling of massed drums. As barrages extended for weeks, French soldiers were unable to leave their bunkers to eat, wash, or shave; their long hair and beards earned the honorific *poilu* (shaggy ones), a title eventually conferred on all French troops who joined the ranks of troglodytes.

One soldier on the receiving end of a barrage on Côte 304 during this period later described the experience:

> The pounding was continuous and terrifying. We had never experienced its like during the whole campaign. The earth around us quaked, and we were lifted and tossed about. Shells of all calibres [*sic*] kept raining on our sector. The trench no longer existed; it had been filled up with earth. We were crouching in shell-holes, where the mud thrown up by each new explosion covered us more and more. The air was unbreathable. Our blinded, wounded, crawling and shouting soldiers kept falling on top of us and died while splashing us with their blood. It really was a living hell.[22]

A less subjective measure of the ferocity of these bombardments was provided by the fact that barrages of German and French batteries progressively reduced the height of Côte 304 by three meters during the offensive. Following the war, the French constructed a monument exactly three meters tall to restore the ridge to its original elevation and to memorialize troops lost defending the high point. The crests of Le Mort Homme and Côte 304 fell to the enemy, but French troops always regained the lost ground.

In hopes of forcing the Germans to shift troops away from the besieged city and to regain the initiative on the Western Front, the Allied high command hurried preparations for a massive attack by late spring 1916. The site was the Somme River in northwest France, where thirteen British divisions supported by five French divisions assembled to attack strong German positions. Unfortunately, the number of divisions was reduced considerably by the necessity of sending French troops to reinforce Verdun. Despite the reductions, British field marshal Sir Douglas Haig remained optimistic that his Somme Offensive could break through enemy lines, free British cavalry to dash northward behind the Germans, and shift the fortunes of war in the Allies' favor.[23]

The British knew they were facing a skilled enemy with stout defenses, but "Haig had been seduced by the potential of massed artillery as demonstrated at least in part by the early German operations at Verdun."[24] Enamored by the promise of the big guns, the British field marshal assembled 1,537 artillery pieces that over five days fired more than one million shells at the enemy.[25] Confident that the barrage had destroyed the five belts of German barbed wire and pierced infantry bunkers carved deep into solid chalk, Allied troops went over the top at 7:30 a.m. on July 1, 1916, and marched forward in neat waves to meet the enemy.[26] The assault battalions were surprised to discover that much of the barbed wire was still intact and that the kaiser's troops had emerged from undamaged bunkers in time to mount and fire their Maxim machine guns. Historian Martin Middlebrook calculated that by the end of the *first day of fighting*, the British had suffered 57,470 casualties, including 19,240 dead.[27] For these sacrifices, the British captured only three small villages and advanced one mile at the farthest point.[28]

On July 11, less than two weeks after the disastrous British attack on the Somme, German troops made a final attempt to capture Verdun; more than 10,000 men were sacrificed in a vain effort to capture Fort Souville and blast a path to the city center. Shortly thereafter, the battle subsided, each side paralyzed by maximum efforts. Some twenty million artillery shells had been fired into the cauldron, and they had done their work well.[29] The Germans could point to 377,231 French casualties (including 162,308 dead or missing) to demonstrate the effectiveness of Falkenhayn's offensive. Unstated, however, was the fact that more than 337,000 German casualties (including approximately 100,000 dead or missing) were required to achieve the Pyrrhic victory.[30] On the Somme, the toll was even higher: The Allies suffered 622,231 casualties, while estimates of German casualties range from a low of 400,000 to a high of 680,000.[31]

Mourning darkened homes throughout France, Britain, and Germany. Among the high command, Pétain won national acclaim, while Haig plodded methodically on to perfect the bloody tactics that would eventually wear down the enemy. On the German side, little notice was paid to the quick disappearance of the generals who had planned and pressed the offensive to "bleed France white." Falkenhayn, replaced as army chief of staff by the rising Paul von Hindenburg, was sent to a remote command on the Eastern Front. Although the general's reputation was buffered by the distance from Verdun, he failed to escape the calumny associated with the disaster.

Falkenhayn's comrade-in-arms, the crown prince, also disappeared from the scene before surfacing some time later in a less demanding command. By that time, however, grieving German parents had awarded him the sobriquet that he would carry until his death in 1951: the Butcher of Verdun.[32] The pain caused by that harsh nickname might have influenced Wilhelm to record in his memoir the numerous occasions on which he had urged Falkenhayn to abandon the attack on Verdun.[33] However, the crown prince's rapturous descriptions of the capture of Le Mort Homme and the village of Haucourt undercut his professed concern about the lives of his troops.

As fall rains stilled major offensive actions for 1916, the Western Front was mired in a stalemate mirroring the situation that prevailed twelve months earlier. Despite the loss of two million men in a single year, trench lines were little changed, and neither side could claim advantage. Like depleted boxers, the combatants retired to their respective corners, totally exhausted. Huddling in trenches and bunkers, neither side could muster enough energy to throw another punch. They were forced to await new developments to mount renewed efforts to win the war. For the Germans, a revolution in Russia would be required to free troops for attacks on the Western Front. As the Germans looked east for relief, the Allies looked west, across the Atlantic. British and French diplomats implored the United States to enter the war, and each new German atrocity on the high seas brought hope that it would be the final spur for American intervention.

The most shocking of these, of course, was the sinking of the British liner *Lusitania* on May 7, 1915, which according to one of President Woodrow Wilson's biographers was "in time what Sunday, December 7, 1941, and Tuesday, September 11, 2001, would be in their times."[34] After a torpedo from German submarine U-20 sunk the ship, 1,191 of the nearly 2,000 passengers and crew lost their lives in the cold water off the southern coast of Ireland. Among the dead were 128 Americans. As the result of these and additional losses in other maritime attacks, Wilson began an agonizing process of weighing alternatives—even as he recalled the carnage he had witnessed as a young Southern boy during the Civil War. The president genuinely hated war, but he knew that events in Europe were outside his control. While Wilson's staff hailed his efforts to keep the country out of the fight, the president admitted candidly, "Any little German lieutenant can put us into war at any time by some calculated outrage."[35]

As public opinion swung wildly between anger with Germany and the basic American propensity to avoid foreign entanglements, Wilson vacillated as well, confiding to a cabinet member, "I wish with all my heart that I saw a way to carry out the double wish of our people, to maintain a firm front in respect of what we demand of Germany and yet do nothing that might by any possibility involve us in the war."[36]

The president insisted on preserving the nation's strict neutrality in hopes that the United States could serve as an impartial mediator to end the conflict—a task that proved none too easy. Through his first term, Wilson wrestled with pressures converging from every direction. Secretary of State William Jennings Bryan resigned because he feared that Wilson's strong stance against German submarines might lead to war, while former president Theodore Roosevelt accused Wilson of cowardice for not confronting the kaiser more forcefully. Edward House, Wilson's personal friend and US envoy to the European powers, compromised the president's neutrality by confiding to the French that "the lower the fortunes of the Allies ebbed, the closer the United States would stand by them."[37] At home, Irish groups lobbied the White House against assisting Great Britain because of its bloody suppression of the Easter 1916 "rising" in Dublin, while German American citizens pressed the fatherland's case for righteous war. From time to time, Wilson's persistent neutrality won a modest victory, as when he wrung a promise from Berlin not to attack passenger liners without warning.

Following narrow reelection over Charles Evans Hughes in November 1916, Wilson readied one more attempt to mediate peace in Europe. He hoped that the twin disasters of Verdun and the Somme would persuade the warring nations that "peace without victory" was the only way out of the quagmire.[38] But the costly battles had made both the Allies and Germany less reasonable and more desperate.

At a meeting in Berlin on January 9, 1917, German military authorities presented to the kaiser their case for stronger measures: because of the effective British blockade, Germany's economy was weakening dramatically, and the war had to be won as soon as possible before the country was exhausted. The only option to break the stalemate, argued Navy chief of staff Holtzendorff, was to resume unrestricted submarine warfare to cut off Great Britain's supplies and starve it out of the war. Acknowledging that such a move might precipitate US action, Admiral Holtzendorff eased that concern by offering a vainglorious declaration: "I will give Your Majesty my word as an officer that not one American will land on the Continent."[39] Holtzendorff's imprudent wager against US determination was extended into a lunatic parlay by what historian John Keegan later called "a clumsy German approach to Mexico, proposing an alliance, baited with the offer to return Texas, Arizona, and New Mexico, if America went to war against Germany."[40] Contained in a telegram from German foreign secretary Arthur Zimmermann, the ploy was intercepted by the British, given to the Americans, and released on February 28. Combined with news of the German submarine offensive and the sinking of nine American ships, the Zimmermann telegram pushed American public opinion decisively toward intervention.

With reluctance and sorrow tempered by firm resolve, the president asked a joint session of Congress to declare war on April 2, 1917. Wilson felt that his request marked a personal failure, and after returning from Capitol Hill, he sat in his study and wept. The declaration, however, was acclaimed by the American public and passed by large majorities in both houses. It swept the nation into a conflict that had scourged Europe for almost three bloody years, costing more than five million lives.

CHAPTER 3

"DO YOU WISH TO TAKE PART
IN THE BATTLE?"

Cursed as "vipers of the battlefield," German machine-gun units were expected
to fight to the death. Many American troops refused to capture members of these
"suicide squads," who exhausted their ammunition, threw up their hands, and
shouted *"Kamerad."* Many were nonetheless immediately shot.

★   ★   ★

We have come over here to get ourselves killed.

—General Tasker Bliss, US Army[1]

F or months, General John J. Pershing had looked forward to August 30, 1918. That was the day the First United States Army would assume responsibility for its own sector of the Western Front. By virtue of the move, Pershing would become the first American general to command a multidivisional force in a foreign war, an army he would soon lead into battle to erase a long-standing bulge in the front near St. Mihiel, southeast of Verdun.

Walking toward his advanced headquarters in the pleasant provincial town of Ligny-en-Barrois in eastern France, Pershing had no reason to doubt that the day's events would unfold just as he had planned. As he bounded through the door held wide by a military policeman, staff members might have been tempted to cheer. But Pershing's stern demeanor and rigid posture eliminated any thoughts of celebrating the day's significance. The chief's presence insured decorum.

While reviewing the disposition of American troops who had begun replacing French poilu in frontline trenches at midnight, Pershing reflected on the whirlwind of the last year and a half. One day he had been chasing the Mexican revolutionary Pancho Villa across the Chihuahuan Desert; it seemed that the very next, he was climbing aboard an express train to Washington to help plan America's participation in the war.

The long train ride gave Pershing time to reflect on his lengthy career and the current state of the US military. Pershing was part of a proud tradition that had fought in the Indian campaigns in the West, the Spanish-American War in Cuba and the Philippine

Islands, the insurrection of the Islamic Moros in the former Spanish Pacific colony, and many smaller actions against rebels and bandits in Mexico and Central America. Throughout the course of those campaigns, the general had seen the army's ranks wax and wane with fluctuating congressional funding, but by 1917, the army had shrunk to a new low. The US Regular Army then consisted of only 107,641 men, ranking seventeenth in the world; the Marine Corps added another 15,500 professional soldiers, while the National Guard consisted of 132,000 part-time troops.[2] All told, the nation could muster only 255,141 men, barely enough for nine divisions.

At that time, Germany fielded 123 divisions on the Western Front; by the time the Yanks were ready for battle, that figure would rise to 185.[3] Some experts reckoned that America would need four million soldiers to defeat Germany and the other members of the Central Powers: Austria-Hungary, the Ottoman Empire, and Bulgaria. To meet the manpower needs, President Wilson developed a new plan for national conscription that historian David Kennedy has described as "a radical departure from the traditional reliance on volunteering."[4] Conscription would set the pattern for US defense policy for the next half century, and at the time, many experts predicted that the services would encounter insurmountable problems in training unmotivated draftees. The burden would fall on a small cadre of experienced Regular Army officers who would be called on to organize and train the raw recruits. Selecting these officers emerged as the most pressing problem facing the nation as it readied for war.

Even before the public celebration of the declaration of war had ended, President Wilson and his secretary of war, Newton D. Baker, began surveying the ranks of US officers to determine who was capable of meeting the organizational, logistical, and physical demands of the conflict. Many senior generals, like Army chief of staff Hugh Scott, were aging and lacked the requisite stamina. The leading candidate, Major General Frederick Funston, died of a heart attack before he could be vetted thoroughly.[5] Others were hidebound in thinking, tied to outdated tactics, or were politically unreliable—like General Leonard Wood, who had irritated Wilson with strident calls for war preparations well before the president and Congress had made the decision to intervene. Such officers would remain on the Atlantic's western shore.

Toward the bottom of the seniority list of flag officers appeared the name of John J. Pershing, who had soldiered in Cuba, the Philippines, and Mexico. He had been promoted to major general the year before, and was a rising star. The secretary of war made inquiries and found that Pershing knew how to manage interservice rivalry, had mastered the complexities of duty abroad, could speak middling French, and, not insignificantly, was the son-in-law of US senator Francis E. Warren, whose support was critical to the war effort. Above all, Baker found that the officer had the reputation of being utterly reliable and compliant with instructions from superiors.

Shortly after Pershing got off the train in Washington's Union Station, he was invited to meet with Baker. Pershing hoped that they would be discussing the possibility of a divisional command in France, but Baker had broader responsibilities in mind. A former mayor of Cleveland who had no previous military experience before being named head of the War Department, Baker was a good judge of character; he quickly took Pershing's measure. He liked the general's cut, his granite face, his military bearing—all bespoke strong character and deep reserves of personal and professional pride. Although the topic was never broached, Baker also was aware that Pershing had consciously stiffened his demeanor to mask an almost unbearable family tragedy: the death of his wife, Frances, and three young daughters in a house fire two years earlier. One son survived. After a pleasant conversation, the meeting broke up with best wishes but without mention of greater responsibility than that normally accruing to a major general.

A day or two later, however, Pershing was once again called

to meet with the secretary of war, who told Pershing that President Wilson had selected the general as commander in chief.[6] He would lead all US troops in Europe, a group modestly designated as the American Expeditionary Forces.

The new AEF commander quickly threw himself into work. In an amazingly short period of time, the fifty-seven-year-old Pershing recruited an experienced staff, helped plan thirty-two new training camps across the nation, and assisted in the design of a basic-training regimen. In short order, the war department rounded up transport ships to carry Americans across the U-boat-vexed Atlantic to France, where they would undergo an intensive program of combat training to put a sharper point on their bayonets. While the logistical achievements were impressive, the test of battle still lay ahead for Pershing's inexperienced doughboys, who had been nicknamed for their khaki uniforms covered in dust kicked up by marching.

As Pershing recalled these and other developments on the pleasant August morning at his Ligny headquarters, he recognized a surprising irony: many of the most difficult challenges of the past few months had been posed not by Germans but by his allies. Repeatedly, Generals Ferdinand Foch and Sir Douglas Haig pressed Pershing to parcel out arriving American soldiers to fill battalion and regimental gaps in French and British divisions depleted by fighting. The Allied generals called the plan "amalgamation," and argued that Yanks needed the direction of experienced combat officers to be effective. The AEF commander believed that such an approach would end in disaster rather than victory, as American troops would adopt the trench-fighting tactics of the Europeans that had led to a stalemate. He adamantly refused to feed his troops piecemeal into the war's grinder.

Developments in Russia forced Pershing's hand. In the first week of November 1917, Bolsheviks deposed the provisional government that had ruled since Czar Nicholas II's abdication and began to nurture their nascent experiment in communism.

Quickly, Bolshevik leader Nikolai Lenin petitioned the Central Powers for an armistice, which was granted by the gleeful Germans. The Allies had lost the service of thousands of Russian soldiers who had insured to that point that Germany would be compelled to fight a two-front war. These developments constituted a bonanza for the kaiser and his warlords, as more than a half million German troops from the Eastern Front were freed to attack French and British positions. Beginning in March 1918, the Germans used their newly amassed total of 185 divisions to mount a series of offensives designed to split the Allies and capture Paris before the bulk of the Americans arrived in Europe.[7] The kaiser knew that his nation and army were approaching the limits of their endurance, and he and his generals threw everything into a gamble to win the war before the Yanks could become an effective fighting force.

Barely established on the Continent, Pershing hoped to reserve the few US divisions in France for action as a unified army, but he recognized that American delay might cause Allied defeat. The flinty general reluctantly freed his men for action. In little-known places such as Château-Thierry and Belleau Wood, the Yanks helped stanch the German flood. At the small town of Cantigny, they even retook some of the lost ground in a small but decisive attack directed by one of Pershing's rising stars, General Robert Bullard.

By the end of August, Pershing and his men had met all the challenges of the Germans, as well as those from the Allies. The American general had reclaimed command of most of his far-flung troops and used them to invigorate the US First Army with fourteen battle-ready divisions, comprising four hundred thousand men—with artillery, tanks, and warplanes supplied by the French. In accordance with agreements reached with Foch, Pershing was poised to lead his army to erase a bulge in Allied lines at St. Mihiel, a relic of Crown Prince Wilhelm's campaign to encircle Verdun in 1914. Aptly termed a "hernia" by the portly

Foch, the German incursion was a few miles southeast of the besieged city, looming over critical supply lines to the *dèpartments*,
or provinces, of France near the German and Swiss borders.
French commanders had awarded their American comrades the
honor of eliminating the threat to the symbol of French resistance. Through months of intense preparation, Pershing's staff
had developed a comprehensive plan directing the moves each
American regiment would make. The effort would be mounted by
the most experienced US units, full of "piss and vinegar," thanks
to their success in halting the German spring offensives.

Little wonder, then, that in the waning days of summer 1918,
everything looked bright to Pershing, who anticipated a successful
fall campaign that would position his growing army for complete
victory over the Germans in 1919. Optimistic officers predicted
that American doughboys would be marching with French and
British soldiers through Berlin's Brandenburg Gate before fall
rain blew in off the Baltic Sea.

Late on the morning of August 30, however, Pershing received
word that Foch was on his way to Ligny for an unscheduled visit.
Appointed supreme commander of Allied troops just in time to
coordinate the response to the German spring offensives, Foch
was a pompous man who had dispatched countless French soldiers to death during the early days of the Great War. Trusting in
the invincible élan of the French army, Foch had flung his spirited
troops against German machine guns in the belief that *l'offensive
à outrance*—aggressiveness to the extreme—could overwhelm the
strongest defense.[8] The outcome was predictable: French ardor
offered scant protection against Krupp steel.

Following this early debacle, Foch's star waned, but his irrepressible ego and France's dangerous situation eventually res-
cued him from the shadows. In the dark winter and spring of
1917–1918, Foch and his jaunty bantam stride were once again
prominent on the Western Front. Strained to the breaking point,
the French Republic called on its toughest son to fill the breach.

The nation honored Foch's success in stanching the German tide by naming him a *Maréchal de France* in July 1918.

Personally, Pershing and Foch had a checkered history. The reserved American could hardly stomach the Frenchman's cocky attitude. Pershing knew enough recent military history to be aware that Foch's flawed tactics had nearly brought about Allied disaster in the war's early days. During the emergency caused by the German spring offensives in 1918, Foch pushed his relationship with Pershing nearly to the breaking point by hounding the AEF commander to commit his troops to battle before the Americans were ready. On May 8 as the Germans pushed close to Paris, Foch met with Pershing to argue for the commitment of American troops. The French general feared that the enemy would take the national capital and push the poilu well south, even beyond the Loire River that runs through the middle of France. To cow Pershing, Foch angrily asked the American commander if he was going to withhold US troops until the French were forced to give up half the country. Maintaining his composure, Pershing replied simply, "Yes." Only the American's strong reserve and the unflinching support of President Wilson saved the AEF general from the intense hectoring, which had been aided and abetted by the British.

Awaiting Foch's arrival in Ligny, Pershing did not know what occasioned the visit. Perhaps its purpose was to salute the US Army's assumption of responsibility for its own sector or to review the elaborate plans for reducing the St. Mihiel salient. Pershing had little time to speculate, as the marshal's entourage soon entered the manor's gate. When the US commander walked through the front door, Foch was stepping down from his long black Renault limousine. After adjusting his splendid tunic and straightening his braid-encrusted *kepi*, the diminutive Frenchman cocked his head, snapped off a salute, and thrust out his hand to the towering American.

After obligatory photographs, the marshal walked with Pershing to the map room, where he unrolled charts of the Western Front, launched into a lecture on grand strategy, and announced superciliously that he had devised a better use for the American troops than the St. Mihiel operation the French had earlier approved. Poised to launch that attack, Pershing was flabbergasted and argumentative, but the wily Frenchman had planned the meeting carefully and was prepared to use a full panoply of flattery, intimidation, cunning, and other psychological techniques to persuade Pershing to reduce his St. Mihiel operation and to take responsibility for a more ambitious attack in the Meuse-Argonne sector. By appealing to Pershing's pride, stoking his anger, and arousing his determination not to divide the US First Army, the Frenchman subtly maneuvered the American into accepting the new—and far more difficult—assignment. Some historians believe that the marshal did not have the requisite guile to finesse Pershing into agreeing.[9] But a thorough examination of the meeting provides ample evidence to the contrary.

After peremptorily announcing the changed assignment to put Pershing off balance, Foch turned to flattery by affirming that the Americans were essential to his new plan, a strategy that both acknowledged the truth and appealed to Pershing's pride. Both men recognized that with more than a million fresh troops on the Continent, the United States would have to play a key role in preventing the disorganized Germans from regaining their footing. To preclude the Germans' shifting their limited reinforcements to meet attacks launched sequentially, the French marshal had developed the most ambitious plan of the war: a near-simultaneous flurry of punches culminating in a knockout of Germany. During one week in September, British, Canadian, and Australian troops would assault the enemy at Ypres. Near the center of the front, British and American divisions would mount a major offensive on the Somme. Farther east, two French armies and the remainder of the American troops would deliver the finale by punching through enemy positions west of Verdun and driving north to seize vital rail facilities between the border towns of Mézières and Sedan.

The attack in the Meuse-Argonne was the most promising of the offensives, as well as the most challenging. Through Sedan's rail lines flowed more than one-half of the munitions and reinforcements destined for German positions farther west. If the Allies could cut the lines, the kaiser's hard-pressed soldiers would soon face a bleak choice: capitulation or starvation. In either case, the war would be over before winter snow came blowing out of the Ardennes—a full year earlier than most experts thought possible.

There was only one small hitch in the plan, Foch paused to explain. To mount the critical attack on Sedan, the Americans would be required to shift most of their troops to the sector west of Verdun and forgo their carefully laid preparations to eliminate the bulge at St. Mihiel. Although Foch did not say so, Pershing suspected that the reassigned and reapportioned US troops would probably be placed under French command.[10]

As Foch finished his crisp presentation, stepped back from the table, and folded his arms with obvious pride in the imaginative scheme, the American staff noticed that their chief's face was flushing, a sign of anger that Pershing was unable to control. But the US general held his temper and explained patiently that it would be unwise to abandon the well-planned St. Mihiel operation that was to begin in less than two weeks. Foch countered by offering to leave a few American divisions to attack St. Mihiel in a much-reduced effort. Still, the Frenchman insisted that the bulk of the US troops would have to be deployed west of Verdun. He argued that the payoff would be an almost certain collapse of the German army that would save countless lives by ending the conflict a year early.

"I realize that I am presenting a number of new ideas and that you will probably need time to think them over," Foch condescended, "but I should like your first impressions."[11]

Through clenched jaws, Pershing replied: "Marshal Foch, here on the very day that you turn over a sector to the American Army, and almost on the eve of an offensive, you ask me to reduce the operation so that you can take away several of my divisions and assign some to the French Second Army and use others to form an American Army to operate on the Aisne in conjunction with the French Fourth Army, leaving me with little to do except hold what will become a quiet sector after the St. Mihiel offensive. This virtually destroys the American Army that we have been trying so long to form."[12] Having spent the past year deflecting attempts to use American troops as replacements in weakened French and British divisions, Pershing was determined not to give up his newly unified army.

At this point, Foch sprung his trap. He casually mentioned that if Pershing could offer an alternative that would meet the plan's overall goals, he would consider it. The American grasped the proffered lifeline by eagerly responding that "one solution might be to withdraw the Americans to put them with their right on the Meuse and extending as far west as possible," in a manner that would preserve the unity of the American army.[13] Trying not to appear overly eager, Foch replied that he considered the general's suggestion a possibility, but he observed that it would be difficult for the US First Army to conduct the St. Mihiel operation and then to move to the Meuse-Argonne in time to launch the attack in concert with the other offensives along the Western Front.[14] Foch's objection was mild, because he realized that Pershing had introduced an attractive alternative in line with his own thinking.

Abruptly changing direction, however, the AEF commander argued that if the well-developed plan to eliminate the St. Mihiel salient were abandoned, the Germans might use the bulge to attack Allied supply lines feeding the proposed drive to Sedan. Warming to resistance, Pershing pressed more forcefully against Foch's plan. After two hours of intense wrangling, the French

marshal grew impatient. He taunted Pershing with an insult designed to arouse the American's legendary sense of pride.

"Do you wish to take part in the battle?" Foch sneered.

"Most assuredly," replied the exasperated Pershing, "but as an
American Army and in no other way."

"Your French and English comrades are going into battle; are
you coming with them?" the Frenchman jeered.

"Marshal Foch, you have no authority as Allied Commander in
Chief to call upon me to yield up my command of the American
Army and have it scattered among the Allied forces where it will
not be an American Army at all," Pershing charged angrily.

"I must insist upon the arrangement," came the supercilious
reply.

"Marshal Foch, you may insist all you please, but I decline
absolutely to agree to your plan," Pershing countered. "While our
army will fight wherever you may decide, it will not fight except
as an independent American Army."[15]

With that, both men jumped to their feet. Pershing later confessed that he had a fleeting notion of swinging at the imperious
Frenchman, but caught himself just in time.[16] The general's characteristic self-control reasserted itself, and he turned away from
confrontation. After the men composed themselves, Foch quickly
departed, tossing on the map table a memorandum detailing the
plan.

As in the run-up to a duel, Foch had flung his gauntlet at
the American. The cocky Frenchman knew that Pershing's pride
would demand a response, and that it would probably take the
form of the offhanded suggestion that Pershing had advanced.
After several days of consideration, the insult and challenge were
too much for the AEF commander to ignore, and he took Foch's
bait. Pershing chose the course that any proud American warrior would take: he would show the French that the Yanks could
handle *both* operations—*at the same time*. The AEF commander
offered to complete the St. Mihiel operation and simultaneously

plan the Meuse-Argonne Offensive, if Foch would delay the series of attacks until the last week of September and would allow
the Americans complete control of the Meuse-Argonne Front,
including command of several French divisions. At a meeting in
Bombon on September 2, Foch gladly conceded both points; the
date for the attack was ultimately set for September 26, 1918.

In the judgment of Pershing's biographer, Donald Smythe,
the AEF commander had thus "committed himself to what was
really too large an undertaking. An American Army, untested and
in many ways untrained, was to engage in a great battle, disengage
itself, and move to another great battle some sixty miles away, all
within the space of about two weeks."[17] In addition to imposing
stiff logistical challenges, Pershing's unwise decision placed several major burdens on his army. First, because the veteran US
divisions—the 1st, 2nd, 26th, and 42nd—were already in place
around the St. Mihiel salient, they would not be able to participate
in the opening days of the Meuse-Argonne Offensive, when their
combat experience would have been most valuable in forcing a
breakthrough. "This single failure," concluded historian Robert
Ferrell, "proved to be a major factor in the initial difficulties in
the new sector."[18]

The second burden was that the attention of Pershing's headquarters staff would be divided during the coming critical month.
It would be impossible for the same number of officers who had
spent months developing the plan for assaulting St. Mihiel to
employ an equal amount of time on the new operation, which
was much larger and more complex. The possibility of mistakes
in planning would increase exponentially, as staff officers worked
around the clock to assemble a plan and draw up orders. At the
same time, they would be forced to keep a wary eye on the operation taking place sixty miles away.

By accepting Foch's challenge, Pershing also doomed his
troops to fight in the most rugged area of the Western Front. As
Falkenhayn and Crown Prince Wilhelm had discovered earlier,

the region between the Meuse River and the Argonne Forest was "the most ideal defensive terrain" that First Army chief of staff Hugh Drum had ever seen.[19] If the area's difficult topography set the stage, the Germans provided all the necessary stage dressing. The region was heavily defended by field fortifications constructed during the battle of Verdun, as well as a newly developed defensive barrier that Field Marshal Paul von Hindenburg, the kaiser's warlord, had designed to stop Allied breakthroughs before they could threaten the Belgian or German borders. Built behind the existing front in 1917, the line eliminated many kinks and curls in the original trenches, cutting approximately twenty-five miles from the previous length of the Western Front and freeing thirteen divisions that had been needed to defend the longer line.[20]

In a fit of uncharacteristic whimsy, the Germans named the new fortification and its features after characters in composer Richard Wagner's operas. In addition to calling the entire defensive barrier the Siegfried Stellung (redubbed the Hindenburg Line by the Allies), German planners named the three principal layers of fortified lines for witches in Wagner's epic *Ring* cycle: Etzel-Giselher, Kriemhilde, and Freya. "They were all bitches," quipped one Yank.

Each position consisted of five or more roughly parallel trench lines protected by countless strands and coils of barbed wire. Dugouts, bunkers, and *stollen* were spread liberally throughout, and potential avenues of attack were covered by massed machine guns and interlocking fields of fire covered by presighted artillery pieces.

In an operation named Alberich in honor of Wagner's evil dwarf, the kaiser's troops destroyed houses, barns, fences, and any other feature that might provide the Allies cover or comfort in the area between the former German front lines and their new fortifications.[21] Engineers paid special attention to the destruction of roads that attacking armies would need to transport equipment and supplies forward, and they blew up or poisoned wells. When the Germans withdrew to their new positions, they left behind a true wasteland: a gray muddy swath that would make it physically difficult for any attacker to advance.

The Hindenburg Line was particularly strong in the Meuse-Argonne region, where it incorporated many of the fortifications earlier constructed by the crown prince. From previous experience in the region, German engineers knew the terrain well and carefully sited fortifications to take maximum advantage of natural features. Attackers would first face the front lines, and then an "intermediate position" linking the Oeuvre du Demon with the Redoute du Golfe along the top of a ridge stretching across the battlefield. A mile and a half farther north, the fortress of Montfaucon served as the keystone of the Etzel-Giselher Stellung, the first of the three principal lines of resistance. The strongest position, the Kriemhilde Stellung, lay five miles beyond the mount. It snaked through some of the densest woods of the sector, where additional strongpoints were constructed on forbidding hills, including the heights of Cunel, Côte Dame Marie, and Côte de Châtillon. The third major position, the Freya Stellung, had not been completed by the summer of 1918, but Russian prisoners who had finished work on the butte were shifted to strengthen the line that stood as a final barrier protecting Sedan.

In addition to preparing these lines, the Germans fortified almost every fence line, ravine, and copse of trees with machine-gun nests, trenches, and dugouts, so that attackers could hardly advance uncontested over any ground in the region. The overall result was a twenty-mile-deep zone that remains one of the most formidable defensive positions in history.

As forbidding as these features were, the most significant German military asset in the Meuse-Argonne proved not to be the concrete and steel of the Hindenburg Line, but a Prussian officer who was one of the most talented artillerists of the entire war, General Max von Gallwitz. At his birth in 1852, few would have

predicted an outstanding military career for the native of a back-
water town in Silesia, now part of Poland. Gallwitz was further
handicapped by the fact that he was neither a nobleman nor a
Protestant, hallmarks of most German officers in the nineteenth
century. But the young commoner had the good fortune to enlist
in the Prussian army just before it began its victorious march
on Paris in the War of 1870. Most enlistees aspired to serve in
the highly visible cavalry or infantry, but Gallwitz chose to join
the 9th Artillery Brigade.[22] It was an auspicious time to feed the
guns, as the Prussians were pioneering the use of breech-loading
cannons that imparted a significant advantage over the French,
who still used the slower muzzle-loading system. An eager student, Gallwitz learned the science of ballistics from the ground
up by firing hundreds of rounds through Krupp breechloaders
that transformed modern warfare.

Because of his outstanding performance and obvious promise,
Gallwitz was sent to the national military academy following the
swift Prussian victory. Upon graduating, the young lieutenant
grew a dashing goatee that put a visible point on his razor-sharp
mind and launched his climb up the army's career ladder. Advancement was swift, and in 1899 Gallwitz was designated a general of artillery, ennobled by the kaiser, and appointed inspector
of field artillery. While in that position, he helped develop indi-
rect-fire and sound-ranging techniques that would make German
guns such a decisive factor in World War I. Using indirect fire,
artillery could remain safely hidden in valleys and forests and rely
on the guidance of forward observers to drop high explosives and
shrapnel on enemy targets. Sound ranging consisted of observing
the time lapse between the muzzle flash of enemy cannons and
the arrival of the sound, and using the interval to calculate the
precise distance to the target.

Gallwitz displayed his skill prominently in the attack on the
Belgian frontier forts at Namur in August 1914. Designed to hold
out for months, the installations consisted of nine forts positioned

to interdict invaders attempting to cross the Meuse River. The Germans approached Namur with caution, because earlier attacks on similar forts protecting Liège, Belgium, had cost the lives of hundreds of young troops and consumed eleven days. On August 20 Gallwitz arrived at the massive fortress with several of the largest weapons the world had ever seen: Austrian 305mm mortars and the even larger 420mm mortars forged in great secrecy by the Krupp works.[23]

Although the attack on Namur was supposed to follow a plan similar to that used at Liège, Gallwitz tossed it away and developed one of his own to better employ the siege artillery.[24] The guns reduced the forts to ruins in three days, and the Belgians surrendered to the Germans on August 24. Gallwitz's achievement, said John Keegan, "spelt the end of a three-hundred-year-old military trust in the power of [a] fortress to oppose the advance of a hostile army without the active intervention of supporting mobile troops."[25]

Always an innovator, Gallwitz was one of the first to advocate close coordination between artillery and infantry units, a combined-arms strategy perfected during the war by Lieutenant Colonel Georg Bruchmüller.[26] With the general's support, the colonel helped develop box barrages that prevented reinforcement of enemy positions under attack by surrounding them with artillery fire, *Feuerwaltze* (fire walls, called rolling barrages by the Allies) to protect advancing assault troops, and a devil's brew of mixed types of explosive, shrapnel, and gas shells to destroy special targets.

Although fearsome images of German machine guns spewing five hundred rounds per minute prompted prewar experts to predict that the fast-firing Maxims would produce most combat casualties, battlefield studies demonstrated that artillery accounted for approximately 60 to 70 percent of the fallen soldiers of World War I.[27] The Great War was, in reality, the Great Artillery War. Gallwitz anticipated this development and taught his gunners to exploit the advantages they possessed. The kaiser's batteries were expert at laying down deadly barrages, not only on fixed targets but also on moving bodies of troops. German field artillery units could rush from one battlefield site to another to confront urgent challenges. When tanks were introduced by the Allies in 1916, speed and accuracy enabled the kaiser's 77mm batteries to stop the new mobile threat, as French, British, and American crews were to discover in the closing years of the war. Much of the success of the German artillery is attributable to Gallwitz's four decades of leadership, and the armies he commanded on the Eastern, Serbian, and Western Fronts were justly celebrated for their sharpshooting.

As the general took over responsibility for the Fifth Army from the crown prince in the summer of 1916, the French launched a series of successful counterattacks in the Verdun sector. One of them recaptured the fortress of Douaumont, an event celebrated by the ringing of church bells throughout France. Although his army was demoralized by heavy casualties, "Tenacious Gallwitz," as the Germans dubbed him, soon stopped the French counterattack in its tracks by using the army's massive complement of artillery. Gallwitz was called away briefly to stabilize the Somme Front, but he soon returned to spend the remainder of the war with the Fifth Army near Verdun.

Across war-torn Europe, there was no battlefield better suited for a general skilled in artillery than the Meuse-Argonne region. Numerous German guns and mortars used in 1916 were still in place in the region, and the ridge-and-valley topography seemed purpose-made to protect hidden batteries and to funnel attackers into pretargeted killing zones. Above all—literally above all—the high-tech observatory on Montfaucon was just the instrument a dedicated artillerist needed to do his worst.

Ultimately, the approaching battle in the Meuse-Argonne would come down to a race between Gallwitz and Pershing. In driving for a breakthrough that would enable his troops to sever

Sedan's rail junction, the American general would have to employ stealth and speed: stealth in assembling his divisions without German notice, and speed in piercing layers of fortifications before the enemy could dispatch reinforcements. Across no-man's-land, the German general would rely on the depth and elasticity of his defenses to hold off the Americans until he could rush additional troops to bolster the understaffed main line of resistance: the Kriemhilde Stellung. The famed German artillery, sophisticated tactics, and magnificent observatory would be valuable assets in the skilled hands of Gallwitz, who would be fighting one of the least experienced divisions of the American Expeditionary Forces as it struggled to take the key butte of Montfaucon.

CHAPTER 4

"THIS APPALLING PROPOSITION"

Encumbered by a large ego and burning ambition, General Robert E. Lee Bullard was set in his ways. He knew only one direction—forward—and only one speed—fast. Bullard scorned orders from General Pershing's staff that required teamwork and coordination.

★   ★   ★

The Meuse Argonne is a hard nut to crack; there are great obstacles to be overcome. But it is all right, your men have the devil's own punch. They will succeed despite everything.—Go to it.

> —Marshal Ferdinand Foch,
> Allied commander in chief
> to Pershing[1]

The Marne-Rhine Canal running through Ligny-en-Barrois, France, was especially lovely in the early fall. The yellowing chestnut trees were reflected by the dark water so intensely that the winding tow path became a favorite stroll for officers stationed at the nearby US First Army headquarters. But as Lieutenant Colonel George C. Marshall headed out for a brisk walk on September 12, 1918, he was in no mood for relaxation. He needed to clear his head. Just moments before, he had been called to a meeting with Colonel Hugh A. Drum, from whom he received a new assignment that would be critical to the Meuse-Argonne Offensive, even as the St. Mihiel operation was about to begin. Marshall's assignment was developing a transportation plan to move the necessary troops and equipment to the new site. The young colonel's meeting with Drum was brief, the guidance minimal. Basically, Marshall was given a list of the available divisions and their locations and told to generate a scheme and timetable to have the troops in place on the date that Foch and Pershing had agreed to launch the offensive. So stunned by the news that he could hardly mumble a question, Marshall returned to his office to weigh the task before him.

"About ten minutes' consideration made it apparent that to reach the new front in time to deploy for a battle on September 25th [later delayed to the 26th] would require many of these troops to get under way on the evening of the first day of the St. Mihiel battle, notwithstanding the fact that the advance in the fight was expected to continue for at least two days," the colonel reasoned. "This appalling proposition rather disturbed my equilibrium, and I went out on the canal to have a walk while thinking it over."[2]

After wandering along the canal for some distance, Marshall sat down beside "one of the typical old French fishermen who forever line the banks of the canals and apparently never get a bite. In the calm of his presence, I composed my mind and, after a half hour of meditation, returned to the office still without any solution of the problem, but in a more philosophical mood."[3]

In solitude, the colonel concluded that the "only way to begin is to commence," and he placed on his desk the list of divisions, maps of France, and a pencil to address the task that was complicated by several factors.[4] To insure the necessary surprise over German defenders, Pershing decreed that troops and equipment could move only at night. During the day, transports and soldiers would have to take shelter beneath trees or camouflage netting to hide their presence from German observation planes. The secrecy requirement halved the hours available for logistical movements, and the stricture was compounded by the fact that there were only three roads and three rail lines that ran from the St. Mihiel area to the Meuse-Argonne region.[5]

Marshall would have to plan the immediate transport of 600,000 troops, 2,775 artillery pieces, 821 airplanes, 189 light tanks, one million tons of supplies, 34 evacuation hospitals, 93,032 pack and saddle animals, and countless mobile kitchens, water wagons, and caissons.[6] After staying up most of the night, the colonel put the finishing touches on the plan outline, slipped it under the door of Drum's office, and stumbled off for a few hours' sleep. Early in the morning, an apprehensive Marshall was awakened and summoned to the chief of staff's office. He was relieved to hear the outline pronounced "a dandy" and "a fine piece of work" by Drum and Pershing.[7]

While the young colonel who would eventually become army chief of staff worked in solitude to complete the logistical plan, Drum and a group of senior officers led by Colonel Robert P.

McCleave were developing the plan of attack for the Meuse-Argonne. Three US Army corps would mount the initial assault. Arrayed across a twenty-four-mile front running from the dense Argonne Forest on the west to the deep Meuse River on the east, I Corps, V Corps, and III Corps (from west to east) would each have three divisions for the assault wave, with an additional division in reserve. Two French army corps under Pershing's command would be stationed west of the Argonne Forest and east of the Meuse River, respectively, but they would maintain holding positions to protect the flanks rather than join the initial assault.

As McCleave's staff made initial assessments of the area, the planners recognized that the region was especially difficult terrain for attackers. Hunter Liggett, a senior general who would command I Corps, put it best when he compared the area to a famous Civil War battlefield:

> The region was a natural fortress beside which the Virginia Wilderness in which Grant and Lee fought was a park. It was masked and torturous before the enemy strung his first wire and dug his first trench. The French had burned their fingers on the German half of it in 1914 and let it alone thereafter; the enemy had been content to do the same but had strengthened his half leisurely in the ensuing years, with all the ingenuity of skilled engineers. The underbrush had grown up through the German barbed and rabbit wire, interlacing it and concealing it, and machine guns lurked like copperheads in the ambush of shell-fallen trees. Other machine guns were strewn in concrete pill boxes and in defiles. On the offense, tanks could not follow, nor artillery see where it was shooting, while the enemy guns could fire by the map.[8]

As tough as the region was, the area was garrisoned by German units that the Americans believed to be demoralized. Veteran divisions weakened by combat and regiments still in training manned the enemy lines. Like US generals who would assign inexperienced troops to defend the "impenetrable" Ardennes Forest before the Battle of the Bulge in December 1944, the German commander, General Gallwitz, believed that no one would be foolish enough to attack through the dense Meuse-Argonne region. He was further reassured by the fact that the sector was only thirty-one miles south of the railways of Sedan, which could flood the area with reinforcements in the event of an unexpected attack. American intelligence officers estimated that during the first day of the offensive, the Germans could rush four divisions to the battlefield; on the second and third days, an additional two; and thereafter, nine divisions could reinforce the four massive lines of trenches and dugouts that made up the Hindenburg Line.[9] The task of the five German divisions in place would be to hold until additional men could arrive and halt the American drive.

Intent on preventing a possible German counterattack, Pershing directed his staff "to effect tactical surprise if possible and overcome the enemy's first and second positions in the area of Montfaucon and capture the commanding heights (Côte Dame Marie) of his third position before he could bring up strong reinforcements."[10]

McCleave and his planners agreed that the first task was the capture of Montfaucon and the elimination of its observatory, which would otherwise target artillery fire on Americans along the front. Once the artillery was blinded by the fall of the butte— by noon on the first day—the Americans would be able to advance quickly to pierce the four defensive layers making up the Hindenburg Line. The capture and quick thrust composed a tall order, calling for a nine-mile advance in a single day on a front that had been fought over without significant movement since 1915.

As planning proceeded, however, the AEF commander in chief was warming to the scheme that Foch had promulgated. In mid-September, Pershing's optimism grew so strong that he remarked to one of his aides, "If we strike hard enough, we may end the war this fall."[11] McCleave's group was determined to meet the general's optimistic expectations, even though the divisions they would deploy were among the least experienced in the First Army. The problem was Pershing's stubborn insistence on completing the St. Mihiel operation, even though Foch had given him tacit approval to cancel the effort. Pershing was, in the words of Donald Smythe, "leaving the cupboard quite bare of experienced frontline troops for the coming Meuse-Argonne operation."[12] Years later, Pershing obliquely acknowledged the mistake by admitting that his decision "compelled the employment of some divisions which had not entirely completed their period of training."[13] Indeed, the AEF commander understated the case: only seven of the nine divisions assigned to the assault wave had completed training in France, and of these, only four had combat experience. The two remaining divisions of the nine had neither completed training nor served in a combat sector of the front, a prerequisite that the cautious Pershing had earlier demanded before permitting any American division to undertake offensive operations. He felt that only by practical experience would divisions and regiments learn the techniques necessary for battlefield success.

Among the assault wave, the 79th Division was the least experienced. The green draftees from Pennsylvania, Maryland, and the District of Columbia had completed only one month and thirteen days of the required three-month training period in France, but for some reason, they were assigned the most difficult task of the entire campaign: capturing Little Gibraltar.

The 79th Division's assignment has remained an enduring mystery, puzzling generations of veterans and historians. Few documents in the National Archives illuminate the deliberations that led Pershing's staff to assign the inexperienced troops the task of taking Montfaucon. An interesting hint, however, is contained in postwar correspondence by General B. A. Poore, who led a brigade of the 4th Division. The general refers to the fact that the 79th was given the difficult objective of Montfaucon for "psychological reasons."[14] The logic was based on the belief that the green troops were bursting with enthusiasm and bored by their long stay in training camps. Like the French in 1914, the US officers hoped that these psychological conditions would propel the troops forward with such force that they would sweep over the Germans.

When discussing that decision in his memoir a decade later, Pershing sought the comfortable camouflage of the passive voice to explain the logic of using green soldiers against Montfaucon: "It was thought reasonable to count on the vigor and the aggressive spirit of the troops to make up in a measure for their inexperience, but at the same time the fact was not overlooked that lack of technical skill might considerably reduce the chances of complete success against well organized resistance of experienced defenders."[15]

As Pershing suggests, McCleave and his planning staff well understood that they were asking a great deal of the green 79th, and they knew that the inexperienced doughboys might be stymied by the fortress of Montfaucon. In keeping with the understanding that the early capture of the observatory was essential, they developed a two-part, fail-safe strategy. The planners assigned the III Corps and positioned its 4th Division to conduct a "turning maneuver" that would encircle the butte from behind and force its surrender—regardless of the success of the 79th. It was for that reason that the experienced, battle-hardened 4th had been placed on the right flank of the 79th.

Pioneered by prehistoric warriors and perfected by Hannibal, Julius Caesar, Napoléon I, Lee, William Tecumseh Sherman, and many others, the turning maneuver consisted of three elements: a holding attack on the front to keep the enemy occupied, an encirclement of the rear of the objective, and then an assault from behind.[16] Turning movements had been taught to generations of students at West Point; Pershing had practiced them in Cuba, the Philippines, and Mexico; and every midcareer officer who attended Staff College at Fort Leavenworth knew the concept by heart. Senior members of Pershing's staff—including Drum and McCleave—had graduated from Fort Leavenworth, and it was second nature for them to call for encirclement by an experienced division to aid the 79th in crushing Little Gibraltar. Following the war, Drum wrote a treatise on military offensives that describes the ideal turning movement: "One force, the weaker, is designed to engage and hold the enemy, while the other, the stronger, makes a detour to strike the enemy in flank."[17] It was this concept that determined the plan of attack for Montfaucon.

Historians have consistently failed to appreciate this feature of the assault. One of the most prominent, John Eisenhower—himself a West Point graduate and retired general—states, "On such a narrow front [as the Meuse-Argonne], large-scale maneuver in the attack was out of the question: all divisions would drive straight ahead."[18] This statement flies in the face of the First Army's successful use of the maneuver on at least two other occasions during the offensive; more significantly it contradicts written orders for the III Corps. First Army Field Order No. 20 issued six days before the attack specifies missions for each of the three American corps involved in the drive toward Sedan. The most important is that for III Corps:

> By promptly penetrating the hostile second position it will turn Montfaucon and the section of the hostile second position *within the zone of action of the V Corps*, thereby assisting in the capture of the hostile second position *west of Montfaucon* (emphasis added).[19]

Drum, McCleave, and the planning staff envisioned a critical role for the veteran 4th Division, which was the unit of III Corps adjacent to the 79th. While the 79th's frontal assault pinned down the Germans on the butte, the 4th was expected to drive quickly through the lightly defended sector east of Montfaucon. Then the

4th would wheel left behind the fortress in an enveloping maneuver to force Montfaucon's evacuation or surrender. The order for an encirclement of Montfaucon by the 4th Division explains the military logic underlying the First Army's decision to assign the 79th Division the difficult task of attacking the butte. Although the planners hoped that the inexperienced division would storm the butte, they incorporated a contingency plan. If the straight jab by the 79th did not floor the Germans, the right hook by the 4th would produce the knockout.

A major risk of turning maneuvers is that the unit that envelops the enemy objective from the side and rear could be mistakenly fired on by friendly troops attacking from the front. To reduce that risk, McCleave inserted explicit language in the orders to both corps involved that the 4th Division's action would take place "within the zone of action of the V Corps." The phrase was intended both to clarify what was expected of the 4th and to warn the 79th that a friendly unit would be operating on the north side of Montfaucon. The First Army order also provided a warning to the 37th Division, on the 79th's left flank, that the 4th Division would be continuing the encirclement around the butte to assist "in the capture of the hostile second position west of Montfaucon."[20]

When First Army Field Order No. 20 was finished by McCleave and the planning staff on September 20, it was approved by Drum and Pershing and then presented to the commanding generals of the three corps and their staffs. It then became their responsibility to develop corps plans to carry out the army orders and oversee the preparation of divisional, brigade, and regimental orders ensuring that coordinated action was taken to achieve the corps mission. Because the attack was to be initiated in only six days, there was little time for the staff of subordinate units to develop detailed plans, to confirm that the subordinate plans meshed with those

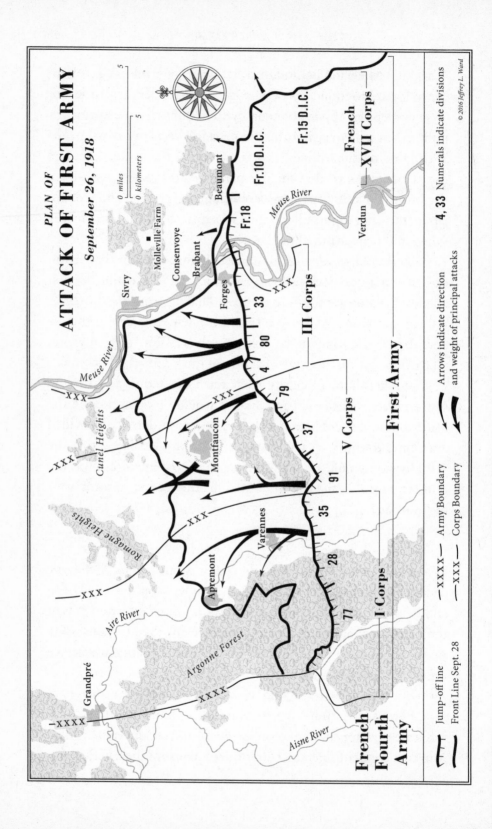

PLAN OF

ATTACK OF FIRST ARMY

September 26, 1918

0 miles 5
0 kilometers 5

Sivry

Molleville Farm

Consenvoye

Brabant

Forges

Meuse River

Beaumont

Fr.18

Fr.10 D.I.C.

Fr.15 D.I.C.

French
XVII Corps

Verdun

Meuse River

33

80

4

III Corps

79

Cunel Heights

Montfaucon

37

V Corps

91

First Army

Romagne Heights

35

Varennes

Apremont

28

I Corps

77

Aire River

Argonne Forest

Grandpré

French
Fourth
Army

Aisne River

Arrows indicate direction
and weight of principal attacks

XXXX — Army Boundary

XXX — Corps Boundary

4, 33 — Numerals indicate divisions

Jump-off line

Front Line Sept. 28

© 2016 Jeffrey L. Ward

from higher authorities, and to review them with the captains, lieutenants, and noncommissioned officers who would actually lead the assault. Apparently there was not even enough time for First Army staff to review the plans developed and returned to Pershing's headquarters by the three corps to make certain that they conformed to the orders issued by planners at the Ligny headquarters. The time pressure of planning the Meuse-Argonne Offensive while fighting another operation at St. Mihiel had injected uncertainty into what should have been a fail-safe process.

Pershing, however, was confident that corps and division orders would be written correctly and the mandated maneuver implemented because he had chosen his most competent generals to head the three army corps. Each of the men had attended West Point, and two had developed strong relationships with Pershing over the years.

The portly Hunter Liggett, who had led I Corps in the first American victories at Cantigny, Belleau Wood, and St. Mihiel, would retain that command on the far left of the Meuse-Argonne front. In the coming offensive, his divisions—the 77th, 28th, and 35th—would attack through the heavily wooded and fortified ravines of the Argonne Forest.

Following graduation from West Point in 1879, Liggett had established a solid reputation during the Indian campaigns, and had mastered higher command in Cuba and the Philippines. From 1909 to 1914, he served in quick succession as a student, faculty member, and, finally, president of the US Army War College, where he earned a reputation for being a brilliant military strategist. At the end of his term as president, Liggett led a staff ride through the Philippines, when he presciently identified the Lingayen Gulf as a doorway open to Japanese attack, should war come to the Pacific. His aide-de-camp on the ride, George Marshall, lived to see Liggett's prediction become reality in 1941.

By 1918, Liggett was sixty-one and had become quite heavy. Some officers in Pershing's headquarters questioned whether he was physically fit to command a corps. Liggett learned of this backbiting, but he never confronted the AEF commander about the matter. Later, when someone asked about his fitness, Liggett answered succinctly: "[U]nquestionably there is such a thing not only as being too old to fight but too fat. That disqualification is the more serious if the fat is above the collar."[21]

In the critical center position along the front, V Corps was commanded by General George H. Cameron, a member of the West Point class of 1883. Of the three corps commanders, Cameron was least known. He remains an enigma. Unlike many other generals, he was a man of few words, and following the war, he chose not to waste any of them in a self-serving memoir. A cavalryman, Cameron fought in the Indian Wars, the Philippines, and on the Mexican border, where he proved reliable. His first assignment in France was as commanding general of the 4th Division, a unit that fought well in countering the German offensives of 1918. As a result of this performance, Cameron was named to command V Corps for the St. Mihiel operation.

During that operation, Pershing expressed some concern about the laconic Cameron, whose troops had not advanced quickly enough from the north face of the salient.[22] But Cameron's earlier success suggested that additional experience would make him an effective corps commander. He was assigned the most demanding task of the offensive: attacking Montfaucon and leading the First Army north along the "humpback" ridge that dominated the central Meuse-Argonne region. Despite the difficult assignment, "For some inexplicable reason," John Eisenhower noted, "Cameron's V Corps . . . was given three inexperienced divisions [the 91st, the 37th, and the 79th]. And within V Corps itself, the division slated for the all-important assault on Montfaucon was the 79th, quite probably in the worst condition of any unit in First Army."[23]

Compounding these liabilities was the fact that Cameron apparently never established a strong relationship with Pershing and other West Pointers who dominated AEF headquarters. Although he had graduated from the military academy, Cameron despised "ring-knockers": officers who banged their heavy West Point class rings on map tables to call attention to their pedigree and to underscore their military sagacity.[24] There was little doubt that Cameron knew soldiering, but weak relations with superiors made him an unlikely choice to lead the most important corps in the upcoming battle.

Supporting V Corps' attack on Montfaucon and protecting the army's right along the Meuse River was III Corps, with the veteran 4th, 80th, and 33rd Divisions. In command was one of Pershing's most trusted lieutenants, General Robert Bullard. A hard-charger who earned his spurs during the campaign that captured the Apache chief Geronimo, Bullard was known for being up front with his troops. He had led the first successful American attack of the war at Cantigny. Pershing had little doubt that the flamboyant southerner would succeed, especially since III Corps' sector—in the words of John Eisenhower—was "the least challenging of those facing the corps commanders."[25] Imbued with a "belligerent spirit," Bullard had a reputation of fulfilling his mission, regardless of the cost to his men.[26]

The son of a Confederate veteran who farmed the cotton-depleted soil of Alabama, Bullard had apparently chosen his life's work by the age of six, when he persuaded his parents to change his name from William Robert to Robert E. Lee Bullard. Entering West Point in 1881, the future general astutely realized that his amended name might offend senior faculty members who had fought for the Union. He wisely registered as Cadet Robert L. Bullard. In his final year at the academy, he commanded the cadet company in which a young plebe from Missouri, John Pershing, served. Bullard later said that the two were not close during their West Point years, but he did remember that the tall Missourian evidenced promise. In a class led by Joseph Kuhn—commander of the 79th Division in France—Bullard graduated a shabby twenty-seventh out of thirty-nine officers.[27]

The war was a time of great change for the US Army, replete
with profound organizational, strategic, tactical, and cultural challenges. As the "old army" morphed into a "new army," there were
few officers more resistant to the transformation than Robert Bullard. In ways large and small, the southerner seemed to be fighting
a rear guard action against many of the adaptations that others
saw as essential to the twentieth-century military. Bullard carried
heavy baggage: the xenophobic and racial attitudes of his heritage.
As talk of American involvement in the European war mounted in
1916, Bullard's hypervigilance about foreigners boiled over, and
he reported officers he suspected of disloyalty. Not surprisingly,
many of these "suspects" bore Germanic surnames. One officer,
Bullard recalled, "a captain of my old regiment . . . was, largely
upon my report, held back [from France] as of doubtful loyalty:
though born in America, he was of German parentage."[28] When
the general found out that another officer had praised the German army, he accused him of "defeatism."[29] On one occasion,
Bullard "made an official report of another officer of my regiment
for dangerous pro-Germanism. No less an official than the Inspector General of the United States Army recommended that I
be investigated for having made such a report!"[30] The lesson was
lost on the self-confident Bullard.

Another concern for Bullard was the use of black troops in
combat. African Americans had fought in every US war, but many
officers felt that they were not reliable in battle. As a result, black
soldiers were often relegated to labor tasks or assigned to serve
with the French, a measure that Pershing resisted for white troops.
One of two African American divisions, the 93rd, was broken up
and its units parceled out to French command. The division's 369th
Regiment—known as the Harlem Hellfighters—was particularly
effective and valued by the French. Led by black junior officers and
white senior officers, the African American 92nd Division served
alongside other US units. The division ultimately was assigned to
Bullard, who professed strong disdain for the soldiers.

"Poor Negroes! They are hopelessly inferior. I've been talking with them individually about their division's [lack of] success," exclaimed Bullard in his diary. "That success is not troubling them. With everyone feeling and saying that they are worthless as soldiers, they are going on quite unconcernedly."[31] Although the III Corps commander knew that General "Black Jack" Pershing had earned his nickname by successfully leading the 10th Cavalry Regiment, an African American unit, in Cuba, that did not deter him from reaching a harsh conclusion about minority troops: "If you need combat soldiers, and especially if you need them in a hurry, don't put your time upon Negroes. The task of making soldiers of them and fighting with them, if there are any white people near, will be swamped in the race question."[32]

As repugnant as Bullard's personal attitudes are, they seldom interfered with his ability to get fighting done in France. More troublesome, however, was his oft-expressed disdain for "textbook warriors," who had been educated at service schools leading the transformation of the army in the early decades of the twentieth century. Fort Leavenworth's Staff College had begun to exercise significant influence on army organizational and operational planning. Because of the lingering effects of the army's seniority system, many "seat-of-the-pants" officers, like Bullard, would command large units in France, but staff officers at almost every other level were beginning to assume responsibility for key planning and operations functions they had mastered at Leavenworth.[33] Tension between the general officers of the "old army," who had learned by doing, and new staff officers, who had studied battle planning and complex coordination in Kansas, was becoming pronounced.

Bullard was certain that he had learned all that he needed to know in the deserts of the American Southwest. For the general, there was only one direction of attack: straight ahead. And there was only one speed: fast, as fast as possible. In this regard, Bullard was one of the most vocal line officers, but he was alert enough to recognize that Pershing relied on and trusted the staff officers who conceived complex maneuvers and drew sweeping arrows on maps. The disconnect between the two groups of officers was a serious matter, and much of the success of the upcoming Meuse-Argonne Offensive would depend on how such disputes between the old and new army were resolved. The bottom line, however, was that Bullard was tough, and Pershing knew he could depend on the crusty general to push onward, however difficult and bloody the fighting might become.

Bullard and Pershing were sanguine about AEF prospects on the new front. But those better acquainted with the area's forbidding topography, its hardened fortifications, and the Americans' naïve bravado were more pessimistic. In fact, many agreed with France's General Pétain. After reviewing Pershing's plans for the Meuse-Argonne Offensive, the revered "Savior of Verdun" shook his head and predicted sadly that the huge AEF enterprise would advance no farther than Montfaucon before winter rains and German resistance stalled progress in a situation that would spell doom for the green American soldiers and the inexperienced US Army.[34]

CHAPTER 5

"FEELING LIKE CRUSADERS"

Bullard's chief of staff, General "Wild Bill" Bjornstad (left), was as headstrong as his commander and frequently issued orders on his own. Entranced by the prospect of higher rank, Bjornstad forged alliances with those at Pershing's headquarters, including future US vice president Charles Dawes (right), who served in the Coolidge administration.

★   ★   ★

The acclaim that greeted us as we drove through the streets en route to the hotel was to me a complete surprise. Dense masses of people lined the boulevards and filled the squares. It was said that never before in the history of Paris had there been such an outpouring of people.

—General John J. Pershing, commander in chief,
American Expeditionary Forces[1]

By the time Captain Harry D. Parkin and the 79th Division landed in France in July 1918, one million doughboys had preceded them. For that reason, longshoremen on the docks of the Atlantic port of Brest hardly raised their eyes to acknowledge the khaki-clad Americans tromping off the SS *Agamemnon*.

Weary from their long voyage, Parkin's men were eager to file off the ship, sling their packs, and hike to camp where they could collapse. As exhausted as their troops, many generals and colonels of the 79th relinquished their responsibilities to seek out hotels with hot baths and soft beds. Senior officers expected their juniors to obey orders implicitly, while they enjoyed the luxuries of the ancient French city. Guided by crude maps, the young officers and men began walking from the dock in a casual manner that disturbed Parkin.

"It was not military. The French would not have done it that way," observed the short, ruddy-faced captain, whom Colonel Oscar J. Charles had designated to lead the 316th Infantry Regiment to its bivouac. "And so I decided to march through the city with full military pomp and display. I knew that this would make a good impression on our men, and then one does not enter a foreign country at the head of a full regiment but once in a life time."[2]

Parkin called his regiment to attention, ordered the band to the front, and unfurled the national and regimental colors to whip in the offshore breeze. To a rousing march, the Americans paraded up from the crowded wharf, past medieval châteaux, and on through Brest's main street, the Rue de Siam.

"The French people cheered us, and we went through with our heads held high, feeling like crusaders come to rescue a friendly country from its foes, and so I think we should have felt. And so I think a fighting regiment, come to help France, should properly enter France, not slip in informally like a lot of labour troops," declared Parkin.[3] As the regiment neared the center of town, the captain rounded a corner and saw a familiar form in the crowd.

> On the sidewalk, looking at us with pride on his face, as we came up in perfect step to the fine band, I perceived Colonel Charles, our commander. Perhaps he had not expected me to come in such fine style, but he could not resist the emotions of the occasion, and giving up his good bed in town, he came out into the street and fell in beside me, and marched through the streets with his regiment. A very right and proper thing for him to do, and a privilege that I, in his place, would not have given up for all the good beds in the world.[4]

The contrast in leadership styles between Colonel Charles and Captain Parkin could hardly be more profound. Charles, like many generals and colonels of the American Expeditionary Forces, had been brought up in the old army, in which strict discipline ordained a wide gulf between officers and enlisted men. The prerogatives of rank were ruthlessly honored, and little time was spent explaining the significance of orders to troops or encouraging their compliance. Harry Parkin intuitively understood, however, that America's precipitous entry into World War I and the quick scramble to assemble a large force had dramatically changed the character of the nation's armed forces. Rather than the disciplined veterans of the Indian campaigns or the Spanish-American War, the new army was composed of young citizen-soldiers, men who enlisted or were drafted for the duration. They were willing to obey the orders of superiors, but they rankled when they confronted the capricious RHIP (rank has its privileges) mentality of the old army.

Parkin was not a professional military officer, but he had a broad education, a firm understanding of human nature, and, above all, the flexibility that enabled him to recognize the needs of this new breed of soldiers. He would not rely on outworn truisms of order, command, and discipline. It was clear that the new soldier required directions as well as orders, inspiration as well as commands.

In a sense, Parkin had been preparing most of his life for that day on the docks of Brest. Born only two decades after the Civil War, Harry grew up in Pittsburgh hearing veterans' tales. His books were filled with war's glories, and he collected colorful artifacts from the conflict, as well as relics from Napoléon's campaigns. As if to extend Harry's informal education in military matters, the Grand Army of the Republic held its national encampment in the Steel City when the boy was an impressionable eleven-year-old. More than five thousand members of the fraternal order made up of veterans who had fought for the North in the Civil War donned faded blue uniforms to march through the streets, commandeer bars, and deliver multitudes of patriotic speeches. The boy was mesmerized. When it came time for him to enter high school, he persuaded his parents, successful immigrants from the industrial midlands of England, to send him to military school.

Parkin trooped off to Michigan Military Academy, a prep school near Detroit. Founded by an obscure Civil War general, the school proclaimed itself the "West Point of the West," although few of its graduates earned military distinction. In fact, its most celebrated alumnus was Edgar Rice Burroughs, author of the Tarzan books. Entering school, Harry had an enticing taste of barracks life, close-order drill, and fancy uniforms before he was forced to leave the next year when funding shortages began to plague the academy.

Parkin's experience at the military institute came a few years too late for him to hear the advice of General William Sherman, who had visited to warn the cadets that "War is hell." It probably would have done little good, because Harry was thoroughly entranced by his new life. His single year at the academy strengthened his fascination with the army and instilled an appreciation for military virtues that he would later put to good use. After completing high school, the young Parkin enrolled in Harvard University, and in 1904 he took his bachelor's degree alongside Franklin D. Roosevelt. A good student with a penchant for writing, Parkin went on to attend Harvard Law School, where classes in contracts and torts bored him. He dropped out and returned to Pittsburgh to join the booming family business supplying equipment to the steel industry. Although business success enabled the young man to purchase a comfortable home in the exclusive Sunnyside neighborhood, he eventually found trade as boring as law. With the start of the war in 1914, Parkin spent evenings in his study, reading newspaper accounts of the European fighting and analyzing the implications of new technologies on the tactics he had studied at school.

When a mania for preparedness swept the nation in 1915, Parkin joined a group of U.S. Steel executives who took leave from their jobs to attend a voluntary six-week military training program in Plattsburgh, New York. Designed by General Leonard Wood, the Plattsburgh plan was the equivalent of an accelerated officer-training course for young men of means who foresaw that war would eventually end American isolation. At the camp in upstate New York, the patriots learned soldiering from the ground up. Samuel W. Fleming Jr., Parkin's friend from Harrisburg, Pennsylvania, went through the course the same summer, and found it challenging.

"We had a strenuous half hour several times a week scaling walls, jumping ditches, traversing narrow planks, and dodging barbed wire, all at top speed," wrote Fleming, who later served with Parkin in France.[5] "After we had more or less mastered these feats, we were ordered to put on packs, sling rifles, and repeat the exercise. We did not enjoy this part of the schedule." In addition to physical training, the men "acquired smatterings of Army Regulations, Rules of Civilized Warfare (imagine a course in that), Infantry Drill Regulations, Minor Tactics . . . Rifle and Pistol Range firing, Manual of Court Martial, Trench digging, barbed wire handling, and field problems."[6] In a few short weeks, the Plattsburgh men gained broad, if not deep, knowledge of the military enterprise in the early twentieth century.

As Parkin expected, the European conflict eventually ensnared the United States. When Congress declared war in April 1917, Harry was among the first to sign up, even though he was thirty-seven years old, and he and his wife, Alice, had a young son named Harry Jr. As the nation struggled to recruit, train, and field its first full divisions, men with any type of military training were prized. Parkin's college education and Plattsburgh experience qualified him for Officers Training Corps. He quickly found himself on the train to Fort Niagara, New York, the oldest continuously occupied military base in North America. In the fort's stone buildings, Parkin studied the finer points of military protocol, close-order drill, small-unit tactics, and other skills needed for success as an officer. At the end of the required ninety days, Harry's leadership ability and exceptional performance won a commission, not as a second lieutenant, which was customary, but as a captain of infantry. After a few days of leave, he packed the Buick his mother had given him and headed to his first assignment, the 79th Division of the recently formed US National Army.

National Army divisions composed the third tier of America's military hierarchy, at the bottom of a rigid structure headed by Regular Army divisions, followed by second-tier divisions made up of National Guard officers and men. The primary distinction was that the vast majority of men in the National Army had been drafted; those in the Regular Army and National Guard had volunteered. Regardless of the difference, the stark truth was that with the exception of relatively few Regular Army units, Pershing's American Expeditionary Forces were the figment of a vivid congressional imagination—much like Camp Meade, Maryland, when Parkin reported on August 29, 1917. Instead of a functioning military base, the new captain found sandy, treeless fields stacked with fresh-cut lumber waiting to be fashioned into structures where the men would eat, sleep, and train. As the cadre pitched in to construct crude buildings, the post resembled nothing "so much as a western mining camp in full blast; workmen here, there and everywhere, with the whole world resounding to the rasp of saws and the clang of hammers as barracks after barracks sprang into being."[7]

The first trainload of men who would make up the 79th arrived on September 21, 1917, little more than one year before they would face the test of battle. By all accounts, the division's human materials were as green as the lumber used to construct their barracks. With twin bars of confidence on his shoulders, Parkin felt prepared to help train the men into an efficient fighting force. The new captain and his fellow officers soon learned, however, that they would face one of the stiffest organizational challenges since General George Washington formed the Continental Army with undisciplined backwoodsmen in 1775.

Struggling to train his troops to mount a coordinated attack on the British at Boston, Washington famously complained that his men were "accustomed to unbounded freedom, and no control."[8] Although the nation had matured since the founding father's time, the men making up the National Army of World War I were in many ways similar to those in Washington's ragtag army. Most troops of the 79th Division came from the remote farms and mines of Pennsylvania and Maryland, while others arrived from the factories and mills of Philadelphia, Pittsburgh, Baltimore, and the District of Columbia. Because it was customary to begin work at an early age, many recruits had little formal education and even less experience cooperating with groups to accomplish complex tasks.

Compounding these shortcomings was the fact that a sizeable percentage of the draftees were either recent immigrants or first-generation Americans. During the three decades preceding World War I, the nation had experienced the largest wave of immigration it had ever seen, with a record nine million arriving from central and eastern European countries in the first decade of the twentieth century.[9] Many of these men moved directly from Ellis Island to hard-labor jobs in rural areas. Others took manufacturing jobs in cities, where they worked long hours. As a result, most of the new arrivals had little time to master English. A survey conducted by the National Army's 77th Division discovered that its troops spoke a Babel of forty-three different languages.[10] According to one apocryphal tale, an officer in the 79th elicited only blank stares as he called the roll of his recruits' difficult foreign names; but when he sneezed, ten men stepped forward.[11]

More serious, perhaps, was the fact that many of the immigrants had not had time to adopt American traditions and customs that established unity of purpose. For these immigrants, the emotional pull of their homeland would remain strong for years. In eastern cities, ethnic, cultural, and national organizations provided support for newcomers that actually reinforced cultural isolation and delayed assimilation. In Philadelphia and Baltimore, for instance, the local German Society offered a full slate of activities, maintained warm contact with the kaiser's government, and exercised substantial influence on local and national politics. When the European war began in 1914, these societies lobbied to keep the United States from entering the conflict and thereby incurred the enmity of those supporting the Allies. Little wonder, then, that after the American declaration of war, one 79th Division soldier of German descent complained that he was being sent back to Europe "to kill my cousins."[12]

Despite these potentially divisive factors, there was something promising about the National Army. Ultimately, it would help push the grand American experiment another step forward. The soldiers represented all the diverse elements of the national melting pot, with Privates Yingling, Wosilesky, Del Sardo, and Rinus joining Privates McCoy, Hezintzelman, Di Pisquale, and Santos in the great adventure. One 79th Division lieutenant observed,

> Looking at the numerous Italians, Russians, Poles, Hungarians, Greeks, Serbs, Slavs, Roumanians [*sic*], and even Austrians and Germans in this vast Army, one at first wondered where the real American was keeping himself. Slowly the realization came that this conglomeration of nationalities was the real body of American people—they were the real Americans.[13]

Forging a unified fighting force out of the welter of humanity was challenging, and the endeavor's success rested directly on junior officers like Harry Parkin. By trial and error, suggestions from others, or personal inclination, the more effective officers discovered that the method recommended by General Washington to help govern his undisciplined recruits was as effective in 1917 as it had been in 1776: "A people unused to restraint must be led; they will not be drove."[14] For Parkin, Washington's brand of leadership involved explaining rather than commanding, inspiring rather than pushing. The company commander initiated this approach early in the training regimen, in fact on the men's first night in camp. After dinner, Parkin assembled his 150 nervous recruits for a talk, and reminded them that they would be proud of their service for the rest of their lives, and for that reason they should do their duty willingly. If they did so, the captain promised they would be treated fairly and no bullying would be permitted.

Fatherly talks like this became a tradition, as Parkin addressed his company to clarify new concepts, boost morale, and build commitment to the AEF's mission. Although the sessions were designed to appeal to the men's desire to prove their mettle,

Parkin's strategy evoked criticism from the regiment's commanding officer, who accused the captain of coddling his troops. Colonel Charles favored crisp orders unembellished by clarification
or encouragement, like those issued in the old army.

"Our sore-headed regular Colonel told me more than once
that I was too soft and too good for my men, but since he also
told me several times that I had the best Company in the Regiment . . . I feel that my attitude towards my men could not have
been very wrong," recalled Parkin. "At any rate, it was my natural
and only attitude towards them, and I, personally, found that they
responded splendidly."[15]

Other senior officers, including the veteran Colonel Claude B.
Sweezey of "Baltimore's Own," the 313th Infantry Regiment, used
a similar approach with equally effective results. A West Pointer
with a face as fearsome as a bulldog's and a voice slowed by stuttering, Sweezey inherited several conscientious objectors among
his recruits. He respectfully examined each one. If the colonel
concluded the man's claim was sincere, he was reassigned, but
if suspicion remained, Sweezey would resort to more persuasive
methods. One day the colonel interviewed an objector who refused rifle drill because "his sister had advised him not to touch
any weapon with which another might be killed."[16]

"Would you object to carrying a stick?" asked the colonel.
The man replied that he would have no objection. Sweezey had
a two-by-four brought to the office and instructed the recruit,
"Shoulder that and walk up and down in front of this office until
relieved." The next morning, Sweezey received a note from the
soldier saying that he had talked with his sister again, and "they
decided the war was just and that he should do his bit as others
were doing it. He asked to be pardoned, and promised to be a
good soldier and to obey all orders. The Colonel sent for the lad,
and after a fatherly talk sent him back to his company. From that
day to this the record of that soldier has been perfect."[17]

As months went by and training fostered unity, many of the

men began to subscribe to a common personal goal. In letters, speeches, and memoirs, the doughboys of the 79th, like their comrades in other units, declared their desire "to make good." Throughout the divisions of the American Expeditionary Forces, the wording of this sentiment was remarkably consistent, with even General Pershing joining in.[18] Coming from an era in which wealth had not yet become synonymous with success, the men understood that the war would be the ultimate test of their generation, and they were determined to earn passing grades. For some, "making good" meant showing bravery in action, but for most it entailed simply doing their duty. For Parkin, "making good" meant fulfilling his mission, caring for his men, and living up to his own high standards. Whatever meaning the ubiquitous phrase took, the men were dedicated to the task. In Europe, they often became the most exacting judges of their own performance. Like any organization, the National Army had its share of shirkers and malingerers. But those who were intent on performing well often applied peer pressure to fellow soldiers dodging duty; this proved to be the most effective remedy in America's new model army.

The egalitarian underpinnings of the National Army worked well for many of the draftees, including John N. "Jack" Bentley, a Marylander who had a solid prewar career pitching for the Baltimore Orioles, and a sterling record with the New York Giants following his service days.[19] A large, popular man, he excelled at close-order drill, mastered quickly the manual of arms, and enjoyed the camaraderie of battalion "sings" around bonfires. Bentley was promoted to corporal soon after arriving at camp, earned sergeant's stripes soon thereafter, and was selected for the third Officers Training School. On April 20, 1918, he was designated an officer and a gentleman by act of Congress.[20]

Another bright draftee, Maximilian A. W. Boll, seemed poised to follow in Bentley's footsteps. The son of a German immigrant who was a Lutheran pastor in Philadelphia, Boll had been raised with strong respect for authority. Although he did not relish the thought of returning to his ancestral home to fight kinsmen, the drive to make good spurred Max on, and he finished army schools near the top of his classes. One day a company clerk whispered that Boll headed a list of enlisted men recommended for Officers Training School. He was soon called to appear before a selection board of officers.

"One of them asked me only two questions: Where was my father born; where was my mother born," Boll wrote following the war. "When I answered 'In Germany' to both questions, I was dismissed, and that was the end of my candidacy for the Officers' Training School. Needless to say, I was disappointed, but I had experienced so much anti-German prejudice already that the turn-down was not the shock it might have been."[21]

By 1917, anti-German sentiment had enflamed the nation, and the army was not exempt. On the battlefields of France, Boll would witness the logical extension of that anger, which grew to fury as American soldiers saw their friends ripped apart by machine guns and blasted by artillery. Yet the discrimination Boll experienced was mild compared with the institutionalized racism suffered by African American soldiers. As egalitarian as the National Army was designed to be, the system clearly worked against African American troops, as well as those of German descent. Nevertheless, the enlisted Bolls, as well as the commissioned Bentleys, soldiered on. Max rose to the rank of supply sergeant and was acknowledged as one of the best. When his superiors learned that he had not been selected for officers training, they "went out of their way to give me such privileges as was theirs to give."[22]

After earning lieutenant's bars, the more fortunate Bentley was assigned to headquarters company of the 313th Infantry Regiment, a slot that entailed a wide array of duties, some of which he did not understand immediately. The men in his company used special weapons such as 37mm cannons and trench mortars, conducted intelligence operations, staffed vital signals operations, and even formed the divisional band. As Bentley mastered the various tasks he was expected to supervise, he remained perplexed about the responsibilities of a unit called the "pioneer platoon," whose job appeared to be wielding picks and shovels. It would require a trip to the front lines to clarify their duties for the former pitcher.

The new lieutenant might have had a lot to learn, but so did the other 28,000 men who made up the 79th. Along with Captain Parkin, Bentley and the remaining 1,600 officers of the division set about their tasks knowing that in a few months their men would be facing battle-toughened German troops on the Western Front. But, as military historian Edward Lengel pointed out, the training regimen taught proficiency in only "two basic principles: drilling and marching. Day after day, week after week, they assembled, drilled back and forth, spun wooden rifles, and then departed for hot and dusty route marches."[23] Shortages of weapons and equipment often prevented instruction in such advanced infantry skills as firing machine guns, throwing hand grenades, and using field telephones for communication.

But as the months at Camp Meade passed, the men welcomed an opportunity to show their stuff. To mark the first anniversary of the US declaration of war, on April 6, 1918, President Woodrow Wilson and his wife journeyed to Baltimore to review a National Army division for the first time. The 79th was chosen for the honor. The fact that one of the division's four regiments, the 313th, was composed predominantly of Baltimore natives added emotion to the event, and the men gladly hiked twenty-two miles to the city the evening before the big parade. When the troops marched down broad North Avenue the next day, citizens by the thousands cheered their native sons in "Baltimore's Own" Regiment. And hundreds of proud parents from Pennsylvania and the District of Columbia, who had taken special trains to attend the event, applauded the spit and polish of units from their areas. Following the parade, President Wilson congratulated the division's commander, General Joseph Kuhn, on his soldiers, who appeared well prepared for anything the Germans could throw at them.

Unfortunately, the division's readiness was largely illusory, because the 79th as a single entity was never fully trained, even by the meager standards of the day. It had become a "feeder division" that provided initial training for thousands of men who then shipped out to fill regiments in other divisions. In fact, 72 percent of the 95,000 officers and men trained at Camp Meade were transferred out of the 79th before it embarked for France.[24] To worsen the situation, 15,000 of the division's final 28,000-man roster had been drafted in May 1918 and trained for only two months before the 79th sailed for France.[25]

Thus the 79th Division that landed in Brest that July was in reality an ersatz unit composed of one-third of men who had been in the division since its inception and two-thirds who had joined the command sometime during its eleven months of training at Camp Meade. According to protocols established by General Pershing, any shortcomings in basic training would be addressed by rigorous combat training in France. AEF guidelines stated that no American unit would occupy an active-sector trench— much less participate in an assault—before it spent one month in small-unit training, a second month in a quiet sector of the front lines mentored by experienced officers, and a final month learning how to attack fixed defensive positions, such as the Hindenburg Line. Then and only then, Pershing decreed, would the new US divisions be ready for combat. Ultimately, however, the 79th would train for only one month and thirteen days, with little more than a week in the line, before it went over the top in the Meuse-Argonne Offensive.[26] A postwar report determined that the division's young recruits spent less time in training than those of any other American division.

A few days after the 79th landed in France, it began to move toward its training area north of Dijon. The first leg of the journey consisted of a midnight march back through Brest, scheduled to avoid the eyes of German spies suspected of reporting troop movements. The doughboys' late-night journey was distinctly different from the parade that marked their arrival. The men were sobered by the knowledge that they were moving toward the front, and Parkin noted that his regiment's mood was appropriately subdued:

> We entered the city of Brest and found the poorly lighted streets gloomy, with light in only an occasional wine shop. There were no citizens on the street to watch us pass. I looked back down the long heavy-laden column, the men's faces showing only when they came into the light of a shop or street lamp. Their heavy hob-nailed shoes made a sort of low rumbling noise in the quiet street. No other noise is like that of a soldiers marching. A thousand soldiers moving in the night impresses one as a great force, not so much as a large body of troops, but as a mighty individual thing. It becomes a unit, a single thing, a force like a strongly flowing river.[27]

The somber troops, however, erupted in incredulous laughter as they reached the rail siding and learned that they were destined to endure torture suffered by every doughboy who journeyed through France during the Great War. They climbed into French boxcars with signs describing their capacity in hopelessly optimistic terms: *Hommes 40—Cheveaux 8*, 40 men or 8 horses. The boxcars were packed with men and empty of amenities. Max Boll, writing later about his war experiences, recalled, "In addition to the men, the cars had to provide room for 3 days rations, our rifles and other like equipment. If they would have put a few more fellows in, we all could have slept comfortably standing up."[28]

As it was, the men had to sleep in shifts, with some lying down and others standing through miles of jolting passage. Because the troops were forbidden to leave their cars except at a few designated rest stops, they were forced to relieve themselves by hanging from open doorways. Officers were provided passenger cars, and unlike enlisted men, they could stretch their legs or refresh themselves in depots wherever the train stopped. The disparity did not sit well with Parkin, who decided to make the trip as comfortable as possible for his troops. At one stop, he took company funds earlier collected from the soldiers and bought two packs of cigarettes for each man, a welcomed treat.[29]

On July 24, after a long three days, the train stopped north of Dijon, and the stiff, sore troops formed up to march to their respective training sites. The First Battalion of the 316th drew villages with the impossibly quaint names of Percy-le-Grand and Percy-le-Petite, in the beautiful region of Burgundy. When Parkin's contingent reached the foot of the hill on which the larger village stood, a gaggle of children greeted them. One of the urchins, he recalled, "a very gritty little girl of eight or nine years of age, cried out at the top of her voice, 'Hurrah, Geis Grise [*sic*], here are the goddam Yankees.' The soldiers roared with laughter, but I was so astonished I could not laugh. Some soldiers of another division . . . the 28th Pennsylvania National Guard, I believe, had been perverted enough to teach this sweet little thing such profanity, which she repeated like a parrot."[30]

As the men crossed the bridge, the children leaped in front to lead the troops up a winding lane to the town square. There the soldiers stacked their rifles and dropped their packs in front of an imposing church, just as Percy-le-Grand's mayor, complete with his tricolor sash of office, dashed from the *marie* [town hall] to shake hands with Parkin and salute the doughboys. Percy offered an Arcadian idyll for the Yanks, a wonderful respite from the boredom of Camp Meade and the cramped Atlantic voyage. Under its spell, the new soldiers found it difficult to envision the combat hell that lay in wait for them, just a short day's ride over the northern horizon.

CHAPTER 6

TRAINING FOR DISASTER

Training exposed the weaknesses of aging senior American officers,
including those of one commander who insisted that trombone players
move their slides in military unison. The resulting cacophony demonstrated
the officer's inflexibility, a mortal liability on the battlefields of France.

★　★　★

Oh! The precious time wasted in our elaborate, useless, murderous "science" called "musketry." It is as
much out of style as the musket from which it takes
its name. Teaching it should be made a court-martial
offense. It is murder in print.

—Lieutenant Hervey Allen, US Army[1]

To Captain Harry Parkin, combat training was pressing business, but few enlisted men shared his urgency. The Yanks had succumbed to the pleasures of the lush Burgundian countryside by helping themselves to the burgeoning orchards, finding the best swimming holes, and spotting vineyards selling wine for a few centimes. March them to the rifle range, however, and their vision faded. The majority of the troops were apt to see more red flags signaling clear misses than bull's-eyes marking direct hits. One afternoon, following a particularly poor showing, Parkin issued a wake-up call to two companies. Sitting astride his black horse, he gave a "vigorous talk on the value of rifle fire. I told them that we were soon going to the front lines, and that they might be subjected to a charge of German infantry at anytime. I said that I could not think of anything more discouraging to troops than to realize that they were maintaining a heavy fire upon an advancing enemy which was not effective and was not stopping them."[2]

Parkin demanded more attention during daily rifle practice, as well as more effort in bayonet drill, an exercise supervised by veteran British instructors straight from hand-to-hand combat on the Somme. One Cockney instructor directed the infantrymen "to shove a bayonet only a 'hinch' into a man's throat, two 'hinches' into his kidneys, or a couple of 'hinches' into 'is 'art. If you git the blade too deep in 'is ribs, you will 'ave difficulty in gittin' it out, and the next Boche will git you."[3]

Preparing the green Americans for combat was serious business, but the time devoted to rifle and bayonet practice demonstrated that the AEF still relied on outmoded tactics enshrined in the US Army *Field Service Regulations, 1914.* The book prescribed a sustained period of long-range rifle fire to wear down the enemy, followed by a bayonet charge to finish off the foe. The Americans' romance with hot lead and cold steel was a dying echo of the concept of élan that had led the French general staff to send massed waves of poilu advancing over open ground toward entrenched German lines in a manner that guaranteed catastrophic losses. Eventually the French found the high casualty rates unsustainable, and Allied armies began to explore and master infiltration, the liberal application of heavy artillery, and combinations of infantry attacks and barrages. As a result of the experimentation, French and British armies transformed their tactics between 1915 and 1917.

As military historian Mark Grotelueschen has demonstrated, however, US Army doctrine stagnated during this period, even as the nation began to build up the size of its armed forces.[4] Ignoring lessons from European battlefields, American tacticians still worshipped the rifle and bayonet. Somehow Americans had not received the message that accurate artillery, fast-firing machine guns, hardened field fortifications, and other defensive weapons and tactics had made infantry waves as outmoded as cavalry charges. When Americans began combat training in Europe, French generals urged the use of their advanced tactics. But the Yanks were new to the war, imbued with enthusiasm, and convinced that they were superior to their exhausted European brothers. Like the French of 1914, the Yanks were eager to test strong American character against tough German steel.

"If the Americans do not permit the French to teach them, the Germans will do so," observed the French prime minister, Georges Clemenceau.[5] The words proved prophetic. After the Americans took heavy losses in attacks against the Germans along the Marne River in the spring and summer of 1918, Pershing and his staff began exploring the new, life-saving techniques. The result was a red pamphlet simply called *Combat Instructions*, which drew a sharp distinction between the old tactics of trench warfare and those new techniques needed to prevail on modern battle-fields. "Trench warfare," read the booklet, "is marked by uniform formations, the regulation of space and time by higher command down to the smallest details, absence of scouts preceding the first wave, fixed distance and intervals between units and individuals, voluminous orders, careful rehearsal, little initiative upon the part of the individual soldier."[6]

To replace the rigidity of trench warfare, the booklet espoused the principles of open warfare: a doctrine granting considerable flexibility to troops attacking fortified defenses, such as the Hin-denburg Line. "Open warfare," said the pamphlet, "is marked by scouts who precede the first wave, irregularity of formations, comparatively little regulation of space and time by the higher command, the greatest possible use of the infantry's own fire power to enable it to get forward, variable distances and intervals between units and individuals, use of every form of cover and accident of the ground during the advance, brief orders and the greatest possible use of individual initiative by all troops engaged in the action."[7]

Distributed on September 5, 1918, the pamphlet was a be-lated attempt to adjust to the new battlefield, as the American army groped its way toward effectiveness. Unfortunately, the talk of innovation was purely theoretical. The new guidelines were published only three weeks before most of the troops marched to their rendezvous with a skilled and ruthless enemy.

Parkin never mentioned the new concepts, and most of the time was devoted to teaching precisely aligned attack formations: "Ten paces between men, and twenty paces between the lines of men," he recorded in his memoirs. "Soldiers are hard to control and lead in this formation, especially in rough country, so consid-erable practice is necessary. Against machine guns and artillery no other formation is possible."[8]

When the troops moved to the front line, however, Parkin learned quickly that such orderly assaults were *impossible*. Experience conclusively demonstrated that the best way to capture a heavily fortified position was for one group to take cover, lay down fire on the enemy objective, and wait for its comrades to zigzag to the next spot of cover. They would then repeat the process in leapfrog fashion until the troops drew close enough to launch a barrage of hand grenades and automatic weapons fire on the enemy strongpoint. But in the early fall of 1918, the AEF, in historian Douglas Johnson's words, trained "infantry that attacked in linear formations of the decades gone by. It produced infantry that only knew how to attack straight ahead. It produced infantry unfamiliar with its normal supporting arms. It produced infantry willing to be killed in straight-ahead attacks because it knew no better."[9]

As the 79th continued to practice direct attacks, it also undertook large-unit maneuvers that tested the command and communication structure and the ability of companies and regiments to work in a coordinated manner. None of these exercises included training with artillery, tanks, or airplanes, nor did the units carry field telephones they would be expected to use in the Meuse-Argonne, a situation that revealed flaws in communications and coordination.

One exercise exposed something more disturbing: the questionable character of Colonel Charles, commander of the 316th Regiment. In the exercise, the colonel ordered Parkin's company to advance past one village, continue through a thick wood, and join the remainder of the regiment just beyond. The reunited 316th was then to conduct a mock attack on a village that was the final objective. When Parkin arrived at the outskirts of the village early in the afternoon, however, no other American troops were visible. Certain that he had interpreted his orders correctly, Parkin waited most of the afternoon and finally sent his adjutant to headquarters. Hours later, the assistant returned with news that the orders had been changed, and the remainder of the regiment had halted several miles behind Parkin's unit. Had the exercise been an actual attack, the enemy would have wiped out the un-supported company.

The adjutant reported that earlier in the day, orders had been sent to all the battalions and companies to halt at their second objectives, but Parkin noted that "the runner from our regimental headquarters had never found me. They should have known this, because all officers are required to initial all such general orders when received and allow the runner to take the order back with him. Of course, I had not signed any such order."[10]

The following day, General Kuhn appeared at Parkin's head-quarters and asked, "So you are the officer who got lost yesterday at the maneuvers, are you?" Parkin replied that he had not been lost, and had "carried out my original orders and reached the third objective. I never received orders directing me to stop at the second objective."[11] As a result of the exchange, Kuhn later asked Charles to explain his inaccurate report about Parkin's battalion. The colonel "made a lame job of it and got his, as was proper. Charles tried to take it up with me, and I told him very plainly just what I told the General, and he dropped it quickly. It was an attempt at a very dirty trick, the results of which might have been serious to my reputation, for an officer who gets lost on maneu-vers would not be considered as fit to lead troops in battle."[12]

Several times Parkin ran afoul of similarly malicious officers. As his troops were slogging through the mud of a rainy forced march, he was visited by his brigade commander, General Robert H. Noble, who arrived in the backseat of a warm, dry Cadillac. Known to be irascible, the general fired a question designed to unsettle the young officer: "How many men have you left on this road?"[13]

Parkin replied that all his men were still with his column, and explained that he had arranged for a truck to pick up stragglers. The brief ride up to the column generally gave the exhausted men enough rest to resume marching. The general appeared skeptical of what he had been told, and departed in the direction from which Parkin's column was moving. A few minutes later, the Cadillac came splashing back up the road with several doughboys on the running boards. Angrily, Noble accused Parkin of misleading him about stragglers. After looking at the soldiers' distinctive collar insignia, however, the captain noted that they were not from his unit. Parkin called this to the general's attention, and Noble "looked at them and ordered them roughly off his car. I had put one over on him, or rather he had put one over on himself. He said nothing but rode off and bothered me no more on that march."[14]

While many senior officers were respected for their integrity and concern for common soldiers, others, like Charles and Noble, focused on finding fault and shifting blame. Some of their concerns could be downright frivolous. Charles, for instance, directed trombonists in his regimental band to move their instruments' slides in strict military unison, an order that produced such a cacophony that the men erupted in laughter. The order was immediately rescinded. Officers such as Charles seemed to believe dogmatic discipline and harsh treatment were the only effective modes of command. In the heat of battle, however, Parkin's methods would prove their worth, while officers who depended on arbitrary techniques failed.

As Parkin trained the 316th at Percy-le-Grand, his friend Captain Sam Fleming was instructing the 315th at the nearby village of Esnomes. Through experiences similar to Parkin's interactions with his commanding officers, Fleming began to notice "an unfortunate strain in Regular Army officers that was not uncommon":

A great many who seemed to have superior qualities, appearance, aggressiveness, and enthusiasm, were more interested in soft jobs, such as staff work, and in getting decorations and promotion, than in taking part in the fighting . . . The officers who talked the loudest and inspired us the most in training camps often faded out as we approached France. Then by mysterious means they appeared in offices and limousines in Paris, London, or Chaumont [the AEF's general headquarters].[15]

This phenomenon became so prevalent that it inspired a joke that spread like wildfire when the 79th reached the front: "Now I know that the Germans have a gun that shoots fifty miles. I heard yesterday that a Regimental Adjutant had been wounded."[16]

As much as they disliked some senior officers, both Fleming and Parkin had great respect for the division's commander, General Joseph Kuhn. Although Parkin had little opportunity to interact with Kuhn, he clearly revered his commanding officer. He might have been less impressed had he known that the Meuse-Argonne Offensive would be Kuhn's initial experience leading troops in battle. After graduating first in his class from West Point in 1885, the slightly built but ramrod-stiff Kuhn had chosen a career in the Corps of Engineers rather than in one of the combat arms. He was quietly proficient as an engineer of harbor facilities and artillery emplacements, in San Francisco; Philadelphia; and Norfolk, Virginia, and taught engineering at West Point for several terms. A few years after the turn of the century, when Kuhn had been in the army two decades, someone in higher command recognized the forty-year-old major's potential for advanced leadership. He was sent as military attaché to Japan during that country's war with Russia, and on his return, he landed a choice position in the army chief of staff's office. In 1915 the newly minted lieutenant colonel was named to the US Military Commission to Germany. With the initiation of hostilities in Europe, American military leaders realized that the international situation might require a larger army, and the commission was dispatched to observe how the German army—reputedly the world's best—was recruited, trained, structured, and led. The group was welcomed by the Germans, who relished the opportunity to demonstrate their prowess to American visitors, perhaps as a warning to stay out of the European conflict. Kuhn was allowed unprecedented access, and was so close to the action on the Eastern Front that he was knocked down by the concussion of an exploding Russian shell.[17] When the commission returned to Washington, Kuhn remained in Berlin as military attaché until German submarine warfare chilled diplomatic relations.

The engineer so impressed superiors with his insightful reports about the German military that he was named president of the War College on his return, a post normally reserved for an officer from one of the combat arms. Because the army had a minute general staff at the time, the college served as the strategic planning group for Chief of Staff Hugh Scott. As de facto chief of planning, Kuhn routinely met with the most senior military and civilian leaders of the nation, and was so skilled in charting the army's development that the *New York Times* reported in September 1917 that he would succeed Scott.[18] When that story proved false, Kuhn set his sights on a combat command in France and was one of the first officers appointed head of a division in the National Army, receiving his assignment to lead the 79th before several combat-hardened officers gained divisional command. One of the disappointed officers was Robert Bullard, who was chagrined that a classmate without combat experience had been appointed to the august command before him.

Kuhn's appointment over qualified infantry, artillery, and cavalry officers placed a large target on his tunic. In the eyes of long-time officers of the line, engineers were not qualified for combat command. Historian Allan Millett notes, "For the individual engineer officer, an army career was a succession of assignments to public works projects. His work contacts and social life were within civilian society; his values were as shaped by the profession of civil engineering as by the army; his life-style was more analogous to that of a civil servant than to that of the majority of the army's officers."[19] This and rumors of cushy assignments fostered a near-uniform belief that engineers simply were not tough enough to lead men in combat.

There is little doubt that senior AEF commanders harbored

similar doubts about Kuhn. Even before the Meuse-Argonne Offensive was launched, officers of the 79th noticed that their general was "not in the inner circle of the AEF High Command," and was "ignored and slighted on occasions."[20] Still, the discipline that Kuhn instilled in troops gave Pershing no pretext for action, and the engineer survived the politics of high command to lead his men over the top. As events played out, Kuhn would have only one fateful day to prove himself worthy of combat command.

Kuhn's military bearing and no-nonsense leadership made him an impressive figure to the men of the 79th; his dedication to fairness and the welfare of his troops won their loyalty. As the division matured, Kuhn was on the lookout for promising officers, and had his eye on Captain Parkin for some time. A few days after their interchange about the botched field exercise, Parkin was assigned to a school for field-grade officers in the ancient town of Langres. Along with a group of lieutenant colonels, majors, and a few captains like himself, Parkin spent two weeks studying the use of tanks and artillery, the power of high-explosive shells, and gas warfare. Regardless of the new weapons, the officers were taught that the infantry would remain the "queen of battle." The school had been developed by Colonel Alfred W. Bjornstad, a graduate of the Staff College, who instilled the Leavenworth spirit in the curriculum. Parkin passed the course with high marks and rejoined his troops in Percy-le-Grand. When he alighted from a truck in the middle of the village square, evening formation was just breaking up. The men from Parkin's company spotted him immediately and, without prompting, came to attention. "Hundreds of heels clicked and hundreds of hands snapped up to smart salute," recalled the captain. "And I stood there amongst them and smiled with pleasure at the sight of them, good men and true and close to my heart, and the smiles and grins spread over all their bronzed faces."[21]

Much later, memories of that evening caused Parkin to reflect on the nature of military leadership: "Be just, be fair, be reasonable with soldiers, and do not fear to take a kindly human interest in them and their troubles, but never be familiar. First you must gain their respect; obedience and loyalty will follow. Harshness and brutality will never make good soldiers. They will fail you in time of need. An officer can be strict, he must be, but he need not be harsh nor unjust."[22]

The benefits of strong relationships between officers and men were often intangible, but in Parkin's case, the reward for the outstanding performance of his men came in the form of two gold leaves that arrived on September 3, 1918. Because of senior officers' absences, Harry had often shouldered the responsibilities of a major. With the promotion, he was in charge of the 316th Regiment's First Battalion, composed of four companies totaling some 1,100 men.

To celebrate his promotion and relieve the stress of impending combat, Parkin hosted his fellow officers at a party in Percy-le-Grand. "Sandwiches and drinks in plenty were served. Speeches of congratulations to me were delivered; the best of these came later in the evening, when the good wines of France had properly mellowed the officers," the major remembered years later.[23] Unfortunately, the party was nearly marred by the sentiments of one speaker:

> Lieutenant Sheridan made the prize oration of the evening, but rather ruined the effect by becoming maudlin in his cups over the approaching death in battle of many of us. Tears ran down his face, and his voice failed him. But the crowd roared with laughter during the saddest part of his speech and refused to have their high spirits dampened. *All of that merry group were either killed or wounded*, but we refused to think about our future fates that evening (emphasis added).[24]

Sheridan got his comeuppance an hour later. Staggering back to his billet after the party, the morose lieutenant fell into a canal and, in Parkin's words, "was fished out a soaking wet but soberer man."[25] Though it might have seemed exaggerated at the time, the young lieutenant's gloomy prediction proved accurate.

As a herald of trouble to come, the beautiful summer weather was slowly waning. It was September, and early autumn rain clouds were sweeping off the North Sea southeastward into the hills of the Argonne and the valley of the Meuse. Before winter's heavy showers could transform Lorraine's gray clay to glutinous mud, Pershing was determined to launch what he had come to believe could be the AEF's final offensive. The commander had been heartened by the September 15 attack on the St. Mihiel bulge, which succeeded spectacularly. In eliminating the salient, the Americans suffered only seven thousand casualties, a much lower total than expected. The welcomed surprise inspired a sense of invincibility at US headquarters. Pershing boasted to his intelligence chief that "the reason for the American triumph lay in the superior nature of the American character . . . Americans had the willpower and spirit that Europeans lacked. With military training equal to that given a European, the American soldier was superior to his Old World counterpart."[26]

What Pershing and his staff were yet to learn, however, was that General Gallwitz had been planning to vacate the St. Mihiel area as part of the continuing effort to shorten German lines. When the assault was launched, the Americans incorrectly assumed that the Germans were so demoralized from recent defeats that they had become "pushovers." In addition to misinterpreting the German withdrawal, the inexperienced AEF had made numerous tactical mistakes: slow artillery fire, placement of command posts far from the lines, communication disruptions, and huge traffic jams that slowed the movement of supplies to the front and the wounded to hospitals in the rear.[27] Pershing's unfounded assumptions about American superiority and the staff's failure to identify and correct procedural errors would be dangerous in the Meuse-Argonne, where the Yanks faced a much more determined foe and tougher obstacles.

Shortly after the St. Mihiel victory, Pershing focused all his attention on the new task at hand. To keep the Germans guessing about his next move, the AEF commander launched a strategic scheme that succeeded spectacularly. He sent three senior officers from the 79th to the far southern end of the Western Front to survey an area that supposedly would be the site of the AEF's next offensive. The Americans expected the Germans to learn of the reconnaissance and to conclude that the next US effort would be aimed at the mountains along the Rhine River.[28]

The ruse worked, and German reinforcements were sent far from the actual point of attack. More demanding and complicated than the hoax, however, was the effort to conceal the movement of a half million American troops to the front that stretched between the Argonne Forest and Meuse River. As Pershing had ordered, *all* movement proceeded at night via blacked-out transportation. During the day, doughboys slept undercover to escape observers in German airplanes that effortlessly flew over Allied lines.

On September 7, 1918, the 79th received word to move to the front, just as rain arrived on an almost daily basis. For many of the troops, the first leg of the journey was by train, and the doughboys found that the boxcars were no more comfortable than they had been on the trip from Brest. Some of them, however, discovered a worse method of conveyance. After they climbed from the train, the men of the 316th were told that the next leg of the journey would be by French camions (trucks). Unaware that they were about to experience one of the strangest episodes of their time abroad, the Yanks stood in a dripping rail yard until a group of large blue vehicles screeched to a halt. What confronted the men was no less than "a scene from Mars for the saucer-eyed doughboys," Captain Carl Glock recalled.[29] Huddled behind the steering wheels of the camions were strange-looking men who appeared to be from another planet. Called Annamites by the French, the diminutive, betel-chewing, fur-coated truckers were actually soldiers from Indochina, who were so tired from endless round trips to the front that they fell asleep as soon as their vehicles halted.

After twenty-two Yanks packed into the back of each truck, the Annamites magically revived and steered into the night, careening along the rutted, rain-slicked roads of eastern France toward distant destinations. There were accidents, and some men feared they might not live to arrive at the deadly front. After a few hours, however, Harry Parkin gained a new appreciation for the drivers' skill: "Practice makes perfect, of course, but it seemed a wonderful thing to us that these Chinese [sic] could drive those great trucks, at good speed, with no headlights and only the small red taillights of the truck ahead to guide them, keeping very close together all the time and yet never touching each other."[30]

As they rode through the darkened town of Bar-le-Duc, thirty miles southwest of Verdun, the Americans first saw damage inflicted by long-range German guns, still growling in the distance. Around dawn, the camions slammed to a stop. The soldiers dismounted to march the rest of the way to the front, a situation that greatly disappointed Jack Bentley of the 313th Regiment. He and a fellow officer had admired the warm fur coats worn by the Indochinese drivers and had resolved to swipe a pair to protect themselves from the increasingly chilly, damp weather. Before the American officers could act, however, the Annamites and their trucks sped off into the gray dawn.[31]

To maintain secrecy, the 79th Division spent the day sleeping out of sight in a nearby forest. Walking around the area, Parkin was amazed to see the lengths to which the Allies had gone to disguise stores of equipment and matériel for the coming battle. "Out in some open grass fields were placed whole batteries of light guns in gun pits, the whole being covered over so cleverly with camouflage cloth screens, as to be invisible until you were within a few yards of it. Some we only discovered by hearing the men's voices as we went by," the major remembered.[32]

After sunset, the troops were reinforced with a hot meal and sent off to find camps two miles behind the front. It was on the final night of the trek that Parkin's battalion escaped its first air raid but was singed by the wrath of its commanding officer. The night was uncharacteristically clear and moonlit, and the major warned his men that if airplanes appeared, they should not look up because reflections from their faces might betray their presence. Shortly afterward, the battalion heard planes, and then "a large bomb with a brilliant red flash burst in the field near the column."[33] Seeking cover, Parkin moved the troops off the road and into a patch of high grass where, "To my dismay, I saw that the whole thousand greenhorns were gaping at the sky, the long line of white faces showing very plainly in the moonlight. I rode down the line, handing out pungent, forceful remarks, which soon put those faces down under the helmets where they belonged."[34]

The Americans needed to conduct all their movements with as much stealth as possible, even amid the ungodly Sturm und Drang of the battlefield. A nearby French artillery battery with harnessed horses helped underscore Parkin's message. The battery's men were motionless while the plane was overhead; even the horses stood quietly. No one was hurt, but Parkin and his men came away shaken by the bombing. In his memoir, the major described the experience:

> First you hear a heavy thud on the ground followed instantly by a blinding, shattering crash and brilliant flash of red, which momentarily lights up the vicinity. The shriek and whiz of flying pieces follows, and you cannot help ducking and shrinking. Your ears are shocked, and you stumble and are confused. You are so demoralized by a close explosion that you do not know at once whether you are hit or not. You cannot help think of how terribly you will be mutilated if a piece of the bomb strikes you.[35]

Following the unsettling incident, Parkin soothed his own fear by reasoning that "bombs and shells are not the great killers of men in war compared to machine guns and rifle fire."[36] The comfort that Parkin drew from this conclusion was misplaced. Artillery was the true killer, as the Yanks learned quickly when they emerged from the trenches to launch the upcoming offensive.

After the bombing, the regiments of the 79th began to locate their bivouacs. About two miles behind the front lines were Camp Normandie, Camp Pierre, and Camp Civil. All three lay in the heavily forested lea of infamous Côte 304, which had been the scene of vicious fighting two years before. In the dense woods around Camp Normandie, where the 316th settled, there were massive ammunition dumps, mobile field kitchens, deep dugouts to shelter troops, huts for officers, assorted war wreckage—and massive graveyards. During one exploratory hike, Parkin noticed "a large purplish sheen on the hillside, and could not imagine what it could be. I found on approaching closer that it was the sun shining on the decorations of this mass of graves." With a start the major realized, "Most of those resting therein had marched up this same road, hopeful of surviving the dangers of the battle to which we were getting nearer at every step."[37]

The omnipresence of death, proximity to the front, and periodic shelling weighed on the men, who reacted in a variety of ways, both humorous and sad. On the dark night of September 20, for instance, Company G of the 314th Regiment became one of the first units of the 79th to experience a gas alert, sounded by a hand-operated claxon signaling the urgent need to don gas masks. Sergeant Joseph Labrum reported that one of his friends, Supply Sergeant Bill Brewer, was overwhelmed by dread on hearing the ominous alert:

"Good-by boys, I am going to die," said Bill, and he meant it. "Good-by Seitz and George, I am resigned to die," continued Bill in awe-inspiring tones. Then the shrill voice of a lieutenant out of the night, "Climb a tree, the gas always hangs on the ground." And the last we saw of Bill before our sides split with laughter brings to mind the picture of our supply sergeant double-timing gamely for a thirty-five-foot tree. The funny part of it was that there was absolutely no gas at all.[38]

Comrades of another soldier noted that their friend had developed a limp in his right leg that worsened as he neared the front. But after an observant officer noticed the soldier limping on his *left* leg, he received no more sympathy.

The massive troop movements, convoys of tanks, and artillery trains convinced the 79th soldiers that they were to take part in the long-expected "big push." Having completed less than half their allotted training period, however, the soldiers reasoned that they would play some secondary role in the coming assault. These hopes, however, were soon deflated by the testimony of men who visited the front lines, only two miles ahead. Soldiers from the 315th Regiment returned from the trenches with the news that the sector they were to occupy faced the dreaded Little Gibraltar of the Western Front. One man wrote later that the rumor mill quickly accommodated that fearful knowledge by generating a completely new—but spurious—interpretation: "Old-timers in the ranks scoffed at the idea of green troops being sent against positions such as those lying opposite the Regiment, and the majority of the Regiment was of the opinion that the initial attack, at least, would be made by some of the more tried and seasoned divisions."[39]

Soon enough, however, US troops would learn the age-old truth that there are no safe places on a battlefield.

CHAPTER 7

"AN OMINOUS, DREAD-INSPIRING PLACE"

From 1914 on the Germans signaled their determination to maintain a grip on France's Meuse-Argonne region by constructing strong fortifications and comfortable living quarters reinforced against enemy shells. Some included Iron Cross memorials for comrades who had fallen to the French.

★   ★   ★

Argonne Forest, Argonne Forest
Soon thou wilt be a quiet cemetery.
In thy cool earth rests
Much gallant soldiers' blood.

—Popular German army song[1]

"It was desolation itself. Ominous, dread-inspiring, it held me silent and deeply impressed," said Major Harry Parkin when he first viewed the front facing Montfaucon in late September 1918. Four long years of war had left the Meuse-Argonne region deeply scarred, with "Broken trees, bare shafts of trees, broken rusted wire, shell holes, weeds, a torn and broken and utterly wasted place."[2]

Nearly a century later, the passage of the seasons and the ministry of foresters have softened the scars that once held Parkin in awe. Decades of falling leaves have partially filled the trenches, and replanted trees shade the frozen convulsions created by exploding shells. But the woods still exhibit a washboard of fighting trenches, collapsed dugouts, and massive chasms, crosshatched by communication trenches running from the rear to the front lines. As rough as the landscape remains, it is a shadow of that encountered by soldiers nearly a century ago. In addition to dealing with the challenges of fractured topography, the doughboys were forced to dodge bullets, shrink from shrapnel, and avoid poisoned gas lurking in the cool bellies of shell craters.

Parkin began his dangerous visit to the front by entering a *bayou* (communication trench) south of Côte 304. Built to convey troops and supplies safely forward, the six-foot-deep trench ran over the top of the ridge and down a hillside exposed to German observation. Looming over it were multiple strands of barbed wire to deter infiltrators. Because of the ever-present mud, trench bottoms were covered with duckboards, and lines from field telephones were bundled low along the trench side. "Cubby holes"—one-man alcoves in the trench sides—offered meager, but welcomed, shelter from barrages.

When the major arrived at the front line, he began scouting the sector that his battalion would soon occupy. He exercised caution, because the Yanks had been strictly warned to stay under-cover, so that the Germans would not see that American troops were replacing French troops. To maintain the secrecy of their arrival, some Americans donned French horizon-blue overcoats and helmets.

Climbing carefully onto the trench's firing step, Parkin peered out over Forges Brook, which divided no-man's-land at the bottom of a valley running from left to right. Normally a shallow creek, the brook was swollen by autumn rains. The major realized that the marshes created by downpours would be formidable obstacles should the 79th be called on to attack. As he looked farther north, Parkin spied the ruins of Haucourt and Malancourt, ancient French villages utterly destroyed by the vicious fighting and shelling of the last four years. Hardly a stone stood on stone, but the rubble provided ideal cover for German machine gunners and snipers. On the hillsides forming a valley just beyond the villages were lines of trenches protected by multiple strands of barbed wire. And to the right and left, blasted woods concealed additional troops, dugouts, and trenches.

Gazing north of Malancourt, Parkin traced the faint outline of a nearly obliterated road climbing the far end of the valley over a low ridge. On the rise sat a network of earthworks that he learned was called the Oeuvre du Demon. According to the French who had learned about the Work of the Demon from a series of futile assaults, the Germans had constructed large bunkers in the area to shelter troops from preattack barrages. A little farther to the right of the ridgetop stood a massive German blockhouse so strong that it had withstood repeated direct hits from French artillery. These fortifications made up what the Americans called the Intermediate Position. Behind it loomed Montfaucon, the

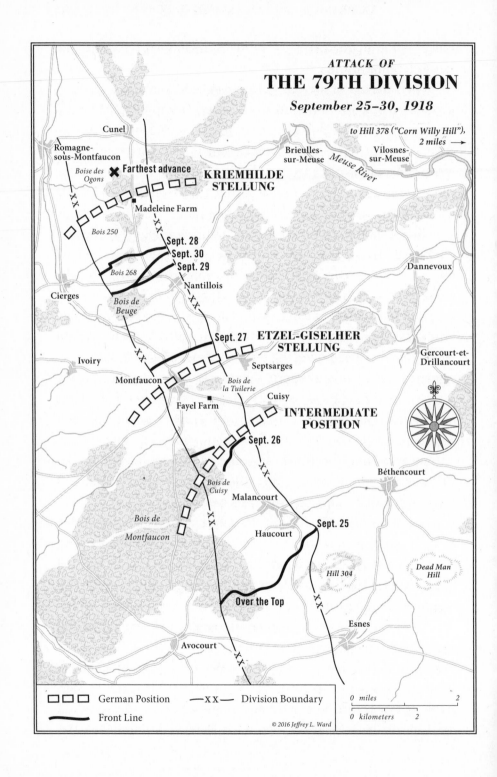

ATTACK OF
THE 79TH DIVISION
September 25–30, 1918

to Hill 378 ("Corn Willy Hill"),
2 miles ⟶

Cunel

Romagne-
sous-Montfaucon

*Boise des
Ogons*   ✗ **Farthest advance**   **KRIEMHILDE
STELLUNG**

Brieulles-
sur-Meuse   Vilosnes-
sur-Meuse

Meuse River

Madeleine Farm

Bois 250

Sept. 28
Sept. 30
Sept. 29

Dannevoux

Bois 268

Cierges

Nantillois

*Bois de
Beuge*

Sept. 27   **ETZEL-GISELHER
STELLUNG**

Gercourt-et-
Drillancourt

Ivoiry

Septsarges

Montfaucon   *Bois de
la Tuilerie*

Cuisy

Fayel Farm   **INTERMEDIATE
POSITION**

Sept. 26

Béthencourt

*Bois de
Cuisy*

Malancourt

*Bois de
Montfaucon*   Haucourt   **Sept. 25**

Hill 304   *Dead Man
Hill*

Over the Top

Esnes

Avocourt

☐☐☐ German Position   —x x— Division Boundary
━━ Front Line

0 miles   2
0 kilometers   2

© 2016 Jeffrey L. Ward

butte anchoring the first of three major fortified belts composing the Hindenburg Line.

After viewing the entire scene, Parkin had to agree with the general headquarters' assessment: the Meuse-Argonne was ideal ground for defensive warfare, but forbidding territory for offensive operations. The major had been told, however, that the quality of the German defenders was questionable, and some units used the distant woods to recuperate from earlier battle. Moreover, "No fighting or raiding had been going on for months, and only occasional shell fire disturbed the absolute peace of the front."[3]

The scene confronting Parkin was quiet at the moment, but the major knew that it was necessary to take precautions. The French had constructed a row of lonely outposts near the brook, two hundred yards in front of the main Allied lines. Each dugout was manned by twenty US National Guard troops, who had been told to stay out of sight during the day to await nightfall when they might be expected to fulfill their unique role. That mission, according to one American general, was to detect infiltrating German troops and then "to die as loudly as possible" to warn the men back in the trenches of an impending attack.[4]

Being stationed in an outpost was one of the most dangerous assignments a soldier could draw. Compared with those troops, the men in the front lines led a relatively safe existence, thanks to numerous dugouts and bunkers punctuating the muddy ground. Poste de Commande Copinard (Command Post, or PC Copinard), Parkin's headquarters, included a bunker thirty feet below the surface, in which two rooms provided space for the commander and his staff, as well as for a dozen French telephone operators who linked observation posts along the front lines to the regimental command post farther back. Many shelters in the area were even more elaborate. Lieutenant Jack Bentley, for instance, examined a bunker "capable of holding a thousand men comfortably. It was narrow in construction and had a great many entrances, each provided with a gas-proof door."[5] Although the shelter appeared safe, Bentley discovered that its protection came with a considerable price: "There's nothing so loathsome as one of the rat-infested places, with water on the floor, and cooties hiding everywhere waiting for a chance to get at you."[6] Rats were so numerous that as Sergeant Max Boll entered one dugout, he could hear "the pitter-patter of what sounded like hundreds of tiny feet: rats fleeing down at our approach."[7]

When it was not raining, Boll stayed outside to enjoy fresh air and relax in some typically French facilities. Because the sector was quiet, "At some points out in the open, the French had built small patio-like lounging spots where they could sit quite comfortably on a quiet day and drink their wine."[8] Yet, as the sergeant was to find out a night later, the peacefulness could be broken by sudden violence:

> It was some time after dusk, a quiet moon-light [sic] night on our front. Everything was so peaceful around us that I ventured to peek out of the trench toward the German lines. All of a sudden I heard a peculiar whistle pass my left ear. Before I could even realize what it was, there came another whistle past my right ear. That I wasn't dead there and then was just dumb luck.[9]

In late September, as regiments of the 79th Division began to take turns manning the frontline trenches, the Germans became increasingly watchful. Relief rotations were carried out at night to keep the Germans in the dark about Allied intentions, but the enemy began to put up more sausage-shaped observation balloons and to send additional airplanes over the lines, a sign of impending trouble. On only a few occasions did French airplanes rise to challenge the German aviators, as the kaiser's planes, with their black Maltese crosses, seemed to hover with impunity gathering intelligence over the hidden doughboys.

Following the war, General Gallwitz, commander of the Meuse River group of the German Fifth Army, claimed that his intelligence officers knew that an offensive was coming but could not ascertain the exact point of attack.[10] After the St. Mihiel operation, German intelligence officers concluded that the next American move would be either west or south of Verdun, and they were determined to find out where. The only sure way to do so was to take Allied prisoners to question. To satisfy that need, the Germans launched a series of trench raids that bloodied units of the 79th unfortunate enough to occupy the front lines at the wrong time. Purely by chance, "Baltimore's Own," the 313th Regiment, took the brunt of these attacks. The unit was responsible for the extreme left of Sector 304, near the ruined village of Avocourt, a mile southwest of the spot where Parkin got his first glimpse of German lines. Around midnight on September 20, Lieutenant Anthony McKim and a detachment of Company E moved into an outpost in a small dugout. Just as they were settling in for the night, two hissing German "potato-masher" grenades rolled through the enclosure's door. By a stroke of luck, the explosive charges at the end of their wooden handles failed to detonate, but they galvanized the Yanks, who charged from the dugout with guns blazing. Then ensued a major firefight in which the raiders were driven off at the cost of two wounded Americans.[11]

McKim and his men spent the remainder of the night on full alert—a wise precaution. Around 2:00 a.m., the Germans returned for a second assault on the position, but the watchful Americans drove them away quickly. First light revealed that the storm troopers had come back to retrieve the body of a German officer, who lay dead just beyond reach. The body, of course, was quite important because it would yield clues about the units facing the 79th. But anyone who ventured beyond the trench to recover it would be shot by watchful snipers. A regimental intelligence officer, however, came up with a solution by fashioning stiff wire into a hook used to snag the body and work it into the trench.

The dead officer's papers revealed that he was Second Lieutenant Frederich von Frienburg of the First Prussian Guards

Division, a crack German unit. The Americans were surprised to learn that he was the son of one of the kaiser's warlords. After intelligence officers examined a gold watch and other personal effects of the dead German, they boxed them up and returned them to his family through the Swiss Red Cross. By recovering the lieutenant's body, the doughboys had turned the tables on the probing Germans. They learned the identity of one of the units they faced, while preserving the anonymity that Pershing valued. A couple of days later, however, storm troopers returned once again, and this time they found what they were looking for.

The second raid began at 5:30 a.m., September 22, with a heavy artillery barrage that fell just behind the American front lines. Then German gunners slowly lifted the barrels of their howitzers and walked the barrage back toward no-man's-land, imposing a steel barrier between the lines and an outpost. "The barrage kept up for an hour and thirty-five minutes and, under its cover, a strong raiding party of Germans came on," wrote Henry Thorn, a reporter covering Baltimore's regiment. "One man was killed and one captured. The Germans suffered more heavily, as they left nine dead, including an officer, and carried off eight of their own, either dead or wounded."[12] From the dead Germans left behind, the Americans learned that in addition to the Prussian Guards, they were also facing the 157th Infantry Regiment of the 117th Division, as well as the 233rd Pioneer Company.

But the captured American soldier represented potential disaster that far outweighed the information the doughboys secured. Interrogation of the Yank should have enabled the Germans to determine that the US Army was preparing a major effort in the forests behind Le Mort Homme and Côte 304—information that should have been acted on immediately. At a very minimum, Gallwitz should have begun to bolster his defenses in the Kriemhilde Stellung and atop the butte. And yet to the amazement of Pershing's intelligence officers, Sector 304 remained quiet, even as the Americans undertook final preparation for the offensive.

As the soldiers of the 79th peered up at Montfaucon, they clung to the belief that they would be spared a direct assault on Little Gibraltar: "No one in the enlisted ranks dreamed that the division, without previous blooding, was to be one of the center divisions in the opening phase of the final drive of the World War," one officer recalled.[13]

Each day, however, brought new signs that the division was to be involved in a massive operation. One soldier recorded, "The first intimation came in the form of a group of French marines, who began the construction of large gun emplacements along the Dombasle-Montzeville Road. A day or two later, batteries of heavy howitzers took up position one by one in the vicinity of Esnes."[14]

Although efforts to maintain the secrecy of the movements remained paramount, AEF officers feared that the massive scale of preparation might eventually betray the plan to the Germans. With the arrival of large howitzers behind the lines, a new concern emerged: that the sound of powerful tractors pulling the guns would awaken the enemy, who, to that point, seemed oblivious to the growing noise. Even louder were the hulking tanks that rumbled through the dark, startling soldiers who had never seen armored vehicles before. As Lieutenant John Kress and his 314th Machine Gun Company moved toward the front, "Suddenly a black rattling monster loomed up before us almost filling the road completely. This was the first time we had seen one of those gigantic tanks we had heard so much about. Several of them came clattering along, making enough noise to waken the dead."[15]

The intense preparations made the American enlisted men as well as their officers increasingly jittery. Bentley recounted the story of one lieutenant from the 313th Regiment who was in such a hurry to take refuge from a German barrage that he failed to hear a sentry's command to halt as he ran toward a dugout. Known as particularly officious, the officer rounded a corner and impaled himself on the bayonet of one of his own troops. Later the unlucky lieutenant became the laughingstock of his regiment when word spread that he had moaned to a pretty nurse at the hospital that his flesh wound was the result of a fierce battle with a German.[16] Other incidents were more serious, as nervous Americans shot in the dark at a strange noise or sudden movement, only to learn later that they had wounded or killed a fellow soldier.

Sporadic German bombardments with high-explosive shells and gas canisters added to the unease. All the American soldiers kept their gas masks ready, and they cocked an ear for the gas-alert claxon. At such times, there was a thin line between readiness and fear, and even the best soldiers sometimes crossed the boundary. Parkin was once called from his bunker during a furious barrage. He confessed that as he neared the top of the steps, "the noise of the shells seemed to be much worse, and I hesitated, fearing to go out among them. But I soon realized that this was a poor attitude on the eve of a battle, and that my chances of making good were small if I did not take hold of myself. So I put aside fear, a thing I had to do many times, and went out of the dugout and back to my P.C. [command post]."[17]

In such circumstances, one's senses became especially keen, and soldiers learned quickly to distinguish between the sound of a German aircraft and an Allied fighter, or between a shell that was out of range and one that would land close enough to kill. Over the course of his service, Parkin became skilled at judging the danger of incoming artillery: "The shell you hear has passed you, except when you hear a certain shell noise, a loud fierce hissing sound, and then is the time that you want to drop flat or throw yourself into a trench or dugout, for that shell is coming right at you and will strike very near."[18]

Some nights, the front was relatively quiet. During such evenings, recalled Frank Barber, commander of the 304th Engineering Regiment, "the most picturesque side of trench warfare presented itself to the men in the thousands of star shells, rockets, and flares which blazed against the night sky from dusk to dawn in a display that cast into the shadows any Fourth of July celebration ever witnessed."[19]

To suggest that Americans were able to relax and enjoy the red, white, and blue fireworks that transformed no-man's-land into a phantasmagorical hell would be to misjudge the doughboy experience. Being on the front lines was deeply disturbing, a feeling enforced by many factors, not least the ubiquitous detritus of war. During one turn in the trenches, for instance, Colonel Barber saw "scattered articles of French and German equipment, rusting helmets, broken rifles and bayonets, half-rotted bits of clothing, here and there a bleached bone protruding from the earth."[20] Such signs led many troops to consider the possibility that they could very well be the next soldier chewed by war's relentless grinder circling Montfaucon.

Late in September, word started to filter out of headquarters that the inexperienced boys from Pennsylvania, Maryland, and West Virginia were indeed to have the "honor" of attacking Little Gibraltar. Pershing's order first arrived at V Corps headquarters, where General Cameron and his staff prepared Field Order No. 6, which detailed the plan of attack for their three divisions: from left to right, the 91st, the 37th, and the 79th. The map attached to the order showed the 79th on the right of the corps attacking through the villages of Haucourt and Malancourt and the Bois de Montfaucon to the ominous butte on the horizon.

To maintain security, information about the ominous mission was at first limited to senior officers. On the evening of September 22, just four days before the assault was to begin, General Kuhn assembled his staff and brigade officers to announce that an attack was imminent. As a precaution, however, no date would be announced until late on the day before the assault. As a substitute for the date, the AEF used the term *D-day*, likely for the first time in US military history. The 79th's brigade commanders

(Generals Noble and William J. Nicholson, each in charge of two regiments) were limited to informing their own staffs and regimental commanders.

On September 24, only two days before the attack was to begin, majors, captains, and lieutenants—the officers who would actually lead the battalions, companies, and squads into combat—were briefed on their assignments and given maps to study. Jack Bentley of the 313th remembered that his briefing ended with a flash of insight about the task his pioneers would be asked to undertake:

> Colonel S- [Claude Sweezey, the regimental commander] in his talk to ninety odd officers of the regiment that afternoon, concluded his speech by calmly saying: "Lieutenant Bentley, with his pioneer platoon, will cut the [barbed] wires up to the jumping-off place tonight, and on the morning of the 26th, will form his platoon into sixteen teams of three men each and will precede the infantry over the top as wire cutters."[21]

The surprise announcement left Bentley speechless, because his short time at the front had taught him that "Cutting wire is one of the most dangerous pastimes known, and about the only thing that will beat it is to get up when you hear a shell coming, to see where it will land."

Nevertheless, the good-natured lieutenant accepted his assignment and, "I kissed myself good-bye, and as my friends gathered around me to tell me to 'go for it,' I gave them the address of my relatives that I wanted notified in case I got bumped off."[22]

Foch had authorized a one-day delay for the offensive, so D-day was to be September 26. Only one day before, Parkin and the other officers of the 316th were briefed fully on the offensive. That afternoon, the major attended a conference at which his brigade commander, General Noble, explained erroneously, "Our plan of attack was that used by the French. We were to advance in very open formation, the men ten paces apart, and the lines or waves twenty paces in advance of each other."[23] Clearly, the new tactics pioneered by the French and advocated by Pershing's pamphlet on open warfare had not filtered down to the brigade level, and Noble ordered an attack in neatly formed but deadly ranks.

Several elements in the First Army's Field Order No. 20, however, reflected a commitment to the new tactics. The first was the use of a short, overwhelming artillery barrage of German lines and supply routes that would begin at 11:30 p.m. on the night of September 25. To maintain surprise as long as possible, only 20 percent of the guns would begin to fire at that hour, so that the barrage would mimic a routine nightly bombardment. At 2:30 a.m. the remainder of the guns would open fire, an unmistakable sign that an attack was on the way.

The second element reflecting the new thinking was the use of a "rolling barrage" that would begin at 5:30 a.m., when American troops entered no-man's-land. As Nicholson's 157th Brigade attacked, its 313th and 314th Regiments would proceed toward German lines following a curtain of hot shrapnel and high-explosive shells laid down by the division's batteries. As the regiments advanced one hundred meters every four minutes, so would the barrage. If the soldiers followed closely enough behind the artillery, German troops who had sheltered in their dugouts would have little time to emerge and set up their weapons before the American infantrymen were on top of them. This combined-arms technique had proved to be very effective on the Western Front.

The third and clearly the most critical element of open warfare in the First Army's plan was the order for the 4th Division of the III Corps, under General Bullard's command, to conduct a turning maneuver to envelop the butte. The tactic was designed to assist the neighboring 79th of General Cameron's V Corps to capture Montfaucon. Cameron realized that this element of the attack was so important that he specifically called the 79th's attention to it in his order for the division:

HQ 79th

American E.F., France

13 H30

F.O. No. 6

Part I (b) the 4th Division (3rd Army Corps is on our
right—) and is to assist:—in turning MONTFAUCON;
and (later) by turning the sector of the hostile 2nd position in our divisional front.[24]

Eyewitnesses recalled that the 4th Division's turning maneuver was emphasized at briefings given at army, corps, and divisional levels. Addressing his engineers, Colonel Barber called
attention to the special circumstances by saying, "While the
Seventy-ninth Division was to make the direct assault on Montfaucon, the Fourth Division on the right was to aid in turning
the stronghold . . . At the same time, the Thirty-seventh Division, on the left, was to contribute its part by assisting in turning
the Bois de Montfaucon [a heavily defended forest on the left
side of the 79th's zone]."[25] The announcements of these incursions into the 79th's zone of operation were especially important
because they alerted General Kuhn's troops to watch for Americans operating in their front to avoid friendly-fire casualties.

The promise of assistance was comforting, but the officers
of the 79th would have been astounded had they known that
the orders issued by Cameron's counterpart—General Bullard—
contained no mention of III Corps' envelopment of Montfaucon.
Instead, the veteran 4th Division—serving on the 79th's right
flank—was ordered by Bullard to charge on, bypass Montfaucon,
and advance as quickly as possible to its corps objective line near
the main part of the Hindenburg Line. To make this order explicit
to his men, the general wrote that he had "called together my
division commanders and told them that in every fight in which I
had thus far taken part I had heard division, brigade, and regimental commanders excuse their failures to continue the advance by

blaming the units on their right or left for failing to come forward with them. 'I shall take no such excuse on this occasion,' I added. 'Each of your divisions maintains its reserve for the very purpose of protecting your flanks.' That was enough."[26]

Indeed, it was enough. With Bullard's injunction ringing in their ears, 4th Division commanders knew that they would face severe punishment for attempting to aid neighboring divisions.

The orders issued by Cameron and Kuhn conformed to the directions of the First Army, and aside from the rolling barrage and the expected turning of Montfaucon, they were quite traditional. At H-hour, Nicholson's 157th Brigade would make the assault, with its 313th Regiment attacking through the wooded ridges on the left side of the sector near Avocourt and its 314th Regiment attacking up the valley containing the destroyed villages of Haucourt and Malancourt. In reserve, Noble's 158th Brigade would follow a thousand meters behind, with its 315th Regiment on the right and its 316th on the left. Two battalions of small Renault tanks and a few heavy tanks would assist the attack regiments when the brigade commanders requested and if the ground where they were to be deployed could bear their weight.

The follow-up regiments, including the 315th and Parkin's 316th, were to mop up areas of German resistance passed by the assault regiments. North of Montfaucon, the fresh troops of the 158th Brigade (the 315th and 316th) would move through the tired soldiers of the 157th to continue the attack northward toward the Kriemhilde Stellung. At the end of the first day, the 79th was expected to create the long-sought Allied breakthrough by puncturing the German main line of resistance that lay some nine miles beyond the division's starting point. This schedule was based on Pershing's optimistic appraisal of American troops, but one historian called it "an attack timetable fit for an army of supermen."[27]

As Harry Parkin contemplated the 79th's formidable task, he found himself somewhat disappointed by the reserve role assigned his battalion, concluding that in the follow-up position "our trouble would be shellfire mostly."[28] On reflection, however, the major realized that his responsibilities were substantial. In addition to shepherding the troops of his own battalion, he would have half of Company F (from another battalion), a heavy-weapons platoon (from the headquarters company), and several squads of pioneers (also from headquarters). By Parkin's calculation, he would direct more than 1,200 men in the coming battle.[29] The major knew that leading so many men with such disparate missions would be challenging. He retired to his dugout to study maps of the area, detailed with tiny blue lines marking German trenches, redoubts, and bunkers.

While Parkin studied his maps, the 28,000 other men of the 79th Division got down to work as well. Supply sergeants were particularly busy. In the 313th, Sergeants Maximilian Boll and Henry Gunther, both Baltimoreans of German parentage, made sure that each doughboy received the requisite two hundred cartridge shells, ten hand grenades, and two days' worth of emergency rations, including hard crackers and tins of corned beef, derisively called "corn willy" by the troops. Although the infantrymen turned in their packs and blankets to be reclaimed later, the men who would advance through the battlefield's muddy shell holes were still weighted heavily.

With the pioneer squads, Bentley sharpened wire cutters and wondered what he was likely to encounter in no-man's-land. In the 314th Machine Gun Company, Kress oversaw the cleaning of the new Browning water-cooled machine guns that would challenge the long-standing battlefield dominance of the Germans' sled-mounted MG08s and the more mobile MG08/15s. All the doughboys put an extra layer of oil on their personal firearms: Enfield Model P-17 bolt-action rifles, French Chauchat light machine guns, or Browning automatic rifles for enlisted men; Colt and Smith & Wesson .45 revolvers for noncommissioned officers; and, of course, the newer Model 1911 Colt .45 automatic pistols for officers. One officer took special pride in preparing the well-made Brownings for combat: Lieutenant Val Browning was the young son of the weapons' designer.

Well behind the lines at the Camp des Gendarmes, the engineers began loading their trucks. Equipped only with picks, shovels, and mule-powered graders, the men had the tough task of rebuilding roads through no-man's-land. Most roads had been obliterated by a combination of four years of fighting and German destructiveness; only hard work could make them passable for the movement forward of vital field artillery, ammunition, and supply convoys, and rearward for ambulances carrying the wounded to life-saving hospitals. Although Barber trusted his engineers, he wondered if he had enough troops to make the repairs necessary to supply and reinforce the infantry.[30]

The 79th's artillerymen were also busy, checking the map coordinates of fire missions they would soon undertake. Although they were not the batteries that had originally been assigned to the 79th, the artillerymen were fully committed to providing the best support available. They were hampered, however, by not having established relationships with the officers with whom they would be communicating from the front lines. The plan that Pershing's artillery staff had developed was a sound one. The heavy artillery, including some fourteen-inch naval guns on railroad carriages, was targeted to disrupt the movement of German reinforcements and supplies well behind the front. The field artillery, with their French 75s and 155s, would pulverize the fortifications making up the various layers of the Hindenburg Line. When the doughboys went over the top, the field artillery would shift its attention to laying down the rolling barrage to suppress German fire. Once the first line of fortifications was captured, the field artillery was to move forward quickly to be in position to support succeeding infantry attacks.

These planning activities kept the doughboys busy, but their minds turned repeatedly to the coming battle. Pressure was building, and the men dealt with it just as soldiers of every age have countered hopes and fears. Many wrote "last" letters home. Others sought the solace of religion. Private Andrew Kachik of the 314th attended Catholic services in an unusual chapel. Using ropes, he and his comrades bent several small trees to form an arch over two boxes serving as an altar. Standing in the rough sanctuary, the priest heard over eight hundred confessions and administered communion to all comers. "I will never forget that evening," Kachik recalled. "Just think, people gripe about fancy altars nowadays. To me that was a beautiful altar. I knew God was here."[31]

While Kachik sought divine protection, soldiers in the 313th were attempting to decipher the supernatural implications of their ominous regimental numeral:

> Privates Bill Conway and Bob Armstrong . . . sat there discussing the strangely persistent presence of the number "13" in and around their immediate neighborhood. It had been Friday, the 13th, when the regiment had arrived in the Bois de Pommes preparatory to taking the Avocourt sector. That day, as soon as midnight had gone, would be just 13 days ago. The date of the attack was just twice 13. And there were 13 active men in the regimental intelligence section, and the regiment itself was the Three Thirteenth! Lucky or unlucky?[32]

Defying augury, junior officers pierced the somber mood with jibs and jabs. "I'll appropriate your cigarettes and dog biscuits tomorrow, when you're yelling for Peter at the Gates," joshed one lieutenant of Italian descent to his friend. "Say, whop [sic], you're mistaken. I'll be taking that five bucks you owe me from the last poker game, when you're with your monkey ancestors," came the tart reply.[33] The bravado could not mask the truth that many men were deathly afraid of what was to come, some so disturbed that they were willing to do anything to avoid combat. In the woods behind the lines, Bentley was sitting in a pup tent with fellow lieutenants, when he heard a shot ring out, followed shortly by another. Two men had put themselves out of action by shooting themselves in the foot. "They were sent to the hospital marked 'S.I.W.' (self-inflicted wound). There were many cases of that kind and you could hardly blame the boys for the strain was exceedingly great," the lieutenant remembered.[34]

The strain *was* great, and no one felt it more acutely than Bentley. On the evening of September 24, he led his pioneers through the bayou to the front lines beyond which they would fulfill the first half of the mission: clipping paths for the attacking troops through Allied barbed wire. On his way, Bentley took steps to protect his troops, including "telling all that I met not to fire on that night, while we were cutting the wire in front of them, and I am glad that I took that precaution, as one machine gunner did take us for an enemy patrol, and nearly killed some of my men, and we would have had a lot more trouble had I not taken that precaution."[35] After the pioneers reached the front trenches, they prepared for four hours of hard, dangerous work under Bentley's direction:

> At dusk we were ready to start, and I led the men, showing them the North Star, and told them to cut due north. I divided them up into eight teams, and they went to it. This was a hard job and the boys were exhausted when twelve o'clock came; I blew my whistle and collected them together at the jumping off trench. We had done our work. Our hands were torn and bleeding, clothing torn and wet, many of the boys had slipped into shell-holes filled with cold water, and the whole party was about all in. It took us two hours to get back to camp and at daylight I was up, and reported to Colonel S- [Sweezey] that the work was complete. He told me we were to go back that night and tape off the front and on the following morning we were to go over the top at five-thirty, preceding the infantry.[36]

Bentley knew that the second night of his pioneers' work would be even more dangerous than the first, because the men would have to wade Forges Brook to clip German barbed wire on the far side of no-man's-land. Placing the white tape was particularly important because on the morning of the attack it would help guide the Yanks through the predawn darkness to pathways clipped in the barbed-wire barriers.

The proximity of the pioneers to enemy trenches would dramatically raise the chance of detection. During the previous night, every clip of the wire cutters sounded like explosions of artillery shells, and the harsh light of enemy flares sent the pioneers flopping on their stomachs and freezing in place. To reduce the danger, the lieutenant issued strong warnings to his men to muffle the noise of their clippers with rags and to avoid being silhouetted against the lighter sky.

As Bentley's men entered no-man's-land and waded across the swollen stream, the enemy remained quiet. Only a random rifle shot and a stray mortar round broke the still night. Although the young lieutenant was too busy to recognize it, his squad's stealthy advance was the culmination of all the First Army's veiled troop movements, truck convoys, tank expeditions, and individual trips—the revelation of any one of which could have betrayed American intentions to the enemy. Even after the capture of the doughboy from the 313th, secrecy had held. Somehow the Germans had not pulled the discrete bits of evidence into a pattern enabling them to discern what had been happening.

Against all odds, Pershing had achieved one of the primary conditions for the success of his offensive: strategic surprise. As historian Edward Lengel concluded, "The failure of German intelligence presented the Americans with a precious opportunity to score a striking victory in the Meuse-Argonne. They would have to move fast to take advantage of it."[37]

PART II

BATTLE AND BETRAYAL

The heart of Montfaucon's secret observatory was a telescopic periscope similar to this portable model. Like today's drones, the device could precisely target American positions for the supremely accurate German artillery that caused havoc across the entire twenty-four-mile-wide front.

CHAPTER 8

TOWARD MONTFAUCON
AND INTO A TRAP

Even Colonel George Marshall admitted that the explosion of shells from Germany's 210mm howitzers shook him up. The gun and its evil sisters, Austrian 88mm cannons dubbed "whizz-bangs," inspired fear in doughboys advancing against German lines in the Meuse-Argonne.

★   ★   ★

Aptly named is the Mount of the Falcon. Sharp are its beak and claws. Before the attackers can even reach it they have to cross rough ground where well-hidden machine-guns give them a rough passage. Rougher still is the handling suffered by those who attempt to gain its forbidding crest.

—B. H. Liddell Hart, British military historian [1]

C aptain Edward V. (Eddie) Rickenbacker awoke well before dawn on September 26, 1918. It was only his second day as commander of the famed 94th Fighter Squadron, and the American ace was eager to get his Hat-in-the-Ring Squadron "up and at 'em."[2]

The captain knew that it was D-day for the Meuse-Argonne Offensive, and he and his pilots were itching to take on their assigned task: destroying German observation balloons in the sector. If the pilots were successful in what they called "balloon busting," the enemy artillery would become dependent on the observation post at Montfaucon. The expected capture of the hill on the first day of battle would effectively blind the German guns, and the infantry could advance with much less danger.

At precisely 5:20 a.m., Rickenbacker pushed the throttle on his French SPAD fighter to the fire wall and followed the rest of his pilots into the air. As he flew north looking for landmarks, he viewed the horizon:

> I saw the most marvelous sight that my eyes have ever seen. A terrific barrage of artillery fire was going on ahead of me. Through the darkness the whole western horizon was illumined with one mass of sudden flashes. The big guns were belching out their shells with such rapidity that there appeared to be millions of them shooting at the same time. Looking back I saw the same scene in my rear. From Lunéville on the east to Rheims on the west there was not one spot of darkness along the whole front.[3]

The roar of the biplane's Hispano-Suiza engine masked the artillery's sound from the American pilots. At ground level, however, doughboys huddled in frontline trenches were exposed to a panoply of terrifying effects: blinding flashes, unbroken thunder, concussions puncturing eardrums, and the shaking of the earth as the huge artillery shells, some weighing as much as 1,400 pounds, ripped into German fortifications.

In memoirs, witnesses to what was called "the greatest barrage in military history" struggled to find metaphors to convey the violence. Captain W. Sinkler Manning, son of South Carolina's governor and a member of the 316th Regiment's headquarters staff, likened the barrage to "a monstrous chorus of destruction, a hundred rending volcanoes," while General Robert Bullard upped the rhetorical ante by describing the bombardment as "the sound of the collision of a million express trains."[4]

The fourteen-inch naval guns mounted on massive rail carriages made the loudest noise, followed closely by French 520mm howitzers. These and other large-caliber guns led off the firestorm a half hour before midnight; at 2:30 a.m., the "big boys" were joined by a mass of smaller guns, including the ubiquitous French 75mms.[5] Despite the September chill and the mist left over from evening rain, gunners sweated profusely throughout the night, loading and firing many of the 4.2 million shells that Colonel George Marshall had helped assemble for the offensive. Doughboys called the show "the million-dollar barrage," which was said to have expended more firepower than both sides used during the entire Civil War.[6] Monetary and historic measures aside, what impressed most observers was the continuous roar of the barrage. As each of the 2,775 American and French guns along the twenty-four-mile front fired as quickly as possible, the individual explosions merged into "one continual stupefying concussion, one pulsating scream of shells."[7]

All along the US line, the barrage evoked patriotic emotions. "America was answering all of the questions about herself that night—she was cleaning away every stain on her good name, and I was mighty proud to be there and do my part," said Lieutenant Jack Bentley.[8] Extending the theme of patriotism, Field Surgeon William Hanson compared the cannonade to fireworks on the Fourth of July, and Lieutenant John Kress thought, "What joy and elation it is to stand under your own barrage and feel that the other fellow is getting his."[9]

The Yanks had little experience with such barrages, so they were bound to be impressed. They had not witnessed the long cannonades that led off the Somme Offensive or the attack on Verdun. Such barrages reduced even the strongest soldiers to whimpering wrecks, as narratives written by the men who crouched in bunkers make clear. In keeping with Pershing's desire to achieve surprise, the Americans limited the Meuse-Argonne bombardment to a few hours. But the ferocity of the barrage more than made up for its brevity. Two of the kaiser's leading generals later testified to that fact. Erich Ludendorff, who had become the chief German warlord, gave credit to the "extraordinarily strong artillery" of the Americans.[10] By describing the cannonade as "drumfire," General Gallwitz awarded the highest accolade to the Allied barrage. The unbroken roar of an endless line of rolling drums rattled the windows in Gallwitz's headquarters, some twenty-five miles behind the front.[11]

The explosions shook Harry Parkin's troops as they marched through the bayou toward the front lines. The young major was eager to get into battle and reached the front ahead of schedule. There he encountered the forbidding commander of the 313th, Colonel Claude Sweezey, who chewed out Parkin for mixing the 316th with his assault wave. The major knew he was wrong and meekly countermarched his men down the lengthy communication trench. Just as day was breaking, he reached the south end of the bayou, immediately turned his troops around, and marched them back up the trench to the front lines, where they would go over the top as the second wave.

"At 5 o'clock to the second, there was a mighty cheer and shouts, which were sufficient alone to inspire fear in the hearts of the Huns and two battalions of the Three Hundred and Thirteenth leaped out of the trenches into No Man's Land on the journey to the Rhine," wrote Lester Muller, a reporter for the *Baltimore Sun*.[12] But other witnesses recalled no such enthusiasm. Their memories echoed those of another soldier: "Doughboys when they're going up to the lines they look straight in front of them and they swaller every third step and they don't say nothing."[13]

Troops in the 316th's Company F were more talkative as they engaged in a cacophony of brave banter and whispered instructions before using ladders to climb over the parapets of their trenches:

"As skirmishers—don't bunch up—keep down, but keep moving," were the orders passed along the line.

There were some scared faces. Others were grim. But as a whole, Company F went into its first battle with light hearts and laughter.

"You never hear the one that hits you," Corporal Bill Sommer told his squad.

"No metal can touch me!" yelled Gene Jacks, waving his famous lavender Boston garters, which he always carried for sentimental reasons.

"Wait till my girl sees me parade down Broad Street in good old Philly!" grinned Warren Sherff.

"Hot damn!" A shell burst with a bang. "The cossackers!"[14]

"Don't cuss, fellows—this is no time to swear," pleaded Slim Holloway.[15]

The chatter subsided when the outfit's most popular officer, Captain Benjamin Hewit, waved his hand forward, noncommissioned officers blew their whistles, and the men of Company F went over the top into no-man's-land.

Assault troops had been ordered to "keep their noses" in the rolling barrage, a technique that consisted of staying as close as possible to the advancing wall of shrapnel to surprise the Germans before they could clamor out of their bunkers.[16] Achieving the fast pace would have been easy on the smooth ground of a drill field, but battlefield conditions made it virtually impossible for the doughboys to keep up. Millions of shells fired during the battle of Verdun had cratered the ground so that it resembled the surface of a golf ball, confounded further by the entwined trunks of blasted trees. Everywhere, footing and sight were uncertain, as a "thick second growth had sprouted up around the shell craters and broken timbers, which concealed the enemy and confused any American commander trying to keep his men together and in touch with the platoon or company on either flank," explained one officer.[17]

Compounding the difficulties of a fractured landscape was a smoke screen laid by US chemical warfare troops. The thick smoke mixing with ground fog from overnight showers obscured all landmarks and rendered maps useless. The disorienting effect was like being "engulfed in the deepest kind of a gloom," according to Sergeant Joseph Labrum of the 314th.[18] A literal "fog of war" descended on the 79th as it struggled through bands of barbed wire, around shell craters, and over fallen tree trunks. Vision was so limited that the initial troops had to feel their way along, a circumstance that led to disturbing experiences. One group of infantrymen burst into a small clearing in the woods where, through the dense fog, they spied "a group of grotesquely huddled figures in American O.D. [olive drab]. The man in the lead putting his hand to the shoulder of one of these figures drew it away sharply in swift enlightenment—murmured a hardly audible, 'Dead!' and stumbled on."[19]

To keep the attack on course through the murk, Parkin instructed his officers to set their compasses to 258 degrees and forge on.[20] Using dead reckoning, the Yanks could be sure that they were making their way toward Montfaucon, which lay to the northwest. For maximum protection, the advancing doughboys tried to keep up with the rolling barrage, but the bombardment slowly began to pull away from the troops. "It is not hard to appreciate the helpless, heartsick feeling of the frontline officers and those others whose understanding of battle tactics was sufficient to convey the significance of it to them, when they realized that the almost essential protection of that great tidal wave of steel missiles was lost to them for good," Colonel Barber explained.[21]

By 7:00 a.m., as the rolling barrage moved on toward the north and the fog dissipated, snipers and machine gunners who had hidden farther back crawled out of holes to begin their deadly work. They ascended to the surface, hastily reconstructed camouflaged nests, and took aim at Americans advancing toward them. Commonly referred to as "suicide troops," these men added resilience to the Hindenburg Line by pledging to fight to the last. Word had it that German snipers targeted US officers, a tactic that was remarkably effective, as a higher proportion of officers than enlisted men was killed on the first day. But any doughboy who presented a good target was gunned down. Little wonder, then, that Americans developed a burning hatred for snipers and machine gunners, whom they viewed as cowardly bushwhackers. Years later, Harry Parkin still grew angry remembering the German covert combat: "We always regarded it as a mean, contemptible way to wage war. It was more like real murder than war. Snipers never stopped an advance nor won a battle and hence, are, in reality, useless in winning a war. I have always thought it took a mean, sneaking man to make a sniper. Our men hated them and killed them ruthlessly like dogs."[22]

On the left side of the 79th's sector, the 313th had hardly advanced one hundred yards into the thick Bois de Malancourt before the first German sniper struck, and Bernard Repp went down with a bullet in his leg.[23] A few more yards into the woods, machine guns opened up, and Privates Jack Mitchell and Brian Pritts took hits. The shots seemingly came out of nowhere, and attempts to locate the gunmen were fruitless.

On the right side of the 79th's sector, assault troops of the 314th and moppers-up of the 315th waded through the knee-deep swamp formed by Forges Brook, a natural obstacle that made the Yanks perfect targets for snipers. Slogging through the wetlands, Lieutenant Raymond Turn was obliterated when an enemy bullet struck and exploded several hand grenades contained in his combat vest. Many other Americans fell to well-aimed single shots before they reached dry ground near the destroyed hamlet of Haucourt.[24] There the doughboys encountered their first concrete pillbox with machine guns, which they quickly knocked out of action. The collapsed structure still sits beside the road to Montfaucon.

The dangerous tasks of mop-up regiments were to locate and eliminate snipers and machine-gun nests that had remained hidden from earlier waves. Some Americans, such as Sergeant Grover C. Sheckart of the 316th, became quite skilled at this work. Rather than charging directly toward the enemy as he had been taught, the sergeant crawled around behind nests and shot the Germans in the head. On one occasion, he eliminated four machine gunners in this manner and won the Distinguished Service Cross for his deadly effective work.[25]

As the morning wore on, some German suicide squads reconsidered their dedication and concluded that they did not want to die for the fatherland. They adopted innovative tactics to survive. When the Americans came upon a nest filled with spent cartridges and a cold gun, they took the Germans prisoner; those men had apparently deduced that they had been abandoned by their fellow soldiers and had decided to expend their ammunition harmlessly in hopes of winning mercy. Occupants of other nests, explained Parkin, "fired to the last minute and then jumped up and tried to surrender, with the American dead lying right in front of them.

Very rarely were they taken alive in such cases, nor should they be. It is very hard to grant mercy to people who have slaughtered your comrades to the very last moment."[26]

Despite the Yanks' hostility, some members of German suicide squads did become prisoners of war. During the advance toward Montfaucon, for instance, Private Casper Swartz of the 314th encountered an astounding sight:

> [W]e came across two men and a boy about fourteen or fifteen years old chained to a heavy machine gun by the Germans, they were left there to hold the American troops back and kill all they could, we had heard of people being chained to their post before we were on the lines, we could not believe it but we seen [sic] it here today, they had plenty of ammunition, so they were taken as prisoners.[27]

More often than not, however, German machine gunners did their utmost to slow the Yanks' advance. With camouflaged helmets, green-painted faces, and remotely controlled "electric clickers" simulating the fire of Maxims, the Germans confused the doughboys.[28] When surrounded, German gunners often resorted to treacherous tactics to take some Yanks with them as they died. Bentley recalled that as the Americans approached one nest, "one of the Boche was standing with his hands above his head calling 'Kamerad' [shouting "Comrade!" in a false attempt to surrender]; the other one was using his machine gun on the advancing ranks. Both men were shot by our automatic riflemen."[29]

It took great bravery to hunt lurking snipers and machine gunners, and throughout the day, more men began to follow the example of Sergeant Sheckart by modifying the tactics they had been taught. Among them was Sergeant Joseph Cabla, who learned to maneuver his 314th platoon to flank pockets of resistance. But as the noncommissioned officer drew within five feet of the rear of one nest and opened fire on the gunners, six other

German nests shot at him. Cabla ordered his men to fall back, but before he could turn, the sergeant took a bullet to the chest. Feeling for the entry wound, Cabla discovered to his amazement that his metal whistle had stopped the round, and he began to maneuver to a spot where he could fire rifle grenades at the Germans. As Cabla launched one of the missiles, a sniper shot him in the foot. The wound was painful, but the sergeant refused to leave his squad until they had knocked out all the enemy nests.[30]

Men like Cabla showed great resourcefulness, and for that reason, the offensive seemed to be moving well. In fact, rumors reached First Army headquarters that khaki-clad Yanks had been seen in the streets of Montfaucon.[31] Around noon, Pershing's staff sent out a reconnaissance airplane to investigate, but all that could be seen atop the butte were shell bursts from the furious American barrage. The photographic images dispelled the false optimism and also disclosed the ominous fact that the Yanks had fallen far behind their protective rolling barrage.

Most of the delay was attributable to carefully built German strongpoints concealed in ruins. As the 314th entered Malancourt, for example, the Yanks were stalled by heavy fire coming from a ruined house to the right of the church. Private Clifford M. Seiders of the machine-gun company circled around behind the structure to find that it contained thirteen Germans firing MG08/15 light machine guns. When Seiders burst through the back entrance, one gunner unwisely resisted capture, and Seiders shot him. The others then surrendered meekly. Not entirely satisfied with his day's work, the private made his way toward the upper end of the village where he captured ten additional Germans and five more machine guns in another house.[32]

Across the sector, more and more soldiers began to abandon army instructions and improvise tactics enabling them to kill Germans without needlessly exposing themselves. Too often, however, Americans continued to advance in orderly rows that benefited only German machine guns. About 10:00 a.m., as Major

Parkin topped a small hill on the left side of the sector, he spied "the most inspiring sight I think I saw in France":

> As far as I could see to the right and the left were great numbers of American soldiers advancing on both sides of us in endless lines. There seemed to be no end of their lines. It was a wonderful sight, and it made us feel better to know there were so many of us going forward all together and at the same time. It was the men of the 37th Division I saw to the left and those of the 4th Division I saw to the right . . . all this mass of infantry and machine gunners going forward together, the best of America's young men, the pride of the land; the sun came out and struck the masses of troops, making the sight even grander.[33]

As inspiring as the parade-ground formations were, Parkin soon learned that such tactics spelled death for the Yanks, as the 79th crashed into two nasty surprises embedded in the German intermediate line. In the waning years of the war, the Germans had developed a new concept of field fortifications complementing their "defense-in-depth" strategy. According to Hindenburg, the German general staff decided that "our defensive positions were no longer to consist of single lines and strongpoints but of a network of lines and groups of strongpoints. In the deep cones thus formed, we did not intend to dispose our troops on a rigid and continuous front but in a complex system of nuclei and distributed in breadth and depth."[34]

Two such fortifications were constructed in front of the low ridge that ran diagonally across the 79th's sector. On the ridge's southwestern end was the Redoute du Golfe, built in 1916. The assault troops of the 313th encountered the earthwork as they emerged from the woods into the large clearing or gulf. Situated just below the crest of the ridge, the massive redoubt survived the initial barrage and was sending streams of machine-gun fire skimming over the battlefield. From the earthwork that was the nucleus, trenches ran like ganglia to the Bois de Cuisy, looming just behind the position.

The defenses along the diagonal ridge ran from the redoubt in a northeastward direction to Hill 282, a high spot hosting another nucleus of machine-gun nests. From that point, two spurs emerged from the southern edge of the ridge aimed directly toward the 314th Regiment advancing from Malancourt. The spurs formed a funnel-shaped valley that narrowed as it approached the main ridge to the north. Through the valley ran the road from Malancourt to Montfaucon, a ribbon of relatively flat, open ground that proved an irresistible temptation to infantrymen struggling northward through the brush and over the hills. Before the battle, in fact, the men had been told that their advance would be like "marching over a boulevard"; misled by that description, they gathered on the remains of the road that provided an easy route north.[35] The valley and the road looked safe enough, but the troops failed to spot embedded machine-gun nests hidden along the crests of the surrounding spurs. From these positions, the Germans could pour enfilading fire—shots from the rear and sides—into the unprotected flanks of troops foolish enough to advance up the bottom of the valley.

At the narrow end of the funnel, a mile beyond Malancourt, the kaiser's combat engineers had constructed an additional defensive nucleus; the Oeuvre du Demon consisted of a network of deep bunkers, redoubts, and trenches that crowned the valley head with machine-gun nests and even an artillery piece.[36] Soldiers who made it through the deadly cross fire of the valley would have to conquer those fortifications before reaching the top of the ridge and moving across a relatively flat plateau toward Montfaucon. The Work of the Demon was a fully realized example of Hindenburg's "defensive cones," works that featured interlocking zones of fire designed to snuff out soldiers' lives and smother enemy offensives.

Both the Redoute du Golfe and Oeuvre du Demon were attached to trenches running near the crest of the diagonal ridge,

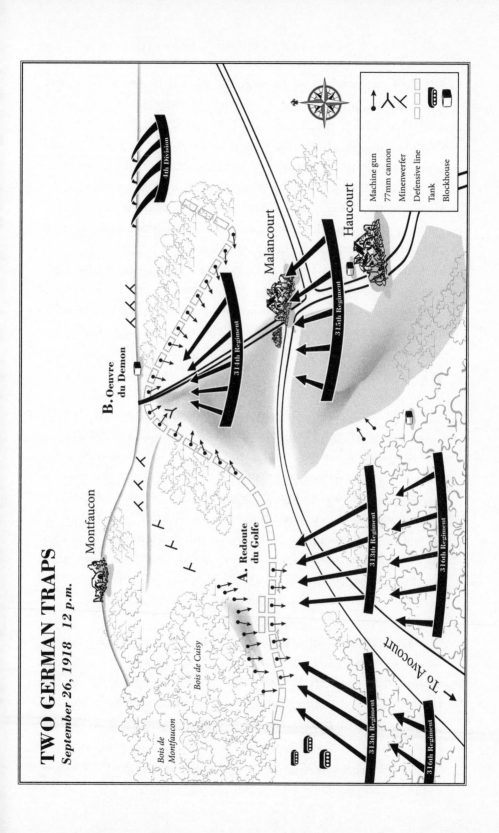

TWO GERMAN TRAPS
September 26, 1918 12 p.m.

Montfaucon

Bois de Montfaucon

Bois de Cuisy

A. Redoute du Golfe

B. Oeuvre du Demon

Malancourt

Haucourt

4th Division

314th Regiment

315th Regiment

313th Regiment

316th Regiment

313th Regiment

316th Regiment

To Avocourt

Machine gun
77mm cannon
Minenwerfer
Defensive line
Tank
Blockhouse

and the Germans had constructed the main defensive features just south of the crest. Unfortunately, the American artillery "concentrated its fire against the tree lines at the top of hills in the expectation that there was where any sensible defender would place his machine guns. When the Americans charged forward, they were mowed down by machine-gun nests camouflaged on slopes of the hills."[37] The Germans clearly understood that the military crest of a hill—the location providing the most extensive field of fire—lies below the actual ridge line.

One of the first Yanks to encounter intense fire from these positions was Captain Arthur Joel, commander of the 314th's Company F, who had been lulled into complacency by the relatively few casualties his unit had taken to that point. As the group walked up the valley beyond Malancourt, said Joel, "the real battle began."

> A lieutenant, Sergeant [John A.] McCawley, and four men had advanced through a network of barbed wire defenses to the crest of a low hill. They were just clearing the knoll in skirmish formation when fired upon by an automatic rifle in a clump of bushes ahead. . . . Then as if by prearranged signal, enemy machine guns, automatics and snipers located in trees, gullies and bushes ahead and on the flanks opened with a hot fusillade which filled the air with snaps, cracks, and whines of flying lead. Cut weeds, flying gravel, and the harsh cracks of the bullets were proof enough that the patrol had located the resistance—and were in a bad trap.[38]

The German ambush was well laid: McCawley and one of his men were killed, and two other patrol members seriously wounded in the initial blast. Thereafter a deluge of fire swept the valley, and the Americans could do little more than hug the ground. One of those caught in the killing zone was Private Swartz of the 314th. "We were in the shape of a horseshoe or [I] should say the Germans were in that position and we were inside of the circle," recalled Swartz. "One fellow was killed by my side; I told him to stay down, he said 'I'll get them with this Brownie Automatic' and the next time he raised up on his knees and was raising his machine gun to his shoulder, the sniper shot a bullet through his helmet and killed the poor fellow, he fell backward and never moved."[39]

Because fire was coming from the sides as well as from the front, there were few hiding places, and tension mounted. Stress drove one doughboy mad. Swartz saw him wildly advancing through the smoke, waving and firing his rifle randomly. He persuaded the man to jump into the shell hole with him but could not prevent him from rising to continue shooting. The soldier met a quick end in the form of a single 7.7mm bullet to the head delivered by an efficient German sniper.

Keeping company with the body in his shell hole, Swartz resorted to a trick from his boyhood to escape death.

"After the Germans shot him I was lying on my chest for one hour and a half or more, every time I would raise up a little, the sniper would shoot over my head; in fact, one time the bullet passed over me *real close*, and that time I left [*sic*] myself drop as though I was hit," Swartz remembered. "I laid still for at least one half hour and 'acting possum' thinking the sniper would take his eyes off my location and by that time I was getting pain in my chest from hugging the ground so long, so I thought I would try and get out of here, so he took another shot and down I went again acting opossum."[40]

By this time in the assault, the rolling barrage had entirely disappeared over the northern horizon, and many of the fragile telephone lines to brigade headquarters and the artillery batteries had been broken by German shell fire. There was no artillery support for the 314th.

The situation was growing desperate, as more and more men were picked off in the valley above Malancourt. Sergeant Joseph Labrum reported that his captain was seriously wounded by a hand grenade. With the company captain and all the lieutenants wounded, Labrum and another sergeant took command.[41] Three officers from the 315th had been killed also, but the men grimly continued their battle to clear the two spurs of deadly snipers and machine guns.

On the west side of the 79th Division's sector, Colonel Sweezey's 313th had run into the other German defensive trap. The ridge across the battlefield cut through the Golfe de Malancourt, where the enemy took advantage of the south-facing slope to place "effectively many more machine guns than would have ordinarily been possible in the same area."[42] To enhance the deadliness of the redoubt, the Germans had chosen it as the site to deploy one of their most fearsome weapons: a flamethrower directing a stream of molten oil twenty-five yards.[43]

"Time after time, the Doughboys attacked machine-gun nests and pillboxes head-on. After the Germans mowed them down or immolated them with flamethrowers, others took their place and attacked anew. The Americans took an average of twenty casualties for each German emplacement," one historian estimated.[44] Unfortunately, the 313th was using the tactics it had been taught by focusing its attack directly on the strongpoint, rather than by moving around its flanks to attack from the side or rear. Just as Clemenceau had predicted, the Germans were teaching the Yanks lessons about warfare, and that instruction would prove long and bloody.

In the first few minutes of the assault on the redoubt, Major Benjamin Franklin Pepper, a Philadelphian who led the second battalion, was mortally shot in the head and his adjutant, Lieutenant Francis Patterson, was killed instantly. Then Major Jesse Langley, of the 3rd Battalion, was wounded in both legs. Only one battalion commander and Sweezey remained to lead the attack. Over and over again, the regiment used the frontal assault tactics, and each time was repulsed with heavy losses.

"The slaughter at this particular point," remembered Barber, "as the infantry left the protection of the woods and emerged in the open of the *Golfe*, commanded as it was by innumerable machine guns, in permanent selected positions, and augmented by the great number of light machine guns, hastily thrown into position by the enemy, was indescribable."[45] German trench maps captured following the assault indicated that there had been at least 113 fixed German machine guns in the gulf, and officers believed that there were at least 50 percent more than that number of MG08/15 machine guns interspersed among the fixed weapons.

American battlefield tactics were so disastrous that they stuck in the mind of German colonel Victor Keller, chief of staff in Gallwitz's army group, who astutely analyzed the flaw: "The young American troops attacked with admirable pluck, though for the most part in unsuitable formations. Swarms of riflemen standing upright were no rarity. The American losses were considerable: 400 American soldiers were found dead in front of a single battalion sector."[46]

Faced with such losses, Sweezey called a temporary halt to the attack and sent a runner back to request tanks. Before they arrived, however, Parkin's follow-up troops—once again demonstrating their overeagerness and exposing their commander's inexperience—advanced to the edge of the gulf. Given battlefield conditions, Sweezey was in no mood to deal with the impatient major, and he called on the 316th's commanding officer, Colonel Charles, to sort the matter out.

It was then well into the afternoon, and Sweezey began to call on additional assets to capture the redoubt. He brought up the 311th Machine Gun Battalion that used its new Browning machine guns to duel the German MG08s. The water-cooled Brownings were more than up to the task, as were the French tanks that appeared from the west side of the gulf. Although tanks in the Meuse-Argonne Offensive experienced an attrition rate of 25 percent per day, the Renault tanks were just beginning their combat duty and "belched forth hundreds of rounds of steel, and each shot was directed at a machine-gun nest."[47] Although the tank fire suppressed the Germans, the redoubt could be taken only by "boots on the ground," necessitating further sacrifices by the 313th. Captain Harry Ingersoll, Lieutenant William Fraley, and Sergeant Harry Fraley were all mortally wounded as they followed the tanks breaching the walls of the earthwork.

The arrival of French tanks from the left flank, continued assaults of the 313th, and emergence of doughboys from woods to the west finally forced the Germans to abandon the redoubt and pull back. The newly arrived troops were from the 37th Division, a National Guard unit from Ohio, which was determinedly following First Army orders to turn the Bois de Montfaucon and threaten the German redoubt from the rear. The Buckeyes' action is powerful testimony to the effectiveness of a properly executed turning maneuver, which in this case freed the 313th to move forward toward Montfaucon.

By the time the Germans retreated, however, it was nearing five o'clock, and the traps set on both sides of the sector by the Germans had more than proved their worth. The Redoute du Golfe and the Oeuvre du Demon had held up the American attack for several critical hours, while General Gallwitz ordered reserve units to rush to the Meuse-Argonne Front. While Pershing had achieved the precondition of secrecy in assembling his troops, the doughboys were losing the critical race to the Kriemhilde Stellung as they encountered German troops much more determined than those at St. Mihiel. The action had been so heavy that there was no time to think about the promised support of the 4th Division, which had already disappeared to the north.

CHAPTER 9

"THE 79TH IS HOLDING UP THE ENTIRE FIRST ARMY"

Destruction fell on this German trench as the result of the powerful preparatory barrage of 2,775 American and French guns. Amazingly, many Germans survived in the corrugated steel shelters lining the front wall of the trench, from which they emerged ready to fight.

★   ★   ★

Storming the Mount of the Falcon was like storming some medieval citadel. Its crest towered above the Americans in the gathering dark, spitting fire. Before them yawned a moat-like valley protecting its foot. They must cross the valley first, then climb the slope, and all under heavy machine-gun fire through the shelling.

—Thomas M. Johnson,
American correspondent[1]

While Jack Bentley's comrades in the 313th and 314th Regiments were stalled by the Redoute du Golfe and the Oeuvre du Demon, the young lieutenant was proving that he was just as ready for the big leagues in combat as he had been in baseball. The former pitcher somehow guided his pioneer platoon along a seam in the center of the battlefield and reached the Bois de Cuisy just as the deadly redoubt to his south was being attacked by French tanks. He encountered a large group of American soldiers and their lieutenant, who appeared to be intimidated by the prospect of Germans in the woods. The lieutenant strongly warned Bentley against proceeding.

"I told him that my orders were to advance, and I intended to do so," said Bentley. "He didn't come along, so, leaving the fifty men behind in the woods, I started onward with my original group."[2] Spurred by their commander's initiative, the pioneers moved rapidly through the Bois de Montfaucon, using hand grenades to roust Germans from deep bunkers, and leaving enemy stragglers for follow-up forces to kill or capture. Turning to the north, the lieutenant and his men quickly came to the edge of the woods and advanced into a large field, above which towered Montfaucon. As he moved forward, Bentley told his men to stay close to a series of wide shell craters in the pasture. "It was a fortunate order, and saved some of our lives. We had gotten halfway across the field, when suddenly machine-gun bullets rained around us. I have yet to see anything like that, four hundred per minute. And did we tumble? No, we simply dropped out of sight into one of those shell-holes, with the bullets cutting the grass around its edges as we went," recalled Bentley, who took shelter to await the rest of the 313th.[3]

It was about 6:00 p.m. before the rest of Sweezey's troops reached the northern edge of the Bois de Montfaucon and peered across the open field and deep valley toward the butte. They did not see any doughboys, and the lieutenant who earlier refused to accompany Bentley reported that the American pioneers had probably been killed in the woods. At that point, Sweezey and the remaining members of his staff paused to take stock. It was late in the day, and they were still well short of Montfaucon.

The 313th officers could not see across the ridgetop eastward to the 314th, nor could they communicate with them through field telephones. Had they been able to do so, they would have understood that the 79th's progress was not satisfactory in either part of the sector. By early afternoon, the division should have taken Montfaucon and been advancing northward to Nantillois. Through that small town, First Army planners had drawn the corps objective line at which the leading American division had been ordered to pause to enable slower-moving units to catch up. When other divisions had assembled on the line, they were to move forward together to attack and pierce the formidable Kriemhilde Stellung, their ultimate objective for the day.

Although the 4th Division had surged past the eastern flank of Montfaucon by the middle of the morning and the 37th would draw even with the butte by late afternoon, the 79th had fallen woefully behind. A careful examination of German trench maps, however, makes clear the cause of delay. The sectors that the 4th and the 37th attacked were not defended as stoutly. There were no defensive nuclei like those encountered by the 79th, and the Germans appeared to have given ground to the two outlying divisions. Clearly, Gallwitz had deployed his troops and arranged his fortifications to insure that the Germans held Little Gibraltar's observatory as long as possible.

But the fierce German fortifications were not the only factor slowing General Kuhn's troops. Other problems were cropping up. The most immediate was the poor roads leading through the 79th's battle sector. At 6:30 a.m., Colonel Barber and his 304th Engineering Regiment had made a "preliminary reconnaissance of the road running from Avocourt northeast to Malancourt—tanks were making very slow progress across No Man's Land, on account of the impossible condition of the ground. They also found that the road to Malancourt entirely disappeared in the maze of shell holes about one kilometer north of Avocourt."[4]

Barber and his engineers launched their repair work as soon as German shelling subsided around 8:30 a.m., and immediately captured the admiration of the infantrymen by working to their very limit, even under intense sniper fire. "By dint of incessant labor, using stones and rocks carried by hand, timbers, tree stumps, and in fact any and every kind of material at hand, the rebuilding of the road was pushed along into the Malancourt Woods by early afternoon," reported the colonel. "Work was continued all night, except for a bare hour or two. Most of the men could have gone to sleep on their feet."[5]

Because of poor road conditions across the twenty-four-mile front and severe traffic jams, Pershing's nine attack divisions were left not only without artillery support but also without hot food and fresh water. Some units went for the next three days without these necessities. The traffic jams also delayed the passage of ambulances carrying the wounded from the front. Although many of the cases were treated at advanced aid stations, some seriously wounded victims had to wait more than forty hours to reach field hospitals. Many died in the interim.

As steady rain set in toward the end of the day, the roads became even more treacherous. But the seriousness of the transportation issues was soon surpassed by poor communications between the 79th's headquarters and its infantry regiments. According to historian Denis Winter, communication was "the unsolved problem of the Great War—to find out what was happening after Z hour. On the instant of advance and in the absence of practicable field radio, fighting men became detached from their order-giving roots with a cut as sharp as a geological fault."[6]

Each of the three existing forms of communication—field telephones, runners, and pigeons—bore inherent weaknesses. Thinly insulated wire for field telephones was unspooled by signal corpsmen walking behind attacking forces. Although technicians were trained to lash lines to trees, the wires could be cut by artillery shells, grounded out by moisture, or slashed by suicide troops. Edwin James, a *New York Times* reporter, described the determination of one young technician who had replaced a line twenty-four times. When it was shot down again, the soldier bravely put it up for the twenty-fifth time and led a squad to kill the enemy soldier who had torn it down.[7]

When telephones were incapacitated or unavailable, the next alternative was a runner. The most reliable enlisted men served as runners, because the job required initiative, resourcefulness, and courage. Most were volunteers. Carrying notes over an active battlefield was dangerous business, and casualty rates were astronomical, as the men exposed themselves to enemy fire on both legs of their journeys. If runners failed to make their delivery, signal corpsmen had been trained to dip their hands into mobile coops and withdraw a carrier pigeon. The birds, about which many heroic tales have been written, carried messages in metal pellets attached to their legs. Using their innate sense of direction, they returned to their home coops at speeds approaching fifty miles per hour.

Sometimes even pigeons failed. Late on the afternoon of September 26, Colonel Sweezey was unable to report to General Kuhn. "So from the little cage that the regimental intelligence section had carried through the fight, he took one of the pigeons, tied a message to its leg, and started it toward division headquarters. The pigeon flew up into a tree and stayed there all night," wrote a Baltimore reporter attached to the 313th.[8]

The failure of an attacking force to report its position was enough to throw any general into a rage. Maintaining liaison with headquarters was an important duty incumbent upon the subordinate unit, because the senior officer had to know where his troops were to direct them effectively. Kuhn realized quickly that his brigade commanders were not fulfilling this responsibility. To regain control, the general moved his headquarters forward to the top of Hill 304 about noon, but communications between brigade commanders and headquarters hardly improved.

The lines from AEF headquarters, however, were functioning all too well. At 2:50 p.m., Pershing sent a stern message to Cameron and Kuhn that the 79th Division was holding up the entire First Army.[9] Composed out of frustration and with incomplete knowledge of the 4th Division's failure to turn Montfaucon, the message would later mislead historians about the cause of the delay. But on the afternoon of the first day of battle, the message was followed by demands from Commander Cameron of V Corps that the 79th move aggressively to the objective.[10] Throughout the afternoon, Cameron's staff pestered Kuhn for information about progress, and tension in Kuhn's command post grew so intense that the worried general dispatched runners to press the attack.

One was Private James M. Cain, a former reporter with the *Baltimore Sun* who, after the war, would become famous as a writer of crime stories, including *The Postman Always Rings Twice*. In 1929 Cain wrote a thinly fictionalized account of his unsuccessful odyssey across the battlefield that began in the early evening of September 26, when he was ushered into Kuhn's command post.

> [M]ost of the time, the General was a pretty snappy looking soldier. He was about medium size, and he had a cut to his jaw and a swing to his back what look like them pictures you see in books. But he wasn't no snappy looking soldier that night. He hadn't had no shave, and his eyes was all sunk in, and no wonder. Because when the Division ain't took Montfaucon that day, like they was

supposed to, it balled everything up like hell. It put a pocket in the American advance, a kind of a dent, what was holding up the works all along the line. And the General was getting hell from Corps, and he had lost a lot of men, and that was why he was looking like he was.[11]

The harried Kuhn directed Cain to deliver a curt message to brigade commander Nicholson: "You must get by Montfaucon tonight."[12] The runner grabbed a horse and galloped toward the last known position of the brigadier somewhere north of the Golfe du Malancourt. As the clock moved toward 7:00 p.m., Kuhn received yet another message from corps headquarters saying that the AEF commander "desires attack pushed."[13] At that, the engineer called for his own horse and rode forward to find Nicholson and light a fire under him. Neither Cain nor Kuhn located the missing brigadier, but the message had already arrived at Nicholson's headquarters. Around 5:30 p.m., telephone communications had been partially restored, and the message ordering an aggressive attack was relayed to Nicholson and on to Sweezey, whose 313th Regiment had been assigned to take Montfaucon.

Sweezey's badly mauled regiment gathered in the northern edge of the Bois de Montfaucon staring out across the field and over the deep valley that lay between them and the fortified butte. The colonel had one fresh battalion, two bloodied battalions, and a few French tanks to undertake what was likely an impossible task: a night attack against a heavily fortified position.[14] Sweezey or Nicholson could have requested reinforcements from the 316th, nearby in the woods. However, there were sound military reasons not to do so. Both men knew that the 316th was a part of the follow-up brigade under General Noble and was being held in reserve to lead the attack north of Montfaucon. Had Nicholson been in communication with his other regiment, the 314th—stalled on the east side of the sector—he might have ordered a concerted attack by both regiments on Montfaucon.

But the brigade commander had long since lost touch with his troops on the right side of the battlefield. Topping all other concerns, Nicholson was unable to contact his artillery to request fire support for the night assault.

The responsibility of taking Montfaucon fell to Sweezey alone. The crusty colonel jammed a cigar into his jaw and began readying his weary troops for another tough fight.[15] In the lead would be the First Battalion under the command of Israel Putnam, great-grandson of the Revolutionary War patriot of the same name who fought bravely at Bunker Hill. At about 6:30 p.m., Sweezey's regiment was ready for the attack. Afflicted by a long-standing case of stuttering, the colonel simply yelled, "Forward!" The 313th stepped out of the woods into the exposed field. Viewing the impending attack with more than passing interest was Jack Bentley, who, with his pioneers, had taken refuge in shell craters that pockmarked the field over which his well-armed comrades began to advance. After the war, he wrote:

> One of my men jumped up waving his helmet, and a rain of bullets greeted him. Our own men were shooting at us, thinking we were Germans. I told the man to stick his helmet up on his bayonet so that the boys could see that it was an American, and I am glad we had done this, for we were recognized at once. The boys were just getting ready to give us a shower of hand grenades. The men were glad to see us and we were glad to see them, for we had spent a very uncomfortable four hours in that hole. I ran forward in the new attack and helped to run out those Boche machine gunners who had been shooting at us. The Boche came out yelling "Pardon Kamerad," while my men were yelling "Kill 'em, kill 'em," but nobody did.[16]

The Yanks advanced farther into the growing gloom. German machine-gun fire swept from the far side of the valley, but the Yanks could not see well enough to respond with accuracy. French tanks led, but as German artillery began to find their range, the tracked vehicles "turned clumsily around and headed back into the woods."[17] Later the French explained that they had withdrawn because the decreasing light limited their ability to maneuver effectively.

Without the protection of armor or the option of retreat, the American infantrymen advanced against the entrenched Germans. "Progress was necessarily slow. Only by short rushes was any advance possible," recorded one officer. "It took three-quarters of an hour to reach the bottom of the valley, and just about that time the gradually deepening dusk gave way entirely to the pitch darkness of night."[18] The blackness actually made it easier for the Americans to spot targets, because the "enemy's lines were red with fire."[19] Company K had just begun to climb Montfaucon's southwest slopes when heavy casualties forced Sweezey to accept the inevitable. There was no chance of success, and the colonel signaled a withdrawal to the woods. Bodies were scattered across the lower reaches of the slope, including that of Major Putnam, killed instantly by a bullet to the head.[20]

Sweezey stood alone in the woods, confronting the grim knowledge that he was the only field-grade officer of the 313th Regiment. And the hardest task still lay ahead. Heavy rain began to pelt the men as they reached the woods, where they wrapped themselves in blankets and bedded down in German bunkers or shallow foxholes gouged just within the tree line.

On the other side of the 79th's sector, Colonel William Oury and his 314th Regiment faced an even more desperate situation in the same cold rain. The Yanks were making slow progress up the slope of the diagonal ridge a mile northwest of Malancourt. For all they knew, the rest of the climb would be as deadly as the first. The men were still scourged by machine gunners and snipers on the ridges towering above them on three sides. The slightest movement or sound from a doughboy would evoke a flurry of German fire, as well as an occasional *minenwerfer* shell.

A few of the officers caught in this predicament were beginning to wonder what had happened to the 4th Division, which
was responsible for clearing the ridge to the east and assisting
the capture of Montfaucon. Hunkering in one shell crater in the
middle of the killing zone was Colonel Gordon Johnston, who
had won a Medal of Honor in the Philippines during the Moro
Insurrection, and was an observer from Pershing's headquarters,
where he had been briefed to expect the envelopment. After the
war, Johnston described his dangerous afternoon to a friend who
served in the Fourth during the offensive: "I awaited your coming to the frontline west of Verdun. I was so sure that you were
coming as hour after hour passed, and my heart sank lower and
lower—'til dark came and the golden opportunity had passed."[21]
Reinforcing Johnston's poignant sentiment years later, John Eisenhower concluded that, "With help from the 4th Division,
Oury [commanding the 314th] might have taken the Butte de
Montfaucon, but no such help was forthcoming."[22]

Darkness effectively ended any hope of rescue and advance,
but it also provided cover enabling the 314th to regroup. Oury
sent word to his battalion commanders that they would begin the
next push at 4:00 a.m. All told, the colonel and his counterpart
on the western side of the sector, Sweezey, were nearly two miles
and twelve hours behind schedule, a fact that General Kuhn was
trying his best to remedy. The commander of the 79th was well
aware that the 4th Division on the right and the 37th on the
left had far outdistanced his division. The latter division, part of
Cameron's V Corps, had driven a mile beyond the 79th and was
dug in for the evening on a plateau west of Montfaucon.

On the 79th's eastern flank, the 4th Division, a part of General
Bullard's III Corps, had won the symbolic but highly prized award
for advancing farthest on the first day of the Meuse-Argonne
Offensive. Ordered by Bullard to ignore the divisions on their
flanks, the Regular Army veterans of the 4th had reenacted the
nineteenth-century cavalry tactic of "galloping for glory"—a

maneuver the general mastered in the American West and the Philippines. Meeting only light resistance, troops of the 39th Regiment on the left of the sector were beyond Cuisy and Montfaucon by noon, and the 47th Regiment troops on the right had suffered the loss of only one soldier to enemy fire by that time.[23] Shortly thereafter, they halted on the corps objective line just east of Nantillois, where they looked across the rolling fields to their left and saw Germans rushing to reinforce the fortress atop Montfaucon. Although they sent patrols to explore the woods shielding the Kriemhilde Stellung to the north, Bullard's III Corps took no action to limit the steady flow of Germans to Little Gibraltar, where they would soon be taking aim at infantrymen from the 79th.

During the course of the day, the 4th Division had encountered two unplanned opportunities to assist the capture of Montfaucon. The first came midmorning, before the fog lifted. Because of poor visibility, the First Battalion of the 4th Division's 39th Infantry Regiment went off course, crossed the boundary between V and III Corps, and wandered into the Bois de la Tuilerie, on Montfaucon's eastern slope. The Germans occupying the woods were not prepared for battle, and the Yanks captured a hundred prisoners from the 11th Grenadier Regiment and entered trenches running straight up the hill to the butte.[24]

The navigational error presented an unexpected opportunity for a major coup, made evident by German alarm at the maneuver. At 11:00 a.m., the fortress sent a message to its commander in the rear: "Enemy [4th Division] on the front of the division on our left [11th Grenadiers] has passed through the hollows of Cuisy and then has swung in the direction of Montfaucon . . . Enemy is attacking strongly."[25]

This and other messages of concern make it clear that had the 39th Infantry Regiment launched an attack on Montfaucon, the Yanks could have captured the butte easily. The odds of success were high: a battle-tested battalion of 1,200 US troops was facing only two German companies totaling 400 men. Had the leadership of the 4th Division invested troops into this yawning crack in Montfaucon's defenses, the butte could have been secured. Then the 79th and the 4th could have linked up at the corps objective line and advanced to the Kriemhilde Stellung.

But an assault by 4th Division troops toward Montfaucon was not to be. Remembering Bullard's stern warning from the previous night, Major Roy Winton, commander of the First Battalion, ordered his men to break off action and swing back into the III Corps sector. When Winton later met his regimental commander, tough Colonel Frank Bolles, he received a severe tongue-lashing for straying from his mission of pressing quickly northward.[26] The 79th Division was on its own, three miles behind the surging 4th Division.

The capture of the butte on the critical first day was still a possibility, however, because an enterprising brigadier general from the 4th Division later envisioned a plan to encircle the fortress. General Ewing Booth's 8th Brigade was following closely behind the 7th Brigade to mop up snipers and machine gunners, and the sounds of heavy fighting from his left indicated that the 79th was having a difficult time with its frontal attack on the butte. At an impromptu meeting, Booth proposed to General John L. Hines, commander of the 4th Division, that the 8th Brigade envelop Montfaucon to aid the hard-pressed troops of the 79th Division. Booth saw that his brigade was in a position to make a decisive difference in the offensive and the war. In full agreement, Hines quickly drew up a proposed order and sent it to III Corps headquarters for review. After considerable delay, it was approved. But before Booth could bring his troops into position, headquarters rescinded the maneuver. Booth put an immediate halt to the preparations and directed his troops to follow the 4th Division's rush toward the north. In the heat of battle, Hines and Booth quickly put the matter out of their minds. The young brigadier had no time to mull over what had happened. He had an important role to play in the hours ahead, one that demanded his full attention.

By late that night, both opportunities the 4th Division had to assist the capture of Montfaucon had evaporated. The 79th Division was stalled in front of the butte, and the telephone lines into V Corps headquarters were growing hot with angry words: "Commander in chief expects the 79th Division to advance tonight to positions abreast of the 4th Division in the vicinity of Nantillois."[27]

No one had to explain the import of this terse message to Generals Cameron and Kuhn. As if to underscore its meaning, however, Pershing soon circulated an explicit order among First Army regiments, demanding, "All officers will push their units forward with all possible energy. Corps and Division Commanders will not hesitate to relieve on the spot any officer of whatever rank, who fails to show in this emergency those qualities of leadership required to accomplish the task which confronts us."[28]

The time for Kuhn to prove himself a combat leader had arrived, but to do so, he would have to perform a miracle. Pershing was furious, and his messages left the engineer little recourse other than to order another night attack on the fortress. Kuhn's choices were limited. On the left side of the general's sector, the 313th was still licking deep wounds after the earlier attack and was in no condition to mount another assault in complete darkness. The only chance that Kuhn saw was to reorganize his regiments on the right side of the battlefield (the 314th and 315th) to form a new provisional brigade and have them attack in a column toward the German fortress in the predawn hours. Kuhn immediately directed General Noble to take command and launch an attack as soon as possible. On the left side of the sector, Nicholson, whose whereabouts were still uncertain, was ordered to take command of a similarly reconfigured brigade made up of the 313th and 316th and to attack Montfaucon. Kuhn also dispatched runner James Cain, accompanied by observer Wilfred Puttkammer, on a near-suicidal mission to move toward Montfaucon to determine what was happening on the butte.[29]

Later that night, General Nicholson began his preparation

for the renewed attack by ordering his regimental commanders, Colonels Sweezey (313th) and Charles (316th), to redouble their efforts at first light. Charles had been slow to advance his head-quarters, but under cover of darkness, he finally made his way to the Bois de Cuisy, where he called an urgent meeting of his battalion commanders, including Parkin. Unfortunately, the order did not give clear directions to the colonel's command post, and Parkin spent a harrowing night wandering through the dripping woods. As the major rounded a turn in the trail, he stopped cold:

> There in the path, very close, was a machine gun pointed at me; a German sat behind it, his fingers on the trigger; and another knelt at one side, feeding the cartridge belt into it. How long I stood thus I will never know. I wondered that they did not fire, and then I realized that there was something peculiar about these men, and I found myself leaning over them. Both were dead and cold and rigid and partly collapsed but still in their positions.[30]

Parkin never located his colonel that night; his confusion mirrored that of many of his AEF comrades, who literally were fighting without direction or coordination. The 79th and many of its sister divisions had seen their communications disrupted, supplies stalled, and momentum lost in the forests and ravines. Like Parkin, the First Army was wandering in the wilderness.

The Meuse-Argonne Offensive was in deep trouble, and American generals from Pershing and Cameron down to Kuhn, Noble, and Nicholson sensed that a long-sought opportunity was slipping away. The generals were well aware that the keys to a breakthrough were the early capture of Little Gibraltar followed by a swift breach in the Germans' strongest defensive line—*before the kaiser's troops could reinforce the formidable Kriemhilde Stellung*. Yet at midnight, the enemy still held Montfaucon and the Etzel-Giselher Stellung, of which the butte was the principal strongpoint.

Although in the late hours of September 26 it might not have been clear to the American commanders, the opportunity for a breakthrough had long been lost. It had disappeared early in the afternoon, as the 79th struggled for hours to capture the Oeuvre du Demon and the Redoute du Golfe. It had been lost as the 4th Division dashed well beyond Montfaucon without turning the fortress or assisting the 79th in any way. It had evaporated as the Germans gained vital hours to rush reserves forward to man the machine guns, *minenwerfers*, trenches, and bunkers of the Kriemhilde Stellung.

The swift American thrust was degenerating into a slow slog through muddy French farmland, and the enemy knew it. German general Gallwitz at Montmedy near the Belgian border took a deep sigh of relief, which he later described to an American correspondent: "Already in the evening, the danger was averted by bringing up reserves."[31] The plain fact was that the Germans had beaten the Americans in a grim race. They had moved their reserve troops to the front with speed and efficiency that Pershing could only envy. The ultimate losers were thousands of doughboys who would sacrifice their lives trying to reestablish the offensive's lost momentum.

CHAPTER 10

"BAYONET AND RIFLE BUTT, PISTOL AND TRENCH KNIFE"

The effects of four years of war were etched into the surface of the Mount of the Falcon. The ruins provided Germans fighting positions, and tunnels enabled the enemy to move without exposure to artillery.

★ ★ ★

We are soldiers, and the weapon is the tool with which we proceed to shape ourselves. Our work is killing, and it is our duty to do this work well and completely. . . . For every age expresses itself not only in practical life, in love, in science and art, but also in the frightful. And it is the meaning of the soldier to be frightful.

—Lieutenant Ernst Jünger,
German Imperial Army[1]

When the sergeant shook Andrew Kachik awake at 4:00 a.m. on the foggy morning of September 27, the young private had no idea that he would soon become the point man in the assault on Montfaucon. He had spent an uncomfortable night huddled in a hole thoroughly soaked by rain. Given the nasty weather, an early wake-up was something of a relief. Kachik rose slowly, mourned the absence of coffee, and met four other men on the southern slope of the ridge north of Malancourt.

The 314th was still smarting from its bloody attack on the Oeuvre du Demon the day before, and the coming day would bring renewed combat against the complex of entrenchments that laced the slopes and the top of the ridge. To initiate the assault, the five scouts were ordered to advance slowly up the ridge and stay a thousand meters ahead of the company behind them. The Pennsylvania doughboy could see no signs of danger in the thick soup, so he plodded slowly up the hill. After about a half hour, however, it began to dawn on Kachik and his four companions that the order was issued so that "if the scouts ran into a machine gun, the Company would have warning. Well, that made us mad. We walked faster."[2]

The scouts were human bait, dangled to draw fire from the hidden enemy. For a while, things went well. The doughboys moved for nearly an hour before they stumbled across an empty machine-gun nest. As they paused to examine the position, they were startled by a German voice from somewhere in the dark, commanding, "Halt!"

"The Captain said to me, 'Let's capture this German,' so we could find out what divisions the Germans are using," Kachik recalled. "The Captain hollered, 'Comrade!' and started shooting his handgun .45, and I shot one shot. We ran toward the voice. Well all hell broke loose. It was a machine gun nest."[3]

The enemy fired star shells to light the area, and then swept it with several MG08s. Kachik crawled into a large shell hole and began to pray. A few minutes later, several other American soldiers appeared, and the reunited scouts lay quiet until dawn. When the weak sun began to burn off the fog, revealing the US soldiers on the barren ridge, the Germans began serious efforts to kill the intruders. Kachik later recalled, "I was next to an opening in the barbwire [sic]. That was across the road when grenades started coming towards us. Everybody tried to get out first. As things turned out, I was the last one out. Maybe that saved my life. Two of our scouts that went out first got wounded so badly that they died later."[4]

Kachik then spent hours bellying down in a fetid farm ditch, keeping low to avoid bullets skimming over the slope. When the squad finally escaped the ridge, its men were angered to find their entire company glued to the ground avoiding the distant fire. In the darkness, the scouts had somehow bypassed five machine-gun nests before provoking a response from the sixth. The ridge was so thick with German suicide squads that it took Company H five hours to take the ground that Kachik and his friends had covered in their hour's walk in the dense fog.

General Joseph Kuhn would have been infuriated to learn that only a five-man squad had responded to his order to press the attack on Montfaucon. It would have confirmed his suspicion that General Noble, whom he had named to command the provisional 158th Brigade on the east side of Sector 304, was not pushing. Kuhn had not heard a word from Noble during the night, so the major general and his chief of staff, Colonel Tenny J. Ross, mounted horses at 5:00 a.m., left their command post atop Hill

304, and galloped toward Malancourt to prod the wayward brigadier, who was better known for prodigious drinking and poker
playing than for hard fighting.[5]

Just as dawn broke over the foggy Meuse valley, Noble wandered into a trench near Malancourt where Colonel Alden
Knowles and Captain Sam Fleming were planning the 315th's
advance behind Kachik's 314th. To Fleming it appeared that
Noble was "without a care in the world as he remarked that it
was a beautiful morning and things were going well. It was not
a beautiful morning and things were not going well." Just then,
Fleming spied trouble: General Kuhn and Colonel Ross "striding,
and I mean *striding*, down the trench apparently trailing Noble.
As Kuhn reached us Noble put out his hand and greeted him with
a cheerful, 'Good Morning, General.' Kuhn paid no attention
to him and jumped to the top of the trench followed by Ross,
and said sternly: 'General Noble, by virtue of the office I hold, I
hereby relieve you of command.' That was all."[6]

Kuhn informed the startled Knowles that he would head the
provisional brigade on the right side of the 79th's sector formerly
led by Noble. The commanding general then left to assess how
things were going on the far side of the battlefield, where other
officers were in danger of losing their commands.

To the left of Kuhn's 79th, the 37th Division used the predawn
hours to launch an attack to take the western edge of Montfaucon and meet 4th Division troops expected to be enveloping the
butte from the east and north. The Ohio National Guardsmen
had spent the dripping night of September 26 in fields between
Ivoiry and the butte. Around daybreak, two companies set out to
attack a cluster of houses at Montfaucon's base. One unit proved
successful, capturing fourteen machine guns and thirty-eight
prisoners from trenches at the bottom of the hill. As the company
made preparations to rush the slopes, it learned that its sister
company had been wiped out after falling for a ruse. Seeing two
Germans wearing Red Cross brassards and carrying a stretcher,

the Americans had stood up in anticipation of a surrender. Hidden German machine guns mowed down almost all the Americans, including their lieutenant, who was struck by fifty bullets.[7] The few survivors, reinforced by the second company, surged up the slope toward a large house they believed to be the crown prince's chateau, but they were stopped by intense machine-gun fire.[8] Afterward, the men claimed they had captured Montfaucon before the 79th appeared later in the morning, but an army investigation after the war determined that they had been isolated on the far western slope of the butte where a new part of the town had been built.[9]

About the time that the 37th Division's assault got under way, Harry Parkin awakened in the Bois de Cuisy, where everything was "dull, gray, and discouraging. Wet and raining. The woods were soaked and dripping wet."[10] Around the major, the troops of the 313th began to prepare for another assault on Montfaucon. The darkness had provided a few hours of badly needed rest for the men following the disastrous night attack, but there was no coffee or food to bolster the troops. Most of the 79th's units would not receive warm food or even fresh water for another three days. The thirsty Yanks were forced to refill their canteens from shell holes, preferably those in which there were live bugs. Rumor had it that water capable of sustaining insect life was not tainted by poison gas.[11]

As Parkin's soldiers foraged for water in shell craters and food from the bread bags of dead German soldiers, the major exchanged brief greetings with Colonels Sweezey and Charles. Sweezey was mourning the loss of three of his battalion commanders, and stress had exacerbated his stuttering. He spoke in monosyllables as he arrayed his men for another attack that he feared would be even bloodier than the one of the evening before. When time came to order the troops forward, Sweezey was so overcome with emotion that he could not voice the order. Looking left and then right down the line of doughboys with fixed bayonets, Sweezey raised his arm as if he were about to throw a football toward the butte. As his arm came forward, the Yanks left the shelter of the Bois de Montfaucon, stepped across the bodies of their comrades lying in the field, and moved toward the fortified butte.

Standing in the margin of the trees, Parkin watched as the men and six French tanks disappeared into thick fog. "I never heard such a terrific roar of machine gun fire," the major recalled. "It was awful and sounded like the cataract at Niagara Falls. To think of human bodies facing such blasts and such sheets of flying lead. It is a wonder that any of these men lived to enter that town. Had it not been for the mist, most of them must have been struck down."[12]

As the roar continued, Colonel Charles ordered Parkin to keep his battalion close behind the attackers to help with the fighting. This was the command for which Parkin had waited. He snappily led his troops across the field, plunged into the valley, and climbed upward toward Little Gibraltar, emerging from the lifting fog. At that moment, however, artillery—the "King of Battle"—chose to assert itself: big German cannons stationed in the Argonne Forest and east of the Meuse River began to pound the Yanks with large shells. From a trench at the foot of Montfaucon, Parkin was alarmed to see his men falling back to take cover from the explosions. Determined to set a strong example, he quickly left cover and advanced with his troops: "I would not have any of my men ever say that I took shelter from shell fire and ordered them to remain out in the open. Men in battle need example and encouragement, and they naturally look to their officers for both."[13]

Directed by observers on Montfaucon, shells burst among the Americans charging up the slopes. All along the front, the story was the same. Bolstered by artillery, German resistance was stiffening perceptibly. "Where it had been possible, twenty-four hours before, to walk upright," one observer noted, "the men now had to crouch or crawl."[14] Moving up Little Gibraltar with the

313th, Jack Bentley described the technique he used as "alternate running and flopping on the ground every few yards."[15] There were few other ways that a soldier could improve his chances of staying alive another day in the Meuse-Argonne, as the observatory directed a storm of high-explosive and gas shells on the exposed Americans. The Germans had become particularly effective at firing a mixture of different gases, including one that made the Yanks "cough, shed tears, and sneeze at the same time. The gas might not be very dangerous, but it was at least exasperating to try and keep on a mask under such conditions," recalled Captain Arthur Joel of the 314th Infantry. Of course, forcing the Americans to remove their masks was exactly what the Germans wanted. After the irritant had done its work, the enemy would fire follow-up shells containing phosgene and mustard gas to add a deadly dimension to what had been merely an aggravation.

By that time in the offensive, American artillery should have arrived near the front to answer German fire and to keep the enemy's heads buried deep in their bunkers. But overnight, only two batteries of 75mm guns had been able to negotiate the ruined roads and horrendous traffic jams to be in position to make a difference to the attacking troops. The two units were stationed south of Malancourt, and they could reach just beyond Montfaucon. Although the guns shelled the upper part of the butte, they failed to make much difference as the 313th continued its charge against the machine-gun nests dug deeply into Montfaucon's ruins.[16] The six tanks ground up the bare southwest flank of the butte, avoiding German tank barriers blocking the main roads. In addition to the concrete-and-steel-cable barriers, the kaiser's engineers had developed improvised mines, which consisted of 210mm shells buried in the ground to be detonated by remote control. The heavy rain, however, had shorted most connections.

The losses of the previous night and the newly killed and wounded Americans enraged the men of "Baltimore's Own" Regiment, who scrambled up the hillside. The Yanks were further

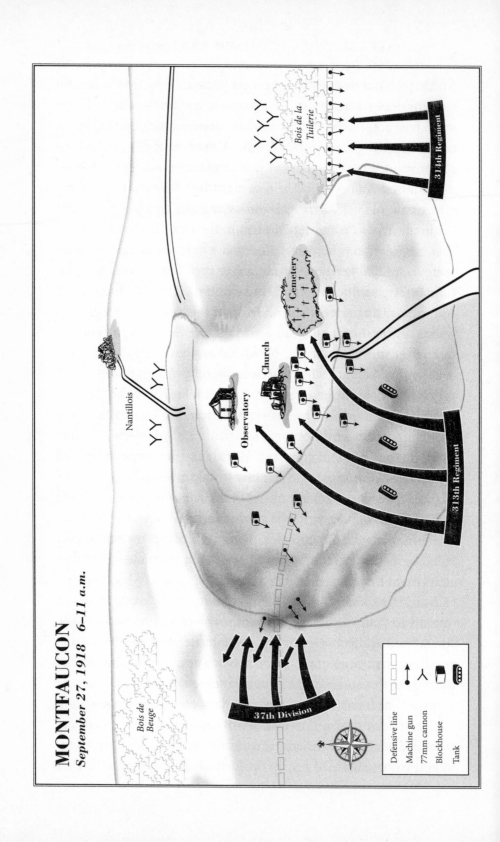

MONTFAUCON
September 27, 1918 6–11 a.m.

Bois de
Beuge

Nantillois

Bois de la
Tuilerie

314th Regiment

Cemetery

Observatory

Church

313th Regiment

37th Division

Defensive line
Machine gun
77mm cannon
Blockhouse
Tank

enflamed by a number of German "tricks," including enemy soldiers dressed in American uniforms, well-concealed snipers, and, according to Bentley, even a woman assisting soldiers in a machine-gun nest. Moreover, the men were outraged by the sight of Germans who had survived, while many of their friends had died. They were ready for revenge. Bentley remembered rousting ten enemy soldiers cowering in a bunker: "My men wanted to kill the Boches, but I wouldn't listen to it. S—, a German-American, but one of my best men, glared at the Boches and threatened them until one of them, a boy of 15, began to cry."[17] At other places, the Germans were not lucky enough to have a cool-headed officer around to control raw emotions. Private Joshua Cockey III found three Germans huddled on wooden bunks in a dugout. He ordered them out by the time he counted to three. "One two three!" the private shouted. "And then he blew out the brains of the German in the middle bunk. The others tumbled out in terror."[18] Cockey never learned whether the men understood English.

The heaviest fighting of the assault, recalled Major Charles DuPuy of the 79th, took place in Montfaucon's cemetery, located on the southeast corner of the butte. Mausoleums concealed German machine guns, and rooting out the gunners required hand-to-hand fighting with "bayonet and rifle butt, the pistol and the trench knife."[19] One of the doughboys in DuPuy's machine-gun battalion "accounted for seven men in less than an hour, three with the pistol and four with the trench knife."[20]

As fighting wound down, Captain Junius Dunford rounded the corner of a ruined building and came face-to-face with a German officer fleeing toward the back of the butte. Both men had holstered their pistols, but the American proved the quicker draw and dispatched his enemy with a single shot. For intelligence purposes, he collected the officer's papers and dog tags. After the Armistice, Dunford was assigned to occupation duty in Germany, where he was billeted in the home of a woman whose two sons had been killed in the war and whose husband was missing. When the American asked where her husband had been serving, she answered that it was at Montfaucon. With a sense of dread, Dunford retreated to his room, found the papers collected from the body on the butte, and discovered that he had slain the woman's husband.[21]

As Dunford and other Yanks continued the search for stragglers, they discovered "peeled potatoes in kettles on the stoves, pots of acorn coffee already brewed, cheese, and small bags of biscuits."[22] This food and cabbages growing in German gardens around the butte were soon devoured. As hungry and thirsty as they were, many doughboys shared their meager supplies with the wounded, even those from the enemy army. Captain Ben Hewit, the popular leader of the 316th's Company F, found a dying German with "ghastly green face and hands." The prisoner held up an image of Christ and begged for water. In what an observer called "a futile act of mercy," Hewit ordered a private to give the German a drink, and then moved on.[23]

The generosity was characteristic of the captain, whose unfailing kindness and customary cheerfulness made him the idol of his men. Born in the West, the tall, muscular Hewit grew up in Pennsylvania, and was educated at Lehigh and Purdue Universities. Although he was well above military age when the United States declared war, he volunteered and earned his bars at Fort Niagara, where he met Harry Parkin.

Hewit's comrades on the east side of the battlefield were finally able to drive through the Oeuvre du Demon and advance across the open plateau stretching from the top of the diagonal ridge toward the butte. The regiment continued along the Malancourt-Montfaucon road to an intersection just a half mile south of Montfaucon, where Sergeant Joseph Labrum had to duck fire coming "from all sides. The doughboys had been marching up the road in platoon columns when ambushed. They immediately dropped into shell holes and narrow trenches on the right side of the road—lost many men here."[24]

Quickly mastering the lesson of dispersing in a combat sector, the Yanks ran toward a patch of woods just east of the butte. It was the Bois de la Tuilerie, which the 4th Division had encountered virtually undefended twenty-four hours earlier. By September 27, however, conditions had changed dramatically. German machine gunners and infantrymen had reinforced the woods, occupying trenches that Bullard's men had found empty earlier. After a tough fight, the 314th "hardly reached the outer edge of the woods before they were met by a terrific barrage of overhead shrapnel which made things unbearable in that vicinity for some time. The entire battalion was forced to withdraw and take up a position in the field just before the city [Montfaucon]."[25]

Although the 314th and 315th had not experienced as rough a morning as the 313th and 316th troops—who had charged up the west side of the butte—they still had seen far too much bloodshed, as Sergeant Boll related in a chilling vignette:

> We came down a slight slope on the side of which a heavy German gun emplacement seemed to have been cut. I see on the farther side of the emplacement a number of German soldiers lying side by side, about four of them. They appear to be dead. As I look, one of them lifts an arm as if in a gesture for help; then a series of pistol shots scream out behind me. There some ten feet in back of me is our bugler, Isaac Kevitch. He is emptying his revolver at the wounded German who throws up his arm then rolls to the side on his face. I am dumb-struck.[26]

As disturbing as Boll's experience was, any American soldier in the Meuse-Argonne could cite similar stories of savagery in which the villain was German. Jack Bentley, for instance, recalled seeing a wounded enemy officer who was being carried by American litter bearers to a field hospital. The German "asked one of our men for a drink of water, and as the man approached his side with the canteen in his hand, the officer shot him through the head, the bullet entering through the lip, and passed out of the back of his head. The officer had a small '25' concealed in the palm of his hand."[27] Bentley recited the story as an example of the "meanness of some of the Germans," but it is obvious that neither side had a monopoly on virtue during the difficult days of 1918.

At 11:30 a.m. on September 27, the 313th secured the top of Montfaucon. The firing, however, continued long after, as Parkin's reserve troops searched for snipers and artillery spotters. In one sheltered niche, "Two Germans were found operating a buzzerphone [telegraph set], and apparently directing the enemy fire, as when they were corralled, the artillery fire began to lose some of its effectiveness."[28]

One of the final positions atop the butte to fall was an observation and machine-gun post built into a massive stone pier at the southwest corner of the church. Under long-range artillery fire from both sides, the structure's nave had been reduced to broken stone ribs and the ravaged steeple, which somehow remained standing. The church's rubble made it nearly impossible to advance toward the last emplacement. Resistance around the pier was stiff, with sustained firing coming from ground-level galleries in the church's crypt. Each nest was manned by determined crews. After the Yanks mounted a stiff assault using grenades, the surviving Germans scuttled down tunnels leading to the back of the butte, where they emerged to continue a fighting withdrawal toward the north.

At 11:55 a.m., Colonel Sweezey scribbled a field message and placed it in a metal capsule strapped to the leg of US Pigeon 47. The bird flew through the heavy German barrage, and despite a torn and bloody wing, made the fourteen-mile trip to divisional headquarters in one hour and forty-three minutes.[29] Unfortunately, General Kuhn was not present to receive the news carried by the brave pigeon, because he was working from an advanced command post near Malancourt. Another message, however, reached him by courier a little after 1:00 p.m. It read, "Took town of Montfaucon 11h 55, after considerable fighting in town. Many snipers left behind. Town shelled to slight extent after our occupation. Am moving on to corps objective and hope to reach it by 16 H. SWEEZEY."[30]

More than a day after the 4th Division was in a position to have captured Montfaucon, the 79th Division finally pushed the Germans out of the observatory. At midmorning, German general Gallwitz had detected the 314th's effort to take the Bois de la Tuilerie, which caused him to issue new orders: "To all appearances, the Americans endeavored to encircle Montfaucon from both sides, in order to pinch it off. The enemy advanced up to Nantillois. I ordered that Montfaucon be relinquished and a new line established, running from Epionville, by way of the heights to the north of Nantillois to Brieulles [the Kriemhilde Stellung position]."[31] As the 79th mopped up, the remnants of the German garrison escaped along the road to Cunel, where they would join five fresh divisions reinforcing the lines. Had the butte been enveloped as planned, these Germans would not have lived to fight another day.

While the enemy artillery lessened momentarily to give the Germans the best opportunity to escape safely, the tired doughboys atop the butte had an opportunity to take a breath, light a smoke, and observe their surroundings. What they saw was nothing less than a fiery panorama of hell.

Through gaps in the smoke of battle, the Americans glimpsed the destruction that their weapons and those of the Germans had created. Massive enemy shells from well beyond the Cunel heights to the north were still screaming southward toward advancing US lines. When the shells burst, explosions dealt death to nearby doughboys and splintered every tree within range. As the dust cleared, new, dark craters appeared on the pocked landscape of old shell holes. And still it continued. Above the deafening bass chorus of massive howitzers soared the soprano clatter of countless machine guns spitting streams of steel to kill unwary Americans who dared enter any German-held clearings.

The answer from American guns was anemic. Keen eyes could trace fire from 75mm cannons stationed in the woods around Hill 304 and Le Mort Homme, but though the offensive had been under way for hours, few of the Allied batteries behind the men had been able to traverse the rough roads forward to support the continuing attacks of their comrades. Farther back, the big guns mounted on railway cars had fallen silent for fear of hitting their own troops in the confused melee. Most often the only response to the massive German barrages was sporadic single shots of .30-caliber rifles or the halting stutter of unreliable French Chauchat machine guns, prone to jam when the smallest particle of dust infiltrated their firing chambers.

If the fighting had not been so destructive, its effects might have seemed beautiful to the Americans on top of the butte. Among the countless explosions wafted brightly colored smoke from flare guns, marking new targets for the voracious cannons. The Americans' hand grenades had set alight many enemy bunkers and trees, even as liquid fire coiled from the Germans' primitive flame projectors. From the Heights of the Meuse to the dark Argonne Forest in the west, the entire scene was an inferno that only Dante could have described.

As the doughboys gazed across the terrain, they gained a new appreciation for what they had accomplished. In a short day and a half, they had pierced the German front line, the intermediate line with its two nasty traps, and now the Etzel-Giselher Stellung, the first of three massive defensive works that stood between them and Sedan. Marshall Pétain had predicted that the Yanks would be lucky to capture Montfaucon before December's rains. But the 79th and its green troops had pierced the line anchored by the butte in just thirty-six hours, an achievement hardly diminished by the unrealistic First Army timetable dictated by rear-echelon planners who seldom heard cannons fired in anger.

For these reasons, the doughboys standing near the ruined church experienced an unusual mix of emotions: pride in conquering battle-hardened German troops, their superior weapons, and their strong fortifications and sorrow at the immense cost required. Each man had his own memories of a comrade shot, a friend obliterated by artillery, or an acquaintance whose limbs had been severed by slashing shrapnel. But no soldier—nor any officer, for that matter—had a comprehensive view of the human cost of the assault.

Because accurate records are seldom kept during desperate fighting, the actual number of Americans killed and wounded at Montfaucon can never be precisely fixed. In the first four days of the offensive, the 79th lost approximately four thousand troops. Simple math suggests that the cost of capturing Montfaucon was around two thousand men, maybe even more. The total losses due to the delayed capture, both to that point and in the future, were far greater and yet incalculable.

But the Yanks did not reckon the cost. When the American flag was hoisted on one of the piers of the basilica, they snapped off a crisp salute, slung their rifles, and marched on north toward the next fight at the bottom of the butte's back slope. About that time, the German artillerymen who had lessened their fire to aid their comrades spied the Stars and Stripes fluttering above the church. Immediately, they directed their guns to the new target. Enemy shells soon began to crash into the butte in a barrage that increased the price that the 79th had paid for the victory.

The officers of the division, however, had little time to consider what had been accomplished. Even as Montfaucon was being secured, Colonel Sweezey walked just beyond the ruined basilica to focus his binoculars on the plateau rolling away to the north. The four miles between the butte and the Kriemhilde Stellung were wrinkled with gently rolling hills and darkened by woods, some many acres in size and others forming thin ribbons between pastures and wheat fields. No matter its size, each copse was fortified by the Germans. In a deep ravine on the right side of the 79th's sector crouched the village of Nantillois, which had been nearly destroyed by shelling but provided numerous fighting positions. On the west side of the 79th's sector—opposite Nantillois—lay a large, trapezoid-shaped wood called the Bois de Beuge, a forbidding area that harbored multiple machine-gun nests and artillery emplacements.

About three miles north, the Bois des Ogons stretched almost all the way across the division's front. Pierced only by the road running from Nantillois to Cunel, the forest concealed the German main line of resistance, the feared Kriemhilde Stellung. In the center of a clearing just east of the road lay Madeleine Farm. Before the US attack, the huddle of stone-and-brick buildings housed a German hospital, but by noon on the second day, the buildings had been converted to a fortress bristling with machine guns. However, the roof of the barn was still marked with a protective red cross, which Americans later contended was a violation of the rules of war. Just behind the large house and barn were the stronger fortifications of the *stellung*: deep concrete bunkers, massive dugouts, and trenches coiling through dark woods.

Even today, the Bois des Ogons and the Bois de Cunel are dense and dark enough to shelter owls, deer, and boars. Massive oak and beech trees cover continuous ravines and rills, broken by a few rocky patches and an extensive array of rusting artifacts. Here lies a blasted steel container that a German once shouldered to bring warm food to frontline comrades. Several bullet holes disclose the fate of the man who ported it to this spot. At the base of an oak lie three rusty German hand grenades, slightly smaller than the baseballs that John Bentley pitched. A few years ago, a similar weapon exploded in the hand of a careless French farm boy who jostled its unstable charge. In a small clearing lie hundreds of brass rifle cartridges mysteriously separated from their 7.7mm projectiles huddling in a nearby pile. And, as throughout the Meuse-Argonne, countless pieces of shrapnel rust under a blanket of leaves on the forest floor, suggesting the omnipresent danger endured by soldiers of both nations.

On the afternoon of September 27, 1918, the deposition of the steel relics had just begun as German batteries searched for targets near Montfaucon, and American long-range guns replied. Once the doughboys eliminated Little Gibraltar's observatory, they anticipated an advance relatively unimpeded by German artillery, but they had not reckoned with Hill 378, a bald ridge on the Heights of the Meuse. The promontory was part of a line of high ridges that followed the meandering east bank of the river as far north as the Yanks could see. The Germans had fortified the ridges and built multistory observation posts in trees on the Borne de Cornouiller, the high spot of the range. From rickety tree houses three or four stories tall, Germans with binoculars and telescopes could spot soldiers on the newly conquered butte or on the plateau beyond.

The next three days of heavy German shelling was what many Yanks remembered most vividly about the Meuse-Argonne. Bentley recalled "terrible shell fire, shells crashing into Montfaucon at a tremendous rate of speed." Later, he was standing with a fellow officer,

watching the line of wounded men going to the First Aid Station, when a shell came crashing through the air and lit under a couple of these men, killing the man who had been wounded and severely wounding the man who had been carrying him. Lieutenant C- and I ran over to the man to render assistance and calling a couple of my men we carried him in to the First Aid Station. The poor fellow kept saying: "What have I done, boys, what have I done?" and soon passed away. When we arrived at the station I found that there were many there already that I knew: Lieutenant M- was lying on his blood-soaked stretcher, dying with a bullet through his lungs. I leaned over and bending near his white face, I said: "Will you make it, Mac?" and his answer came back: "You bet"—but he couldn't.[32]

Years later, one veteran summarized the situation succinctly: "A man on Montfaucon or around it in those days simply carried his life in his bare hands."[33] In the early afternoon, the Germans concentrated fire on the highly visible church steeple, a convenient aiming point just south of the crown prince's observatory. They were desperate to destroy the telescope and maps, which could be used against them. In the midst of the shelling, however, a detail of American intelligence troops arrived to salvage what was left. Among them were Privates Cain and Puttkammer, dispatched by General Kuhn the previous night. They emerged carrying metal cases, parts of the huge telescope, and armloads of maps. While they were laboring with these burdens, a huge German shell skimmed over their backs and burst just beyond. Two men were badly wounded, but the others scooped up the intelligence treasures and moved on to shelter.[34]

When word of the telescope's capture reached Kuhn, he rushed another group to reassemble the instrument within its secure concrete structure. A squad under the direction of Sergeant Thomas Rivel put the scope to good use. The Germans deduced quickly from the improved American gunnery that the observatory was back in action, and directed a daylong barrage on the manor house. Rivel and his men, however, persisted to identify targets; they were awarded Distinguished Service Crosses.[35]

The heavy artillery barrage was not enough to discourage the dead-tired Colonel Sweezey from moving on to his regiment's next objective: the Bois de Beuge. Infested with machine-gun nests, trenches, and large bunkers, the woods lay just beyond one of the narrow-gauge German railroads that crisscrossed the battlefield. The colonel knew that taking the woods would be difficult, so he requested artillery preparation. Awaiting the American barrage, officers strengthened the battered 313th by asking Ben Hewit to join the attack with the 316th's Company F. He was not obligated to do so but agreed readily. The remainder of the 316th, including Parkin's First Battalion, was deployed on the northern slopes of the butte to stanch a potential German counterattack.

Although the requested US artillery barrage never appeared, Sweezey ordered his troops and tanks forward at 3:30 p.m. German artillery and machine guns took a fearsome toll as the attackers crossed the fields. The men continued, exhorted on by their officers. "Come on, fellows!" shouted Hewit. "See that narrow-gauge railroad cut on the edge of the woods? Run like hell for that. Follow me!"[36]

At first, the troops cheered as they surged down the grassy slope, but soon enemy machine guns found their range and drenched American enthusiasm with German steel. The cheers quickly died as doughboys dropped and survivors dived into shell craters. Then, inspired by their captain's courage, the majority rose again and continued up the slope to the shelter of the roadbed.

The Yanks were furious about the losses they had taken, and small groups spontaneously began to forsake cover and fight their way into the margin of the woods. One of the first platoons to reach the forest was led by Corporal Paul Runkle, who had taken over command when Lieutenant Hank Welling was seriously wounded in the meadow. A football star at Pennsylvania State University, Welling refused to be left behind while his men fought their way into the woods. Carried by his men, the lieutenant continued to direct the assault as he sat exposed on top of a trench—until he was carried away on a litter. Confronted by such determination, the Germans retreated, abandoning their automatic weapons and *minenwerfers*. Foot by foot, the 313th moved forward, with one American yelling at his slower compatriots, "Come on boys. Don't go back on us."[37]

Despite heavy machine-gun fire from deep in the woods, more Yanks began to dash into the thickets, where they established a tenuous toehold. Sheltered in a shallow depression, Private Adam Matlawski heard "a voice loudly praying in Polish, and in a shell

hole found a German-Pole with a shrapnel wound in the abdo-
men. Hewit questioned the man about machine-gun positions
and enemy strength, with Matlawski interpreting. The enemy
soldier was Waclaw Pietruszka, a corporal in the 42nd Regiment
of the Prussian Guards, from Posen, German Poland. 'Take care
of him, Mat,' said Captain Hewit. 'It doesn't matter if he is in the
German army. He has to fight, the same as we all have to fight.
When it gets dark, take him to the first-aid station. Then settle in
for the night, because tomorrow will be a tougher day.' "[38]

As the sun of September 27 began to set, the Yanks dug in
along the southern edge of the Bois de Beuge. The Germans
driven from their trenches in the woods, however, had reported
the Americans' new position on field telephones. As soon as the
information was relayed to distant batteries, a massive barrage
began falling on the Americans. Some of the Yanks swore later
that the blasts were coming from their own artillery; soldiers
experiencing flanking fire for the first time often drew that inaccurate conclusion. With increasingly heavy casualties from the
huge shells, the Yanks were eventually forced to surrender their
hold on the woods and to fall back to a trench on the lower slopes
of Montfaucon.

Parkin observed the assault from the ruins of Little Gibraltar, where he had established a command post. Toward evening,
a drawn and weary Colonel Sweezey trudged back through the
streets, and the major offered him shelter to serve as his P.C.
"P.C., hell," cursed the colonel. "I want to get in touch with Division P.C. and have your regiment relieve mine tonight instead
of in the morning. We are all shot to pieces."[39]

On the east side of the 79th's sector, the 314th had also been
"shot to pieces." After resting in the Bois de la Tuilerie and pawing
over several captured German artillery pieces, the troops moved
forward in waning light to assault Nantillois. About a kilometer
north of the woods, the 314th met stiff resistance and suffered the
same heavy barrage that was falling on Americans on the west side

of the sector. They dug in for the night. Nantillois, which could have easily been captured by the 4th Division the previous day, would not be taken by the 79th until the following day, forty-eight hours later.

At German Fifth Army headquarters, news from the battle-front sparked a modest celebration. General Gallwitz was pleased to learn that "Along the new line, a strong attack launched from Montfaucon was repelled! Subsequently we took Nantillois. Beginning at 3 p.m., a number of powerful enemy attacks . . . between the Argonne and the neighborhood of Nantillois, proved abortive. Also, between 7 and 8 p.m., a strong attack with tanks from the direction of Montfaucon-Septsarges was repulsed. Our situation seemed satisfactory once more."[40]

Conditions were less satisfactory for Harry Parkin, who settled in for a few hours of fitful sleep on a bed of broken rubble. But in the middle of the night, he and Major Baird Atwood of the 316th's Third Battalion were awakened to attend a meeting in Colonel Charles's bunker. Their regimental commander had just received an urgent message to take over the front and was meeting with Sweezey for a briefing on the deployment of the 313th. "Col. Sweezey gave Col. Charles the information he had for him about the front and the position of his men," reported Parkin. "Then Col. Sweezey got into his bedding roll, which had been brought along for him. Col. Charles seemed confused and undecided about what to do. He kept asking Col. Sweezey over and over. Finally, Col. Sweezey, who was tired out, spoke to Col. Charles very sharply and said he had already given him all the information he had. Then Col. Charles subsided."[41]

Recognizing that Charles's indecisiveness was keeping him from taking charge, the two majors promised they would relieve the 313th and prepare the next day's assault. Given the darkness and the continuing artillery barrage, Parkin and Atwood knew the mission would not be easy, but they decided not to consult Charles again for fear he would complicate the task. Outside of the colonel's earshot, the officers developed a plan and agreed "to help each other all we possibly could. We were to advance our battalions side by side," recalled Parkin. "Poor Atwood, that was the last time I saw him until I stood and looked down on his dead body three days later, although he was killed early the next morning."[42]

The majors gathered their men and moved down Montfaucon's northern slopes to relieve the exhausted 313th. By the light of star shells and artillery explosions, Parkin made his way to Captain Hugh Kelly's command post located in a long bunker crammed with sleeping men and illuminated by only two candles.

"The dim light made the tired and haggard faces look ghastly and drawn. What a scene to stay forever in a man's memory," Parkin recalled later. Without a word of welcome, Kelly glanced at the major's fur-collared coat and tall boots and predicted bluntly that Parkin would not last long the following day: "Your fur collar and your boots will show the German snipers that you are an officer. With that fur collar, they will think you a general. Better throw away that coat," said the captain. Reluctant to part with his warm cover, Parkin turned the collar under and plastered his boots with mud. Kelly also advised him "to take a place in the line with the men and carry a rifle," recalled Parkin, "which I did for a while next morning, but found the rifle a nuisance to me and dropped it. I had messages to write and receive, and the field telephone to handle at times. I could not be bothered with the rifle."[43]

Parkin settled in for a restless night in the bunker as German artillery thumped the ground outside. He was proud of what his battalion had accomplished in the last two days. Although the 1,200 men had played a supporting role in the attack on Montfaucon, they had fought German stragglers well. Now it was time for the 316th to take the lead, and for Harry to face the full test of battle. The major was optimistic about his doughboys' ability to clear the Bois de Beuge and sweep on to pierce the Kriemhilde Stellung.

Parkin's confidence, however, was based on a limited understanding of the battlefield situation, which had changed dramatically in the previous forty-eight hours. The failure to capture Little Gibraltar on the first day had exposed the entire US First Army to the skilled brutality of German artillery, and their massive guns had slowed the offensive across the entire front. Hunter Liggett's I Corps was stalled in the ravines of the Argonne Forest, and George Cameron's V Corps had advanced just half the distance it had been expected to cover on the *first* day. On the right the offensive had gone well. Near the Meuse River, III Corps had "been making history"—in the words of one exuberant reporter—but only because of the sector's light defenses and Robert Bullard's refusal to assist Montfaucon's capture. By the end of the second day of battle, however, Bullard's strategy to charge quickly forward had begun to sputter, and his troops were stalled well south of the Kriemhilde Stellung.

In the precious time afforded by the stout defense of Montfaucon, General Gallwitz had used efficient German railroads to rush a total of ten divisions to reinforce the front that protected the vital rail line near Sedan. As Parkin dozed fitfully in the bunker on the night of September 27, thousands of fresh German troops were awake only two miles to the north. Preparing for a bloody morning, they labored all night digging in near the Kriemhilde Stellung, placing their machine guns and artillery pieces to cover avenues of American advance, and using skills mastered over four years of combat to halt the largest offensive the US Army had ever mounted.

Although Generals Kuhn, Cameron, and Pershing would not face the fact for another two days, the game was nearly up. They had accomplished the impossible by assembling their troops without the notice of the enemy. But having satisfied the need for stealth, they failed to maintain the speed necessary to crash through the Hindenburg Line. The hope for a quick break-through had been eliminated by the stubborn German stand on Montfaucon. Over the next three weeks, the Yanks would learn the futility of attacking well-constructed defenses over open terrain, just as the French and British had before them. The lessons would be costly.

CHAPTER 11

"ALL AMERICA IS BEHIND US"

On September 27, 1918, as doughboys marched by the Crown Prince's Observatory, they could see in the attic the concrete substructure protecting the telescopic periscope that enabled the enemy to direct artillery onto any spot of the battlefield.

★   ★   ★

Time after time, the Doughboys attacked machine-gun nests and pillboxes head-on. After the Germans mowed them down or immolated them with flame-throwers, others took their place and attacked anew.

—Edward G. Lengel, military historian[1]

When dawn arrived on September 28, conditions were not promising. Rain fell steadily, German troops had reoccupied the Bois de Beuge, and the enemy artillery, which had diminished overnight, began to reassert its dominance. And as usual, there was no warm food, hot coffee, or fresh water.

Parkin and Atwood roused their men from cold, wet trenches, and formed them for battle. Parkin's First Battalion, reinforced with two additional companies, would take the left side of the Bois de Beuge, while Atwood's Third Battalion would assault the right side of the woods. Although the men had been promised artillery support, the telephone line to the batteries was down, and no American shells threatened the Germans peering up at Montfaucon from their trenches in the woods. Parkin waved his troops forward, and walked just behind the lead company as it entered the valley that had seen much death and destruction the previous day.

"Already the German shells were bursting in the meadow, the Germans having seen Major Atwood's men forming there for the attack," recalled Parkin. "We were now experiencing the heaviest and worst shell fire we had yet endured. Shell fire is terrifying and demoralizing, and it takes good [sic] disciplined troops to endure it and not break or be driven back. I am proud to say that my men not only endured it, but advanced under it and through it without flinching and were scarcely free from it for the next two days."[2]

As they attacked the Bois de Beuge for the second time, Captain Hewit's Company F was trapped in the open before reaching the railroad grade it had captured the day before. Always out front, Hewit yelled, "We've got to reach that railroad cut or be

shot to pieces . . . Come on men. Keep on your feet—they're
shooting low!" In the assault, the captain took a bullet to the wrist,
but he continued forward, demonstrating to his men that they
could fight when wounded.[3] Adding to the misery, shells emitting
telltale yellow puffs of smoke began falling among the men, who
struggled to pull on their masks. Before they could do so, however, mustard gas brought several of Hewit's men to their knees.

On the right, Atwood's troops were taking terrific fire from the
edge of the woods. Machine guns, *minenwerfers*, and the feared
"whizz-bangs"—Austrian high-velocity 88mm guns—fired as
quickly as possible. Crouching in a shell crater, Atwood sent a
strong note to regimental headquarters: "Being fired at point
blank by field pieces. For God's sake get artillery or we'll be an-
nihilated."[4]

When Parkin received the order, he ran back up the butte's
slope to underscore the urgency of Atwood's request with Colonel Charles. On a road near the base of Montfaucon, Parkin
found Charles, who stood in the midst of the German barrage
with a newly arrived artillery liaison officer. Although the colonel was brave physically, he was frozen by indecisiveness. The
liaison officer easily could have called for artillery support using
a nearby telephone line, but Charles argued that there *might* be
Americans in the woods. Impassioned by Atwood's desperate situation, Parkin argued that his troops were in the lead and had not
yet entered the woods. There was no way that Atwood's troops
could have reached the trees. Charles's answer was a curt order to
continue the advance, a command that he also relayed by runner
to Atwood.

After receiving the order, Major Atwood waited until Parkin's
battalion was ready for the assault to launch his own attack. As
Atwood rose to his knees to order the troops forward, he was
struck by a German bullet just left of his nose and was dead before his body hit the ground. But the assault went on as Charles
had ordered.

"It was just such a command which had sent the Light Brigade to destruction and eternal glory at Balaclava," recalled one angry officer who watched the action. "It did the same for L and M Companies of the 316th on that September day in the depths of the woods. Someone had blundered. Officers and men of the Third Battalion paid with their lives for the fatal error. Two full companies, well-nigh 500 men, went forward without the slightest bit of artillery or machine gun fire to cover them."[5]

The fighting was vicious, as the Germans hung tenaciously to their positions in the woods. While most of the troops followed army doctrine by assaulting the trenches and machine-gun nests directly, Parkin had begun to sense the flaws of American training. He sent a platoon to the left of the Bois de Beuge. Because all the officers had been killed, the group was led by a corporal, George Livelsberger. Miraculously, the men managed to flank the trenches and attack the Germans from the side and rear, a move that led immediately to enemy withdrawal. In one encounter, Private John Thomas, an Albanian restaurant owner from Philadelphia, crouched and ran a quarter of a mile until he outflanked a machine-gun nest. He killed one gunner, captured another, and put the third to flight: "I tried to shoot fast enough to make them think a whole Platoon was on top of them," said Thomas. "But I was more scared than they were."[6]

Thomas escaped the exploit unscathed; other Americans were not as lucky. Private Emil Greimann crawled back from the firefight holding something in his hand. "'I've lost a lamp,' he grinned. It was his right eye, ripped out by a machine-gun bullet."[7] Incidents like this drove men wild with anger, including Sergeant Grover Sheckart, who saw his captain shot dead by a concealed sniper. The American, who had been wounded in the foot on the first day of battle, "was so infuriated that he rushed into the bushes, drove out the German and another, and killed them with his bayonet."[8] Parkin noted that Sheckart "was of German parentage, but nevertheless he was the best German killer in my battalion."[9] Although the sergeant was limping severely, he was far from finished. Looking up, he saw an enemy officer fleeing and called on him in English and German to stop,

> but the officer kept on and, looking back, laughed at him. Then the Sergeant leveled his rifle and shot the German between the shoulders. He went up to him and seeing that the officer was dying, he tried to help him pass out as easily as possible. He turned him over and put a rolled up coat under his head as a pillow and was offering him water when the German drew his pistol, which Sheckart finally got and threw away from them. The German officer died very quickly, his end hastened no doubt by the struggle.[10]

For his actions, the sergeant was awarded the Distinguished Service Cross.

The Yanks slowly took command of the Bois de Beuge, but the cost of victory was high. Parkin went into battle with twenty-two officers, of whom only five were still standing at the end of the day. In one company, all the officers were killed, while another lost all but one.[11] At 10:15 a.m., Colonel Charles informed divisional headquarters: "Estimated casualties so far: Officers 17—men 250."[12] Recognizing the plight of the 316th, General Kuhn sent back a message promising "to send forward [a] company of big tanks to assist you in capture of Bois de Beuge . . . Organize the assault and give necessary instructions to insure co-operation between infantry and tanks. Maintain liaison with Colonel Oury's P.C. by frequent courier service if not possible by wire."[13]

On the eastern side of the 79th Division's sector, Oury and the 315th were fighting for survival. Their objective was the village of Nantillois, a goal that drew them out of the woods into open ground exposed to aerial observation. "Enemy planes spotting for their artillery flew over, and as soon as a plane would see an advancing line, it would wheel back, and in a minute accurate fire would be registered on us," recalled Captain Sam Fleming.[14] Rarely did Yanks see their own planes contesting the air space, and, despite the fact that Captain Eddie Rickenbacker's pilots had "busted" ten German balloons on the first morning of the offensive, the enemy seemed to have a limitless supply of the inflatables.[15] Once again, the ominous balloons had begun to rise from the hills to the northeast.

The lack of American air cover and the absence of artillery support exposed the Yanks to terrific barrages. Sergeant Joseph Labrum, whose 314th Regiment was following just behind the 315th, recalled, "It was at this juncture that the Huns fired minnies [*minenwerfer* shells] and three-inch shells [77mm] almost point-blank at us . . . keeping us in a box barrage that for its intensity of fire could hardly be equaled."[16] Under such conditions, advances are purchased by the blood and bravery of individual soldiers, and the 315th Regiment did not lack men up to the task. After being stopped for nearly an hour, Captain William M. Carroll of the 315th finally had enough. He and a sergeant moved down a sunken lane and attacked the enemy crew from behind, killing one, capturing another, and putting the others to flight. The elimination of the position opened the way for the 315th, which promptly captured the town. For "extraordinary heroism," Carroll was awarded the Distinguished Service Cross.[17]

By 11:00 a.m., the 315th had forced its way into Nantillois, albeit at heavy cost. The regimental historian recorded that the "front line companies had each lost a third of their men killed or wounded, and the other companies of the advanced battalions had sustained losses almost as heavy."[18] As the doughboys climbed the hill just north of Nantillois, several French tanks led the assault. "It was rough because the Germans were shooting their cannons right at the tanks. Some shells missed and came at us," recalled Private Andrew Kachik.

On the west side of the sector, Parkin and the 316th continued to push through the Bois de Beuge and soon emerged from the northern edge of the woods. Beyond them were Bois 268 and then Bois 250, the western extension of the Bois des Ogons. To the northwest, the men spotted a long column of Germans retreating across the hills toward Romagne, as well as a group preparing to evacuate a 77mm gun that had been firing at the advancing Americans. Jumping at this opportunity to avenge the morning's slaughter, Parkin ordered a company of heavy Browning machine guns forward. The group of German artillerymen was only five hundred yards away, and the heavies hosed the crew and their field piece with steel.

"A team of six galloping horses came tearing over a rise, swung into place very neatly behind the gun, which was quickly attached to the limber," Parkin recalled. "There was a wild scramble among the gunners to climb into their places on the gun and limber, and away the whole unit went at full gallop, bumping and bouncing, and were quickly out of sight under a hail of bullets."[19]

The American machine guns then turned their deadly attention to the column of retreating German troops and finally to the machine-gun nests in Bois 268, the next woods that lay astride their path to the Kriemhilde Stellung. As the Browning barrage took a toll on both targets, a group of strangely arrayed French officers emerged from the Bois de Beuge. Dressed in the black leather coats, gray breeches, and black leggings of the French tank corps, the men offered to help Parkin push his attack. After they agreed on a plan, a squadron of six large tanks rolled out of the woods and crawled toward the next objective. Parkin and his men were astonished to see a French officer walking in front of each tank, calmly using a cane to test the ability of the ground to bear the weight of the armored vehicle. Stating that the officers' actions were "one of the bravest things I ever saw," the American major watched as German observers in balloons floating above the battlefield noted the coordinates of the tanks and launched a terrific barrage.

The shells were dropping fast now about the tanks hurrying back to cover. Suddenly one of the tanks farthest out was squarely hit by a shell, and to our astonishment great tongues of fire poured from it . . . To our horror not a door of that tank opened. Not one of the six men in it survived. The tank stopped when hit and stood there smoking and burning, the brave men within killed by the explosion, or if wounded, slowly roasted to death there before our eyes.[20]

The American infantrymen were once again on their own to attack the woods. As the senior officer of a rapidly shrinking assault force, Parkin gathered the remnants of his own battalion, survivors of Atwood's unit, and some men of the 313th. When the troops were reorganized under the few remaining officers, Parkin led them over the open ground to the ribbon of trees ahead. Frightened by the tanks, some Germans had fled, but others remained to fight and die in their trenches. Parkin's surprise assault was successful, and the victorious Americans sprawled in the meager woods to catch their breath.

As German artillery shells deluged the men in Bois 268, Parkin called a meeting of the few surviving officers, including Captains Hewit, Louis Knack, and Lauriston Knowlton. After noting that the promised American artillery fire had not appeared and that their flanks were unsupported by other US units, Parkin solicited the advice of his comrades. One officer suggested retreating, but Ben Hewit reacted strongly: "Never. We helped capture the Bois de Beuge twice and it's too costly to cross these open spaces."[21]

"Our men will get blown to pieces," argued another officer. Ignoring the danger they were in, Hewit laughed gently and gave his fellow officer a poke in the ribs. "It was a friendly laugh," Parkin recalled, "and the others joined in. His actions were incongruous, ludicrous: 'Old Man War Himself,' they had jokingly called him, because he had been so earnest in preparing for war—and there he stood, laughing, with shells crashing all about. It struck their funny bone. Tension was relieved."[22]

The major decided that the best course was to report his position and request further orders. Hewit volunteered to deliver the message, joshing, "I've got nothing better to do."[23] Shrugging off danger, the good-natured Hewit struck out through the continuous barrage and found Colonel Charles near the Bois de Beuge. Oblivious to the peril of trekking through heavy fire, the colonel thoughtlessly sent the captain back with orders for Parkin to return for consultation. After a half hour of dodging high-explosive and gas shells, the major joined the meeting. The unpredictable Charles seemed on the verge of pulling the men back from Bois 268, but Parkin argued that his men could hold their position through the coming night. As usual, the colonel could not make up his mind. Just at that time, a shell burst above the command group, and the colonel collapsed to the ground moaning loudly and shouting, "Tourniquet, tourniquet!" Two medical officers rushed to attend the wounded officer, but after close inspection, all they could find was a bruise on his hip. It seemed that a piece of the shell had hit Charles's canteen, smashing it, and he assumed that the moisture was blood.[24] The colonel's overreaction became quite a joke among the regiment, eroding any remaining respect the men had for him. Thereafter, as the 316th marched through France, an anonymous voice from the ranks would cry out, "Tourniquet! Tourniquet!" and the men would break into gales of laughter.

Because the officers' attention was focused on the colonel, they initially failed to note that the blast had indeed injured one soldier, Sergeant Major Howard A. Bair, who was lying nearby with a thigh wound. Bair had been away attending Officers Training School when he heard about the impending offensive and the inclusion of the 79th. He insisted on leaving school to return to help his friends. After Bair's wound was bandaged, the command group dusted itself off and continued discussing Parkin's battalion. One officer with binoculars noticed that Hewit, back in Bois 268, seemed to be pulling back the men. In one of the quick, abrupt reversals for which the colonel was infamous, Charles decided the 316th should stay put. He dispatched Parkin to inspire his troops to spend another dangerous night on the battlefield.

While the 316th was taking Bois 268, the 315th had left Nantillois and was pushing toward the Bois des Ogons. Led by two heavy tanks and four light Renaults, the men braved the same intense shell fire endured by Parkin's men. Despite losses, they surged into the southern edge of the woods. Their appearance drove the Germans to a frenzy of machine-gun and artillery fire, which eventually pushed the Yanks back to the reverse slopes of Hill 274. From that promontory, one of the officers noted that the Germans seemed to be preparing to follow the American withdrawal with a counterattack from the woods. A noncommissioned officer of the 315th recalled that his company and two others were quickly formed into a skirmish line to break up the impending German attack. The men surged back into the Bois des Ogons. There the Americans went on a rampage, capturing German weapons and destroying emplacements. More importantly, they took invaluable maps of German positions. Emboldened by success, the doughboys advanced farther north until they saw a large building with a Red Cross flag floating over it. "We found out later that it was a regular fort. They had a machine gun in every window," recalled one Yank.[25]

Although the men of the 315th did not realize it, they were only one hundred to two hundred yards south of the famed Kriemhilde Stellung, the German main line of resistance in the Meuse-Argonne and the heart of the Hindenburg Line. The largest building was Madeleine Farm's barn, still flying the Red Cross flag designating a hospital in contravention of accepted military conduct. For the next three weeks, the farm would repel waves of Yanks who sacrificed their lives attempting to take it. As the Americans considered attacking the barn, they were ordered to pull back because the Germans were setting fire to the woods. Just as a particularly heavy barrage began to level the front half of the woods, the 315th made it back to the relative safety of the reverse slopes of Hill 274. Known thereafter as Suicide Hill, the low ridge sheltered the Yanks, who soon learned that it was self-destructive to raise their heads above its crest.

Farther back, the engineers continued to repair the roads that carried urgently needed artillery batteries, ammunition, food, and medical supplies for the troops. The engineers' efforts were increasingly ineffective, however, because of a breakdown in discipline among vehicle drivers. Tough military policemen were brought up to supervise the movement of vehicles, and they gave ambulances conveying wounded to field hospitals the highest priority. Given the congestion, however, the medical trucks simply were unable to get through in time to save the lives of many severely wounded men. The 79th Division medical staff had set up a casualty collection station and triage area just south of Montfaucon near the Malancourt road. The physician in charge, Major Hanson, had grown frustrated by the increasing number of patients left lying in a field where only the most rudimentary medical aid was available. With two hundred casualties who needed immediate evacuation, the doctor sent a motorcycle messenger to request more help, and he commandeered every empty truck to convey the most desperate cases to field hospitals.[26] Doctor Hanson's initiative saved lives and led to substantial improvement in the treatment of the 79th's wounded. A mobile field hospital, a corps of doctors, and more ambulances were dispatched forward.

Inadequate medical support resulted from poor American planning for the Meuse-Argonne Offensive. AEF staff had vastly underestimated the number of casualties. Based on the results of the highly successful St. Mihiel operation, general headquarters had projected only ten thousand wounded and dead for the coming operation. St. Mihiel, however, had been carried out against Germans withdrawing from their positions. But the Meuse-Argonne was a much tougher region, defended by more determined Germans. In the final accounting, American casualties in the offensive amounted to more than ten times the estimate.

Inaccurate projections increased the number of dead by reducing the availability of urgently needed medical facilities, equipment, and staff. But the inability to manage the traffic was ultimately the more destructive factor, as evacuation of seriously wounded slowed to a snail's pace. Because of poor traffic planning, the 79th Division bore a disproportionate part of the burden. General Kuhn's division was not permitted to send supplies over the road from Hill 304 to Malancourt, the very stretch of road that his division had just captured. Instead, munitions for the 79th were diverted three miles west to Avocourt and then detoured back across an exposed part of the battlefield to Malancourt, where the trucks merged with traffic proceeding toward the 4th Division. The 4th Division used the direct, shorter route, while artillery support and supplies to the troops beyond Montfaucon were often delayed interminably by the long detour.

On Suicide Hill, Sergeant Boll of the 315th scraped a foxhole for himself out of the rocky soil just south of the ridge crest. He pulled a poncho over his head to protect himself from the downpour and, in relative comfort and safety, realized he had nothing to eat. Some of his friends had taken bread bags from killed or captured Germans, but Boll had not had the forethought to prepare for another night without rations. Just as the young Philadelphian was adjusting himself to that miserable reality, the Germans decided to make things even more uncomfortable.

> The shells began to whistle around and over us increasingly in regular exasperating rhythms. It was whizz, whizz, whizz —————whizz, with a slight pause between the third and fourth whizz; then followed the boom, boom, boom—————boom as the shells struck. That last delayed shot had a certain effect on the nervous system. If that was artillery psychology, it served its purpose.[27]

On the western end of the 79th's line, Parkin also hunkered down against shell fire, as rain pooled at the bottom of his hole in Bois 268. The major knew that the regiment's assault on the Kriemhilde Stellung the following morning would likely make the day the toughest of the campaign. Compounding that bleak knowledge, Parkin's troops had "[n]o food, not even a piece of old bread, not even water, no blankets, absolutely nothing to give us courage and strength for the terrible ordeal of the morrow," the major recalled. "Nothing but the 'will to do,' and our own sense of duty and self-respect to carry us on and help us in the attack we all knew must be made in the morning. It rained most of the night and shells fell, and we lay in the mud under the dripping bushes, cold, weary and hungry with the thoughts of tomorrow's battle and wounds and death to wear down our courage."[28]

The evening of September 28 was to be Parkin's dark night of the soul. Worn by responsibility for the 316th's attack and discouraged by the death of friends, the major called on his last reserves to steel himself for the coming attack on the Bois des Ogons and the feared Kriemhilde Stellung. Farther along the woods, similar challenges were confronting the men of Company F. According to one veteran, "We looked like wild men, with our three-day beards and hollow eyes and ragged, mud-spattered uniforms. We acted like dazed men with every sense dull; only remained the instinct to fight and save ourselves."[29]

But on the far right of the line, the irrepressible Ben Hewit retained a sense of grim optimism and used the late-night hours to visit every sentry post. Despite the worsening pain in his wounded wrist, the captain moved along the line, cheering up troops. "Fellows, it's going to be a tough battle tomorrow," he said. "But don't forget to keep up the old spirit the way Hank Welling did yesterday. A good soldier is one who will fight and keep going to the last. And if we are all knocked off, there are plenty more back home to take our place. All America is behind us."[30]

CHAPTER 12

"REGARDLESS OF COST"

Little Gibraltar was honeycombed with tunnels, galleries, and bunkers, like this one used to store ammunition. The underground fortress was built to hold out for a long siege, so that it could continue to direct artillery fire on any force that might assault it.

★　　★　　★

In having to grope its way to victory, the AEF succeeded not because of imaginative operations and tactics nor because of qualitative superiority in open warfare, but rather by smothering German machine guns with American flesh.

—James W. Rainey, World War I historian[1]

S ome fifteen miles behind American front lines, the provincial town of Souilly was sheltered by several ridge lines that softened the rumble of artillery from the north. Despite its secure setting, the town was always bustling. Souilly's main street was the celebrated Voie Sacrée, the "Sacred Way" that the French had used to supply the fortified city of Verdun during the siege of 1916. In 1918, instead of serving a defensive purpose, the highway had taken on the more aggressive function of fueling the American offensive against Gallwitz's Fifth Army. Heavy truck traffic feeding the battle sped by every hour of the day; a slower procession of ambulances carried seriously wounded Americans back to hospitals in Paris.

The frenetic activity, however, was not permitted to disturb deliberations taking place behind the thick walls and massive doors of the Marie, the three-story town hall that served as First Army advanced headquarters. Inside, General Pershing insisted on a rigid sense of order, strict decorum, and quiet confidence, all to create a calm atmosphere in which staff could reach dispassionate decisions affecting the lives of a million soldiers.

During the evening hours of September 28, however, the mood was decidedly tense. Lights burned brightly behind blackout curtains throughout the night, and the latest battlefield dispatches were rushed immediately to the chief's map room. Pershing was increasingly concerned about the Meuse-Argonne Offensive. He had first confessed unease about the halting pace of the drive in an ambivalent diary entry the day before: "On the whole I am not very much pleased with the progress made, though it should not be called unsatisfactory."[2] Over the course of the night, however, the commander's uncertainty evaporated, and by morning, he had resolved to take decisive action to accelerate the First Army.

Climbing into a khaki-colored touring car at daybreak, Pershing set out to visit all three corps and several divisional commanders to rivet their attention on the mission. As the general traveled from west to east along the battlefront, he grew alarmed by the incompetence of some senior officers he met. At one stop, an officer seemed so confused that the general left an aide to sort things out. Dodging dense traffic jams and navigating muddy roads made for a long day, and when Pershing returned that evening, he wrote in a defensive tone, "I gave orders for the advance to be resumed, and certainly have done all in my power to instill an aggressive spirit in the different Corps headquarters."[3]

The commander's extraordinary efforts were necessary because the campaign had reached a critical point. As historian John Eisenhower observed, "By taking Montfaucon in a day and a half, the Americans had done better than [French General Henri] Pétain had predicted, and by that criterion they had scored a great victory. But that victory had fallen short of Pershing's need to take not only Montfaucon but Romagne as well, in the course of forty-eight hours . . . It was a victory, but an ominous one."[4] While the First Army commander had achieved strategic surprise, he had not attained the second element necessary for success: a speedy advance and quick breakthrough of the Kriemhilde Stellung. But Pershing clung to one remnant of hope: the Yanks still might just pierce the Hindenburg Line before the majority of the German reinforcements arrived—*if* they moved decisively on September 29. And *if* the doughboys could break through the main line of German resistance into the relatively unfortified area beyond the heights of Romagne and Cunel, the commander would have space to employ the life-sparing maneuvers of open warfare. If they failed, a reversion to trench warfare and its deadly direct assaults on fortified positions appeared inevitable. Some officers whispered that if the attack stalled, the First Army would have to surrender the hard-won butte of Montfaucon and withdraw for the winter to more defensible positions farther south. It would be nothing less than a disastrous return to the status quo ante.[5]

To avoid the unthinkable, First Army staff underscored the effect of Pershing's tour by working through the night pressuring commanders thought to be lagging. Many of those at Souilly believed that two generals who could profit most from a good prodding were George Cameron of V Corps and Joseph Kuhn of the 79th Division. Headquarters' anger had been stoked by an indignant Bullard, who complained that the 79th was not keeping up with the advance of the 4th Division and was exposing III Corps' flank to German fire. As a result, headquarters unleashed a barrage of telephone calls and messages demanding aggressive action. One call from Chief of Staff Drum severely bruised Cameron's pride, but a short time later, the V Corps commander issued Field Order No. 46 directing that "Divisions will advance independently of each other, pushing the attack with the utmost vigor and *regardless of cost*" (emphasis added).[6] Less than a half hour later, Kuhn echoed the imperatives: "The 79th Division will attack at 7h, 29th September, 1918, and will advance rapidly in the sector previously assigned. Brigade, regimental, and battalion commanders will use every means *regardless of cost* to prevent the advance from being delayed" (emphasis added).[7]

Regardless of cost: the phrase emphasized the desperate measures commanders were authorized to use: the sacrifice of any number of American lives to break the Kriemhilde Stellung. In the middle of the rainy night, a messenger bearing that order began searching for Major Parkin in battered Bois 268, where he huddled under a blanket with his adjutant, Lieutenant Dan Kellar. Roused by the sound of someone calling his name, the major shouted to guide the visitor through the darkness. Shortly afterward, Lieutenant Ivan Lautenbacher "stumbled over our feet and fell full length upon us, with his weight of some two hundred and twenty-five pounds. There was a scramble to get ourselves separated, and strange as it seems now, much laughter among us at our ridiculous position. He got up finally and apologized and gave me some orders from the Colonel relative to the attack of the morning. I have forgotten now just what they were."[8]

As exhausted as Parkin was, he did not require new orders to explain the importance of the task that lay ahead or the sacrifices needed for its completion. Nor were the demands of Colonel Charles, General Kuhn, or General Cameron necessary to coerce his compliance. Shaking off the rain and cold, the major arose to get his men ready for the assault. Parkin was heartened by the divisional commander's promise of a one-hour artillery barrage on the Bois de Cunel and the Bois des Ogons scheduled to begin at 6:00 a.m. In addition, Kuhn had assigned a battalion of smaller French 75s to provide close fire support for the assault regiments: the 316th on the left and the 315th on the right side of the sector. Clearly, the divisional commander understood the high risk of the attack and had used the hours of darkness to arrange as much support as possible for his men.

Unfortunately, the Germans had been busy as well. More reinforcements had poured into the front, including the 5th, 15th, and 37th Bavarian Regiments, and units of the 117th Landwehr Division.[9] Overnight, the fresh troops had moved additional batteries of 77mm field guns, as well as the dreaded Austrian 88mm high-velocity cannons, into the woods and ridges along the Kriemhilde Stellung. They were echeloned in depth to fire over the heads of newly arrived machine gunners, who used the evening to scrape shallow nests for their Maxims. During the hours of darkness, German long-range artillery east of the Meuse and in the Argonne Forest had concentrated fire not only on the US front line but also on "the back areas clear to Malancourt, and with special concentration on the ground lying north of Montfaucon where the American reserve and support units waited."[10] To greet the dawn, the Germans sent aloft an observation balloon that directed the fire of the big guns on the east side of the Meuse River. According to one divisional staff officer, the balloon loomed over the battlefield most of the day, daring Rickenbacker's pilots to react. It was hauled down only twice when Allied planes were nearby.

As the 79th readied for assault, heavy concentrations of German high-explosive, shrapnel, and phosgene-gas and mustard-gas shells began crashing into Bois 268 and Suicide Hill. The dough-boys eagerly awaited the American barrage that would answer the German guns. When the US bombardment finally appeared, however, it was so tepid that it had little effect. The 75s assigned to the 315th remained "all but incapable of action."[11] Moreover, the guns designated to support the 316th were simply unable to make their way up the muddy, jammed roads south of Montfau-con, so Parkin's men had no artillery support whatsoever. The major and his officers were stunned; even the irrepressible Ben Hewit recommended postponing the attack until the 75s came forward. But Parkin insisted on initiating the attack on schedule, and the officers promptly complied.

So many men of Hewit's command had been killed or wounded that he was well short of a company. Because he was assigned orig-inally to another battalion, he was not technically subject to Par-kin's orders. Hewit was determined, however, to play a role in the assault and volunteered to help. Because several companies had lost most of their officers, Parkin asked Hewit to take command of Company A and lead the attack—a dangerous assignment. The major added, "That's not an order, you know." Hewit's reply was swift: "I know. I want to help."[12]

Both men recognized that attacking the reinforced German position without artillery support was little short of suicide, yet once again the 79th advanced on schedule. At 7:00 a.m. sharp, the 316th charged into the open fields between Bois 268 and Bois 250, the western extension of the Bois des Ogons. Parkin recalled that the ensuing action was his battalion's "most severe trial," an assessment echoed by another member of the staff, who characterized the assault as "the most desperate fighting of the entire operation."[13] The Germans responded with the infantry equivalent of drumfire, as the massed field artillery and machine guns poured an unbroken stream of steel on Yanks emerging from Bois 268. As the 316th scrambled across the open space, Parkin noted that "a small bomb, probably fired from a trench mortar, came bounding along the ground, jumping from side to side, the fuse sputtering and crackling, and actually passed between my feet and exploded beyond me. I remember my thought at the time was 'What a ridiculous thing to try to kill a man with.'"[14]

Up ahead, where the fire was more deadly, Hewit "strode from group to group, waving his bandaged left arm toward the woods looming up through the rain and smoke about 200 yards ahead. Inspired by his courage, the ragged line advanced, stumbling and splashing into shell holes."[15] Some men were so shaken by the unprecedented fire that they fell to the ground out of sheer fright. Following behind Company A, Parkin responded with stern action. He ordered the laggards to get up and move forward, but they would not budge. He was so angry that he could have shot them—an action authorized by army regulations. But that type of punishment was not in the major's repertoire. Instead, he grabbed a shovel lying nearby and "I hit each of these two terrified men a resounding whack on the seat of his breeches, putting my back into the blow, and was about to repeat the treatment when they jumped up and made off at full speed after their company, fearing the spade more than the shells."[16]

The artillery and machine-gun fire took a tremendous toll on the depleted 316th, but Parkin pushed the drive toward Bois 250, where automatic-weapons fire winked steadily through the morning murk. To silence the Maxims, the major called up an officer with a 37mm gun that fired a dozen explosive rounds at the target. At the completion of the volley, the commander of the weapon predicted that German field pieces would soon reply.

At that moment, enemy fire blanketed the area, killing Parkin's adjutant, Lieutenant Dan Kellar.

The next officer to fall was Hewit, who took a shot to the chest while leading Company A toward the woods. When his men reached him, Hewit was pale and his breathing difficult. A machine-gun bullet had pierced his right lung, and he was placed on an improvised litter formed by two tree limbs and a German overcoat. Asked if he was all right, Hewit replied, "I will be. Goodbye till later. Keep up the spirit—and God be with you."[17] Three Americans and a German prisoner carried the improvised litter toward the rear, as a few men left from Hewit's company stood watching, wishing that their concern could protect their fallen commander. But before the litter made it fifty yards, an enemy shell fell directly on the group, blotting it out. Parkin watched as the blast vaporized the men into red mist. He later recalled that "absolutely no trace was left, and a hole in the ground marked the spot where they had been obliterated."[18]

Many survivors of the attack recalled that the bombardment was the heaviest they had ever seen: "It was more like hell, as they had dreamed of it, than anything else our boys had ever experienced or ever hoped to experience again," reported the *Baltimore Sun*'s Lester Muller. "Tanks were called for and word was received that the tanks refused to operate against the enemy positions unless afforded artillery support. The tanks did not come, and neither did the artillery support. I have never heard the reasons for the lack of artillery support satisfactorily explained."[19]

German shelling forced Parkin and his lead element to take cover in a shallow ravine. Within a few minutes, the fire lifted, and the men peered over the edge. Parkin was surprised to see a group of Germans off to the left rise up and start toward the rear in a leisurely manner. Clearly, they believed that the fierce artillery fire had killed most of the Americans. The Germans were preoccupied with repositioning for the next assault, and the situation was ripe for revenge.

"All over our position, officers and men arose and began firing rifles at the Germans as fast as they could work the bolts," Parkin recalled. "The excitement caused a too rapid fire, which was not as effective as it should have been. I picked up a rifle myself and emptied it several times." Then the major began to take more time and squeezed several rounds off with his P-17. "I remember distinctly one German soldier on the flank of the retiring company nearest us. When I first saw him, he was marching along leisurely with his big pack on his back and his rifle on his shoulder. When the bullets began to fly around him, he walked faster and then began to run awkwardly. I was firing at him slowly and carefully. Suddenly he stopped abruptly and fell down on his face."[20]

As German artillery fire increased once again, Parkin's men returned to the ravine, while to their right, a battalion of the 316th surged into the extension of the Bois des Ogons near the road to Cunel. Led by Captain John Somers, fifty men who survived crossing the deadly open ground struggled "forward in the woodland, frequently in hand to hand encounters with machine gunners, they pushed at last to the northern edge of the woods and set up a defensive position."[21] From there the men could look across a shallow valley to the ominous Bois de Cunel, in which the German main line of resistance lay. With the exception of Somers's small success, the outlook for the 316th was bleak. Losses were extremely heavy. At 10:10 a.m., General Nicholson complained to Kuhn, "Troops being cut to pieces by artillery and machine-gun fire . . . Hostile artillery fire practically unopposed by our artillery."[22]

On the opposite side of the 79th's sector, the 315th had launched its dawn assault with a flourish. Enflamed by a report that General Bullard had accused the 79th of exposing the left flank of the 4th Division by moving too slowly, the men began "with a yell that carried above the scream of Boche machine guns."[23] Although some of the regiment's companies consisted of only two platoons and another was led by only two officers, the survivors charged into the open fields toward the east end of the Bois des Ogons. Beyond Suicide Hill, they faced a withering artillery fire that equaled that endured by Parkin's regiment.

Most of the fire came from the Bois des Ogons, but additional casualties were inflicted by flanking (enfilading) fire from the Bois de Brieulles, which lay slightly behind and to the right of the 315th. Capturing those woods was the responsibility of the 4th Division. The fact that German artillery still operated from the position demonstrated that Bullard's claim that the 4th Division had advanced farther than the 79th Division was not accurate. Colonel Oury reported this fact immediately to divisional headquarters. With evident pleasure, General Kuhn quickly dispatched a message to the 4th Division that redirected the blame: "My Division [the 79th] cannot advance because of enfilading artillery fire from the right. Cannot advance unless your left brigade also advances at the same time."[24] Clearly, the fighting on September 29 was not limited to the battlefield, as the struggle to enhance reputations was under way among American generals.

Despite the heavy fire, the 315th again forced its way to the edge of the Bois des Ogons, where a massed chorus of machine guns silenced the Yanks' exuberant yelling and stalled the assault. In a written note, Oury pleaded for artillery fire. "The advance has been stopped," he confessed to headquarters. "The enemy fortifications at Madeleine Swamps [lowlands south of Madeleine Farm] consist of antitank guns, machine guns, renders imperative further artillery preparations before advance can be resumed. Bois de Cunel is also strongly held. Request that heavy artillery be again laid on Farm de la Madeleine."[25] The men in the front line saw little, if any, change in the volume of American fire that could generously be described as desultory.

In the early afternoon, German barrages continued tearing huge holes in attacking American regiments. Parkin estimated that his command had about 250 "effectives": men capable of walking and fighting. There were some 50 additional Yanks in Somers's small group clinging to a defensive position in the Bois 250. On the right side of the sector, the 315th Regiment reported that it had no more than 500 men capable of fighting.[26] The rest of the doughboys were dead, wounded, missing, or dispatched to the rear.

Throughout the day, wounded members of the 79th hobbled or were carried to first-aid stations near Nantillois and the Bois de Beuge, and then on to the field hospital that lay at the southeast foot of Montfaucon just south of the Bois de la Tuilerie. Enemy shells fell on or near the disabled Yanks and their stretcher bearers much of the way, but when the men entered the hospital, they believed they were safe. The hospital tents were marked with large red crosses clearly visible to German planes that circled unmolested over the area for hours at a time.

In the hospital, a corps of doctors led by Lieutenant Colonel John McKenna tried to meet the needs of more than five hundred wounded and dying men. As they worked, the physicians and orderlies began to hear rumors of German planes attacking first-aid stations north of Montfaucon. McKenna dismissed the reports as apocryphal tales of German atrocities. In the afternoon, however, seven airplanes with Maltese crosses began to circle above the hospital tents and then abruptly broke out of the pattern, leaving the Americans puzzled about their purpose.

> Then the whole grim story came forth [recalled the detachment's adjutant]. It was explained in the roar of high explosives as the boche heavies from up around Romagne began deliberately to shell the hospital. The great missiles came whistling through the air to churn up the ground in all directions . . . The officers and men under Lieutenant Colonel McKenna went quietly ahead with their work, encouraging the wounded and making light of the attack, although there was not a soul but expected the next minute to be his last.[27]

Twenty-one soldiers were killed by the barrage, including a captured German captain and an enlisted man who were being treated, as well as two American medical officers and two men who attempted to carry the wounded to safety.[28]

Although most of the officers and men who survived the attack believed that it was proof of German treachery, some American observers pointed to the proximity of a US artillery battery in the Bois de la Tuilerie, a hundred yards away. "Under these conditions, there may have been some extenuating circumstances connected with the shelling," one officer ventured later, "although the red crosses should certainly have been an incentive to a humane foe to be cautious in his firing."[29] The agony of those wounded in the attack was compounded by the fact that there were no ambulances available to carry the men back to more secure field hospitals in the rear. The pouring rain had made the roads impassable, as an engineering officer reported graphically to 79th Division headquarters: "All movements between Avocourt and Malancourt blocked. If rain continues, a personal reconnaissance satisfies me that conditions will grow rapidly worse."[30]

Although the engineer did not know it, the impassable roads and snarled traffic would cause a great deal of personal trouble for General Pershing. At that exact moment, an important official was doing his utmost to complete a pilgrimage to Montfaucon. Elated by the recapture of the prominent town that had been under German rule for four years, Premier Georges Clemenceau was determined to be the first French official to celebrate the historic liberation atop the butte itself. On the morning of September 29, "the Tiger," as Clemenceau was called by his countrymen, arrived unannounced at Pershing's headquarters, declaring his intention to motor to Little Gibraltar. Knowing that the firing was still hot on the butte and traffic glacially slow, Pershing made "the best argument that could have been presented" to dissuade the premier from proceeding.[31] But the crusty Frenchman summarily rejected the advice. Using his own Renault limousine and the authority of two US staff officers detailed as minders by Pershing, the premier made it only as far as Esnes, where a jam of trucks, ambulances, and cannons had congealed into an unmovable mass.

As the Tiger sat stranded in the car, his joy about the liberation of Montfaucon curdled into indignation at the jammed traffic and stalled American offensive. Mentally, he began composing a venomous letter to Allied Commander in Chief Foch that would sully Pershing's reputation and undercut the success the First Army had achieved:

The French Army and the British Army, without a moment's respite, have been daily fighting, for the last three months [Clemenceau wrote] . . . but our worthy American allies, who thirst to get into action and who are unanimously acknowledged to be great soldiers, have been marking time ever since their forward jump on the first day; and in spite of heavy losses, they have failed to conquer the ground assigned them as their objective. Nobody can maintain that these fine troops are unusable; they are merely unused.[32]

Although the American First Army was fighting amid the most rugged topography of the Western Front and against the Germans' strongest fortifications, there is some truth to Clemenceau's angry analysis. While other Allied armies—indeed other US divisions under British and French command—were moving smartly into enemy territory, Pershing faced an unpalatable truth: the Meuse-Argonne Offensive had ground to a halt in French mud.

CHAPTER 13

THE COST OF "REGARDLESS"

World War I was the first mechanized conflict, and keeping the new weapons of war repaired was essential. Some 25 percent of the tanks broke down each day, and the US Army's new Browning water-cooled machine guns, seen here, needed frequent maintenance before being rushed back to the battle, in some cases by motorcycle.

★　　★　　★

Our company numbered two hundred men. Within a few minutes about half of them were either killed or wounded . . . Everything happened that never happens in the storybooks of war. There were no bugles, no flags, no drums, and as far as we knew, no heroes.

—Lieutenant Maury Maverick, US Army[1]

About the same time that Premier Clemenceau was stalled in traffic south of the battlefield, ferocious German fire had stopped Parkin and the survivors of the initial assault on the Kriemhilde Stellung. They lay in a shallow depression north of Bois 268. Although some demoralized men wanted to withdraw to the woods, the major decided that they would stick it out. Given Parkin's physical and mental exhaustion, the decision to hold fast was a supreme act of courage. The major did not express his pessimism to his comrades, but he confessed later that he had reached "a state of mind which did not leave me hope of surviving the battle. I could not see any hope of that—it was now only a question of how long I would last and how I would be hit."[2]

Just as the troops were at their lowest, they were cheered by the improbable sight of General Nicholson dashing "on horseback through an area swept by intense artillery and machine gun fire in full view of the enemy to order a new attack on Bois 250."[3] The general's big white horse made him a conspicuous target for every German sniper on the left side of the Nantillois-Cunel road. As Nicholson galloped forward, even those who doubted his leadership ability, including Parkin, could hardly question the general's courage. After a meeting with the officers, Nicholson quickly grasped the ruinous condition of the 316th, and called for sturdy Colonel Sweezey and his 313th.

"Sweezey," [Nicholson] said, "your regiment has got to take over the front line and keep this division moving forward."

"It c-c-can't b-b-be done," interrupted an officer of the brigade who stutters.

"I b-b-bet y-y-you my l-l-life it c-c-can," retorted the Colonel, who also stutters.[4]

Although the 313th had been in reserve for the past two days,
it also had suffered from the massive shelling of Bois de Beuge
and the areas south of the front line. One observer estimated that
not more than five hundred men remained "effective"—able to
fight—but Sweezey set out to crack the Kriemhilde Stellung.[5]
As the colonel prepared his troops for attack, Nicholson turned
his attention to the 316th. As usual, the regimental commander,
Colonel Charles, was nowhere to be seen, so Nicholson consoli-
dated what remained of the unit under Parkin's command. They
were to follow six hundred yards behind Sweezey's doughboys.
At the time, neither Nicholson nor the commanders of the two
regiments were aware they were about to encounter a situation
that had turned even more deadly. Shortly after Nicholson left
his command post to ride forward, General Kuhn issued orders
demanding a massive artillery barrage blanketing the Bois de
Cunel and Bois des Ogons late that afternoon. Kuhn was acting
on the last reports he had received that the 79th was stalled well
south of the woods and behind Suicide Hill, and therefore was
not in the barrage's target zone. He applied the full weight of his
authority to force the hitherto unresponsive artillery brigades to
deliver as never before. As a result of conflicting orders issued
by Nicholson and Kuhn, however, the 313th and 316th not only
would be attacking in the face of massed German firepower but
also would be advancing into an area that was soon to be targeted
by a powerful American bombardment.

The assault was launched at 2:00 p.m., when the 313th burst
into the open area between Bois 268 and Bois 250. The rested
troops moved quickly through the men of the 316th sheltering in
the ravine and rushed the woods flickering with machine-gun fire.

Reinvigorated German artillery fire filled the air with shrapnel and gas, as Sweezey's men entered the southern fringe of Bois 250. When they exited on the far side of the woods, the officers saw that the center of German resistance was to their right, clustered around the road from Nantillois to Cunel and Madeleine Farm. As the soldiers had been taught, the depleted regiment turned toward the mass of German machine guns and field cannons. The unfortunate move placed it in the middle of a cross fire laid down by Germans in two wings of the woods.

"That was an awful afternoon, and nothing that we had ever been through could compare with," Jack Bentley recalled. "Two big tanks started out with us, the Joan-De-Arc, and the Charles Martel; these both drew the artillery fire of the enemy and were blown up. An aeroplane started to blaze up in the air, and the aviator, jumping out, fell to his death. An ammunition dump was set on fire, and thousands of rounds of ammunition were set off and created a terrific racket."[6]

As high-explosive and gas shells intensified the chaos, "Baltimore's Own" sustained its heaviest casualties of the drive. "Captain D- dropped by my side shot through the leg, and Lieutenant C- rushed over to us with his face all bloody," Bentley remembered. "On reaching the woods, I found that my men were still with me, and halting there found two of them crying. I patted two of them on the back, believing it to be the last act of my life, and said, 'Let's go,' and started forward into the clearing. Jumping into a shell hole, I looked around and saw Captains R-, G-, R- and H-, with but very few men."[7]

Shortly thereafter, the former Baltimore pitcher had what he called his "narrowest escape from death." Taking cover in a garden, "My ears were deafened with a tremendous explosion and the concussion was something awful, and as I gathered my wits together again I discovered there, not over two feet away, a brand new shell-hole."[8]

Finally came the command for the survivors of the disastrous

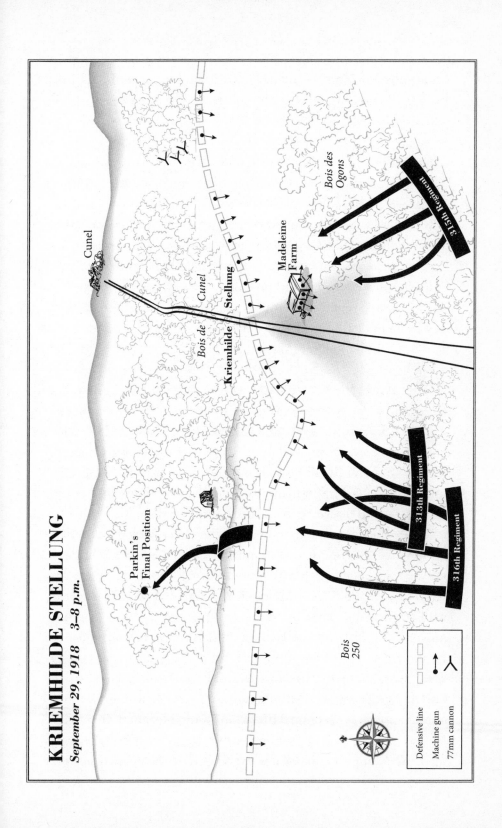

KRIEMHILDE STELLUNG
September 29, 1918   3–8 p.m.

Cunel

Bois des Ogons

315th Regiment

Madeleine Farm

Bois de Cunel

Kriemhilde Stellung

Parkin's Final Position

313th Regiment

316th Regiment

Bois 250

Defensive line
Machine gun
77mm cannon

assault on the Cunel Wood to fall back to the cover of Bois 250. As Bentley shepherded his platoon to the rear, he recalled the casualties.

> I had seen both Captain R- with Captain R- killed, not over ten minutes apart. Captain R- was carrying a sergeant back to the rear when hit, and C- Riley had almost reached his destination when hit. A shell had exploded in front of him, and a fragment caught him just at the bridge of his nose, killing him instantly. I saw a lieutenant rush over to him, and then break down, crying like a baby. We had a hard time of it that day, and as I walked back with Lieutenant—I noticed that his trousers were soaked with blood, and asking him about it, I was surprised to hear him say: "I am shot in three different places."[9]

After the 313th retreated to relative safety, Bentley noted that the strain of battle was beginning to affect the senior officers. "Colonel Sweezey wasn't himself at all, and Captain H- broke down and cried all night," he observed. "Lieutenant C- and I kept a stiff upper lip and would kid one another to keep a-going. I made the remark, 'Sherman wasn't emphatic enough, was he, old Cookie?'—and he would come back with 'Hell, no.'"[10]

While the destruction of the 313th had been taking place, Parkin remained behind Bois 250 until he calculated that Sweezey's unit had advanced six hundred yards north, as he had been ordered. Then the 316th advanced through the woods into the maelstrom. The 313th had knocked out many of the machine guns in Bois 250, but the artillery became even more intense as the Germans added fearsome new munitions, shells containing metal discs about the size of silver dollars. Fired from Austrian 88mm guns, the new "Whiz-Bangs burst in the air like shrapnel, and the discs whiz around with the most terrific shrieking noise," Parkin recalled. "It is almost impossible not to drop flat when one hears them, but we could not stop there in the open and must get on into the woods, where we might have a little protection."[11] To move his men out of the killing zone, the major blew his whistle ordering them to double-time across the muddy, crater-filled field.

As the men sprinted toward Cunel Wood, they heard a terrific din emanating from Madeleine Farm, located east of the Nantillois-Cunel road in the sector assigned to the 315th Regiment. Assuming that the battle noise was caused by the 315th, Parkin's men surged forward to locate Sweezey's 313th, which they believed had gone straight along a forest road into Cunel Wood. In fact, the sound of heavy action was caused by Sweezey's regiment: it had unexpectedly veered east toward the heavily fortified buildings of Madeleine Farm. As the Germans in the Bois de Cunel focused their fire on the 313th crossing their front toward the farm, Parkin's men sprinted directly north into the western extension of the same woods. A neck of Cunel Wood obscured Parkin's view to the east, and he had no idea that Sweezey's regiment had swung toward the farm. Because of the divergent movements, the 316th never saw the 313th until much later that night.

Parkin's regiment moved deeper into Cunel Wood, where German resistance seemed less severe. More troubling was artillery fire, which Parkin believed was caused by short rounds from US guns. When the shelling abated, the 316th pushed farther into the woods. The thick forest and a ridge to the east muffled the sound of gunfire from the farm, while Parkin and his men advanced stealthily through the heart of the Kriemhilde Stellung. As they reached a forest crossroads, the Yanks saw a large frame house, which they rushed with rifles and pistols. After determining that there were no Germans inside, Parkin and his men discovered that the building was outfitted with bedrooms, a living-dining room, and a kitchen. The structure hosted German officers "in the greatest of comfort. The living room was well furnished with tables and comfortable, large chairs, and an upright piano stood against the wall, some German music on it. The interruption of life here was apparently very sudden. A half-eaten meal of meat, potatoes, cabbage, and bread and wine still remained on the table, the chairs thrown back as if hastily vacated."[12]

Although it was not obvious to Parkin, the German occupants must have been summoned to help repel the 313th's assault on the Madeleine Farm. The rush to reinforce the critical position to the east left a gaping hole in the defense of the Hindenburg Line, a critical mistake that Parkin was determined to exploit. After grabbing boiled cabbage from the stove, his first warm food in several days, the major continued along the forest road to the north. Accompanied by his orderly, Parkin came to the northernmost tip of the woods, where he stood among the trees, looking out over a wide expanse of open fields.

"There slightly to our left and in full view and within a half or three-quarters of a mile away, lay the town of Romagne, our final objective. I knew the name of the town from my map. Between us lay open fields and no more forests. An advance would be fairly free from machine guns, but terribly and for a long time exposed to artillery fire," Parkin recalled later. "I thought as I stood there that if I had fresh troops with me or proper support for my weary half-starved men, I could easily pass those fields in the dark and surprise and capture that town."[13]

Had Parkin been able to advance, he would have fulfilled Pershing's most optimistic hope: a breakthrough into the area behind the German main line of resistance. But given the major's devastated regiment, he had as little chance of exploiting the opening as he had of taking Montfaucon on September 26. His men were depleted, he lacked artillery support, and his flanks were dangling in the air. And yet on the bleak afternoon of September 29, the major and his determined doughboys had advanced farther than any other US troops in the Meuse-Argonne Offensive.

Several of Parkin's officers were so unnerved by their advanced position that they recommended withdrawing to the area they had left two hours before. But the major was not inclined to give up captured territory, and he opted to defend the position in hopes that he could persuade Colonel Charles to send reinforcements to exploit the gap in German lines. For that purpose, Parkin dispatched Lieutenant Mowry Goetz to undertake the hazardous journey back to headquarters near the Bois de Beuge.

Awaiting orders, the officers established outposts to defend their small perimeter, while Parkin used the time to take stock of his men. He knew that most of his troops had used up their rations on the first day of the assault and had practically been without food for three days. The major himself was past hunger, but he had gone five days with very little sleep and was feeling the strain. Given the lack of rest, minimal food, harsh weather, and persistent German fire, Parkin began to wonder how he and his troops were still standing: "What is it that keeps men up under such awful strain? Why did we not all get up and run away far to the rear where safety for our lives and good hot food and good quarters were?" he pondered. "Pride, proper pride in oneself and one's life, is the answer. Real men had rather be dead than disgraced as cowards."[14]

Meanwhile, Goetz reached Colonel Charles's command post just as the sun began to set over the Argonne Forest. Breathlessly, the young officer reported his unit's position and requested additional troops to exploit the gap. Charles cut him off with more urgent news. An American barrage was about to deluge the woods that Parkin's regiment was holding. Making matters worse, the rest of the 79th Division had pulled back two kilometers to form a defensive line just north of the Bois de Beuge and Nantillois. The colonel explained lamely that he had dispatched several messengers to order both the 313th and the 316th to withdraw. When the runners sent to Parkin did not return, and no messages from the 316th were received, Charles assumed erroneously that Parkin's command had been wiped out.[15] Just as in the botched training exercise near Percy-le-Grand, the careless colonel had undercut Parkin's initiative. But on this occasion, Charles's failure to confirm that the withdrawal message had been received resulted in more than confusion. It placed the doughboys in extreme danger. The barrage to blast German positions in the Bois de Cunel and Bois des Ogons was almost due to begin, and it would certainly kill many of Parkin's surviving troops. To forestall a tragedy, an officer was dispatched to the batteries in hopes of delaying the barrage, and Goetz was sent back streaking across no-man's-land to order the 316th's immediate withdrawal.

A half hour later, Parkin was flabbergasted by Goetz's report. Isolated and unsupported, his command was in danger of becoming the "lost *regiment*"—or being destroyed by friendly fire. To escape the imminent barrage, the group faced a perilous two-kilometer dash in near darkness to the distant American lines. After allowing himself a flash of anger, the major began an orderly but rapid withdrawal. Parkin was the last to leave, and as he made his way south, he and the other members of the rear guard searched for wounded comrades. They found no surviving Americans, but many dead ones.

Seeing one soldier lying wrapped in a blanket to his shoulders, Parkin paused to touch his face, which was cold as stone. It was Sergeant Major Bair, who had been wounded by the same shell that had punctured Colonel Charles's canteen. Unlike Charles, the sergeant major had his injury bandaged and returned to the fight. Parkin was strangely comforted by the fact that Bair's face had a smile.

Under the light of flickering star shells, the survivors of Parkin's regiment stumbled through the dark, blasted woods. Just as the major watched the last Yank leave the Bois de Cunel, the first American shells began crashing into the woods. Ironically, General Kuhn's demand for artillery support had finally yielded spectacular results. Crossing the remainder of the battlefield was not easy, as the Yanks used their final reserves of energy to dodge German fire and jump shell craters. Running toward the distant US lines, the men realized they were giving up trenches and machine-gun nests that would soon be reoccupied by the kaiser's troops. As Parkin would recall:

> Back of us in the dark woods, left there alone with their dead comrades, lay I knew the bodies of my good friends and comrades. Lt. Kellar, my adjutant, Capt. Lukens, and many others. I hated to leave them there unburied on the cold, wet ground, their comrades gone so far away from there, and their bodies to be rifled by the enemy. But no living man that I knew of was left behind us.[16]

When Parkin finally made his way through American lines late that night, he first saw to the needs of his men, who were treated to a generous supply of canned salmon and hard crackers—a feast after the privation of the past three days. Parkin was so angry that he did not permit himself to eat, but charged directly to Charles's headquarters to express outrage about being abandoned. Before Parkin could confront the colonel, however, he was intercepted by his friend Captain Sinkler Manning, a respected regimental staff officer who had repeatedly requested a combat assignment. The captain explained that the colonel was sleeping, and, in a move designed to lessen his friend's anger, he volunteered to take Parkin's report. With no hesitation, the exasperated major fired away:

> I asked Manning why they had retired and left me out there in the front alone. He said they had not done so, but had sent at least two messengers to me and in the confusion of retiring in the dark did not know, and could not find out, whether I had rejoined or not. Apparently Manning felt he had done his duty by me and was surprised to learn, when Lt. Goetz had so informed him, that I had not received my orders to retire.[17]

The explanation was not satisfying, but Parkin began calming down as he described the opportunity that had slipped through the First Army's hands. He was soothed further by news that the depleted 79th was being relieved by the veteran 3rd Division the next day. Parkin did not express the depth of his feelings, and he continued to stew: "We had been practically lost to the regiment and in great danger of being surrounded and cut off, and our return and my report caused about as much excitement as that of the officer of the guard at Camp Meade, who would report, 'All's well and no change.'"[18] To top off the situation, Charles had gone to sleep before determining whether the missing regiment had returned to American lines.

What Parkin did not know and Manning concealed was that Charles was suffering from shell shock. The events of the past four days, the bruise to his thigh, the failed assault, and the precipitous American withdrawal had pushed the colonel past his breaking point. As Parkin had sensed many weeks before, the aging officer simply could not stand the stress of battle. After a medical examination during which he complained of "a lack of energy" and not being "his old self," Charles was sent to a hospital.

In the following days, as news of Parkin's exploit made its way up the chain of command, General Kuhn recognized the 316th's advance with a citation for bravery.[19] The recognition also staked the 79th Division's claim to have made the farthest advance in the initial phase of the Meuse-Argonne Offensive, a fact later confirmed by the recovery of bodies of 316th soldiers at the area in the Bois de Cunel marked on Parkin's map.[20]

Following the war, the penetration of German lines was verified by the testimony of another officer, but army historians failed to contact Parkin for confirmation.[21] Two independent witnesses were required for official recognition of the achievement, and the army did not acknowledge the advance on its postwar maps. For that reason, few historians are aware of what the thrust might have meant to Pershing's sputtering offensive. Parkin and the 316th had discovered and exploited a gap in the Kriemhilde Stellung that could have enabled American troops to penetrate the main line of resistance. Poor communications, however, kept the First Army from even knowing that the opportunity for a breakthrough existed. But the bloody events that occurred after the 316th withdrew are clear. For nearly three weeks, the most experienced troops the First Army could muster threw themselves against the Kriemhilde Stellung between Cunel and Romagne; according to historian Robert Ferrell, at least six thousand American deaths—*in that sector alone*—were required before a doughboy once again stood where Parkin had rested on the northern edge of the Bois de Cunel.[22]

What might happen in the future, however, was not Parkin's concern late on the night of September 29. He was recording the 316th's dead and wounded to determine the number of remaining men. As Parkin led the survivors into American lines a few hours earlier, he asked one of his sergeants to count the men in his ragged column.

> There were one hundred and sixty of us left out of three hundred and sixty men with whom I had entered the woods that day. The other two hundred were killed, wounded, lost, sent back with wounded—at any rate they did not return with me. I knew that many of them would never again march with me.[23]

In keeping with his training, the weary major compiled the most critical data about any combat unit: the number of men available to fight. Parkin's attention to this vital measure of strength revealed an alarming statistic. On the morning of September 26, the major had entered the offensive with some 1,200 troops; on the night of September 29, he returned with 160 men. The cost of the battle is almost beyond comprehension. Only 13 percent of the battalion remained capable of fighting as a feeble dawn broke on September 30. By following their commanders' orders, the men of the 316th Regiment made tangible what otherwise would have remained the uncalculated expense of an attack conducted "regardless of cost."

CHAPTER 14

RELIEF AND DISGRACE

Commander of V Corps, General George Cameron (third from the left, with mustache), was summarily dismissed by Pershing when his men, including the 79th Division, failed to capture Little Gibraltar quickly and move forward. The demotion helped disguise the cause of the bloody debacle at Montfaucon.

*   *   *

Those Americans will lose us our chance for a big victory before winter. They are all tangled up with themselves. You have tried to make Pershing see. Now let's put it up to President Wilson.

—Premier Georges Clemenceau,
Republic of France[1]

The battle-hardened troops of the 3rd Division who relieved the 79th on October 1, 1918, were appalled by the carnage they encountered on their march toward the front lines. Although the veterans had seen tough action near Château-Thierry and the Marne, they were astonished by the evidence of ferocity they found on the battlefield in front of Montfaucon.

"The elements of the 79th advanced steadily against the withering fire of the machine guns, but with frightful losses in killed and wounded," observed 3rd Division colonel George Duncan, who called on his extensive military experience to interpret the disturbing scene he encountered north of Malancourt. "The German gunners, though, paid dearly for their stubborn resistance. We saw a number of German machine guns along the ridge badly wrecked and broken. Surrounding their guns were the bodies of gun crews, shot and bayoneted, lying cold in death."[2]

As the colonel moved closer to the butte, more evidence of fierce fighting appeared in the form of a remarkable procession. Marching to the rear, members of the 79th Division bore litters with dead soldiers; others carried deceased comrades on their shoulders. Nearby the colonel saw "a long shallow trench, freshly dug, and not over 15 feet from the road," in which more than 200 bodies rested.[3] Because of poor record keeping, it is difficult to ascertain precisely how many 79th Division troops were killed or wounded in the four-day attack, but in a briefing after the battle, Jack Bentley was told that the division sustained more than 3,900 casualties in four days.[4]

When the 3rd Division passed over Montfaucon and began

to descend the valley toward the Bois de Beuge and Nantillois, its men were more shocked. Private L. V. Jacks, a loader in a field artillery battery, was sickened by what he discovered: "There were so many corpses of the 79th Division on the hillsides that some had to be dragged away to make a path through which ammunition could be brought to the guns without driving across the bodies . . . A perfect windrow of the 79th lay behind our battery, 39 bodies being piled in one heap."[5]

These recollections from veterans support the contention that the 79th fought fiercely, if not wisely. The survivors took pride in their first combat. "We were glad to be alive and felt that we had done well in our first fight," reflected Major Parkin. "I looked upon these fine young soldiers with a heart full of pride and affection. They endured so much, complained so little, and made so little of their splendid services in battle."[6] Clearly, the major and his men thought that relief came in recognition of their performance; after all, the 316th Regiment had advanced farther than any other unit in the initial phase of the offensive. The novice soldiers did not understand that being relieved is seldom a reward for outstanding service. More often, it is punishment for poor performance. Thus it was in the Meuse-Argonne, as several National Army units were replaced on October 1 by Regular Army divisions in which Pershing placed more trust. The 79th was sent to the quiet Troyon sector near St. Mihiel to sharpen its combat skills.

As fall days grew shorter, Pershing realized that he had lost the race to crack the Kriemhilde Stellung with a swift thrust, and he paused to reorganize the First Army so that it could regain traction on the muddy battlefield. Both I Corps and V Corps were stalled. Bullard's III Corps had come closest to the mark, but only because it bypassed Montfaucon and had encountered few German strongpoints. John Eisenhower astutely observed that Bullard had drawn the easiest sector, and, "[f]rom his relatively comfortable vantage point, viewing the plight of his fellows, he was almost smug. It seemed to him, he wrote, that the rest of

First Army was near a standstill, making small gains at the cost of heavy losses."[7]

First Army headquarters concluded that the mistake was trusting that the spirit of undertrained National Army units could sustain the advance. As one senior officer observed, "We carried to the seemingly quixotic limit our confidence in our ability to transform on short notice citizens into soldiers who would go bolt from the drill-ground into a charge that was to take an elaborate trench system as the prelude of from five to six miles of advance in the days of mobile interlocking machine-gun fire."[8] If that judgment were accurate, reestablishing the attack's momentum would be a simple matter of replacing green National Army units with battle-tested soldiers from the Regular Army.

There were some experts, however, who believed that the Americans' troubles were more deep seated. Early in the month, Clemenceau's chief of staff, General Jean-Henri Mordacq, visited Pershing and, after reviewing the situation, wrote a perceptive assessment:

> His [Pershing's] soldiers were dying bravely, but they were not advancing, or very little, and their losses were heavy. All that great body of men which the American Army represented was literally struck with paralysis because "the brain" didn't exist, because the generals and their staffs lacked experience. With enemies like the Germans, this kind of war couldn't be improvised.[9]

Mordacq's conclusion was not one that the AEF leadership was prepared to accept. Instead, the analysis of Pershing's staff cited the poor roads and resulting traffic jams, breakdowns in communication, the artillery's inability to keep pace with infantry advances, and a shortage of replacements compounded by a rapidly spreading outbreak of Spanish influenza. There had been breakdowns in command and control, but the First Army staff believed that most of these failures occurred in National Army units at the divisional and brigade levels; replacement with Regular Army divisions was the answer.

When the replacements were completed on October 4, the AEF commander launched the second phase of the Meuse-Argonne Offensive. The battle-tested veterans, however, soon met the same difficulties that their National Army colleagues had encountered, leaving Pershing embarrassed once again.

"The attacks were not going well, and the whole world knew it," observed Pershing biographer Donald Smythe of the abortive second phase of the offensive. "One AEF division, moving up in support, suffered 5,000 casualties from German artillery without firing a shot. In one attack by the 1st Division, over 12,000 men went in; only 2,000 came out."[10]

Pershing still refused to draw hard conclusions. Many senior officers turned to scapegoating, trying to determine who was responsible for failing to move quickly enough on the first day of battle to pierce the Kriemhilde Stellung. The most obvious culprits were the 79th Division and V Corps. Parroting Pershing's snap judgment on September 26 that "the 79th Division is holding up the entire First Army," many of the staff concluded that the failure of Kuhn's troops to capture the fortress of Montfaucon and its observatory on schedule provided the hours the Germans needed to bring reserves to stall the offensive. Word of the high command's judgment began to circulate among the officer corps, providing general absolution for other assault divisions, none of which had pierced the Kriemhilde Stellung. As Pershing's rash comment reverberated along the battle line, the 79th's culpability gained credibility in hundreds of conversations.

Early in October, for instance, pioneering neurosurgeon Harvey Cushing, a senior officer on the AEF medical staff, welcomed a distinguished friend for dinner at his headquarters in Fleury. André W. Brewster, the urbane inspector general of the First Army, had been assigned by Pershing to determine the causes of the failures of the initial phase of the Meuse-Argonne attack.

Sharing a bottle of wine with Cushing, Brewster confided, "We have unquestionably been severely handled." He continued that the 79th had come out "much bedraggled; because of its poor record, it will probably be broken up or have its number changed, as there's no use trying to build up an esprit from a unit with a bad name. The National Army has not made such a good showing as was expected."[11] Cushing responded by providing additional damning information. Inspecting several army hospitals, the doctor confided he had encountered "some foreigners of the 79th Division with nothing much wrong with them."[12] Over the next few days, the consequences of such conversations would become clear to Kuhn's division.

As Harry Parkin and the rest of the 79th marched to exile in a quiet sector, they got word that Colonel Charles, who in Parkin's ironic description had "gone to the hospital as a result of the wound in his canteen," would not be returning to the regiment.[13] Most of the officers were overjoyed because the pompous, indecisive colonel had failed to lead effectively. A few days later, however, Parkin and other officers were chagrined to see a car arrive and the colonel step from the vehicle shouting a hardy, "Well, how's everybody?" Apparently Charles had not gotten word in the hospital that he had been relieved. As much as they disliked him, the regimental officers were pained to see their former commander's humiliation as his adjutant, Captain Manning, handed the colonel the written order saying he had been relieved.[14]

In addition to being removed from the front line, the 79th had by October 4 witnessed the relief of a brigade commander (Noble), a regimental commander (Charles), and several lower-ranking officers. On the afternoon of October 5, Brigade Commander Nicholson arrived to drop the next bombshell.

"To our astonishment and anger," Parkin later recalled, "he gave us a thorough bawling out for our conduct during the battle of the Argonne Forest. He accused us of everything but cowardice. It was a most unfair arraignment of a new regiment in its first battle. I was thoroughly incensed and mad clear through."[15] Although the indictment of the brigade was all-encompassing, Nicholson's accusations centered on the high number of stragglers reported in rear areas during the attack. Ever scrupulous, Parkin later professed ignorance of the issue, while granting that it might have been true. "I and all the other officers were up at the extreme front all the time, doing our best with the men we had," he explained. "With new men in their first battle and with the confusion and lack of possible control due to the thick and frequent woods, it is not surprising that many men straggled."[16]

Parkin was more angered by two unfounded stories that had circulated through the division about his 316th Regiment. The first was based on a statement of Colonel Sweezey on the morning of the fourth day of fighting. After Parkin's troops disappeared into the dense Bois des Ogons, the colonel concluded that the 316th had fallen apart and that Sweezey's troops were the only force standing between the Germans and Montfaucon. The 313th commander passed this erroneous information to Nicholson, who used it to impeach the 79th.

"This incorrect information, which the General believed, without making any attempt to verify it, no doubt prejudiced General Nicholson against my regiment and most unfairly at that," argued Parkin.[17] The major knew that his troops by that point in the battle had advanced to the northern edge of the Bois de Cunel.

The other damning—and mistaken—rumor arose later that day when the 316th was urgently recalled under threat of the expected American bombardment. Parkin's men had been ordered to run to escape the barrage, and as they jumped trenches and shell craters, the men of the 37th Division on their left saw the hurried retreat toward the Bois de Beuge. The Buckeyes erroneously reported that the 79th had broken and run from the enemy. Parkin and others were aware, however, of the facts of the case and took action to correct the misimpression. Fortunately, Nicholson did not cite the story in his tirade, but undeniably he delivered stiff medicine to the officers, who were troubled by the unjust charges for the rest of their lives. To avoid undercutting morale, most of the officers chose not to pass along Nicholson's criticism to the rank and file; most doughboys never learned of the situation.

The 79th was humiliated, but the crowning blow came a few days later, when V Corps commander Cameron was relieved. In an attempt to disguise the major general's disgrace, AEF headquarters put out word that Cameron had requested relief and had been reassigned to his old command of the 4th Division.[18] After a few days, however, this cover story fell apart as Cameron was relieved again, reduced to the rank of colonel, and sent home a broken and bitter man. He was the most senior of the AEF commanders that Pershing removed during the war in France. Somehow General Kuhn retained his command of the 79th, perhaps because he had powerful friends in Washington whom he had met while serving at the War College. But sentiment at Pershing's headquarters was decidedly against him, and odds were long that he would be given another opportunity to prove himself. Earlier, Cameron had recommended Kuhn for the Distinguished Service Medal, but Pershing took no action on the recommendation. After the Armistice, a rumor circulated among the 79th's veterans that Kuhn was the only general in the AEF not to be awarded the DSM during the war.[19]

Although these actions clearly focused blame on V Corps and the 79th Division, criticism of Pershing was also mounting. Following the Armistice, Pershing admitted, "The period of battle from October 1st to the 11th involved the heaviest pressure on the army and on me."[20] Much of the pressure was applied by Pershing's implacable critic, Clemenceau. Still smarting from the massive traffic jam he encountered while trying to reach Montfaucon, the prime minister fired off his letter to Foch demanding that he go over Pershing's head: "Those Americans will lose us our chance for a big victory before winter. They are all tangled up with themselves. You have tried to make Pershing see. Now let's put it up to President Wilson."[21] Clearly, the French head of government hoped that the American president would relieve the AEF commander. Pershing became increasingly aware of the criticism, which was underscored by the success of other Allied armies on the Somme River and in Champagne. In those areas, the performance of US divisions under foreign command undercut the proud American general. Commanded by British general Sir Henry Rawlinson, the 27th and 30th Divisions had broken the Hindenburg Line near Bellicourt on September 29. The US 2nd and 36th Divisions and the Marine Expeditionary Brigade won acclaim while serving in the French Fourth Army in Champagne. On October 5, in fact, the Marines completed the capture of Blanc Mont, a heavily entrenched hill in Champagne that was the last German barrier before the Aisne River.

Under the pressure of the stalled US offensive in the Meuse-Argonne, the successes of American troops under foreign command, and numerous brickbats aimed by the French, the AEF commander was coming to the end of his rope. According to Smythe, Pershing was "weary and worn, his hair whitening, his face lined and aching from overwork and overtaut nerves, not quite knowing what to do that he hadn't done, he felt indescribably saddened and alone."[22] Perhaps the most revealing indication of Pershing's state of mind was disclosed later by the general's aide-de-camp, Colonel John Quekemeyer, who recalled that during this period he saw his commander in the rear seat of his command car bury his face in his hands and sob aloud the name of his late wife, "Frankie . . . Frankie . . . my God, sometimes I don't know how I can go on."[23]

A few days later, however, Pershing had regained his determination. Unable to sleep, he made a late-night visit to an old West Point friend leading the 90th Division, General Henry Allen. "Things are going badly. We are not getting on as we should be," Pershing confessed. "But by God! Allen, I was never so much in earnest in my life, and we are going to get through."[24] The deep reserves of character that Secretary of War Newton Baker discerned in his initial interview with Pershing were coming to the fore, but the general faced a formidable task in reorganizing his army for victory. Included was a rough meeting with his bête noire, Marshal Ferdinand Foch.

On October 13 Pershing was summoned to the headquarters of the Allied supreme commander in Bombon. By that time, Foch had decided to reject Clemenceau's advice to seek Pershing's relief, but he would goad the American general to advance more rapidly and, in particular, call his attention to a near-fatal flaw in AEF's planning that had contributed to the debacle at Montfaucon.

In a meeting as tense as that of August 30, Foch asked the AEF commander to assess the progress of the First Army. "General Pershing remarked that we had met with very hard fighting and the Germans were putting up a very determined resistance," recorded an aide. "Marshal Foch stated that on all other parts of the front the advance was very marked; that the Americans were not progressing as rapidly as the others; that he would like to see them advance."[25]

In defense of his army, Pershing argued that the Americans' fighting was facilitating the rapid advance of other Allied armies by drawing German troops away from their battlefronts to protect the vital rail connections near Sedan. According to the AEF commander, his troops had faced twenty-six German divisions by that date. Suggesting that Pershing's analysis was exaggerated, "Marshal Foch shook his head and said that he would show General Pershing his figures on this."[26]

Most military historians conclude discussions of this meeting with a detailed analysis about how many German divisions confronted the Yanks, or with an examination of the difficulties presented by the Meuse-Argonne's terrain and fortifications— excuses cited by Pershing during his discussion with Foch. The failure to review the transcript of the entire conference is unfor-

tunate because the most significant part of the conversation occurred as the French marshal raised a seemingly trivial complaint
regarding the First Army's battle planning.

Like a West Point instructor addressing an inept plebe, Foch
lectured Pershing that "in order to have an attack succeed the
commander must go considerably into details so far as corps, division, brigade and even regimental orders are concerned; that the
commanders should be required to bring their orders in writing
so that they could be examined and operations of different units
coordinated; that if they were not required to bring them up [to
headquarters] in writing, sometimes they were never written."[27]
When Pershing replied that the procedure was followed in the
American army, Foch merely shrugged and said, "Yes?" in apparent disbelief.[28]

The pointed comments of the Allied commander in chief apparently refer to the First Army's critical order to the III Corps
"to turn Montfaucon" and the failure of the 4th Division to conduct the required maneuver. Whether Foch's information on this
incident came from a French observer at American headquarters
or from General Mordacq's inspection in early October, the marshal had put his finger on the most likely cause of the failure of the
Americans in the first phase of the Meuse-Argonne Offensive.[29]

In fact, the flaw had been identified by First Army chief of staff
Hugh Drum soon after the debacle at Montfaucon. In a postwar
letter to John Hines, commander of the 4th Division during the
offensive, the former chief of staff stated that he had immediately
reviewed the original First Army orders for the initial assault on
the butte, as well as the subordinate III Corps orders. "Candidly,"
wrote Drum, "I was greatly surprised and much disturbed at the
time as I realized the opportunity that had been lost. My investigation gave me definite knowledge as to the cause of the failure
and I can assure you that I realized the predicament you and your
division were placed in by III Corps orders."[30]

Drum had discovered that III Corps leadership had eliminated the envelopment prescribed by First Army headquarters. As a graduate of the Staff College, Drum had mastered the art of complex military maneuvers. Later, as a staff officer to General Frederick Funston, he designed a plan of attack on a theoretical "stone city" in Mexico that greatly resembled the fortified butte of Montfaucon.[31] Reportedly, the treatise called for a turning maneuver, with one unit conducting a holding attack at the front while another enveloped the objective from behind. With Drum looking over their shoulders, Colonel Robert McCleave and his planning group naturally adopted the same technique, which they also had learned as students at Fort Leavenworth.

Unfortunately, no one checked the orders returned from III Corps to guarantee that they conformed to First Army orders. The officer responsible for doing so was Colonel McCleave, the First Army's chief of operations. Drum's discovery of this oversight might account for the fact that McCleave was never promoted to general as most colonels at headquarters were; in fact, he was soon reassigned to be the 3rd Division chief of staff, a demotion that stung.

McCleave's sin of *omission* paled beside the sin of *commission* committed by someone in III Corps who had disobeyed the orders of the First Army. Although Drum probably knew who the guilty party was, he had little time to deal with the offender while he was attempting to revive the failing offensive. Instead, Drum took swift action to preclude repetition of the failure. He wrote First Army Field Order No. 33, which Pershing signed on October 1. The order outlined the next series of offensive actions against the Germans; more importantly, it concluded with a pointed direction that applied to only three senior officers who would supervise future attacks:

> *Corps Commanders* within their own corps and by mutual agreement with adjacent Corps Commanders will insure cooperative flanking maneuvers between adjacent divisions and brigades. *The*

*personal attention of Corps Commanders will be given to this feature
of the attack* (emphasis added).[32]

By addressing this order specifically to corps commanders,
Drum implicitly repudiated the verbal order that General Robert
Bullard had given his divisions and brigades just before the initial
attack: to ignore units on their flanks and advance as quickly as
possible. The order is also a restatement of the doctrine of maneuver espoused by Drum and other AEF senior officers, as well
as a demand for cooperation rather than competition.

As if to demonstrate what could be accomplished by turning
maneuvers and interdivisional teamwork, First Army headquarters promptly planned one of the most successful envelopments
in US Army history to relieve German pressure that had stalled
Liggett's I Corps in the Argonne Forest. The 82nd Division was
ordered to cross divisional and corps boundaries on October 7 to
penetrate the German flank near Châtel-Chéhéry from the east.
"This would be a daring maneuver," observed historian Edward
Coffman, "since the right flank of the attack force would be in the
air—that is, open toward the enemy—while the infantry moved
laterally across the front. It would be an imaginative stroke in a
period characterized by direct frontal assault."[33]

Coffman's description of the 82nd's attack replicates the turning maneuver that the First Army had envisioned for Bullard's III
Corps at Montfaucon. At Châtel-Chéhéry, the tactic worked perfectly, as the All-American Division broke through the German
flank, enveloped enemy positions in the Argonne Forest from
the rear, and forced the retreat of Gallwitz's forces. The success
of the 82nd's tactic is convincing evidence that had the III Corps
encircled Montfaucon in the early afternoon of September 26,
the Germans would have almost certainly retreated, and the 79th
could have joined the 4th to crack the Kriemhilde Stellung on the
same day. Then little would have stood between Pershing and the
critical rail line near Sedan.

In the stressful days of mid-October, however, Drum had little time to fret about the lost opportunity or to identify the guilty party in III Corps. He and Pershing needed everyone operating at peak efficiency to overcome the obstacles that lay along the Romagne-Cunel heights just to the north. There would be plenty of time to deal with the responsible officer after victory. In the meantime, the 79th Division was left to bear the burden of the failed attack and the disgrace inevitably attached to the incident.

CHAPTER 15

INTO THE CYCLONE . . . ONCE AGAIN

By 1918, German combat engineers had developed methods to install field fortifications quickly. The armored walls of this machine-gun bunker could be erected in a matter of hours and sheltered crews from small-arms fire and hand grenades while they fired from the ports.

★　　★　　★

God would never be cruel enough to create a cyclone as terrible as the Argonne battle. Only man would ever think of doing an awful thing like that.

—Sergeant Alvin York, US Army[1]

In their lyrical manner, the French named the highest ridge east of the Meuse the melodic La Borne de Cornouiller. After suffering artillery fire directed from the promontory, however, angry doughboys translated the lovely French phrase into Corn Willy Hill, in ironic homage to the despised canned meat that—like the ridge—left a bitter taste. To meet the requirements of clipped battlefield communication, Allied generals designated the rocky peak Hill 378 for its height in meters. But the men of three American divisions who fought to conquer the mount devised the most evocative tag. They simply called it Hell.

After the fall of Montfaucon's observatory on September 27, First Army officers had expected relief from the German artillery, and for a few hours, their hopes were realized. But in less than half a day, the enemy began using telescopes in rickety treehouses atop the *borne* to spot Americans across the Meuse River. Using telephones and telegraph lines, the observers directed 210mm howitzers, 150mm guns, and 77mm cannons in deadly fire missions on the advancing Yanks. Barrages killed unprecedented numbers, wounded even more, and enraged survivors who had mounted bloody attacks on Montfaucon, Nantillois, Romagne, Cunel, and Brieulles.

Because the firing came from the side and not from behind the German front lines to the north, many Yanks believed mistakenly that the shells were short rounds of their own artillery. Anger against the suspected American batteries boiled over among frontline troops until word filtered down that the fire was not from US guns but from German artillery stationed on the east side of the Meuse. Pointing out the ridgetop observation post on the Borne de Cornouiller, an officer from the 314th Regiment explained to his troops, "German big guns from that hill shot us up at Montfaucon . . . Their shells were what we thought was our artillery falling short."[2]

After enduring a week of artillery fire directed from Corn Willy Hill, Pershing and Drum realized that they had to eliminate the observation post. Before the offensive began on September 26, the AEF commander had assigned the east side of the Meuse to French general Henri Claudel's XVII Corps, with instructions merely to hold the line north of Verdun until the great mass of Americans broke through to Sedan. But Pershing had underestimated the damage that the observation post on Hill 378 could do in the interim. When the offensive stalled at the end of September, the AEF commander demanded that the thorn be removed from his side. To reinforce Claudel's corps so that it could take on the task, the First Army moved the 26th, 29th, and 33rd US National Guard Divisions to the east side of the Meuse.

On October 8, doughboys from the 33rd dashed over hills near the river in an attempt to flank the Borne and capture it from the rear. Strong German resistance at Sivry-sur-Meuse, however, forced back the Americans with heavy losses. The impetuous failure demonstrated that the Yanks had no other alternative than to fight their way up into the ridges shielding Hill 378, a forbidding area that General Gallwitz had used to great advantage.

On the east side of the river, the topographic challenges of the Meuse-Argonne region are exaggerated. The hills are steeper, ravines deeper, valleys narrower, and forests denser than on the west side. As Gallwitz constructed the eastern end of the Hindenburg Line in the Grande Montagne sector, he bolstered these natural features with bunkers and dugouts and large numbers of machine guns and artillery pieces. Because the soil on the east side of the river is quite rocky and hard, the Germans dug fewer trenches, and many were quite shallow. To improve protection, the enemy often added rock parapets to the forward-facing sides of the trenches.

Compared with the area west of the Meuse, there were also fewer roads on the east, and those that did find a narrow gap, broad valley, or bridge were registered precisely by German artillery that could slaughter soldiers and wreck equipment at any time of day. Adding to the attackers' stress, almost every step the doughboys took was uphill, sometimes on slopes so precipitous that the men had to creep on all fours.

To strengthen the resolve of the kaiser's soldiers, officers made sure that their men understood the desperate situation: Hill 378 was the strongest remaining German bastion along the Meuse. The gray-clad troops had been ordered "to resist at all costs."[3]

These elements made attacking Corn Willy Hill daunting, but on October 10 the 29th Division began its uphill fight from the town of Brabant through a broad valley that was continually shelled by German guns. After escaping the barrages, the boys of the Blue and Gray Division entered Belleu Wood, where it seemed that every wrecked tree was defended by entrenched German machine guns and *minenwerfers*, weapons that made the area as memorable to the soldiers as the similarly named Belleau Wood was to the US Marines who fought a hundred miles to the west. But the most difficult task lay ahead in the deep ravine containing Molleville Farm, a treeless, bowl-shaped valley with German machine guns clustered around the high rim. Foot by foot, wound by wound, and death by death, the men fought their way up the bare slopes, across a road running eastward, and through a line of concrete bunkers and trenches. After securing a hundred yards of relatively flat terrain that lay beyond the bowl, the depleted 29th could advance no farther, even though Corn Willy was less than a mile ahead through thick woods.

It was time for the 79th Division to come forward. A month on the less dangerous front near St. Mihiel had given the Yanks a chance to practice vital military skills: patrolling to probe enemy positions, coordinating with artillery batteries, and using their machine guns and 37mm cannons effectively. Despite a continuing shortage of replacements, they had become a more effective fighting force. Not all the units that Pershing had relieved in September could make that statement—and the 79th was given a second crack at the great offensive.

Parkin's officers and men did not know immediately where they were headed as they packed their equipment, slung their rifles, and trudged toward Verdun, some twenty miles to the northwest. While the men slogged through the ever-present rain and mud, the major rode his black stallion in the downpour until, by a stroke of luck, he came across Captain Sinkler Manning. Parkin's old friend from regimental staff offered the major a ride in his enclosed Dodge.

In a day and a half, the 79th reached the besieged bastion of Verdun. While the men dried out in the city's cavernous citadel, Manning and Parkin continued along the east bank of the Meuse to reconnoiter the terrain where they would fight. Some eight miles north of Verdun, they reached the village of Brabant, where a military policeman evicted them from their warm car. He explained that vehicles were not permitted to enter the broad dale, an area so pummeled by enemy artillery that it had been renamed Death Valley. So the officers hiked the trail blazed by the 29th Division, through the valley, Belleu Wood, and Molleville Farm.

On their way, Manning and Parkin happened to meet General Kuhn, descending after surveying the mountainous battlefield. The general stopped to talk, and surprised the major by congratulating him on penetrating the Bois de Cunel on the drive north of Nantillois. Kuhn soon turned to business by asking if the 316th Regiment could hold its position on top of the ridge.

"I had not yet examined my position and did not know whether I could hold it or not, but I did know the answer the General wanted, so I replied, 'Yes, Sir,' " Parkin recalled. "That's right, Major," the general said, "don't you give the Germans a damn inch of it."[4] From the brief conversation, Manning and Parkin deduced that their task would be to hold the ground captured by the 29th. They would learn otherwise.

After making arrangements for the relief with officers of the 29th Division, the men retraced their steps down to Brabant. Manning and Parkin knew that their troops were advancing up the west bank and would use a bridge that crossed two channels of the Meuse and an island at Consenvoye, a mile north. The officers drove there to rendezvous with their men, who were not yet visible on the far bank. Before they could cross the bridge, the Dodge was stopped by another MP, who advised them not to use the span in daylight because it was under German observation from the Borne de Cornouiller.

"I asked the sergeant if the fire on a single car amounted to much," recalled Parkin. "He replied that six shells per car was the usual allowance. Our troops were on the other side. We must choose either a short and fairly dangerous ride or a long, safe one down the east side of the river to Verdun and back up the west side to the regiment. As I have said before, on the front, one gets fatalistic about shells. Manning and I decided to take the chance and cross the bridge."[5]

The driver put the car in gear, gunned the engine, and began what Parkin called "a race with death."[6]

> We were halfway across the first channel when we heard the first shell coming after us. By the sound of it we knew it was going to be very close, if not a direct hit. But we were committed to the test, and there would be no turning back now. The shell passed close on our right with a terrifying roar and struck the water just ahead of us near the bridge. We sped past before the water thrown up by it had fallen back. "One," counted the smiling Manning. A weak smile was all I could give him.[7]

With both officers urging more speed, the driver jammed the car into high gear just as round two hit the end railing of the first span. The third shot fell onto the road on the island. As the vehicle jolted by the edge of the crater, the fourth shell splintered a nearby tree.

> Two more of our allowance were yet to come. We were going at terrific speed now. I was convinced that either the shells or an accident to the car would finish the lot of us. I realized we were fools to take such chances with death to save a few miles of travel. The roar of the car lessened the noise of the fifth shell, which was close and burst in the water of the second channel at the side of the bridge. I don't know where the water thrown up by this shell was when we passed. I did not care at the time. The car was simply flying now. But the good Manning counted, "Five." He was a man of wonderful nerves and self-control.[8]

When the sixth shell approached, however, the officers' fatalistic bravado faded. The massive round appeared to be coming directly for the car, and both men instinctively "crouched low behind the back of our seat, as if the thin steel body of the car could afford us any protection. The shell came upon us with a hissing scream and passed so close over our car as to leave us breathless with fear and emotion."[9]

Just as the car bounded off the bridge, Parkin noticed that they were approaching a sharp left turn at a speed that would not permit the vehicle to stick to the road. The driver locked the brakes, and the sturdy Dodge somehow made it around the curve and coasted to a stop in the lea of a stone wall. After all three men recovered their breath, "We decided that no more should that bridge be burdened with us by the light of day. And I could not help chaffing my good friend Manning, and I said to him, 'Sinkler, you forgot to count the sixth shell.' "[10]

In keeping with the officers' resolution, the men of the 79th crossed the Meuse in the dead of night, but the enemy launched huge flares to expose targets. To reduce risk, MPs spaced out vehicles on the span, and Lieutenant John Kress, commanding the 314th Machine Gun Company, ordered his squads "to maintain a considerable distance between the carts [bearing machine guns] so that if the artillery came down upon us, the casualties would be fewer."[11] After reaching the safety of the east bank, the men continued along the route reconnoitered by Parkin and Manning. Kress recalled:

> The road followed this narrow valley in and out among the steep hills. There was no other way to get to the front lines. The Germans were well aware of this, and at all hours of the day and night, at irregular intervals, they poured shells into the valley on the theory that once in a while they would get something for their efforts. The appearance of the valley upheld this theory. The route was marked by the crosses of fresh graves, the bodies of men and horses that were not so fortunate in securing burial, smashed kettles, and even quantities of food dropped by some ration party—perhaps massacred in their attempt to get it to their fellows in the front lines.[12]

The detritus of war set the men on edge; more disturbing were the haggard faces of ragged, muddy men stumbling down the hill. Wounded and bandaged soldiers with sunken eyes mingled with more sturdy men dispatched on missions to the rear—all in deplorable shape. Sergeant Joe Labrum of the 314th "tried to elicit information from them as to the condition of things up there, but either through fright or that we might prove to be Boche, they would tell us nothing. Once in a while a whispered 'It is hell,' could be heard."[13]

Labrum would soon get a taste of exactly what the word meant. As his unit crossed Death Valley, shrapnel from a bursting German shell killed one of his squad, wounded two others, and neatly clipped off the end of his rifle barrel, narrowly sparing his neck. Every now and then, a frontline refugee would stop for a cigarette, and newcomers would quickly press around the man for insight. It was invariably unsettling: "This is the worst sector we ever had . . . At least 75 percent of our boys who started up here are now casualties."[14]

Deep in the night of October 28, the 79th relieved the 29th Division on the flat ridge lying south and east of Corn Willy. On the eastern end of the line, the 315th manned shallow trenches under direct enemy observation, while the 316th assumed responsibility for a portion of the line running farther west. To the left of the 316th, a division of French colonial troops held the ridge running down to the Meuse River. Directly in front of the 316th and the French lay the deep Ravine de Moyemont. On its east end, the ravine climbed steeply and terminated just below a forest road that ran north across the relatively flat ridgetop directly to the Borne.

Because the men had entered the positions at night, they had little notion of where they were fighting, but the bright morning sunshine of October 29 revealed a scene of destruction so profound that it deeply impressed Parkin:

> The great trees of the wood were shattered and torn, and the ground was gashed everywhere by shell fire. The open land across the road, sloping into the ravine of the Molleville Farm, was pock-marked, and the farm at the bottom was a crumbled heap of stone. On the far side of the ravine, both to the east and the north, the Germans held the woods, and had the P.C. [command post] and the road leading northward to the crossroad under perfect observation. The death-dealing road was lined with broken water carts, dead horses, ammunition boxes, empty marmite cans, and every description of equipment left by men killed while carrying supplies up to the lines.[15]

German observation from Corn Willy had zeroed in on the American positions, and hour after hour, heavies launched fusillades that always found targets. Sometimes only a wagon or caisson was hit, but often the damage was deadly. One afternoon as Parkin was walking back from a "crawling tour" of frontline positions, "I met and passed a military policeman escorting four young red-cheeked German prisoners to our rear. All saluted smartly, and they were smiling and seemed happy to be prisoners and out of the fighting."[16] As he walked on, Parkin envisioned the prisoners' return to Germany after the war, and—thinking of his own wife and son—the warm welcome the soldiers would receive.

At that instant, Parkin was stunned by a huge explosion just behind:

> I turned and saw a horrible sight, and one which filled me with pity. A shell had struck squarely upon the group I had just passed and had annihilated all five of the soldiers composing it. Blood and raw flesh and entrails covered the ground. All of the bodies were horribly torn and mutilated.[17]

At other locations on the ridge, the ferocity of battle failed to tear bodies apart but instead froze men into poignant vignettes that the eyes of combat veterans read as narratives of violence. "Here lay a German, his arm drawn back and in his hand a grenade, caught at the critical moment by the messenger of death," John Kress deduced while examining a destroyed machine-gun nest. "There lay another with a flare pistol in his hand, crouched as if he were about to fire, even as a final bullet pierced his brain. There a machine gun with a heap of burned cartridges and two bayoneted Germans beside it. A few paces away, several unburied doughboys payed [sic] silent tribute to the work of the machine gun."[18]

Even those in reserve encountered 29th Division veterans with terrible stories of destruction. Jack Bentley, for instance, relieved one captain who told him that "[h]is company had charged up a hill and held it, but not one man walked away; they were all killed or wounded. A sergeant was acting as Battalion Commander, and the battalion which before had consisted of one thousand men now had fifty left. The Captain said, 'We went over at Soissons, but this is the worst place of all.'"[19]

Atop the ridge, the 79th sought safety from barrages in bunkers captured from the enemy, but somehow German artillery seemed able to infiltrate the deepest recesses of the fortifications. The bunkers' entrances were at the back, facing toward the German artillery. On two occasions, the enemy had the good fortune—or from the American perspective, the *bad luck*—to find these doorways. Parkin himself suffered a close call, as an enemy gas shell landed directly at the entrance to his bunker and spewed its deadly contents down the concrete steps into the subterranean command post. The men quickly donned masks, while the gas crew swept and fanned the heavier-than-air fumes up the stairwell and out of the bunker.[20] Despite the lucky shot, there were no casualties.

The second incident had the makings of a catastrophe. Captain Carl Glock and his officers had gathered in one compartment of a multiroom bunker when a German shell flew through a north-facing window and exploded with a massive blast. Because the officers were in the front room protected by a steel-reinforced concrete wall, they were not hurt by the shell, which managed to blow the back off the bunker.

During their first few days on the ridge, the 79th's doughboys stayed undercover in bunkers, dugouts, shallow trenches, or any other source of protection. Some men, however, had to brave the frequent barrages to work. One was a slightly built, heavily bearded lieutenant by the name of Kingdon Gould. Heir to the railroad fortune of his deceased grandfather, Jay Gould, young Kingdon was a Columbia University graduate who volunteered for the AEF, in which he was assigned to be an observation officer for the division. Atop Corn Willy Hill, Gould faced a familiar challenge. He could stay on the ground, peer over the

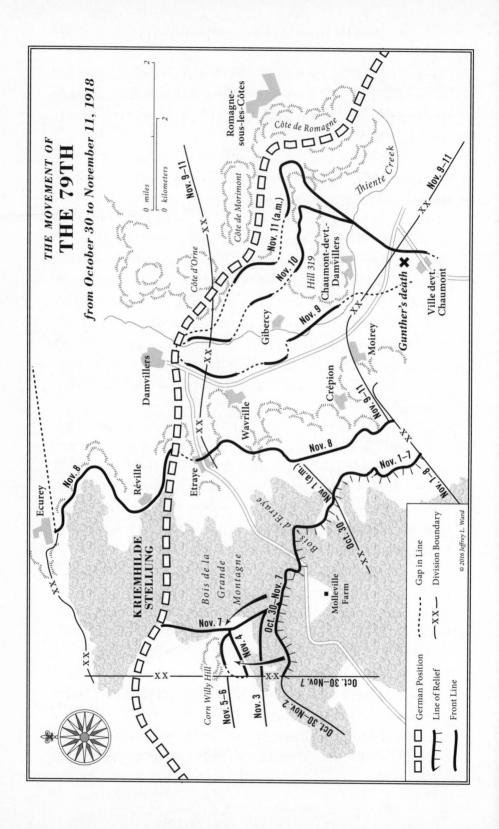

THE MOVEMENT OF
THE 79TH
from October 30 to November 11, 1918

Romagne-sous-les-Côtes

Côte de Romagne

Côte de Morimont

Côte d'Orie

Thiente Creek

Nov. 9–11

Nov. 11 (a.m.)

Nov. 10

Hill 319

Chaumont-devt.-Damvillers

Gibercy

Nov. 9

Gunther's death

Ville devt. Chaumont

Damvillers

Moirey

Crépion

Wavrille

Nov. 8

Nov. 8

Ecurey

Réville

Étraye

Bois d'Étraye

Nov. 1–7

Nov. 1 (a.m.)

Oct. 30

Oct. 30–Nov. 7

Nov. 1–8

Nov. 11

KRIEMHILDE
STELLUNG

Bois de la
Grande
Montagne

Molleville
Farm

Nov. 7

Nov. 4

Corn Willy Hill

Nov. 5–6

Nov. 3

Nov. 2

Oct. 30–Nov. 7

Oct. 30–Nov. 7

2

2

0 miles

0 kilometers

© 2016 Jeffrey L. Ward

German Position   Gap in Line

Line of Relief   XX   Division Boundary

Front Line

top of trench parapets, and see virtually nothing, or he could seek a higher vantage point, observe a great deal more, and risk death from German snipers. As he had in the past, the courageous Gould chose the latter option.[21]

The young multimillionaire stole a page from the Germans by constructing an observation platform in a lofty oak. Thereafter, Kingdon and his assistant—Private Wilfred Puttkammer—could be seen ascending the shaky structure before dawn and descending only after the sun had set. Relying on Gould's spotting, Puttkammer scribbled notes dropped to runners who sped them to the regimental staff. Gould and his assistant survived the war; some of his runners were not so lucky. The lives of messengers atop Corn Willy were often very brief. On November 1, for instance, Private Eugene Watkins was "mortally wounded while acting as a runner between battalion and regimental headquarters, but continued and covered a distance of approximately 300 meters to deliver his message. He died a few minutes after reaching his destination."[22]

Death was always nearby on Hill 378, and threats arrived in many forms. During one barrage atop the Grande Montagne, Private Andrew Kachik—the scout who led the 314th along the road to Montfaucon on the foggy morning of September 27—huddled with a friend in a small shell hole. Spotting a larger crater a few yards away, the private and his companion decided to move ahead. "Two of our buddies in back of us jumped into the hole we left," Kachik recalled. "In about two minutes, a shell hit that hole. One was killed [and] the other wounded so bad he died later that afternoon."[23]

For the moment, the two survivors thought they were safe. But Kachik soon became thirsty and crawled to a nearby spring to fill his canteen. "There was a funny smell around that spring. There were a few French soldiers there. They had their gas masks on. They kept pointing to their masks. I guess they were trying to tell me to put my mask on," Kachik reckoned.[24] After filling his canteen, the private bellied back to his hole where he related the strange tale to his companion, while swallowing a big gulp of cool water. "After awhile, I started to get pains in my chest. I told my corporal about it, so he sent me to a field hospital about a mile in back of us."[25] Because of a case of gas poisoning, Kachik never returned to action.

Life on Corn Willy brought hell in many dimensions, just as the 29th Division had promised. But like soldiers everywhere, the men honored a few "arrangements" with the enemy that made life somewhat more bearable. One day, for instance, Parkin was crawling along the front to visit his forward positions when he saw across the narrow no-man's-land "a German walking about unconcernedly and with not the least effort at concealment."[26] The major inquired about the situation and was told that "the men that they had relieved had told them that they did not fire on the Germans nor did the enemy fire on them. Sort of a mutual agreement to let each other alone."[27] Parkin knew the situation was contrary to regulations. The British had been quick to quash the 1914 "Christmas Truce" in Flanders, Belgium, when British soldiers fraternized with Germans during an informal break in the fighting on the holiday. The stricture against such interludes stood among the Allies ever since.

But the major decided to ignore regulations and leave the situation as he found it, reasoning that "[p]iecemeal killing in the front lines leads to no real result or advantage to either side and only makes the lot of the men there more miserable. Had I ordered them to fire upon the enemy, I would simply have brought death and wounds to my own men. Enough men were being killed and wounded every day."[28]

A similar accommodation was a lull in the shelling at 7:00 a.m. every morning, an unwritten arrangement explained by the 316th's French liaison officer, Colonel Paul Rickard. As Parkin worked in a bunker on his first morning in the sector, Rickard glanced at his watch and said, "Gentlemen, we can go up now and have breakfast."[29] For the next half hour, the men feasted on hot corned beef, bread, jam, butter, and coffee, after which they sat around the outdoor table enjoying cigarettes—just like their German counterparts. At 7:55 a.m. sharp, Rickard suggested going below, as German shells began once again to plow into the ridge.

Arrangements like these helped make life less onerous, but the most common comfort enjoyed by the Yanks—officers and enlisted men alike—was camaraderie with their fellow soldiers. Born of a fierce determination to protect one another, these bonds were stronger than those normally experienced in peacetime. One of the most enduring was the friendship between Parkin and Manning. One dark evening on the Grande Montagne, Parkin heard fire near the regimental command post where Manning was stationed, and became so concerned that he called to check on him. "He said yes they had been attacked, but had withered and crushed the onslaught with machine-gun fire, and it had never reached their trenches. I told him I had been greatly worried over him," Parkin recalled. "He laughed and said I need not be. He had enough machine guns to lick a German brigade. Splendid, courageous soldier and affectionately remembered comrade."[30]

On the evening of October 29, Parkin was surprised to see the South Carolinian duck into his bunker and announce, "Sir, *Major* Manning reports as adjutant of the regiment." As Parkin recalled:

This was his way of telling me that he had received his promotion at last. I jumped to my feet and, grasping his hand, congratulated him heartily. I then asked him if he had any major's insignia, gold oak leaves, to wear on his shoulder straps. He replied that he had none and could get along without them. To do so would take away a great deal of the pleasure of his well-earned and well-merited promotion. I had an extra pair of gold oak leaves in my pocket, which I had taken off the shoulder straps of my overcoat. . . . I produced the oak leaves and told Manning it would

be a pleasure to me to give them to him and that I wanted to pin
them on his shoulders.[31]

Extending the impromptu celebration, the two majors then
turned to their friend, Lieutenant Mowry Goetz, the 316th's
regimental scout. The young officer—who had dashed over the
darkening battlefield to plead for reinforcements to extend Parkin's advance in Cunel Wood—had been promoted to captain,
and Manning lent him the silver bars he had worn since Officers
Training School.

The warm fellowship was soon dampened, however, by a
discussion of the news that the 79th's mission had been altered.
Rather than holding the line against the Germans as Kuhn had
intimated, the division had been ordered to take Corn Willy Hill.
Although the promontory lay less than a mile ahead, the men
knew that the attack was daunting, given the dense defenses and
the weakness of the 316th.

The regiment had just received 180 replacements: green soldiers fresh from the States who had no time to master critical
infantry skills. This situation was exacerbated by a severe shortage
of officers and the assignment of a new general and colonel as
brigade and regimental commanders, respectively. While Parkin
welcomed the new leaders, whose arrival excused him from serving as regimental commander, he recognized that he would have
little time to become familiar with the personalities of the men
who would coordinate the 79th in battle.

"None of us felt that our regiment, which had had no rest
since reaching the Front, was in proper condition for battle. We
were all tired out, and our spirits were not high by any means,"
Parkin confessed. "Also, we had been in battle, and no man enjoys
the prospect of going into another one. No rational human being
could enjoy a battle, with its risks of death and wounds."[32]

The plain fact was that by the waning days of October 1918,
the Yanks had witnessed more than enough death. After little

more than a month of combat, they were emotionally spent. And there were few hopeful signs to cheer them. The Germans appeared to be surrendering in increasing numbers, but there were scarcely any other indications that the enemy was near giving up. The three German divisions holding the area were tough veterans who had mastered the craft of killing over four years. They would not easily forfeit the prime observation post.

Much the same conditions prevailed along the entire Western Front. The British and French had made inroads in Flanders and Champagne, but Pershing's headquarters was then working under the assumption that the war would extend into 1919. German general Erich Ludendorff's plan to consolidate a new defensive line behind the Meuse River seemed to have a reasonable chance of success. If the Germans were able to fall back skillfully and winter contributed its usual share of bad weather to stall offensive operations, the Yanks would be forced into another round of bloody attrition. The river would become an unfordable no-man's-land with Germans sitting in commanding positions on the high ridges east of the river. Through the freezing months, the Americans would be stranded on the exposed bottom land of the west bank, perfect targets for enemy guns. Come spring, the Allies would have no other option than to attempt river crossings on pontoon bridges or in small boats, when they would be subject to massed German machine guns on the far side.

There was little to look forward to, and less to remember with pride. The offensive that had been launched with such optimism had ground to a halt in the sticky clay of northern France. Even the veteran US divisions that had driven the Germans from the St. Mihiel salient enjoyed only modest successes when they appeared on the Meuse-Argonne Front. At the same time, the costs of these operations had been excessive. Rumor had it that American casualties—men killed and wounded—were much higher than those of the better-trained French and British. The doughboys were still throwing their bodies against machine guns, advancing en masse across artillery-blasted battlefields, and attacking strongpoints head-on rather than probing for softer paths around the flanks. The tactical errors added bodies to a total that would ultimately shock the nation.

To Pershing's staff, casualty statistics were a calculation of battlefield efficiency; for Harry Parkin, they were flesh, blood—and faces. The faces of friends who had slipped into the battlefield abyss: Atwood, Bair, Hewit, Kellar, and so many more. As he contemplated the attack on Hill 378, Parkin wondered whether he and Manning would survive the next few days. The odds grew even longer on October 31, when the newly promoted major secured his long-sought transfer to a combat unit. Henceforth, Manning would lead the Third Battalion, currently positioned just to the right of Parkin's unit on the front line.

For the next few days, the regiment was deeply engrossed in preparing for the assault on Corn Willy. The first step was to mount a reconnaissance in force of the promontory to test enemy strength and to determine which route of assault appeared most promising. Although the primary mission of the incursion was to locate German defenses, the force would be strong enough to occupy and hold the ground if that seemed possible. Three large patrols of approximately thirty men each would move toward the ridge from different directions. Led by Captain Francis Johnson and Lieutenant Ira Lady, the left patrol would descend into the Ravine de Moyemont and attack up the steep face of the Borne from the southwest, while a patrol under Lieutenant Harry Gabriel would test an advance along the forest road in the center of the front line that led directly to Corn Willy. A third patrol led by Lieutenant Frank Stevens would attack from the right end of the line to explore the strength of German defenses in the area southeast of the Borne. At the same time, the French 15th Colonial Division was expected to send a strong patrol toward Corn Willy from its position at the extreme left of the line.

At 5:30 a.m. on November 3, all three groups jumped off, and the right and center patrols immediately encountered strong machine-gun fire. After advancing a few hundred meters, both groups found that Germans, who knew the trails on the ridge well, were infiltrating *around* them, reoccupying ground the Yanks had just passed over.[33] Circling back to kill infiltrators, the Americans became disorganized and were forced to pull back. As they did so, the Yanks could hear enemy troops repositioning machine guns in their recaptured lines. With the two patrols on the right effectively stalled, attention turned to Johnson's patrol.

Covered by a low morning mist, the unit on the left managed to descend to the Ravine de Moyemont and climb some distance up the slope of Hill 378 before Germans became aware of their presence. Then machine guns and artillery opened up with a vengeance, creating a cyclone of destruction. A gas shell took out two men forging upward, while a 77mm artillery round partially severed the arm of Private Raymond Naylor before exploding fifty feet away. Naylor's friend tried to complete the amputation with a pocketknife to be able to stanch the bleeding, but finally gave up and helped the wounded soldier back to the far side of the ravine to an aid station. Meanwhile, Private Jimmy Jordan took a shell fragment in his back and crawled into a crater, where he discovered a severely wounded German, who pitifully showed the American a picture of his wife and baby. "I must live. I will live for them," he gasped. "Help me to a doctor." But the wounded American was unable to move under the heavy fire, and watched helplessly as the English-speaking German slipped away.[34]

Just as the Yanks emerged from the broken tree line two-thirds of the way up the steep face of the ravine, Captain Johnson was killed, and Lieutenant Lady was mortally wounded. Command devolved to two sergeants—a Finn and a Pole—who set about reorganizing the fighting line in the lea of the first enemy trench they had crossed. While the Yanks hunkered in their new position, the Germans launched a stiff counterattack, demonstrating their determination not to surrender the promontory.

> Suddenly through the mist, six men with coal-scuttle helmets clumped in their heavy boots. [Private John] Thomas's automatic pounded out a stream of bullets and one of the Germans fell; the others threw down their weapons. Thomas marched all six back to the dugouts, where the wounded German, who had been supported by two others, collapsed. He motioned Thomas to bend over.
>
> "I die," he said. "But take this ring, me to remember."
>
> "I don't need the ring—I'll remember this day as long as I live," said Thomas.[35]

A little to the right, a few reinforcements arrived, led by Lieutenant Harold Alston. When he made it almost all the way to the captured trench held by the first group of Americans, the officer was trapped by a German machine gun pouring fire on the shell crater to which the wounded Lady had been carried. To eliminate the threat to the injured men in the hole, Alston drafted three infantrymen and led them to a spot where he could see the Germans. "Having a grenade, I tossed it over and it luckily landed just a few feet in front of the gunner, tearing his head completely off," the lieutenant recalled. "This was our signal to rush, and we did so. On the rush, two of my men were killed about 25 yards from the gun. I rushed on with the other man, and we got to them before they could fire. My one remaining man was wounded. I emerged from the woods with fourteen prisoners and sent them to the rear."[36]

On the east end of the ridge, firing was initially fierce but dissipated gradually. The survivors of the patrol, however, were in a precarious spot. Just beyond the crest of Hill 378 were scores of German *minenwerfers* and machine guns, which unleashed barrages throughout the day. The shells and bullets—along with high explosives from distant guns—spurred the doughboys' use of combat shovels, captured German spades, empty corn willy cans, and even thin bayonets to scrape out rocky soil from the shallow trenches and shell holes in which they crouched. Although the survivors of the patrol were keeping as low as possible, nothing could obscure what they had achieved. Against long odds, a single patrol had converted a reconnaissance into a capture: a toehold on the most dangerous hill in the Meuse-Argonne. After less than a week on the line, the 79th was demonstrating that it was a new unit; the division was well on its way to erasing the brutal memories of Montfaucon. To keep the hill in the Americans' grasp, Parkin dispatched his friend Captain Louis Knack with more reinforcements from Company B.

Word of the unexpected success was telephoned quickly to General Kuhn, who proudly relayed it to Claudel and Pershing. Just as swiftly, the next order was relayed to the front: "The 158th Infantry Brigade, Brigadier General Johnson commanding, will capture and occupy the Borne de Cornouiller, maintaining close combat liaison with the 15th French Colonial Division."[37]

The newly installed brigade commander designated the 316th Regiment to mount the assault, and quickly called Colonel George Williams, the new regimental commander, and Majors Parkin and Manning to a stout bunker atop Molleville Farm. The group decided that the assault would begin at five o'clock the next morning, following extensive barrages from both regimental and divisional artillery. For one hour, the American heavies would plaster the crest and north face of Corn Willy, followed by a rolling barrage to protect the troops' advance.

Parkin's First Battalion would attack through the Ravine de Moyemont, west of the forest road, while Manning and the Third Battalion would deliver a right hook by crossing through the woods on the east side of the road, over the top of the rise designated Hill 370, and out of the trees toward the barren Hill 378. Parkin met with his counterpart in the French division to his left, who pledged to cover the southwest slope of the Borne de Cornouiller and to maintain contact with the Americans. In addition, the 315th Regiment would launch a diversionary attack from the extreme right of the line.

All was set for the morning of November 4, a day that would be momentous in the history of the 79th Division.

CHAPTER 16

REDEMPTION ON
CORN WILLY HILL

The assault on Corn Willy Hill was bloody, taking the lives of hundreds of Americans and Germans, like these collected for burial near Molleville Farm. The enemy fought tenaciously to keep Hill 378, because it was the last observation post providing a view of the American advance across the Meuse.

★　　★　　★

Death is not the only thing an officer fears in battle. Failure and consequent disgrace have an equally large place in his mind.

—Major Harry Parkin, US Army[1]

The first German shells screamed down into the Ravine de Moyemont just as Major Harry Parkin was aligning his companies to climb Corn Willy Hill, some three hundred feet above the deep gorge. A few soldiers were still working their way single file down the rain-slickened trail from their trenches, but most stood nervously in ranks, grabbing a last smoke or fixing their bayonets to rifle muzzles.

The men and their battalion commander had hoped that the heavy fog blanketing the area would shield them from German observation until they neared the top of their climb, but something—a stifled cough or the snapping of a twig—betrayed the Yanks, proving that sharp ears are as valuable in combat as keen eyes. Whatever exposed their position, the effect was the same. German 77mm and 210mm high-explosive shells descended almost vertically into the pretargeted ravine, blasting holes in Parkin's companies. Making matters worse, the enemy artillerymen included gas rounds among the high-explosive shells, creating a devil's brew of death. The soldiers slid their masks into place, and veterans began to climb the slope ahead to escape the gas settling into the ravine. Officers immediately intercepted the few green replacements who panicked and ran back toward US lines. With a swift kick to the rear, they were sent on their way up Corn Willy, as the gas dissipated with each step they took.

Using the sides of their shoes to bite into the muddy hill or scuttling along on all fours between areas of cover, the doughboys moved through vines, underbrush, and barbed wire until German machine gunners got a fix on them. Then the real fight began, as men dropped to the ground and crawled in the nearest shell hole. Progress was slow, but as the Americans cleared the tree line and walked out onto the grassy margin of the bald ridge, they encountered the men of Captain Johnson's patrol who had survived a dark night terrorized by German counterattacks and artillery blasts. One veteran said that the Germans were "fighting like wildcats" to maintain control of the key ridge.[2]

Although the fog made it difficult to locate areas of resistance, Parkin was pleased with the progress. At 7:55 a.m., he messaged regimental headquarters, "My right is on the objective. My left approaching under machine-gun fire. Am protected by heavy fog. Expect to be shelled if fog lifts . . . Would ask for counter-battery [artillery fire] if fog lifts."[3] The major's only other concern was that he had not seen anything of the French troops who were to advance from his left and defend the gains the Yanks had made.

Masses of German machine guns were stationed on the north slope of Hill 378, as well as in a forest to the east. Throughout Parkin's advance, the enemy's automatic weapons were firing blindly into the fog in hopes of catching an unwary American. With the First Battalion in position on the left of the ridge, Parkin peered into the fog for Manning's Third Battalion, which would secure the right side and roust the machine guns in the trees to the east. The two battalions would then form a strong battle line that would advance toward the crest, still concealed by fog.

Carefully avoiding the forest road that bristled with German machine guns, Manning's battalion cut northwest from its frontline position toward the Borne de Cornouiller. It made good progress. By 7:35 a.m., the group had taken Hill 370 and was setting its sights on Corn Willy. Like the First Battalion, Manning's unit caught up with the Americans' rolling barrage, and had to slow its pace. Shortly thereafter, it was pinned down by a horrific German machine-gun barrage blasting the meager sliver of the hill held by Americans.

Parkin's men had little time to celebrate their arrival on the

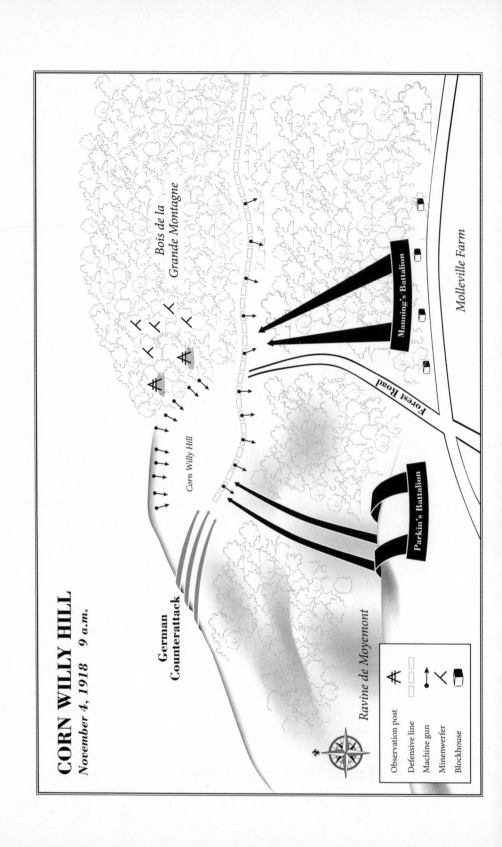

CORN WILLY HILL
November 4, 1918   9 a.m.

German Counterattack

Corn Willy Hill

Bois de la Grande Montagne

Manning's Battalion

Parkin's Battalion

Forest Road

Molleville Farm

Ravine de Moyemont

Observation post
Defensive line
Machine gun
Minenwerfer
Blockhouse

southern margin of the ridge, because their commander recognized quickly that enemy machine-gun fire was preparation for a counterattack. He set about organizing his troops to repel the Germans. Realizing that the battalion was most vulnerable to an attack from the northwest, Parkin ordered two machine guns to anchor the flank, but the officer sent to find the guns was wounded before he could follow through on the order. With few other resources than infantrymen with rifles, the major arranged two lines in arcs facing the northwest corner of Corn Willy Hill. He used every available man in the defense, including Corporal Aniseto Ortega, a Pueblo Indian who until that time had been a runner. "Anybody can take messages back!" shouted Parkin above the roar of the machine guns. "We need men on the front line."[4]

As the major crawled through the shallow trench at the front of his defensive position, he "found that the heavy machine-gun fire had resulted in our having no observation whatever of the enemy, as all the men were keeping well down in the trench. As this would result in our being surprised, it was necessary that some of the men be put on watch. In some angles of the trench, men could observe the enemy and still have some protection from fire. By crawling along the front, I placed a number of men so, and ordered them to open fire on any visible enemy. To encourage these men in their dangerous work, I remained with them some time, and taking a rifle from the ground, opened fire upon two individuals walking up and down behind the German position. They dropped abruptly."[5]

Not one to shy from danger, Parkin seemed always to be out front, leading and instructing his troops in effective combat methods. He soon had a chance to demonstrate leadership again when he saw a line of distinctive "German war helmets topping the rise" to the northwest.[6] The long-expected counterattack was materializing, and Parkin and his men were ready. Using a tactic drawn from the Civil War exploits of Joshua Chamberlain on Gettysburg's Little Round Top, the major called for a bayonet charge down the slope in hopes that a bold surprise would disrupt the German assault.

"I went forward with Capt. Knack. We discharged our pistols at the Germans, and an automatic rifleman also opened up on them. The men did not fire, but followed with the bayonet," Parkin recalled. "Seeing us coming, the Germans halted, and stood in line with their rifles at the ready. We charged to within about twenty feet of them when the Germans broke, and turning their backs, ran down the hill."[7]

Seeing the vaunted enemy running away cheered the doughboys. They had taken too many poundings from the Germans and felt that some payback was due. The Americans surged down the hill fully intent on pushing the kaiser's troops all the way to Berlin.

"The officers had great difficulty in stopping them and did not succeed until we were all well out on the face of the hill," Parkin remembered. "As soon as the German infantry had descended far enough, the German machine guns opened on us, and caused us heavy loss. It was at this time that I received four machine gun bullets in my legs and was no longer able to keep on my feet."[8]

Four men carried Parkin back to the trench, where they had difficulty stanching the flow of blood from his wounds. Using tourniquets fashioned from rawhide thongs, the men finally controlled the bleeding. But shock had blurred the major's vision, and he faded in and out of consciousness. After a few minutes, Parkin recovered sufficiently to assess the battalion's situation. He learned that Knack had sent a messenger requesting reinforcements, but the captain had been killed shortly thereafter. Parkin now had only three young lieutenants left, and while he trusted them, he realized that they were not experienced enough to direct the entire battalion in the fighting that was sure to recommence. Although he was still woozy, the major resumed command of his battalion, stationed lieutenants to direct units at the ends of the line, and "impressed upon them as forcibly as possible my absolute conviction that the Germans would attack us again very soon, and urged them to get their men ready to meet the attack."[9] Parkin was left to direct troops in the middle of the line, assisted by Sergeant Major Robert MacCormack, the highest-ranking noncommissioned officer in the battalion.

Just as the men had begun to take a swig of water or break off a square of chocolate, a German observation plane appeared, circling ominously two hundred yards above the exhausted Americans. The fog was clearing, and the pilot hurled a yellow smoke signal near the front line, before peeling off north. The sound of the plane's motor had barely faded before "German shells began to burst on the hill in great numbers," said Parkin. "In the ensuing hour, we endured the heaviest concentrated shell fire we had ever experienced. The continuous crashing and bursting of shells deafened and confused us. It seemed that everyone on the hill must be killed or wounded, and most of us were."[10] During the barrage, MacCormack sprawled on top of the major, using his own body to protect his commander.

Suddenly the shell fire ceased, and almost immediately a mass of German troops emerged from the dust of the barrage.

"Here they come, Major!" MacCormack cried.

"Who?" asked Parkin, dreading the answer.

"The Germans," the sergeant major replied.[11]

MacCormack fired a couple of shots from Parkin's Colt .45 before the major ordered him to cease fire. The game was up. Armed with rifles and submachine guns, the Germans had followed just behind the artillery barrage, appearing at the top of the American trench the instant the shelling ceased. Huddled below, the doughboys hardly had time to raise their rifles. Parkin saw that further resistance would end in a bloodbath, and he ordered his remaining troops to put down their arms, as he lay looking up at the fierce *Stosstruppen*:

> The faces of the enemy were set and white. They had the appearance of men doing a desperate deed, and their attempt to

capture the hill soon proved to be exactly that. They were led by a short, stout Lieutenant and a number of noncommissioned officers, all older men than the rank and file. These leaders were armed with pistols and hand grenades. Their warlike helmets and bristling moustaches and drawn faces gave them a very fierce appearance. That long line of helmets coming into view was the most terrifying sight I have ever beheld, as I saw it as I sat there in the trench helpless and with nearly all my men lying around me dead or wounded.[12]

Harry knew not what to expect. In similar circumstances, he had witnessed Americans shoot prisoners out of rage, and he feared what was to come. Even worse was the sense of personal responsibility that accompanied the surrender: "Never have I felt more humiliated and miserable than at this time. I was filled with bitterness at our failure."[13]

At the direction of a German officer, Sergeant Major Mac-Cormack and another soldier helped Parkin to his feet, and the group began to make its way north and into captivity. Because the major could hardly walk, the three men had to rest often, and during their slow trek, they passed a long line of heavily armed German troops headed south to drive the Yanks off the ridge. To Parkin's surprise and great relief, most of the enemy were kindly; two offered him their canteens containing welcomed gulps of coffee and brandy. They soon encountered a medic, who examined the major's wounds and directed the group to a German field hospital in the valley north of Hill 378. Before departing over the crest of the Borne, the medic offered some encouraging words: "Don't worry, the War will soon be over; we are going to kick out the damned Kaiser."[14] Comforted by the unexpected prediction, the Americans hobbled on toward the rear, where the major was placed aboard a German hospital train to Trier, a German town founded by the Romans.

South of the Borne de Cornouiller, across the Ravine de

Moyemont, General Johnson and his staff had been listening to the sounds of battle with growing alarm. Obviously a terrific fight for Corn Willy was under way, and they had not heard from Parkin's battalion since about 8:00 a.m.; it was then well after noon. A few minutes later, a muddy messenger was spotted stumbling and scrambling up the narrow path from the ravine. Completely exhausted from running down the northern slope of the ravine and then struggling up the steep southern face, the man could barely speak.

He was half carried to the general's command post near Molleville Farm. In a state of alarmed excitement, the messenger managed to report only that the battalion was being attacked from the flank—whether it was the left or right flank, he could not recall. He collapsed on the floor as the regimental and brigade staff pondered their next move. It was clear that the Germans were willing to bring to bear all their resources to hold Corn Willy. Airplanes, heavy artillery, machine guns, and masses of veteran infantrymen—Gallwitz was throwing everything into the fight for the rocky piece of soil that commanded the Meuse River Valley.

But the 79th was determined too, and General Johnson and Colonel Williams began to assess how they could assist Parkin and Manning. Finally, Lieutenant Colonel George Haedicke was ordered to lead the regimental reserve onto the hill to find and reinforce Parkin's battalion. After the colonel dodged barrages to reach the rocky ridge, he became deeply alarmed. All that remained were a few Americans who had hidden from the counterattack that captured Parkin and his men. They were then holding a thin line on Corn Willy's slopes near the left end of Manning's troops, who were confined to a captured trench by flying shrapnel.

Shortly after Haedicke departed for the front, the regimental commander ordered his adjutant, Captain Glock, to gather up as many spare soldiers as he could find and move left of Parkin's last known position. Glock grabbed two Browning machine guns; recruited nearby cooks, mechanics, and clerks; ran down into the ravine; and charged up Corn Willy's slope. As the ragamuffin group advanced, a line of German airplanes used the weakening afternoon light to swoop into the ravine and strafe the Americans, who advanced toward the southeast corner of the ridge where Parkin had led the bayonet charge.

When Glock arrived, he found only "the dead left by the morning attack. But there remained not a living soul, not one man of the battalion that had swept up the hill in the morning."[15] The captain was sickened by the American bodies, abandoned rifles, and other signs of annihilation. He quickly dispatched a messenger to tell headquarters the sad news. At dusk, Glock and his men formed a perimeter to defend the meager toehold that the survivors of the 316th held on Corn Willy.

The terrible night that followed was filled with repeated German incursions aided by flares rocketing from north of the ridge to expose American positions.[16] The garish, flickering light inadvertently revealed enemy patrols stealthily probing to identify weak points on the hill, signaling their intent to return in force to put an end to the doughboys. Germans spotted one of the new American machine-gun posts and tossed potato-masher grenades, disabling the weapon. The resourceful crew quickly positioned an abandoned enemy machine gun to replace the damaged weapon.[17] The largest attack came around 10:00 p.m., when an estimated fifty Germans crept along the edge of the woods on the right end of the thin American line. Manning had wisely placed two Browning heavy machine guns there to cover the flank, and the weapons took a toll on the unwary Germans.

Through the horrific night, Corporal Ortega, who had somehow survived the German counterattack, conducted a one-man search to locate doughboys who had accompanied him to the hilltop. "I went back and could find none of my company. They had been all shot to pieces and captured," recalled the Native American. "I found two in a dugout; the first two men that I found. I kept on searching; found two in another dugout."[18]

Ortega's courageous forays across the deadly battlefield eventually assembled twenty-five survivors, many of them wounded. "They were a discouraged lot of men, feeling the loss of their comrades, but were greatly cheered to find even so few left to fight on," he later recalled. "I rallied the men, got them together in a dugout, [went] out to provide them something to eat—some had had nothing since they went on the firing line. I then got them guns and ammunition and rations."[19]

Like so many men whose bravery emerges when necessary, Ortega cared for his fellow soldiers by assembling supplies retrieved from the bodies of dead Germans and Americans. In the morning he would again lead by inspiring the men to return to battle. His outstanding efforts later merited a Distinguished Service Cross.

That night, General Kuhn ordered the remaining troops of the 316th to attack at 9:00 a.m. the following morning, with one battalion in the assault and another in support. But as one officer observed, "It was easier to draw that order than to find the necessary available infantrymen for the attack."[20] The few survivors of the First and Third Battalions were already committed to the fight, and the Second Battalion had lost heavily in the armed reconnaissance on the first day of the battle. Regimental commander Williams decided to commit his last two companies to Manning's battalion, and he secured the service of one additional company from the neighboring 315th Regiment. As the next attack gained momentum, these men would gather those clinging to the left side of Corn Willy under command of Colonel Haedicke and Captain Glock, as well as survivors shepherded by Corporal Ortega.

The attack was an act of desperation. If it failed and the men were slaughtered at the rate of those who had attacked Hill 378 the prior two days, the First Army would be forced to write off the 316th Regiment, and Corn Willy would be lost. Although no one recognized it at the time, the Germans and the Americans both were playing their final cards in the bloody battle for the promontory.

Throughout the dark night in his trench on the southeast corner of the Borne, Major Manning planned his assault, burdened by the news of Harry Parkin's disappearance. From what Manning learned from regimental staff, it was obvious that Parkin's battalion had fought its way onto the ridge alone, unsupported by either the French on the left or by Manning's battalion on the right. In his first combat command, Manning had not kept pace with his friend, a fact that cut deeply. Wearing the oak leaves that Parkin had given him, Manning was determined to lead his command to victory in the morning, both for his comrade and himself. Perhaps he would even find Parkin alive, burrowed in some deep hole on the ridge.

As the preparatory barrage began lashing Corn Willy at 8:00 a.m., Manning had difficulty locating all the companies that were to participate in the assault. Rather than delay, however, he placed Company K of the 315th on the left end of his line and Company L of the 316th on his right, and shoved off promptly at 8:30 a.m. Just as Manning had been taught, he followed slightly behind the lines of doughboys to marshal the units under his command. From the west, Glock and Haedicke's men joined in as the Third Battalion attack surged out of the grassy margin of the ridge toward the crest of Hill 378. Just then, however, German heavy guns began firing in response to the American barrage. As the enemy shells blasted massive craters in the rocky ground and flung shrapnel in every direction, the doughboys reflexively began to slow and dodge, even though they knew such tactics were futile.

Sensing that his troops needed inspiration, Manning reacted instinctively, as a battle participant reported later to the *New York Times*:

[T]here was a touch of more colorful days in the advance of the Third Battalion through the murderous barrage, for at its head strode the tall, lean figure of Major Manning, with a flowing black cape over his shoulders, flying in the wind that emerged from the woods behind, a heavy cane in one hand and an American .45 in the other.

There may be a question of advancing against machine-gun fire and snipers' nests—of which Cornwillie Hill was full—in so conspicuous a costume as an old-fashioned army cape. But there can be no question of the inspiration of a sight like that to your hero-loving soldier in the stress of battle, and the Third Battalion went forward through artillery fire and a hail of bullets from a ridge alive with machine guns until its leader [Manning] fell, shot through the head with his pistol extended before him toward the goal.[21]

The 316th had lost two of its three battalion commanders; more deaths would follow. Farther to the right, German machine gunners focused on officers leading Company K of the 315th; in short order, they cut down Lieutenants Lawrence Ayres and John Owens. Luckily, the group had a veteran officer in tow to assume command. Captain William Carroll, who had already won a Distinguished Service Cross for capturing a machine-gun nest near Nantillois, stepped forward to lead the way toward the crest.[22]

On the Borne de Cornouiller, heroism was not the sole domain of officers. Sergeant Joseph Kilroy attacked a German machine gun with a group of five Yanks. When all five were wounded, Kilroy picked up a Browning automatic rifle and finished off the fight by killing the Germans. During the opening moments of the assault, Corporal Ortega caught a piece of shrapnel in his back but remained determined to avenge the deaths of his friends the day before. He rounded up his survivors and joined the line of Manning's troops. "I found two Boche in a little hole, 3 feet square, covered with brush and leaves," he recalled later. "They called out 'Kamerad.' They had used their last shell on me, and then called 'Kamerad.' I answered them with my bayonet."[23]

As the charge surged near the crest of Hill 378, word of Manning's death reached the regimental command post, along with an urgent request for a heavy barrage to be fired beyond the crest of the hill to prevent an expected German counterattack. All over the Grande Montagne sector, fierce German drumfire was falling, so heavily that it cut the telephone lines to American batteries and made a dash by a runner impossible. "Sergeant Major Davitt bethought himself of a lone pigeon still available," wrote an officer later. "Colonel Williams hurriedly wrote the message, it was tied to the pigeon's leg—and unmindful of the shelling, the bird was off and away to the cote at Division Headquarters in Vacherauville. Within a remarkably short time, a deadly barrage was curtaining the Americans from German attack."[24]

Disturbed by news of Manning's death, Williams waited for the German barrage to abate and then announced to his staff that he was going to the ridge to assume command of the attack. Suffering from gas exposure, Williams charged up the steps of the bunker but, at the top, collapsed and fell. Unconscious, he was carried to a bunk, where he later revived. In the meantime, Haedicke was recalled from the ridge to assume command of the regiment.[25]

To replace the lieutenant colonel on the exposed ridge, Major Harrison Smith was sent forward from divisional headquarters to take command of the 316th. Before climbing the ridge, however, the young officer was called to the commanding general's bunker, where he underwent a rigorous interrogation by the impassioned Kuhn, who emphasized the heroism of the depleted regiment.

"They have done the impossible. You must hold the position at all costs. Do you understand what that means?" Kuhn asked.

"Yes sir," Smith answered.

"Don't ask me for reinforcements for I have none I can send

you; you must hold with what men you have. For the honor of your Division, for the honor of your Regiment, for the honor of yourself, you will hold at all costs. Do you understand, Major Smith?" the general said gravely.

"Yes sir," the major replied, as he saluted, about-faced, and made his way toward the Borne de Cornouiller.[26]

As a result of the surge mounted by Manning's battalion, the 316th controlled Hill 378—but just barely. Although the Americans took cover somewhat south of the crest, the three Browning heavy machine guns of the battalion finally denied Gallwitz's use of the hill as an observation post while scattering concentrations of German troops poised to launch counterattacks. Naturally, the doughboys' automatic weapons attracted enemy attention, and one became the particular object of a German sniper whose shots edged uncomfortably close to the American emplacement. Finally, Sergeant Adam Colaizzi, a member of the crew, had seen enough. Crawling across the battlefield, he found and killed the sniper and captured another German with him. Before withdrawing, Colaizzi had the presence of mind to search the dead man. In so doing, he made a spectacular discovery: a map of German defenses around Hill 378. After delivering the invaluable document to the rear, Colaizzi made his way back to his crew to resume normal activities—if being under intense enemy fire on a barren ridge can be called "normal."[27]

Although it did not become immediately clear, the capture of the map slowly tilted the balance of battle in favor of the 316th. The Yanks had the key to victory, and they began deciphering its information. When the map made it to divisional headquarters, Kuhn used it to direct his three artillery regiments and a pair of mammoth 240mm howitzers to destroy German strongpoints that were clearly marked.[28]

Late on the afternoon of November 5, General Johnson delivered to divisional headquarters a frank appraisal of the 316th Regiment, then committed fully to the fight for Hill 378:

The objective was gained but at a very heavy loss. The Lieut. Colonel now in command of the regiment . . . estimates that the present effective strength of the regiment is about 600 [versus 3,600 in a typical regiment]. In one instance, he told me that out of three companies which he immediately commanded, that the loss due to machine gun and minenwerfer fire was 50 per cent, and there were similar losses, in his opinion, in other parts of the line . . . The position is organized and will be held, but I believe that the regiment should be relieved and re-organized before it can be effective for any further work.[29]

As a result of this assessment, the Second Battalion of the 313th Regiment and the Third Battalion of the 315th were ordered to relieve the survivors of Parkin's battalion and to attack on the morning of November 6.[30] This order came as welcomed news to the men of the 316th, who had been defending the ridge under constant fire for nearly two days. During that period, they had not been resupplied with food or water. Relief was coming in the nick of time.

Or was it?

As the expectant men of the battered regiment peered south on the morning of November 6, they saw no sign of their replacements. As usual, a heavy German barrage was falling, and the men burrowed deeper into their trenches and shell holes. Finally, just before eleven o'clock, a single platoon was spotted marching—in perfect order—on the forest road. The sergeant in command said he had lost contact with the units on his right and left but decided to press on to the front.[31] They rushed into the line, just as two enemy patrols began to advance up the north slope of the ridge. More ominously, German planes circled the positions, strafing the doughboys and directing precise artillery barrages on the front lines. As usual, no US planes were to be seen. Still, the 316th held, but in its final hours on the line, the regiment lost one of its most popular soldiers, Pasquale Minello.

Minello liked to joke that he had been drafted "by mistake" while on an extended visit to a family member who had emigrated from Italy to Pennsylvania. Although the international visitor explained to draft officials that he was not an American citizen, the authorities pointed to Pasquale's job in a local coal mine as evidence that he was enjoying the benefits of the United States. Soon thereafter, the good-natured foreigner found himself dressed in army khaki and training at Camp Meade. A veteran of the Italian army, Minello made many friends by helping raw recruits adapt to life in the AEF. He went on to prove his worth in combat on Montfaucon, in Cunel Wood, and, finally, on Hill 378.

On the afternoon of November 6, as Pasquale lay in a trench atop the Borne, a German machine gunner tested the jovial Italian's patience by aiming bursts at his position. Pulling on his big black mustache to stifle his growing anger, Minello swore, "I'm going to get that fellow."

"Keep down, Pasquale," warned his friend.

"He's no tougher than the Turk. I fought the Turk when I was in the Italian army. They were tough, baby— Listen!"

The soldiers heard something that sounded like footsteps running toward their position, and Pasquale raised his head slightly to look over the rock parapet. Then he lowered his head. With alarm, his friend rolled him over in the trench. There was a blue hole right in the center of the Italian's forehead one inch below his helmet.[32]

Just as Minello's friends and the other men of the 316th had begun to despair of seeing relief troops, runners from the regiment located the battalions, which had been shelled and lost in the woods below the Grande Montagne. Around 5:00 p.m., the guides led them back onto the right trails, and the relief was completed late that night. Because they arrived so late, the attack was postponed to the following morning. In the meantime, the situation changed dramatically.

Late that evening, General Kuhn received a dispatch spelling doom for the German army. The First Army had finally broken through, and, west of the Meuse, the enemy was in retreat. The Germans maintained good order, however, and the veteran troops conducted an effective fighting withdrawal. Pershing demanded that the Americans maintain pressure on the enemy, and Kuhn obliged by ordering the new battalions to charge across the crest and take the valley beyond. The operation would begin with a barrage at 7:55 a.m. on the morning of November 7.

"From the very moment that the American artillery preparation began, the absence of heavy enemy retaliatory fire became noticeable," an officer of the 79th reported. "There were no such concentrations as had broken up the attacks planned for the day before. Evidently the enemy was hauling back his heavies, and the artillery fire was less severe than during any of the days which had gone before."[33] Although it was not apparent, the prediction that the German medic had made to the wounded Harry Parkin was coming true. The enemy was slowly withdrawing.

Given the inviting conditions, the men of the 313th and 315th leapt forward but found few Germans remaining on the hill. Captain Sam Fleming was leading a company through the trees to the east of the Borne, but the lack of resistance caused him to question whether he was in the right place. "I was sure we were advancing toward our objective, but so far as we knew, we seemed to be the only men of the AEF in France, and the Germans had disappeared," Fleming recalled after the war. "We saw many signs of German retreat, equipment and ammunition scattered in the woods. We reached our objective at four-fifteen."[34] Because the 313th was moving over barren Hill 378, it advanced more quickly than Fleming's unit, and by midafternoon had captured two kilometers of ground beyond Hill 378. After reaching the Sivry-Reville road, their objective, the men dug in awaiting further orders. It soon became clear that the new battalions had enjoyed a walkover, secured primarily by the sacrifices of the 316th doughboys, including Majors Harry Parkin and Sinkler Manning.

In a formal citation issued a few days after the capture of Corn Willy, General Kuhn rendered tribute to the regiment:

In the final offensive on the heights east of the Meuse and north of Verdun, the task of breaking the enemy's resistance at the Borne of Cornouiller (Hill 378) devolved upon the 316th Regiment of Infantry. Stubbornly defended by the enemy, this tactically strong point presented an obstacle of the most serious character. In spite of all difficulties, the regiment succeeded after three days heavy fighting, November 4th to 6th, in capturing and finally holding the Borne de Cornouiller, in breaking the enemy's resistance, and contributing materially to driving the enemy from the heights east of the Meuse a few days later.

Numerous authenticated instances of gallantry, tenacity, and endurance have come to the Commanding General's notice, proving beyond question that the Regiment acquitted itself with the greatest credit and in a manner worthy of the best American traditions.[35]

Long-sought redemption for the 79th Division had come high on Hill 378, as it broke through the Kriemhilde Stellung and captured the critical German observation post that had made the advance of the First Army such a torturous exercise. By means of a successful operation eerily similar to the assault on Montfaucon, the division had answered every doubt about its combat performance. But the achievement had been purchased principally by the courage and blood of the 316th Infantry Regiment, the death of Major Manning, and the wounding and capture of Major Parkin, who would no longer be present to inspire his men.

CHAPTER 17

MAKING GOOD . . . AT LAST

At eleven o'clock on the eleventh day of the eleventh month of 1918,
a 79th Division artillery battery celebrated the Armistice by hoisting a flag
and tossing their hats in the air. Unlike many of their comrades, they had
survived the bloodiest and largest battle in American history.

★   ★   ★

The mere discussion of an armistice would not be
sufficient grounds for any judicious commander to
relax his military activities.

—General John Pershing,
Commander in Chief,
Allied Expeditionary Forces[1]

No one knew just how the news made it from Germany to Corn Willy Hill, but as the 79th was gathering its wounded, burying the dead, and regrouping for another attack, hope finally arrived. Peace was at hand, or so it seemed. On November 6 Berlin had dispatched a commission to negotiate an armistice with the Allies, and the kaiser's troops were retreating all along the Western Front. The doughboys were overjoyed—all, that is, except Private Henry Gunther. When Gunther heard the rumor, the handsome, muscular private from Baltimore did not crack a smile. He still had some matters to settle, and the prospects of an armistice indicated that time was growing short. He had only a few days left to "make good."

Gunther was somewhat older and considerably more serious than the typical doughboy. The son of German immigrants in East Baltimore, Henry had excelled in Roman Catholic schools, and once professed a call to Holy Orders. But his German mother, who ruled the family with an iron hand, vetoed the idea. She was not content to let Henry be swept into the massive church bureaucracy and taken away from her control. He was meant for better things. Things closer to home.

Raised in the city's large German community, Henry was not a member of the favored class of Anglo-Baltimoreans who prepped at Boys' Latin School, studied at Johns Hopkins University, and then moved seamlessly into white-shoe positions at one of the city's banks, insurance companies, or law firms clustered around German Street. Despite Henry's unprepossessing heritage, the young man's erect bearing and easy smile caught the eye of a manager at the National Bank of Baltimore, and he was awarded an entry-level job. Ahead of him rose a daunting career ladder that years later might lead to one of the innumerable assistant vice presidencies and a gold watch thirty years on. If anyone from East Baltimore could master the intricate footwork necessary for advancement in the alien world of privilege, it would be Henry.

But history intervened. As Europe accelerated recklessly toward war, tension rose between Baltimore's German Americans and those harboring French or British sympathies. In a city boasting ninety-four thousand Germanic citizens, eighty-eight societies fostering ties with the fatherland, and a daily newspaper named the *Deutsche Correspondent*, the growing anti-German sentiment spreading across the United States was sure to evoke strong reactions.

One of the earliest shots in the rapidly heating verbal war was fired by Paul Prodoehl of the Civic Committee of Baltimore, which was made up largely of Germans. Prodoehl inveighed against the singing of "America" (also known as "My Country, 'Tis of Thee"), then contesting "The Star-Spangled Banner" to become the official national anthem. In a comment disclosing the true target of his enmity, the civic leader complained that the United States should not borrow "its national air from a country against which it fought two wars, one to procure independence, the other to maintain it."[2] The melody of "America" is also that of the British national anthem.

Another Baltimorean, Miss Nellie Miller, founded the Organization of American Women for Strict Neutrality, which papered East Coast cities with posters urging Congress "to stop the exportation of arms and ammunition from the United States to Europe."[3] Miller and her cohort knew that 80 percent of the munitions escaping President Wilson's porous ban was destined for the British, with most of the remainder going to France. All would be used to kill German soldiers on the Western Front. As a result of Miller's efforts, many Baltimoreans speculated that her name was actually Muller. Others dubbed one of Miller's neighbors, Paul Hilken, "the Hindenburg of Roland Park," for the swank neighborhood in which they lived. Worse verbal brickbats would soon fly.

In 1915, when the cargo submarine *Deutschland* evaded the British blockade and docked in Baltimore, the Germania Club hosted a dinner for Captain Paul Koenig, who announced exuberantly that one of his nation's zeppelins would soon visit the city, floating far above Allied aircraft just as his submarine had passed silently beneath British warships. Although the captain said that his submersible was carrying only commercial merchandise, rumor had it that the cargo included bundles of cash to fund German spies and saboteurs in the still-neutral country.

On December 7, 1915, President Wilson turned up the heat when he confessed to Congress that he was "sorry to say that the greatest threats against our national peace have been uttered within our own borders." Sharpening his verbal rapier to inspire vigilance, Wilson went on to declare, "There are citizens of the United States, I blush to admit . . . who have poured the poison of disloyalty into the very arteries of national life."[4]

A few months later, Wilson's inflammatory metaphor became grim reality, as the "Black Tom" explosion in a New Jersey munitions depot was attributed to German saboteurs. After Congress declared war in 1917, German-spy rumors blossomed into full-blown conspiracies. The most flamboyant was that of a foreign cell headquartered in Baltimore led by a prominent German American attorney who dispatched enemy officers in American army uniforms to infiltrate Camp Meade and the shipyards of Newport News, Virginia. Shortly thereafter, the Baltimore City Council formally changed the name of German Street to State Street, incidents of harassment of German Americans rose precipitously, and boycotts ruined businesses owned by those of German heritage. In 1918 successful florist Edwin Seidewitz saw his business collapse as a result of the boycott and suffered the ignominy of being expelled from the Rotary Club he had once served as president. He promptly went home and shot himself.[5]

A modest, hard-working bank clerk might reasonably expect to escape the fallout of such ethnic enmity, but Henry Gunther was not so lucky. Like many of those living in East Baltimore, Henry did not relish the thought of taking an expense-paid trip across the Atlantic to kill his relatives. He did not volunteer when war was declared. But a local patriot surreptitiously tipped the draft board that the Gunther family had two grown sons, both of whom were avoiding service. When the inevitable call arrived, Henry responded in character, cheerfully accepting orders to report to nearby Camp Meade to join the 79th Division. His mother was furious, but Henry recognized that he would have no future in Baltimore if he failed to respond. Before leaving, Gunther took the symbolic step of moving his clothes and himself out of the family home and down the block to the apartment of the beautiful Olga Gruebl. The two had been sweethearts since grammar school, and Henry was determined to cement their relationship before embarking for Europe. Gunther also relished the fact that his stern mother did not approve, a circumstance that made his modest move a declaration of independence at the advanced age of twenty-two.

Just as he had in every other endeavor, Henry excelled in the army. But the anti-German sentiment that limited his prospects in Baltimore also prevailed in the military. As a result, Gunther—like another German American in the 79th, Maximilian Boll—was perfunctorily precluded from Officers Training School. Undiscouraged, he pitched into barracks life and rose quickly through the ranks to earn sergeant's stripes, an achievement recognized by the *Baltimore Sun*.[6] The meticulous record keeping that served him well at the bank made him ideal to manage and distribute his company's equipment. The duties of a supply sergeant could be challenging, as soldiers complained vociferously about ill-fitting uniforms and defective equipment they were issued. But the friendly Gunther worked patiently with his men to find clothing that fit even the most extreme physique.

Like many members of the 79th, Gunther was shocked by what he found in northern France. Destruction was total, both materially and psychologically. Inhabitants of Champlitte, the town where the 313th trained, were deeply demoralized by the deaths of sons, brothers, and fathers. Little enthusiasm remained for helping to drive away the enemy. Inevitably, French pessimism seemed to rub off on Henry. In a letter, the young sergeant shared his impressions with a friend at home, who had intended to enlist. Henry urged him to reconsider, in light of the French passivity and the hardships soldiers faced. Posting that missive would be the biggest mistake of Gunther's life.

Letters from American soldiers were routinely reviewed by army censors, and a conscientious lieutenant flagged Henry's note for "defeatist sentiments." The fact that the letter had been written by a man with a Germanic surname and mailed to another of similar heritage sealed the case, as far as the army was concerned. Henry was "busted" to private and had to rip his hard-won sergeant's stripes from his tunics. Compounding the punishment, he was assigned to an infantry platoon under the command of an old friend from Baltimore, Sergeant Ernest Powell. A man who had once been Henry's peer was now his superior.

A few days after the demotion, the 313th moved out for the front, and a long truck ride gave Henry time to reflect on his situation. According to friends, "Gunther brooded over his reduction in rank and became obsessed with 'making good' in front of his officers and fellow soldiers."[7] Henry's deepest fear was that he would be branded a German sympathizer.

When the 313th arrived at Montfaucon, the men were assigned to the west end of Sector 304 near Avocourt, an area the enemy often probed in search of information on the defenders. There were numerous firefights and raids, and the novice American infantrymen were cautioned to keep their heads below trench tops to stay safe. But safety was not on Henry Gunther's mind. When a call went out for volunteers to serve as runners, the disgraced private spoke up immediately: "Sergeant, I'll take that."[8] Henry became an expert at navigating the paths connecting sectors of the American front lines, as he delivered messages in the dangerous, shrapnel-filled ravines north of Côte 304.

"When Gunther returned to my unit after a week of messenger duty," recalled Sergeant Powell, "I noticed he had his left wrist bandaged. A sniper had given him a flesh wound. Most soldiers would have welcomed a chance to get away from the front, but Gunther stayed with the action."[9] He merely wrapped the wound in a dressing, took a day off to rest, and then returned to running.

When the offensive began on September 26, the 313th's assignment to lead the assault on Little Gibraltar guaranteed that Gunther had more opportunities to continue his quest for the lost stripes. Future novelist James Cain, the 79th's unofficial chronicler, recalled that Henry "displayed the most unusual willingness to expose himself to all sorts of risks and to go on the most dangerous kind of duty . . . He repeatedly volunteered for duty when communication had to be established over terrain raked by machine guns and subject to heavy shelling."[10] As the regiment plunged into the toughest fighting on Montfaucon and near Cunel Wood, Gunther continued to serve as runner and established a fine record for bravery, proving "to be a man of the finest mettle."[11]

Rumor had it that the same was not true for some of Gunther's senior officers. Reporters from Baltimore stationed at headquarters wrote anonymous stories speaking of "blunders which had been made by the officers commanding units of the 79th Division." But the victory on Hill 378 lifted a burden from the men of the formerly disgraced division.

Regardless of the 79th's success, Gunther continued to grieve his demotion, and news of an impending armistice placed additional pressure on the private. As Henry and his fellow soldiers trooped down the east side of the Grande Montagne toward the German border, he searched for opportunities to replicate the achievement of the 79th, just as he had mirrored its earlier disgrace.

Although the Yanks were constantly shelled by long-range German artillery and harassed by suicide-squad machine guns hidden in the deep woods, they were seldom able to sight the enemy, who melted away silently toward Germany after doing their bloody work. Death, when it came, arrived anonymously and without warning—jolts of violence that heightened the doughboys' dread. Describing one ambush, Sergeant Joseph Labrum recalled, "The men on the patrol were fired on from all angles by machine guns, trench mortars, hand and rifle grenades, with the result that the patrol was forced to withdraw hurriedly, but not without severe losses."[12]

The loss of close friends and the promise of an armistice began to alter the Americans' behavior. Officers noticed that their soldiers' courage was slowly dissolving into caution. Many of the Yanks advanced haltingly, keeping their heads down and looking for cover that would enable them to survive the war.

On November 7 an American reporter in France cabled his New York office that the Allies and the Central Powers had reached agreement. The news spread quickly around the globe, and spontaneous celebrations broke out in cities on several continents. Later, citizens and soldiers alike learned the sad truth that peace talks were lagging at Compiègne, France, where the belligerents met in a rail car.

About the same time, Harry Parkin was also in a train car, traveling toward an uncertain future in Germany. After his capture, Parkin feared he might face the same abuse that he had seen his soldiers mete out to those they seized on the battlefield. But Harry was in for a great surprise: "I can truthfully say that during

all the time I was a prisoner, I was never the object of an un-
friendly look, nor an ungracious word from my captors."[13] In his
long rail trip with wounded enemy soldiers, he met a variety of
Germans who provided him with assistance, food, even friendship.

One of the most engaging was an enlisted man who had been
featured in Barnum & Bailey's Circus in the United States. As a
strongman, he had performed in Chicago, Cincinnati, and even
Parkin's hometown of Pittsburgh. When the war broke out, the
performer had rushed home to Germany to join the army, and had
done well in the service, earning the Iron Cross for bravery in the
trenches. Parkin remembered that the German confessed, "He
was a damned fool for doing so and would never do it again."[14]

To escape the fighting, the German had feigned a case of
appendicitis, which he exaggerated when necessary. Every time
medical officers appeared, the strongman "began to give every
evidence of suffering and groaned and writhed and held his side,
actually getting pale in the face," Parkin recalled. "The Red Cross
man was quite concerned over him; but as soon as he had left,
my friend laughed and lit up his pipe again, and the whole car
roared."[15] Parkin's suffering, however, was quite real. His four
bullet wounds were painful, he could not walk a step, and he was
forced to rely on the kindness of Germans to find a bunk, relieve
himself, and change trains as necessary. At one point, the major
was left lying on a stretcher between busy train tracks while one
of his new German friends persuaded medics to move Parkin to
a connecting train. One of the most helpful fellow travelers was a
chaplain from the Austro-Hungarian army, a cultured man who
interceded with authorities to send the wounded American to a
military hospital, rather than to a prison camp where the medical
care would not be as professional. When the train reached Trier,
the American was particularly gratified as "All of the officers who
had traveled with me crowded around and shook hands heartily,
wishing me good luck and a safe return home. They were gentle-

men of the finest kind. It has not often been my privilege to travel in better company."[16]

The camaraderie of a crowded train trip had forced Parkin to meet and know the "enemy" personally. What he found was not the fearsome Hun that most Americans had been warned to expect, but men very much like himself. Men with wives, children, professions, and—above all—a burning desire for normal lives. They treated the major well, and he survived because of their ministrations and kindness.

To a man as sensitive as Parkin, the erosion of his misconceptions about Germans must have raised serious questions—maybe even doubts—about the war. He smoked their tobacco, drank from the same cup, and ate food they prepared for him, and these shared moments deeply affected him. Although Harry had not become a pacifist, he naturally began to wonder about the death and destruction he had witnessed—and helped cause.

Meanwhile, as Parkin recuperated in the German hospital, he began to sense unrest sweeping through the streets outside his window. When the revolution reached Trier, the major understood the consequences, as "the nurses and the attendants were greatly alarmed over it. They told us that the officers had been locked up in their quarters, their shoulder straps cut off, their pay reduced to that of a private, they were saluted no more, and a soldiers' committee would handle the local government."[17]

None of the Germans broached the subject, but Parkin knew that peace was on its way, an armistice that heralded several painful leg surgeries and months of recuperation in an American hospital in Paris. When the ordeal was over, the major would return to America a vastly changed man. Although warm memories of friendships with American comrades and altered perceptions of the enemy were beneficial, the overall effect of the war on the major was disastrous. Harry had seen too much anger, too much blood, and far too much deceit. He was profoundly disillusioned and protested in his memoirs that the war was "an outrage committed by man, who claims he is civilized. The war has made a joke both of civilization and religion. Neither had any restraining influence upon man during this terrible struggle."[18]

As Parkin lay in his hospital bed brooding over war's brutality, General Pershing also had begun worrying. Peace rumors were circulating through the regiments, and the American commander in chief feared that his troops might lose their fierceness. To forestall that eventuality, Pershing pushed divisional commanders to stoke their soldiers' fighting spirit. As a first step, General Kuhn issued Field Order No. 46 directing that

> All members of this command are prohibited from starting or repeating rumors relative to the war, intentions of the enemy or intentions of the Allies. Rumors at present being circulated in this command are not substantiated by facts and tend towards careless conservation and the spreading of false information. All authentic information and news will be published from time to time as soon as received.[19]

Aside from demonstrating the futility of ordering soldiers to ignore rumors, the note had little impact on the troops, who hugged the ground with increased fervor. Officers could command, shout, and cajole all they wished, but their men knew that the war would end soon, and they were determined not to be the last American to make the ultimate sacrifice.

Still, the draftees from Pennsylvania, Maryland, and the District of Columbia did their duty. Moving cautiously off the Heights of the Meuse, they reached a broad valley containing one of the larger towns they had seen since passing through Verdun. Wavrille had been abandoned by the Germans, who left little more than offensive graffiti to welcome the conquering Americans. "Gott strafe England!" ("God scourge England!") invoked one sign, suggesting that it had been scrawled before the kaiser's troops met the Yanks. The town offered little comfort for the doughboys, who moved on quickly to confront two looming ridges: the Côte de Morimont and the Côte de Chaumont.

Between these lengthy ridges running east and west was a natural avenue that beckoned the troops, just as the deadly valley north of Malancourt had enticed the unwary men of the 314th on the first day of battle. A road leading through the valley offered the quickest way for the Yanks to move toward the final barrier standing between them and the flat plain that would speed them toward the German border. That obstacle, the Côte de Romagne, was a crescent-shaped hill looming against the eastern sky; intelligence reports indicated that it was bristling with interlocking machine guns, punctuated by bunkers, and covered by multiple artillery batteries. Like Montfaucon and the Grande Montagne, the final objective was a ridge, so it was only natural that the 79th would be called on to take the promontory, just as it had captured Montfaucon and Hill 378. Somehow that seemed fitting.

On November 8, however, events came to a head in Germany: An outright revolt was under way. Troops and citizens marched through the streets under the red banner of communism, while cooler heads called for founding a republic. To defuse the situation, the newly appointed chancellor, Prince Max of Baden, called on the kaiser to abdicate, a demand seconded by the man who had replaced Hindenburg as army commander, General Wilhelm Groener. Petulantly, the kaiser demanded an opportunity to march at the head of his army to put down the revolt. He was told bluntly that he could march wherever he liked, but the army would not follow him. The next day, the deflated Kaiser Wilhelm II signed an abdication proclamation and made arrangements to flee to Holland, as the General Staff struggled to hold the front long enough to secure favorable peace terms.

The revolt and abdication were *public*—not secret—events, announced by officials and reported to the entire world. The

German Empire was finished, and within a few days, the whole apparatus would come crashing down. But General Foch relentlessly drove his armies on, and Pershing, who had suffered painful weeks of static warfare in the Meuse-Argonne, was determined to keep the Germans on the run to demonstrate the toughness of American troops.

In pushing the offensive east of the Meuse, General Henri Claudel, who commanded the II Colonial Army Corps to which the 79th was assigned, accentuated Pershing's desire for aggressive action:

> The First Army, U.S. has made known the fact that the enemy continues to beat a retreat from the Meuse towards the north . . . The Army orders the execution of a general pressure upon the entire front and the vigorous following up of every withdrawal of the enemy. The action will thus be followed upon the entire front of the II Colonial Army Corps, and from daybreak with the very greatest energy.[20]

On the morning of November 10, as Kaiser Wilhelm boarded an express train to exile, Henry and the 313th woke in the dripping Bois de Brabant, a few kilometers from the battlefront. Over the past few days, as the Yanks moved forward, Gunther had become increasingly silent and moody. When he spoke, he grumbled about "making good." Sergeant Powell noted Henry's remarks but had little time to ponder them as he readied his men for the approaching assault.[21]

On the same day, General William Nicholson of the 157th Brigade was developing an imaginative plan to capture the Côte de Chaumont that appeared designed to protect his troops while seizing the objective. The hill had twin summits: Hill 328 to the west and the lower Hill 319 on the eastern end near the Côte de Romagne. A saddle between the two knobs lay just above the small village of Chaumont-devant-Damvillers, clinging to the southern slope of the ridge. Having finally mastered the disastrous lessons from earlier frontal assaults, Nicholson proposed to Kuhn that the 314th avoid the inviting valley to the north, swing around the fortified front of the ridge on Hill 328, and attack the Germans' exposed flanks from the south. For the time being, Henry Gunther and the 313th would remain safely in reserve.

Without acknowledging Nicholson's plan, the division commander ordered a direct assault on the ridge, with the 314th sweeping up the front of Hill 328, dashing through the saddle, and capturing Hill 319 in one bold but dangerous move. Aware that he was still suspected of a lack of aggressiveness by First Army headquarters, Kuhn seemed determined to live up to Pershing's demanding expectations, no matter how many lives the attack might cost.

After repeatedly witnessing the same American tactics, the enemy high on the Côte de Chaumont knew what was coming. Soon after daybreak on November 10, German biplanes began systematic attacks on American staging positions in the valley, dropping bombs and strafing men to break up assault units. Dodging bullets from the aircraft and from machine guns in a large concrete bunker atop Hill 328, the 314th scaled the bare hill, sustaining heavy losses. After blowing up the bunker with TNT, the Yanks continued eastward down toward the saddle, where machine-gun and artillery fire forced them to shelter in shell craters and supply trenches. All attempts to take Hill 319 failed, as more Americans fell.

By that point in the war, AEF artillery had mastered close infantry support, and the target was well within range. Nicholson ordered 155mm guns to blast the second knob. Although a few of the massive rounds landed uncomfortably close to American troops, the barrage devastated the Germans. By eight o'clock, the 314th reported that it had secured the Côte de Chaumont, and everything looked propitious for an assault on the Côte de Romagne the following day: November 11, 1918.

During the overnight hours, Kuhn issued orders calling on Nicholson's 313th Regiment to mop up Chaumont-devant-Damvillers before crossing a broad valley south of Hill 319, harassing the southern slopes of Côte de Romagne, and moving on to capture the tiny village of Azannes, a kilometer beyond the fortified ridge. If the sweeping maneuver worked, the Côte de Romagne would be cut off from supplies and reinforcement. Knowing that rumors of an armistice were growing stronger, Kuhn added a sentence to reinforce the 313th's aggressiveness: "Should it at any time appear that the resistance of the enemy is materially weakening, the ground in front will be immediately occupied and the attack pressed vigorously."[22]

By six in the morning, Gunther, Powell, and the rest of the 313th's First Battalion began their move across the exposed valley toward Chaumont. The first part of the march was masked by heavy ground fog, and by eight o'clock, the Yanks had rousted the remaining German stragglers from the hillside village.

Fifteen minutes later, Kuhn's headquarters received the long-awaited news from Foch: "Hostilities will cease on the whole front beginning at 11h (French time) November 11."[23] Across no-man's-land, German soldiers were also informed that the Armistice had been signed and directed to take defensive actions only. Kuhn did not signal his units for another thirty minutes, and when he did, the general added a deadly coda to the good news: "Hostilities will cease on the whole front at 11 hours today, French time. *Until that hour, the operations previously ordered will be pressed with vigor*"(emphasis added).[24] To underscore his support for the aggressiveness of his superiors, Nicholson appended even stronger words for the 313th and 314th regiments: "These orders will be strictly complied with and *there will be absolutely no let-up in carrying out the original plans until 11 o'clock*."[25] Each senior officer seemed determined to amplify the ferocity of Pershing's order, as if last-minute bravado could recapture the confidence of the AEF commander.

The American generals' eagerness provided the opportunity that Henry Gunther sought. As the mist began to lift across the shell-cratered pastures south of Hill 319, the 313th, with Gunther's Company A on its southern flank, advanced toward a low line of brush and trees stretching across a road toward the Côte de Romagne. The road to Azannes bisected the line of American skirmishers moving cautiously over the rain-soaked fields.

Henry Gunther's trained eyes scanned the distant line of brush as he moved forward. It was probably the distinctive profile of a small mound of earth concealing a machine gun that alerted the private to the enemy's presence. A burst of fire aimed well above their steel helmets caused the doughboys to drop. Although the Germans easily could have shot many of the advancing Americans, it was clearly the enemy's intention to warn rather than to kill.

The US platoon had already received word that the Armistice would commence at 11:00 a.m., and Ernest Powell's attention was focused on his watch.[26] Although the achievements of World War I generals were gauged primarily by the amount of territory they conquered, Powell recognized that his success would be measured by the number of platoon members he returned safely to Baltimore. He was content to wait out the war on his belly as he watched the minute hand on his watch near the top of the hour.

The men of Company A, James Cain reported later, were all well aware that Henry Gunther was "fired by a desire to demonstrate, even at the last minute, that he was courageous and all-American. At a few minutes to 11:00, he announced that he was going to take that machine-gun nest. Though his companions remonstrated, and told him that in a few minutes the 'war would be over,' he started out, armed with a Browning automatic rifle."[27]

Perhaps Gunther hoped to capture the German crew as a means of regaining his lost stripes. Or maybe he realized he could not bear to return to Baltimore in disgrace. More likely, he felt that only his sacrificial death on the battlefield could atone for his mistake. Whatever Henry's motivation, there is no doubt he knew the war would end soon. All he had to do to survive was lie prone.

But Henry chose to stand.

And he chose to advance.

Astonishingly, members of the enemy gun crew stood and motioned the lone American back to safety. Using broken English, they urged him to drop to the ground. Neither gesture was effective, as Henry continued to walk slowly but decisively forward. To underscore his determination, Henry fired a few shots from his Browning automatic rifle. Finally taking cover to protect themselves, the German crew knelt over their weapon and ominously racked a bullet into its receiver. But the doughboy strode on, and a five-round burst ripped from the machine gun. Just as Sergeant Powell's watch reached 11:00 a.m., Henry toppled forward with a bullet in his brain.

Across the gray, ruined ridges of the Meuse-Argonne, the rumble of the large guns ceased instantly. One member of the 79th Division recalled later that the Armistice arrived "amid silence so deep as to be oppressive and almost overwhelming."[28]

It mattered little to Henry Gunther, who had finally "made good." Officially, he was the last American to die in World War I.

PART III

THE WAR
AFTER THE WAR

At the end of the war, little remained of Montfaucon's church.
Germans had incorporated the ruins into the defenses of Little Gibraltar,
with crypts hosting machine-gun nests and the west-front pier
transformed into a small observatory.

▶ Before the Germans came calling in 1914, Montfaucon was a prosperous farming village in the French countryside. Its commanding view and proximity to Verdun made it a prime asset to the invaders.

1

▼ German soldiers stationed on the butte enjoyed a number of amenities, including a cinema, dining halls, and tavern with a ready supply of German beer. Aside from an occasional shell fired by the French from the valley below, there was little to disturb the peace on the Mount of the Falcon.

3

▲ After French shells collapsed the roof of Montfaucon's church, Germans warmed themselves near a fire in the baptistery font while more energetic soldiers cavorted on broken rafters. Over the war years, the historic structure would be slowly destroyed by artillery fire.

2

◀ Crown Prince Wilhelm's capture of Montfaucon was one of the most important German victories early in the war. To prove their participation in the proud event, groups of German soldiers had picture postcards taken in front of the famous church.

4

◀ Trenches lace the forests of the Meuse-Argonne region, like these in the Bois de Montfaucon. Expertly camouflaged, the field fortifications and their machine guns and trench mortars excised a terrific toll on the doughboys.

5

▶ "All is kaput," a German soldier scrawled on this postcard of Malancourt, a village in the 79th's sector. The invaders were eager to share with home audiences the destruction they had visited on their French neighbors.

6

◀ The tiny village of Haucourt was destroyed during the war. In keeping with the savagery, an Allied soldier placed the skull of a German in a distinctive enemy helmet among the ruins.

7

▶ Concealed inside a ruined manor house, the German crown prince's observatory consisted of a three-story telescopic periscope. Observers on three floors could use the device and retreat to the basement during strong enemy barrages.

8

▶ Painted in dazzle camouflage to confuse U-boats, the captured German steamer *Vaterland* was renamed *Leviathan*. Crewed by the US Navy—including future movie star Humphrey Bogart—the ship carried up to fourteen thousand American troops, including the 79th Division.

▶ Smiles soon faded to rancor as Allied commander in chief Ferdinand Foch (left) explained to AEF commander John Pershing his new plan to put an end to the war in 1918.

◀ Joseph Kuhn (right), commander of the 79th Division, confers with his French corps commander, Henri Claudel, on a cold day in November 1918. Claudel wears a wolfskin coat favored by many senior officers.

▶ Doughboys fresh off the farm thought they had landed on another planet when they climbed aboard trucks steered by fur-clad French colonial troops from Indochina. Without headlights, the strange drivers careened over rural roads at night—with surprisingly few accidents.

12

13

◀ A wicked surprise lay in wait for the 79th Division as it attacked along the road toward Little Gibraltar on the horizon. German machine guns and trench mortars lining the ridges beyond the ruins of Haucourt and Malancourt (foreground) pinned the doughboys down for nearly eighteen hours.

▶ A well-concealed part of the Work of the Demon, this German bunker directed machine-gun fire on Americans advancing toward Montfaucon. Yanks were forced to hug the ground through the afternoon and night of September 26, 1918.

14

Tremendous Strain Under Which Our Men Were Laboring

HE TERRIFIC STRAIN UNDER WHICH THESE MEN OF THE 314TH REGIMENT HAD BEEN IS CLEARLY SHOWN B HEIR HOLLOW EYES AND HAGGARD FACES. THEY HAD JUST PUSHED THE GERMANS BACK FOUR AND A HAL MILES IN TWENTY-FOUR HOURS.

15

◀ The anxious faces of men of the 314th Regiment betray the stress the soldiers experienced as they drove through the Oeuvre du Demon and into German-held woods east of Little Gibraltar, as reported here in the *New York Times*.

◄ After capturing the church, Yanks raised the Stars and Stripes to ensure that Montfaucon would join other promontories that were sites of US victories. For reasons that have remained hidden for nearly a century, the butte never secured that notoriety.

▼ Following French tanks, the 313th and 316th Regiments stormed Montfaucon's southwest slope. Every ruin was fortified, with the strongest resistance in the cemetery to the far right, the white church piers towering in the center, and the observatory in the ruined manor house on the far left of the hilltop. The village has been left in ruins as a memorial.

◄ Signs of relief show on the faces of Germans captured on the first day of battle by the 79th Division. These lucky veterans were given loaves of bread while many of their American captors would have nothing to eat for three days.

▼ When the terrain permitted, Renault tanks led the way for Americans in the Meuse-Argonne. George Patton, who captured fame in World War II, led the primitive vehicles forward until he was wounded.

NO. 15 TANKS NEAR VARENNES 27-12-18

◄ French premier Georges Clemenceau was enraged when an American traffic jam thwarted his desire to be the first official to celebrate the capture of Montfaucon on the butte. Stewing in his car, "the Tiger" drafted a letter urging Foch to relieve Pershing for inability to drive his American army forward.

◄ As doughboys of the 79th Division climbed the ridge north of the village of Esnes, they passed a ruined crucifix that suggested they were entering a combat zone where the old standards of morality were no longer honored.

21

▶ After the battle, an American aircrew inspected a German 77mm cannon that Harry Parkin and his battalion destroyed north of Nantillois. The men were gleeful about repaying the enemy for numerous high-explosive, shrapnel, and gas shells.

22

◄ Sharp-shooting German artillery knocked the right track off this tank that led Parkin's battalion toward Cunel Wood. The major marveled at the bravery of the French crews and mourned their heavy losses as many burned to death trapped in their vehicles.

23

▶ After the fall of Montfaucon, the Germans established a replacement observatory atop Corn Willy Hill east of the Meuse River. Rickety tree houses enabled the enemy to mount telescopes to direct a rain of shells on the Yanks to the west.

24

25

◀ One historian observed that Americans smothered German machine guns with their bodies, a sad truth demonstrated by a doughboy slaughtered in front of a bunker on Corn Willy Hill.

▶ On bloody Corn Willy Hill, Chaplain Sam Wright conducted a burial service for American dead. Years later the chaplain revealed the circumstances of the Montfaucon debacle in a story that haunted Parkin for the rest of his life.

26

CHAPTER 18

CONTROLLING THE NARRATIVE

Located near Hill 304, the village of Avocourt was completely destroyed by the war. It was rebuilt on the same site, but several destroyed villages—including Montfaucon—were preserved in their devastated state to serve as permanent reminders of invaders from the east.

★   ★   ★

It's the objective which counts, not the incidents.

—Captain (later, General) John Pershing,
US Army[1]

B attles following wars are often just as brutal—if less deadly—than those occurring during conflicts. Skeptics labeling this observation hyperbolic are invited to consider the career of General James Longstreet. Following the Civil War, the Confederate corps commander became an object of hatred, as disgruntled rebels searching for someone to saddle with the South's loss settled on the retired general.

Seizing on Longstreet's preference for defensive warfare and his delay in attacking the Union left flank on the second day at Gettysburg, diehards of the Lost Cause accused him of subverting the orders of the revered Robert E. Lee, causing the loss of the pivotal battle, and ensuring the South's ultimate defeat. For these and other trumped-up offenses, Longstreet was driven from New Orleans, assaulted by viperous journalists, and burned out of his home in a suspicious fire on April 9, 1889—the twenty-fourth anniversary of Lee's surrender at Appomattox.

Robert Bullard, Hunter Liggett, John Pershing, and other senior generals in World War I had been schooled on such cautionary tales from the Civil War, and were well aware of what happened when battles past were refought in the present. The innocent as well as the guilty often caught loads of shrapnel.

Pershing demonstrated that he mastered that lesson early in his career, as a telling anecdote from the Spanish-American War confirms. In 1898, before the Rough Riders captured national attention, the Cuban campaign was floundering in the island's tropical jungles. In charge of the American assault force was General William R. Shafter, an overweight sixty-three-year-old who many felt was incapable of command. One day, as Captain Pershing and his African American troops cut their way through the underbrush, the future general overheard a young officer complaining about the "Old Man's" poor leadership.

"The fat Old Man you talk about is going to win this campaign," lectured Pershing. "When he does, these things will be forgotten. It's the objective which counts, not the incidents."[2] Pershing's point was that once a war is won, battlefield mistakes fade from public consciousness in the limelight of victory. The principle might be true, but unstated is the fact that reaching the happy conclusion of history often requires what euphemistically might be called firm editorial management—or, in other words, controlling the narrative.

When Pershing received Secretary of War Newton Baker's call in 1917, he stepped from his train into a capital already convinced of the need to shape public opinion about the war. In charge of the effort was former journalist George Creel, a Wilson political supporter who had proposed engaging reporters, sponsoring public speakers, and producing compelling posters and movies to generate support for the war effort. Some military hardliners urged strict censorship, but Creel's proactive approach won Wilson's support and an appointment to head the US Committee on Public Information, history's largest public relations organization.

While the committee's methods were anathema to old-army generals, Pershing promptly fell in line with the program. The AEF commander was aware, however, that he needed a skilled assistant to direct press operations in France. One day in the spring of 1917, Pershing spotted a likely candidate walking by the door of his office: Frederick Palmer, the dean of American war correspondents.

As a youth, Palmer had sought appointment to West Point but abandoned his dream when he discovered that a congenital heart defect made him ineligible. As events developed, however, Palmer's physical limitations would not prove insurmountable.

While attending college, he captured his first job as a reporter by writing a trial story for a local paper about the memories of his hometown's Civil War veterans, and soon moved to New York City, where he grasped an opportunity to cover an obscure conflict in the ever-contentious Balkans in 1897.

From a hillside uncomfortably close to the action, Palmer watched fierce Turks vanquish poorly trained Greeks in the battle of Mati.[3] He then moved on around the globe to cover fighting in the Philippines, China, Manchuria, and other countries where he proved capable of composing stories that informed and entertained US readers. If Palmer had a flaw, it was a fascination with high rank. His deference to generals, admirals, and field marshals fueled friendships with those in command; his discretion often provided access to those planning and directing military operations. The same qualities, however, could sometimes blind Palmer to the failings of the military and the larger responsibilities of his profession. For instance, when he met Admiral George Dewey, the internationally acclaimed winner of the battle of Manila Bay, he was immediately taken by the modest, plainspoken officer, who invited the reporter to join his victory tour of world ports, proclaiming America's newfound naval prowess.

At one port of call, Dewey encountered a haughty German diplomat who insulted the Americans as "Johnny-come-latelies" to international politics. "The Kaiser and the Germans are going to make trouble in the world. They are too pushing and ambitious," confided the American admiral to a group of admirers.[4] The prescient remark was picked up by a reporter, and the resulting diplomatic furor caught up with Dewey in Gibraltar.

After conferring with the admiral, Palmer issued an obfuscatory press statement proclaiming, in the correspondent's words, "the Admiral's indignation at the publication of so preposterous a remark; and this [statement] the public accepted as denial in their conviction that their Dewey could never be so untactful."[5] The misleading dispatch defused the controversy, but it also revealed the correspondent's willingness to shade the truth to protect those he admired.

When European war drums began to beat in the summer of 1914, Palmer was offered a job covering the coming conflict. Soon he was dodging shells on the battlefields, as the only American correspondent accredited by the British Expeditionary Force. To help Americans understand the unprecedented violence of the conflict, Palmer wrote hundreds of stories for the Associated Press, United Press, and International News Service. He soon developed a reputation as a reporter who would go to hazardous lengths to give readers a new perspective, even venturing into no-man's-land on a British trench raid and entering the trenches to cover the disastrous first day of the Somme Offensive.

In addition to writing news stories, Palmer also churned out vast quantities of copy during his off-hours. In fact, the correspondent composed a book called *My Year of the Great War*, published in 1915, a volume followed quickly by *My Second Year of the War* just two years later. In the winter of 1916–17, Palmer came home to embark on a lecture tour promoting the volumes and to negotiate a new contract before returning to Europe. In exchange for combat dispatches, a syndicate of American newspapers agreed to pay the correspondent $40,000 a year—a princely sum considering that President Wilson's annual compensation was $75,000.

After the US declaration of war, Palmer sought out army friends to get a line on what to expect when the American Expeditionary Forces landed in France. It was on one of his visits to the War Department that he ran into General Pershing, whom he had first met during the Russo-Japanese War in 1904–5. Palmer inquired about plans for the AEF, while Pershing sought the correspondent's firsthand insights into trench warfare, new fighting methods, and the state of the Allies. As the conversation wound on, Palmer asked about regulations for reporters who would follow the doughboys abroad. Pershing seized the opening.

The AEF commander invited the correspondent to serve as his press officer in Europe and help develop the procedures.[6] Envisioning the prospect of $40,000 flying from his pocket, Palmer demurred respectfully, but he was intrigued. The general was not one to give up easily, especially as he had earlier received a confidential recommendation of Palmer from presidential aide Edward House.[7] In hopes of eventually persuading the correspondent to undertake the task, the AEF commander offered Palmer a stateroom on the SS *Baltic*, the liner carrying the vanguard of the army staff to Europe. The correspondent joined the group when it sailed from New York on May 28, 1917.

On board, Pershing did not press Palmer about the job, but included the correspondent in an intensive round of meetings taking place during the voyage. Recognizing that Palmer knew more about the fighting in Europe than anyone else on board, the AEF commander invited him to give a series of lectures about new modes of combat. The general knew that there is nothing quite as flattering as being asked to talk about one's expertise, and Palmer soon became a valued member of Pershing's inner circle. He was plied with good meals, numerous cigars, ample whiskey, and the heady esprit of a group asserting American idealism in a world gone mad.

Years later, Palmer admitted that the Yanks' mission had stirred his latent idealism: "Deep down, I did think of the World War as a war to end war . . . After this exhibition of mass murder, we would relegate war to past savagery in common with witch-burning, imprisonment for debt, drawing and quartering, the torture chamber, and hanging for thievery."[8] When Pershing offered the job again, Palmer accepted the opportunity "to get the truth out of hell," as he termed it later.[9]

As AEF chief press officer, Palmer was appointed to the rank of major, and set about managing the flow of information from the battlefield, through a corps of reporters, and on to the American people. He had traded a contract worth $40,000 per annum for a pair of brass oak leaves, a yearly stipend of $2,400, and the exacting task of controlling the narrative of what would shortly become his nation's largest military expedition.

Palmer structured his organization for two primary tasks: exercising censorship and disseminating propaganda. In 1917 the terms did not carry negative connotations. Palmer believed that "Censorship is in human nature, its warrant and excuse in protectiveness."[10] By controlling reporters' access, the press chief sought to protect AEF plans from the enemy; by editing correspondents' stories, he eliminated information that might be useful to the Germans. Reporters were forbidden to mention, for instance, specific names, places, or units that could help the enemy learn about the AEF. The tone was set by Pershing, who strictly limited references to himself in official dispatches, in favor of emphasizing the AEF as the embodiment of America. The censors' blue pencils ruthlessly cut details—and much of the color that home-front audiences sought—from reporters' dispatches.

As opposed to censorship, *propaganda* during Palmer's time denoted positive information designed to motivate recipients. On the front lines, stories about victories could inspire soldiers to fight harder, while on the home front, propaganda would enhance the sale of war bonds, encourage diligence in munition factories, or alert citizens to the danger of saboteurs.

It did not take long for Palmer to discover that his skills were better suited to propaganda than to censorship. When the press officer imposed stiff restrictions on American reporters covering the arrival of the first US troops in France, he was embarrassed to discover that European correspondents who were not subject to American regulation broke news of the landings before papers in the United States received dispatches from their correspondents. The press corps blamed Palmer for the debacle. The incident damaged the press chief's credibility with American reporters, who began to devise various stratagems to escape AEF restrictions.

The situation came to a head when cold weather blew out of the Ardennes in 1917. US soldiers began to grumble about the lack of winter clothing, cases of pneumonia increased, and American doctors complained of a shortage of medical supplies. Reporters quickly learned of the matter and began filing dispatches to inform American mothers and fathers of their sons' privation. As the stories flowed into the press office, Palmer's censors refused to approve them, citing the need to keep the army's unpreparedness from the enemy. Two correspondents who pressed the issue had their AEF credentials revoked, and even Palmer's defenders began to conclude that "censorship was being administered in the narrow interest of the military clique rather than in the interest of the American people."[11]

The story broke when a brash correspondent, twenty-three-year-old Westbrook Pegler of United Press, conveyed his frustration to his superiors in a smuggled letter, just as another disaffected reporter, Heywood Broun, returned from France to write articles critical of the AEF. Broun's story and its headline, "Supply Blunders Hampered First U.S. Units in France," provoked US senator Hiram W. Johnson's famous dictum: "The first casualty when war comes is truth."[12]

Incensed by the matter, Johnson and his fellow senators William Borah and George Norris threatened to investigate military censorship. After several newspapers weighed in with critical editorials, Pershing realized that he had to dampen the outcry. He hit on a solution that would mollify Palmer's critics and enhance the correspondent's ability to manage the AEF narrative. The first step was sending Palmer to Washington as his "confidential agent" to quiet the uproar, an action that convinced correspondents that the press chief had been banished because of their complaints. On the mission, Palmer pacified the angry senators by explaining that news of supply shortages could inspire German attacks. He also promised to loosen the reins on reporters as soon as military operations began in earnest. The meetings went so well that Palmer was welcomed to the White House, where he briefed President Wilson and Edward House.

Settling nettlesome issues quietly is a widely respected skill, inside the military and out. When Palmer returned to France, he was greeted as a hero by fellow officers, promoted to the rank of lieutenant colonel, and posted to Pershing's headquarters. Ensconced a few doors from Pershing's office, Palmer was placed in charge of the AEF war diary and welcomed to meetings of the general staff. The press chief was positioned perfectly to do what he did best: write glowing reports, dispatches, and books about how the Americans were achieving the grand objective of defeating Germany.

Palmer spent most of his time converting the dry narrative of the AEF war diary into two colorful books—*America in France* and *Our Greatest Battle*—published in 1918 and 1919, respectively. Pershing understood the importance of getting his version of the AEF story to the public first, and encouraged the colonel's literary efforts. The volumes reflect strongly the views of Pershing and other senior officers; because of this influence, historians have a tendency to sneer at them. While the books must be evaluated carefully in the light of documentary evidence, they offer one distinct advantage: Palmer's books portray the "party line," the accepted version of truth as headquarters saw it *at the time the books were written.*

One interesting passage bears directly on the delayed capture of Montfaucon, an event the colonel witnessed. Just as Palmer had seen the British go "over the top" in the Somme Offensive, he was determined to view the launch of the doughboys' biggest push of the war, the Meuse-Argonne Offensive. Although he was on deadline for mailing the manuscript of *America in France* to his publisher, Palmer included one chapter about the opening of the battle as a teaser to readers about the book that would follow. To do so, he journeyed to Hill 304 and moved forward with the 79th Division on September 26, 1918.

Palmer soon got an eyeful: "Quite distinctly through the [field] glasses you might see our men advancing up the slope toward the woods to the left of Montfaucon and how, when they came to the sky-line, as the machine guns began rattling, they turned to the right, keeping under cover of the crest," wrote Palmer. "To the east of Montfaucon, there were other figures feeling their way forward. The town was now hidden from view in the valley by a hill in front of it; and in a sunken road on the slope of the hill we found the men of a platoon concealed. They had started over the crest to be met with machine-gun fire from both flanks as well from the town—a cross-fire hurricane."[13]

Palmer's description of the two-pronged attack described accurately the 79th's encounters with the Redout du Golfe and the Oeuvre du Demon. More importantly, the passage dramatically revealed the original intent of the First Army's orders regarding Montfaucon. Below the fortified ridge running diagonally across the front, Palmer wrote, the 79th's soldiers "were *waiting under orders until the flanks had done their work in 'pinching out' Montfaucon*" (emphasis added).[14] The flanking units were, of course, the 37th Division on the left and the veteran 4th on the right, under Bullard's command.

Palmer's detailed knowledge of First Army plans acquired from attending staff meetings at headquarters enabled him to provide this explanation. Echoing the orders, he described a turning maneuver in which the unit directly assaulting the objective makes a holding attack, while two other units proceed around the flanks to attack, envelop, and "pinch out" the objective from the rear. Palmer finished the chapter and mailed the manuscript to New York before the Montfaucon controversy erupted.

After *America in France* was published in 1918, however, questions began to arise, and the AEF command developed a different interpretation of its orders and the action. Palmer's next book, *Our Greatest Battle*, clearly reflects the shift:

Cameron's Fifth Corps [of which the 79th was a part] relied, in mastering the distance it had to cover on the first day as the "bulge" of the Army movement, upon the freshness of its troops, whose inexperience would be only another incentive to hold up their end.[15]

Instead of describing a pause by the 79th Division while the 4th and 37th Divisions "pinch[ed] out" Montfaucon, the revised history described V Corps as the tip of the AEF spear, being out front, forming the "'bulge' of the Army movement" by powering over Montfaucon on its own.

To make this interpretation credible, Palmer argued, "No aspect of the plan of our command was more audacious or more thrilling than the decision to expend in one prodigious ruthless effort the energy of the 37th, 79th, and 91st Divisions and their impatience for action accumulated in their long period in training camps."[16] *Audacious* and *thrilling* are not adjectives normally used to describe a strategy of sending untrained troops to attack entrenched Germans. But Palmer seemed to be motivated by justifying the slaughter of American troops in the bloody attack. By 1919, when *Our Greatest Battle* was published, complaints about Pershing's heavy casualties were circulating in Congress, which was considering an investigation of the matter. Pershing's public-relations expert felt compelled to rationalize the sacrifices by citing the convenient party line about the enthusiasm of untrained troops and the glowing prospect of ending the war quickly.

"The great prize," Palmer explained to readers, "was the hope of an early decision of the war; in expending a hundred or two hundred thousand casualties in the autumn and early winter, instead of a million, perhaps, during the coming summer."[17] The AEF achieved that objective—albeit at high cost. In light of Germany's defeat, Palmer and Pershing hoped the nation would accept the heavy casualties with equanimity.

After finishing his own book, Palmer helped Pershing prepare a raft of after-action reports and accompanied him to the peace conference. In recognition of his contributions, Palmer was presented a Distinguished Service Medal, an award denied General Joseph Kuhn, who had participated in the Meuse-Argonne Offensive from a more dangerous vantage point.

Pershing's final reports emphasized the magnificent objective secured by the Allied victory: the capitulation of Imperial Germany. The scrapes, slips, gaffes, and incidents of battle pale in light of that achievement. The preliminary draft is a short affair, broad in scope and bland to the point of dullness. To protect the deficient, it omits the names of those who excelled.

When the draft was published in 1919, the general invited the army's top commanders to review it and to offer comments. In addition to using the document to smoke out controversies, Pershing appeared to be saying: Gentlemen, here is the story of the AEF. It contains the positive elements of our endeavor and none of the rancor that could diminish the glory of our achievement. See that you keep it that way!

De facto, the pamphlet became the party line, and the general expected that the respect he had earned in France would command the loyalty and discretion of subordinate officers when they returned to peacetime pursuits. To underscore his determination to concentrate on the objective, not the incidents, Pershing confided to aides that his official reports would not cast blame on any person or unit.[18] As intended, word of the general's pledge leaked widely among the officer corps, bringing enormous relief to the deficient and chagrin to those who felt they had been wronged. But the overall effect was a collective sigh of relief heard in US army posts throughout Europe and America.

Despite these efforts, sniping became endemic among officers who felt compelled to defend the honor of their former units, and Little Gibraltar loomed large on the list of postwar conflicts. Although most of the infighting remained sub rosa, from time to time during the early 1920s, the controversial attack bubbled to public view. One episode represented a personal disappointment for Pershing, because it was caused by a friend whose reputation he had protected, Robert Bullard. In 1925 the retired lieutenant general published an account of the AEF that criticized Pershing's leadership and offered a stout defense of every action Bullard's III Corps had undertaken in the Meuse-Argonne. In the volume as well as on the battlefield, Montfaucon stood front and center.

Conveniently forgetting that his corps had been ordered to envelop the fortress, Bullard condemned neighboring V Corps and, in particular, the 79th Division for exposing his flank by not keeping pace. "My left division, the 4th (General Hines), in the first day's advance had gone entirely past the right division of the Vth Corps upon my left, leaving it, the 79th Division, in front of Montfaucon," charged Bullard. "In that neighborhood the 79th remained struggling with the enemy two days or so some kilometers behind the 4th Division. I had in vain tried to induce the General [Cameron] commanding the Vth Corps to take concerted action with me to unite our two flanks. The fire caused steady losses among my front-line troops."[19]

Bullard's account represented the height of perfidy, in light of the general's disobedience to orders. More startling was Bullard's commitment of the statement to print, which many of those who participated in the battle would read. Read it they did, and angry they became. The Montfaucon controversy was given new life.

After returning to the States and being rewarded with a fifth star and the position of US Army chief of staff, Pershing tried to view the controversies sprouting up about the AEF from an Olympian perspective. Half jocularly, he responded to those inquiring about the possibility of his writing a memoir by saying, "If I publish a book now, it would probably cause another war."[20] Spurred by the harsh words of Bullard's volume and the probing investigations by congressional committees, however, Pershing recognized that he would eventually be required to speak on the record.

Early in the 1920s, the general began penning a rough draft. After reviewing the manuscript, however, Pershing dismissed the effort as "dull" and abandoned the project. He complained, "It is the worst and most difficult job I have ever undertaken . . . I should prefer to go through the war again to writing about it."[21] After retiring from the army and being appointed head of the American Battle Monuments Commission (ABMC), which was planning memorials in France, he consulted George Marshall, who offered wise counsel: let officers serving in the ABMC historical division try their hands at composing chapters. To avoid drudgery, Pershing leapt at the suggestion, parceling out responsibility to staff officers, one of whom was Major Dwight D. Eisenhower. It was rumored that the future general and Supreme Allied Commander wrote the chapters on the Meuse-Argonne Offensive.[22]

In keeping with his pledge to avoid criticism, Pershing skirted controversial subjects in his own drafts of the book. For that reason, the general was surely surprised when he saw that Eisenhower's draft addressed the Montfaucon issue forthrightly—in a manner that would enflame the matter. Seeking to avoid controversy, Pershing penciled numerous changes on the draft that is now housed in the US Library of Congress.

The draft launched the Meuse-Argonne chapter by citing the primary tasks of Bullard's command: "The III Corps was directed to penetrate the enemy's position, turn Montfaucon, protect the right flank of the attack and organize the line of the Meuse for defense."[23] The passage accurately reports the corps' subordinate role and the order to turn Montfaucon, and Pershing made no changes at this point. A few pages later, however, the general spied a paragraph that edged too close to the heart of the matter.

The draft stated: "The left of the 4th Division, 39th Regiment, passed beyond the line of Montfaucon on its eastern flank but failed to turn or capture the position. The 79th did not reach its objectives and that stronghold remained in the hands of the enemy at the end of the first day."[24] Clearly, the original draft blamed the

4th Division and, by implication, III Corps for the failure—an interpretation that disturbed the former AEF commander. Pershing firmly struck out the entire paragraph, and in his own hand substituted an innocuous interpretation: "The advance on the first day was rapid. The opposition was taken by surprise."[25]

Near an earlier description of the attack, Pershing inserted a handwritten passage explaining that "through some misinterpretation of orders of the First Army the opportunity to capture Montfaucon that day was lost."[26] By using the passive voice, Pershing avoided identifying the unit or person responsible for the "misinterpretation"; he clearly hoped to leave the matter in the shadow of ambiguity. Ultimately, however, someone persuaded Pershing that the book should present an interpretation of the Montfaucon attack consistent with widely known facts. Thus, additional changes were made so that the published version stated:

> The 4th Division (Hines), on the left of the 80th, took Septsarges and was firmly established in the woods to the north. It was abreast of Nantillois and its left was more than a mile beyond Montfaucon, but through some misinterpretation of the orders *by the III Corps* the opportunity to capture Montfaucon that day was lost (emphasis added).[27]

The printed version clearly placed the onus of misinterpretation on the III Corps staff, a relatively small group of officers. But the explanation is vague enough to shield individuals. The writer or editor—perhaps Eisenhower—whose judgment prevailed in shaping the printed version, however, saved Pershing from making the grave error of eliminating mention of the debacle. Yet the circumstances hardly present Pershing at his best. The general was clearly attempting to control the AEF narrative by dampening discussion of an incident that precluded the success of the Meuse-Argonne Offensive.

Today Pershing's editorial machinations immediately would be labeled a cover-up, but in the less contentious age of the 1920s, they might more generously have been characterized as changes proffered in the cause of propriety. Whatever the motivation, Pershing's revisions to the manuscript make three facts clear. First, the general of the armies initially sought to erase the Montfaucon incident from the narrative of the conflict. After recognizing the flaws of that strategy, however, he characterized the cause of the incident as a "misinterpretation of orders," even though it was clear that Bullard had disobeyed orders. Finally, Pershing obscured the agent of the supposed misinterpretation by assigning blame to III Corps' staff. Whether the general's efforts to control the narrative amount to a cover-up or not, they were profoundly dishonest.

Although *My Experiences in the World War* won the Pulitzer Prize for history in 1931, it received a lukewarm public reception. The effort to cleanse the book of controversy also eliminated much of the human interest. The product of so much effort from so many different hands fell flat among readers, but it did provoke anger among some senior army officers who felt slighted. Army chief of staff Peyton March quipped that the book should have been entitled *Alone in France*, because it focused so tightly on one man.[28]

In the meantime, other officers, enlisted men, historians, and reporters were publishing books that cited mistakes and named names. In particular, a number of war correspondents, freed of censorship, wrote books exposing the flaws of Pershing's crusade in Europe. One of the most respected was Thomas M. Johnson, a correspondent for the *New York Sun* who had chaffed under AEF regulations. Not one to lounge at press headquarters and file dispatches based on optimistic communiqués composed by army scribes, Johnson journeyed to the trenches to dig further into stories. When he submitted his dispatches, censors routinely used blue pencils to cut interesting details and intriguing insights.

Accepting the rules of the game, Johnson maintained cordial relations with press officials while carefully packing away his notes
as ammunition for the postwar battles he knew would come.

Ten years later, Johnson dug out his notebooks, interviewed
retired officers, and published a book that set Pershing's teeth on
edge. Entitled *Without Censor: New Light on Our Greatest World
War Battles*, the volume described the army press operation's functions and product: "Propaganda *and* Censorship, indispensable if
rather ghastly, created a popular version of what happened that
was sometimes simply a fable agreed on."[29] Johnson did not define
precisely which "fables" he had in mind, but many of his questions
echoed the concerns of Harry Parkin, Ewing Booth, and Hugh
Drum about the attack on Little Gibraltar.

In the Meuse-Argonne, Montfaucon was "the key to the situation," said Johnson.[30] Had it been captured on the opening day
of battle, the correspondent posited, the First Army could have
surged on to cut the main enemy rail line near Sedan, and "when
those trains stopped, the German Empire stopped, and with it,
the most enormous war in history."[31] After noting that the 79th
had been held up by strong defenses south of the butte, Johnson
identified what he believed to be the chief cause of the debacle:
"Because the 4th Division, which had got three miles past Montfaucon, did not cut over and take it, notwithstanding that it was
in the 79th sector."[32]

Knowing that some III Corps and 4th Division officers had
complained that the First Army attack orders were unclear, Johnson proceeded to demolish that excuse.

> It is difficult to understand any real misconstruction, if there was,
> of General Pershing's intentions and the First Army attack order.
> It had been issued six days before the attack, discussed in one
> conference after another. It would seem that if there were errors
> in the order or in comprehension of it by corps and division
> commanders they would have been ironed out.[33]

This judgment and the book that contained it were well written and well received. The volume commanded a full-page review in Johnson's rival newspaper the *New York Times*, an admiring appraisal in *Foreign Affairs* magazine, and positive notice across the country. But other stories were competing for national attention, not the least of which were the still-emerging scandals of President Warren Harding's administration and the surging stock market of the Roaring Twenties.

Although Johnson was on the right trail, the scent of disobedience to orders, betrayal, and needless deaths eventually gave out. Ultimately, only two men knew the whole story and could explain what had delayed the capture of Montfaucon: Robert Bullard and his former chief of staff, A. W. Bjornstad. Neither had incentive to disclose who had changed the original attack order or who was responsible for calling off the attack designed to capture Montfaucon late on the afternoon of September 26. It would take another veteran officer who understood the military situation to uncover the truth.

CHAPTER 19

BULLARD, BJORNSTAD, AND BOOTH

General Ewing E. Booth was a "soldier's general" who cared for his
men and sought to rescue the 79th Division from disaster on Montfaucon.
His efforts were rebuffed, and Booth spent the next twenty years
investigating the cause of the debacle.

★   ★   ★

Every way of a man seemeth right unto himself . . .
[but the end thereof are the ways of death].

    —Proverbs 14:12
      Quoted by General Robert L. Bullard,
      who omitted the second half of the verse.[1]

B ut for a chance event on the plains of eastern Kansas, the Montfaucon controversy would probably have passed into obscurity. Perched high on a plateau above the Missouri River, Fort Leavenworth is the intellectual center of the US Army. Shortly after World War I, the post's Staff College began an intensive effort to analyze, digest, and teach the lessons of the American Expeditionary Forces to rising military officers. One of those entrusted with this critical task was Colonel Ewing Booth, former commanding officer of the 4th Division's 8th Brigade in the Meuse-Argonne Offensive. Reduced to his permanent rank from the generalship he held in France, Booth was the school's assistant commandant, a prominent position reporting to Commandant Hugh Drum, a widely respected general who had served as chief of staff of Pershing's First Army. While working hard to impress Drum, Booth enjoyed the camaraderie of other officers who lived in long rows of brick quarters parading west across the prairie.

The senior officers who taught at the school, as well as the captains, majors, and lieutenant colonels who studied under them, had the opportunity to become top-echelon leaders in the postwar American army. All were acutely aware that their performance in classrooms and administrative offices would determine their success in the service that was already dramatically reduced in size from the record three million men wearing khaki on Armistice Day. As the army was thinning ranks that would eventually shrink to only 130,000 men, the number of officers was reduced from 200,000 to fewer than 18,000. Given these cuts, competition for advancement was intense, and any shortcoming, infraction, or insult—actual or perceived—could cripple or end a career.

Ewing Booth understood these realities well and proceeded in his usual cautious manner. But a lecture he heard in the fall of 1920 tested his determination to avoid trouble and posed a challenge that would consume the next twenty years. As part of his duties as assistant commandant, Booth visited classes to monitor the curriculum. For the most part, he heard standard discussions about World War I tactics and strategy, but a lecture the assistant commandant happened to audit in the fall of 1920 advanced a startling new claim about the Montfaucon attack.

In a discussion of the Meuse-Argonne, the instructor declared that "had the Third Corps assisted the Fifth Corps by turning Montfaucon the battle would have been a much more glorious victory for the American Army."[2] As an officer of III Corps, Booth was deeply concerned about the allegation and marched to the lectern to take issue. Confronted by someone well above his pay grade, the startled instructor said that he was only repeating what the commandant, General Drum, had said a year before.

Disregarding the perils of challenging his commanding officer, Booth took the issue to Drum. The general, who had been second only to Pershing at headquarters during the planning and implementation of the final offensive, confirmed that he had made the statement—moreover, he declared that he believed it to be accurate.[3]

"I then asked him if he did not know that such a movement [to turn Montfaucon] had been ordered by the 4th Division Commander on the night of September 26–27, but had been stopped by someone whom I believed to be higher in authority than the Divisional Commander. He replied that he did not," Booth recalled. "At that time, I got the impression from what he said that the official A.E.F. final report would contain a statement to the effect that the Third Corps was expected to assist the Fifth Corps by turning Montfaucon. He added that the Army order had so directed."[4]

The possibility that the reputation of Booth's beloved 4th Division—which would have been responsible for conducting the turning maneuver—might be tarnished by an official report galvanized the colonel. After mulling over what he had just learned, he wrote Drum that

> future students of the history of this battle are sure to bring up the question of the apparent lack of proper cooperation between these two corps on September 26. It appears, therefore, that justice for the troops that participated in this part of the engagement demands that the question of responsibility for the lack of cooperation between the two corps mentioned should be cleared up at this time when most of the participants having knowledge thereof are alive and able to give definite information concerning this operation.[5]

Booth proposed writing senior officers in the battle, assembling their recollections and documentary evidence, and composing a definitive report explaining the incident. Drum approved the plan, and Booth embarked on a long and perilous task.

The colonel understood well that by investigating the matter he would be taking his career in his hands, tossing it high into the air, and inviting fire from all parties, particularly from those in III Corps. To protect himself and to gather evidence supporting his personal recollections, Booth began a low-key inquiry by writing those involved in the battle. His first two correspondents were close friends: General Benjamin Poore, who had commanded the 7th Brigade during the assault on September 26, and Colonel C. A. Bach, the 4th Division's chief of staff, who had been well aware of the various orders and their disposition. Once he had received and digested his friends' responses, Booth planned to widen the circle slowly to seek the views of others about two critical matters: changes to the original First Army attack orders made by III Corps and the fate of the turning maneuver Booth had proposed on the afternoon of September 26.

Looming at the end of Booth's indirect method were Bullard and Bjornstad, the men he suspected of besmirching the 4th Division and abandoning the 79th. In investigating their actions, Booth was delving into two of the most complex, problematic men ever to wear the stars of a US Army general.

In most apparent ways, the two were utterly dissimilar. Bullard was a southerner through and through, firmly ensnared by the attitudes of his region, while Bjornstad was a Minnesotan, raised on the fringes of the frontier. The midwesterner did not complete a degree after dropping out of St. Olaf College and the University of Minnesota; Bullard was a proud graduate of West Point. For thirty years, Bullard knew only the privileged life of an officer, while Bjornstad hacked his way through the Filipino jungles as a private before earning a commission. The chief of staff had mastered the complex maneuvers of modern war in classes at Fort Leavenworth, but Bullard was convinced that he had learned on the western plains all the tactics he would ever need. As a result, he insisted on the blunt wave attacks and slashing cavalry charges of an earlier age. Physically, the southerner was thin, wiry, and susceptible to a variety of illnesses, many of which appeared psychosomatic in nature. Bjornstad was powerfully muscled and seldom had a sick day in his life.

As wide as their differences were, Bullard and Bjornstad were actually doppelgängers: twins so similar in emotion, thought, and deed that they took an extreme dislike to each other at first sight. The proximity of two large egos in the cramped headquarters of an army corps sparked a dangerous chemistry destined to end in explosion, one that would endanger not only the principals but also bystanders.

At the heart of the two men's mutual repulsion was the fact that each claimed the absolute right to reject the orders of superiors, even though they denied the same freedom to subordinates.

Allan Millett correctly diagnosed "Bjornstad's inclination to run his own war," but the historian failed to extend that indictment to the III Corps commander, who warranted the charge more.[6] In his memoir, Bullard proudly proclaims six examples of his own disobedience to orders, and in each case, he argues that the judgment of history confirmed the wisdom of his insubordination. During the insurrection of the Islamic Moro warriors in the Philippines, for instance, Bullard ignored the orders of his commanding officer and attacked two enemy villages in reenacting the Old West cavalry tactic of "galloping for glory." After the young captain was put on report for "heinous offences," he boldly told his commander that he would disobey again if confronted by similar circumstances.[7] The unrepentant Bullard remarked later to fellow officers that he was determined to "run a little war of my own, and be heard from."[8]

The captain soon made good on his promise by leading another charge against the *cotta* (fortified village) of a Moro leader named Hassan. When Bullard's commander sent a message for the captain to slow so that a battalion on his flank could assist the attack, the courier returned to report:

> The active *commandante* [Bullard] didn't like being stopped one bit, and the order to get in touch with Ronayne's battalion on his left wasn't cheerfully received or obeyed. He is most ambitious, and was figuring on holding his advanced position, and rushing and taking Hassan, and his *cotta* before the arrival of the main body.[9]

Twenty years of army service would normally correct a tendency toward insubordination, but this did not prove true in Bullard's case. By the time he arrived in France, autonomy of judgment had become the cornerstone of his philosophy of leadership, one that was soon reinforced. While commanding a division during the German spring offensives of 1918, Bullard disobeyed his French commander's order to withdraw in the face of an imminent enemy attack.[10] Temporary withdrawals were standard operating procedure for the French, who used the tactic to escape preattack German bombardments, after which they would return to their trenches to confront the enemy. But Bullard's troops endured the barrage *and* fought off the enemy attackers as well. Thereafter, the American general proudly carried the sobriquet "No Retreat Bullard," awarded by a group of correspondents eager to publicize—or create—an American hero.[11]

Buoyed by the acclaim, Bullard became so convinced of the soundness of his judgment that he criticized those who slavishly complied with orders, including Pershing. In his diary, excerpts of which were published following the war, the general condemned the AEF commander for his "loyal adherence to the orders, plans, and wishes of his superiors. These were almost always contrary to the views and desires of brother officers and soldiers about him, and he was steadily and severely criticized for his strict adherence to those orders when he might have deviated from them; all to no avail—he still adhered."[12] Bullard believed that Pershing's compliance undermined his staff's respect so that he "nowhere arouse[d] enthusiasm except upon success; not a personal leader; admirable but not magnetic."[13] The southern general apparently wished to be Pershing's foil—or perhaps even his successor. At any rate, Bullard hoped to be remembered by history in a much different way, most likely as the reincarnation of impetuous Confederate cavalryman Jeb Stuart. Perhaps he had forgotten that Stuart's disobedience at Gettysburg had betrayed his namesake, Robert E. Lee.

Although General Bjornstad was more subtle in exercising his self-conferred prerogatives, he, too, believed that he had accumulated so much military wisdom during his career that he should be granted great latitude. An honor graduate of Fort Leavenworth, the imposing Bjornstad cited recent discussions of the role of chiefs of staff at the school as justification. According to James J. Cooke, who has studied command structures of the AEF,

Bjornstad's concept was basically that the staff advised the chief
of staff, who then put plans and operations into motion. The
chief of staff's duty was to be a key player and keep the commander either out of trouble or free to oversee the subordinate
commands in combat.[14]

On a modern battlefield, such an arrangement might be a necessity, but it will fail unless the chief of staff acts in a manner
consistent with his superior's directions. In running III Corps,
Bjornstad did not always follow this rule; more than once, he was
accused of issuing orders in the commander's name without prior
approval.[15] Bjornstad's claim to autonomy was bolstered by the
fact that he had been appointed III Corps chief of staff on March
30, 1918, three months before Bullard was named to command
the corps.[16] During the interim, as Bullard was fighting the German spring offensives, Bjornstad recruited the headquarters staff,
trained them in his procedures, asserted his domineering control,
and won such loyalty as his abrasive personality would permit.
"He held all actions in his own hands," Cooke observed, "and the
corps staff became literally Bjornstad's appendage with no real
responsibility except to tell Bjornstad what was going on."[17]

When the chief of staff and his commander finally met at the
new III Corps headquarters in the ruins of Meaux, France, in July
1918, Bjornstad had already developed several habits that irritated
Bullard. The chief of staff communicated with commanders of
other corps, a privilege normally reserved for peers, and he spoke
frequently with high-ranking friends at Pershing's headquarters—
men he had met while studying at Leavenworth. Matters worsened when General George Duncan, leading one of III Corps'
divisions, disclosed to Bullard that Bjornstad was issuing orders
without the corps commander's knowledge. Surprisingly, Bullard
took no immediate action other than advising Duncan to ignore
"damn fool" orders from headquarters until they were confirmed
personally by Bullard.[18]

The first open clash between the two headstrong officers occurred in late August, when Bullard was ordered by his French commander—the bluff General Jean Degoutte—to defend a fingernail-thin bridgehead at Fismette, directly across the Vesle River from the larger village of Fismes. Degoutte hoped to expand the slim position by shoving the Germans back, and Bullard readily agreed in keeping with his aggressive philosophy. The bridgehead, however, was exposed to heavy artillery and machine-gun fire from surrounding hills, and all efforts to expand the bridgehead were rebuffed by the Germans, whose intense fire picked off the Yanks one by one and forced survivors to huddle in cellars. After several weeks of grim attrition, the Americans began to hear noises from the German line portending an attack, and they appealed for permission to withdraw. "No Retreat" Bullard did not relish the notion of a withdrawal under any circumstances, but he surveyed the situation on August 18 and returned to his command post professing his intent to disobey Degoutte's instructions on maintaining the bridgehead.[19] When Bullard arrived at headquarters, however, he had a surprise waiting for him. He had been one-upped by Bjornstad. As Bullard explained later:

> My chief-of-staff, who was very much in favor of the French general's idea of "bridgeheads," knew of the order which I was going to give. When I returned from Fismes late in the afternoon, I found the French general at my corps headquarters and learned that my chief-of-staff had informed him of my order to withdraw the company. The French army commander ordered me at once to replace it. This was done.[20]

Bullard's humiliation stung, especially because it came at the hands of his subordinate. Worse was to come. In a predawn attack on August 27, the Germans dispatched a fierce *Stosstruppen* unit armed with flamethrowers, submachine guns, and demolition charges to wipe out the bridgehead. Only thirty-nine of two hundred Yanks escaped with their lives. Bullard wrote a strong letter informing Pershing of Degoutte's intervention but did not mention Bjornstad's role in the matter. There is evidence that the incident might have occasioned a negative report that the corps commander placed in his chief of staff's file—a document that hung over Bjornstad's head as a perpetual warning against repetition of the behavior.[21]

Bullard's mild response to Bjornstad's insubordination is puzzling. Allan Millett—the corps commander's biographer—concluded that Bullard's restraint arose from fear of the possible repercussions from "his chief of staff's Leavenworth friends at AEF headquarters."[22] Having just been awarded command of III Corps, Bullard could not risk alienating the headquarters officers he called the "Leavenworth clique," a group known to exercise great influence over Pershing's personnel decisions. The Leavenworth graduates had helped select Bjornstad as chief of staff before naming Bullard commander, ensuring that the Minnesotan's allegiance would be to those at headquarters. Requesting Bjornstad's relief, Bullard recognized, might raise questions about his own fitness for command, just as he was recovering from severe stomach problems and an attack of neuritis that nearly paralyzed his right side. During the time that Bullard was hospitalized for these ailments, Pershing had shielded his old friend from officers calling for a medical review of the general's physical fitness. Best not to rock the boat under such circumstances. But the uneasy truce between the III Corps commander and his chief of staff would disrupt their working relationship as the AEF prepared for St. Mihiel and the Meuse-Argonne.

In addition to Bullard's and Bjornstad's mutually exclusive claims to independence of judgment, another factor complicated their relationship. Both generals harbored a mean streak, a vein of malice just below the surface of their personalities. When malice was aggravated by anger—as was often the case with Bjornstad—eruptions could be spectacular.

In 1898 Bjornstad enlisted as a private in the 13th Minnesota Volunteer Infantry, a unit federalized during the Spanish-American War. The 13th was sent to the Philippines and with two other regiments formed the Manila Provost Guard, which fought insurgents infiltrating the city. Before long, Bjornstad's intelligence and leadership won him a battlefield commission as a captain, commanding Company H. When the new officer began to exercise his authority, the soldiers discovered that their commander was a strict disciplinarian, inflexible and unyielding. Being volunteers and not professional soldiers, the men complained vociferously about their officious captain.

One day as the 13th's company commanders assembled for a conference in Bjornstad's second-story office, a loud voice floated through the open window from a courtyard below: "If I could catch him without those shoulder straps, I would show him!"[23] Sensing that the comment was about him, Bjornstad dashed downstairs immediately, as the other officers moved to a balcony off the office. They saw the captain stride into the courtyard, where a group of his enlisted men had congregated.

"Who was that? Who said he would like to catch me without my shoulder straps?" Bjornstad demanded. As the men hemmed, hawed, and shuffled their feet, the captain singled out a soldier: "Did you make that statement?"

"Yes," the man replied. "I guess so."

With that, Bjornstad stripped off his tunic and said, "I'll just give you a chance. I've just taken off the straps, and nothing will be said about this. Come on, one at a time."

The man rushed the captain, who knocked him flat. Bjornstad stood back and taunted, "Come on. Who's next?" to which there was no response. "If you won't come one at a time, I'll take two or three of you, or all of you." But the fight was over; the men were thoroughly cowed.[24]

Although the soldiers of Company H despised their captain, they had to admit that he was a courageous fighter. On August 13,

1898, Bjornstad rushed from his headquarters to direct an attack against insurgents. He was quickly wounded in the shoulder but grabbed a rifle and shouted, "I'm going to get that guy." Before he could respond, he was shot again but continued shouting encouragement to his troops until he was carried away. Afterward, Bjornstad was reported killed in action. When the news made its way back to Minnesota, St. Olaf College dipped its flag to half-staff for three days in honor of its late student. A short time later, as the happy correction that Bjornstad had survived came over the wires, there were cheers all around.[25] For extraordinary heroism, "Wild Bill" Bjornstad—as he soon came to be known—was awarded the Distinguished Service Cross.

While Bjornstad recuperated in a Manila hospital, however, rumors circulated that both his wounds came from behind. The incident might have been an attempt at what has come to be known as "fragging": the assassination of a disliked officer by his own troops. To dispel the rumors, the captain's defenders countered that at least one of the bullets was from a Mauser rifle, a weapon commonly used by the Spanish and the Filipinos.[26] Whatever the truth, there is little doubt that the captain was cordially disliked—if not hated—by his troops. This was made clear by events occurring on the 13th Minnesota's return to the United States.

The volunteer regiment was mustered out of federal service in San Francisco, and as the men rode the train back to Minneapolis, they were civilians, no longer subject to orders. By telegram, the veterans received an invitation from their governor, John Lind, to participate in a grand homecoming celebration. The men would march through their hometown streets, under a specially constructed triumphal arch, and to a building where they would be greeted by the nation's commander in chief, President William McKinley. Still resentful of Bjornstad's autocratic ways, however, the men of Company H rebelled: "If he is going to march, we will not march." To resolve the impasse, Bjornstad agreed to follow the lengthy regimental column, while his company of blue-clad troops was led by a subordinate.[27]

The insult apparently had little impact on Bjornstad's career, as he was soon awarded a commission in the Regular Army, and returned to the Philippines to fight the Moro Insurrection. His rise to prominence began when he was selected for Fort Leavenworth's School of the Line, from which he graduated first in his class and posted the highest score recorded by any student to that time.[28] Afterward, Bjornstad was assigned as military attaché in Berlin, and wrote treatises on German army methods, military preparedness, and infantry tactics cited throughout the army.

Over time, Bjornstad established a reputation for writing, planning, and teaching; when the AEF landed in France, he was destined for a significant post. In line with his expertise, the newly minted lieutenant colonel was assigned to develop the General Staff School in the town of Langres to educate junior officers chosen for higher AEF command. "He was excellent, and no one doubted it, but his personality was that of a professor addressing obtuse students," James Cooke observed.[29] This abrasive demeanor dominated Bjornstad's personality, and he quickly became known as an officer who did not tolerate fools gladly, whatever rank they might hold.

Although the length of time allotted for officers to attend Bjornstad's school was foreshortened by the pressing demand for graduates, most agreed that Bjornstad had done a remarkable job. His performance attracted the admiration of headquarters, won him an assignment as chief of staff of III Corps, and secured him a promotion to brigadier general. During World War I, Bjornstad's rapid advancement through the ranks was equaled by only one other officer, General Douglas MacArthur.[30]

As successful as Bjornstad was, however, his imperious behavior continued to cause trouble. Several generals—including Pershing's close friend General James Harbord—complained about Bjornstad's abrasiveness, but in the busy days of 1917 and 1918, there was little time to address personality flaws.[31] As the

AEF prepared for the final offensive, Bjornstad moved upward, leaving a list of alienated army officers behind him.

"Wild Bill" Bjornstad's rage usually found expression in physical or psychological brawls, but Robert Bullard's malice assumed a more stealthy form. The wily general had long since learned that he could best accomplish his ends by mounting subtle campaigns against his enemies, who—if Bullard were especially skillful—would be disposed of by others. Ambition and envy were the prime movers of Bullard's aggression, as would become obvious in the case of his fellow Alabaman William L. Sibert, who graduated from West Point in 1884 and joined the Corps of Engineers.

Before the AEF moved to Europe, Sibert and Bullard were both considered for positions in the 1st Division. Competition was fierce for the prestigious posts, because the officer corps had long been starved for opportunities for advancement. In the process, Sibert won the top spot of divisional commander, while Bullard was assigned to command the division's second brigade. The appointment of Sibert, an engineer, to lead the most prominent division in the Regular Army—the Big Red One—raised eyebrows throughout the service and was especially galling to Bullard, who was skeptical of any officer from a service branch appointed to line command. Sibert had served all but six years of his career in the engineers and had been promoted to the rank of general by a special act of Congress—a reward for having helped construct the Panama Canal. The extraordinary promotion exposed Sibert to the same type of envy that AEF commander Pershing had encountered in 1911 when he was advanced from his captaincy to a generalship by President Theodore Roosevelt.

"As compared with his future generals, colonels, and even other field officers, [Sibert] had little experience in the command of troops," observed Bullard, with an eye jaundiced by envy. "I doubted the wisdom of his selection. . . . Getting so you can understand 'em [enlisted men] may, of course, come to an officer by the gift of God: but generally it does not. In the main it comes from experience with soldiers, rarely in any other way. General Sibert had not had that experience."[32]

According to Bullard, signs of Sibert's unfitness for duty appeared even before the division sailed for France. Incensed that Sibert was not in New York to oversee embarkation, Bullard noted that confusion reigned: "Men were sent to ships unprepared to receive them. Supplies were piled in pell-mell. Many had to be unloaded. Some ships received too many troops, some too few, and had to be changed . . . But the troops all got aboard *somehow*. That is all one can say—somehow."[33]

Shortly after Bullard arrived in France, Pershing appointed him to a staff position to establish a series of army training schools, a pet project of the AEF commander. The post gave the Alabaman ready access to Pershing, as the two met to develop plans for the facilities. In a few months, the first schools were up and running efficiently and their enrollments swelled with each new transport. Bullard, however, reported to Pershing that there was resistance to his efforts to train AEF troops; not surprisingly, one prominent source was the 1st Division commander, who felt that his troops should proceed immediately to the front. Bullard wrote later:

> The division commander and many of his officers seemed to regard the school idea as puerility, a fad of schoolmen; very troublesome and irritating at a time when everybody was getting ready to fight. These ideas remained among Americans until they had seen real war at the front. Then every commander wanted officers and men who had been through the schools. The demand for school instruction soon became so great that it could not be met.[34]

Sibert's carping was no doubt reported to Pershing, probably with the interpretation that the resistance betrayed a desire to avoid regulations. Shortly thereafter, the 1st Division commander compounded his error by complaining to Pershing that Bullard was taking away too many of his men.

During the same period, pressure was mounting on Sibert to
get his outfit in shape. Pershing took a special interest in the 1st
Division and expected its soldiers to meet high standards. On his
first inspection, the AEF commander found that the officers and
men were not measuring up, and he turned the full glare of his
attention on the unit. When Pershing returned a few weeks later,
he pointedly invited Bullard to accompany him for the review,
which was an utter disaster. Sibert became ill in front of the AEF
commander and could not recover to conduct a planned tour of
the encampment, which Bullard volunteered to lead. On October 3, as Pershing returned to observe an exercise, the division's
training appeared to be improving. But the AEF commander surprised Sibert by calling on him to assess the various elements of
the infantry demonstration. The divisional commander fumbled
the critique, revealing a thin understanding of the "open warfare"
principles Pershing was pushing troops to master. In front of the
entire divisional staff, Pershing dressed down the hapless Sibert
in a move that effectively destroyed his ability to command.

Throughout the fall of 1917, Bullard was a general without
a command, an officer-in-waiting. He inspected army schools
and visited frontline French troops to study combat techniques.
Pershing clearly had bigger plans for his old friend, who played
the patient courtier at headquarters. Bullard's safe position in the
wings presented numerous opportunities for him to speak con-
fidentially with the AEF commander about personnel matters,
including Bullard's conviction that engineering officers should
not command combat troops. A few months later, this belief led
Bullard to replace an engineer commanding an artillery unit. "To
go to war with such an artillery commander, however able an engineer," said Bullard, "would have been a crime against the men
whose lives were entrusted to me."[35] The statement provides a
gloss on Sibert's perilous position in the 1st Division, and likely
echoes the advice Bullard conveyed to Pershing.

The fall months at headquarters also gave Bullard an excellent opportunity to turn a critical eye on his commanding officer. Even as the southern general waited hopefully for the American chief to grant an expected promotion, he confided to his diary a startling conclusion: "Our General Pershing is not a fighter; he is in all his history a pacifist and, unless driven thereto by the A.E.F., will do no fighting in many a day . . . He is a worldly-wise, extremely ambitious, and confidence-inspiring man, but not a warrior."[36] After the Armistice, Bullard conceded that his judgment had been mistaken, but he undercut the admission by publishing it *and the original charge* in his memoir—a strangely ambivalent way to pay his former commander a compliment.

Bullard's disenchantment with Pershing did not keep him from responding to a call from headquarters on October 20, when the AEF chief confided that he intended to relieve Sibert. He was considering Bullard as his replacement. On December 8 the two spoke again about the matter, but Pershing did not act until a week later, when Sibert was replaced by the newly promoted *Major General* Bullard.

Some historians doubt that Bullard nudged Pershing toward relieving Sibert, but a critical passage from the general's memoir dispels that generous but mistaken assessment. In describing the formative days of the AEF, Bullard recalled,

> In all these preparations, there were some failures. Two brigadier generals and one major general who were slow and unenergetic or careless, who were not impressed by their responsibilities in preparation, shortly lost their commands upon my recommendation; and later, in battle, I know of two other major generals who lost theirs in other corps near me. [37]

In addition to confirming Bullard's role in Sibert's demise, Bullard's gratuitous boast also explains what happened to General Cameron following V Corps' delay in taking Montfaucon, and provides a glimpse of the lengths to which Bullard was prepared to go to fulfill his ambition. Offered without apparent insight into what it revealed about himself, this testimony discloses that Bullard—like his chief of staff—left a long line of bodies on his climb to the AEF pinnacle.

The generals whose demise Bullard plotted paid for their failings with their careers; the soldiers that Bullard led often paid for his ambition with their lives. Historian Edward Lengel has demonstrated the high human cost of such actions in the attack on Cantigny and the bridgehead at Fismette.[38] Bullard's willingness to order his troops into difficult assaults against fortified positions was well recognized and admired by AEF leaders. Pershing knew when he ordered Bullard to attack, the assault would be pressed with vigor and without regard for cost. Perhaps the best example is the Armistice-morning attack Bullard made special arrangements to witness.

Like other US generals, Bullard received advanced news of the Armistice, but in keeping with Pershing's orders, he directed his men to use the last minutes of the war to assault powerful German positions along the Moselle River. Bullard was so enthusiastic about the attack that he made a special trip forward to witness what he described as the "occasion of great history and great happening. Our men showed great zest in the striking of the last blows against the enemy."[39]

Although Bullard was clearly gratified by the aggressiveness of his troops, he was quite angry the following day when he learned that the final combat communiqué from AEF headquarters did not give "*my* army much credit for its effort yesterday. I felt that it was—and so, on inquiry, it turned out to be—the fault of our own [Second] Army's too modest report. I was out of patience to see that on its last day's fighting *my* army did not get the credit for what it had done, so I 'blew up' the people who had failed to report correctly" (emphasis added).[40]

Putting this episode in brutal perspective, Alden Brooks, a former American journalist who volunteered as an officer in the

French artillery, recorded his own observations on Bullard's callous disregard for his doughboys:

> Although the General held in his hand at 6:30 a.m. the official announcement that the Armistice was signed and that the territory his men were attacking would be surrendered to them outright at 11:00, he not only let many of them go to their death in that attack but also went out there himself near front lines to watch them.[41]

Bullard was not alone. On the final morning of the war, enthusiastic attacks by Pershing's generals may have enhanced reputations, but they also resulted in the needless death of approximately 320 American soldiers, and the wounding of thousands more.[42]

Ambition, malice, envy: as Ewing Booth initiated his postwar investigation into the actions of "No Retreat" Bullard and "Wild Bill" Bjornstad, he well understood the status these officers had achieved. He knew that as the two men faced the stiffest challenge of their careers on September 26, 1918, they carried a great deal of personal baggage onto the muddy Meuse-Argonne battlefield. Their obsessions were so powerful that they distracted the officers' focus on the task at hand: working with their peers, subordinates, and even the "Leavenworth clique" at headquarters to develop a smooth-working machine that would roll quickly over the Germans and sweep on north to cut the rail line at Sedan.

As cliquish as Pershing's staff officers might have been, their Leavenworth experience helped them develop a valuable trait that many headstrong generals of the "old army" never acquired. Staff College graduates learned that *teamwork* was a key element of military success. It was drummed into their core as an essential factor that would enable them to implement complex maneuvers depending on close cooperation with sister units and other combat arms, such as artillery, engineers, tanks, and the air service. Teamwork among these assets is a "force multiplier"—to adopt a modern concept—a powerful catalyst enabling military units to accomplish much more working together than the sum of what they could achieve individually.

This lesson from World War I was so important that future US Army chief of staff George Marshall insisted that a commitment to teamwork was an indispensable characteristic for those he selected to lead the army in World War II. According to military analyst Thomas Ricks, Marshall was leery of individualistic officers like "the brawler and the adventurous cavalryman," epitomized by Confederate generals Jeb Stuart and Thomas "Stonewall" Jackson.[43]

> In contrast to those two latter-day cavaliers, Marshall called for steady, levelheaded *team players*. He wanted both competence and cooperativeness. The biggest difference between American commanders in World War I and World War II would be that in the latter war, they were adept at coordinating the efforts of infantry, artillery, armor, and aviation branches, especially in breaking through and then exploiting that penetration.[44]

The lessons that George Marshall learned in attempting to direct the individualistic generals of the Meuse-Argonne paid dividends in the 1940s at places such as Omaha Beach, Saint-Lô, and Bastogne. But the battles of World War II lay far in the future as the First Army prepared to assault the Hindenburg Line in 1918. To pierce the fortifications and exploit the penetration as Pershing hoped, AEF headquarters needed to rein in freelancers such as Bullard and Bjornstad—men who were willing to sacrifice coordination for independence, cooperation for competition, and even victory for ambition. Inclinations like these led directly to their betrayal of the 79th Division at Little Gibraltar.

CHAPTER 20

BETRAYAL AT LITTLE GIBRALTAR

Following the Armistice, the expansive ego of Robert Bullard nettled
his old commander, Pershing, who called attention to the Alabaman appearing
"in all his glory" in a cigarette advertisement. For this mercenary act,
Bullard reaped the scorn of former comrades.

★   ★   ★

The truth about the war, when it is written, will
please neither pacifist nor militarist; neither preacher
nor business man; but it may help free them from
errors long deluding.

—Henry Seidel Canby,
American commentator, 1919[1]

Two days before the start of the Meuse-Argonne Offensive, the last thing that "Wild Bill" Bjornstad expected was a grammar lesson. Nearly overwhelmed by details of the massive operation, the III Corps chief of staff had a great deal more to do than debate the fine points of English. But that is exactly what his commanding officer, Major General Robert Bullard, had in mind as the two prepared to go over plans that Bjornstad had developed to carry out the First Army's attack orders.

Well aware that he was under scrutiny because of undercutting Bullard's orders at Fismette, Bjornstad prepared meticulously for the briefing. In accordance with Bullard's wishes, the chief of staff had already held a major conference with divisional commanders, chiefs of staff, and regimental commanders to review First Army orders. One of the few substantive questions that arose during the meeting was voiced by the 4th Division chief of staff, Colonel C. A. Bach, who asked what was meant by the First Army order for the III Corps to "turn" Montfaucon. Was the 4th Division expected to make a flank attack on the butte from its own zone or cross into the V Corps zone to envelop the position from the rear?[2]

Several officers who were present at the conference recalled that Bjornstad had replied without hesitation: the order called for the 4th to envelop the butte by entering the zone of operation of V Corps.[3] Once the rear of the hill was encircled, the Germans would surrender or die, the observatory would fall, the German artillery would be blinded. Then the First Army could advance unhindered by the "hostile observation" that prompted headquarters to name Little Gibraltar as the primary objective of both V Corps and III Corps, acting in support.[4]

The order for "turning" the butte made immediate sense to Bjornstad, because it was one of the standard maneuvers he had studied at Leavenworth. The fact that the orders featured a turning maneuver also explained why the 4th Division—the most experienced of the nine in the attack—had been assigned the sector just to the right of the 79th. In the lightly fortified zone, the veteran 4th was positioned to dash by Montfaucon to envelop the fortress. After Bjornstad discussed these features of the attack, Bach and his colleagues were dismissed to write orders for their particular divisions, documents to be examined by Bjornstad and then forwarded to First Army headquarters for review by Pershing's chief of operations, Colonel Robert McCleave.

After the conference with divisional staffs on September 23, Bjornstad's next step was briefing his commander on what had been decided by his subordinates, normally a routine exercise followed by pro forma approval. The chief of staff was confident of his preparation, as he arrived at Bullard's office to lay out maps that indicated how the three divisions of III Corps would pierce the German line. In fact, Bjornstad might have been a bit cocky as he pointed out topographic features and enemy fortifications to his superior officer, whom he considered his inferior in preparing orders in precise Leavenworth style.

To the equally self-confident Bullard, the setup was perfect. In fact, he likely watched with amusement as his chief of staff marched into the trap. As Bjornstad began to discuss the order for the envelopment of Montfaucon, the general interrupted to propose a different interpretation of the First Army order.

General Bullard "pointed out that it [the order] did not necessarily mean 'to penetrate promptly the hostile second position and be in position to turn Montfaucon, etc., and to do so if necessary,' but it might mean merely that 'if the Third Corps promptly penetrated the hostile second position, [then] Montfaucon, etc., will automatically be turned, and the Seventy-Ninth Division will thereby be assisted, etc.' "[5] Bjornstad described this key conversation with Bullard in a 1924 letter composed in response to Colonel Bach's questions about Montfaucon.[6] In this lengthy missive, which became a critical part of Booth's file, Bjornstad undercut the validity of Bullard's alternate interpretation: "I believe we had no doubt it meant the former [an envelopment] and my recollection is that it looked like a Third Corps job to initiate it."[7]

Bullard and Bjornstad might have agreed tacitly that the orders called for an encirclement by their corps, but their subsequent actions demonstrate that their commitment to follow that order was nonexistent. By the time Bjornstad was briefing Bullard on the plans, 4th Division chief of staff Bach had already drafted and submitted for Bjornstad's review an order based on the conference of the previous day. According to Bach, that order

> read, in effect, that the 4th Division would assist the progression of the division on its left by an envelopment of Montfaucon from the north and east. The paragraph was disapproved at Corps Headquarters and the Division Commander was directed to operate only in his own divisional area and to rewrite his order to show this fact.[8]

According to Bach, the offending paragraph was "rewritten to suit the Corps Commander [Bullard]," a fact that incensed senior officers in the division, including Booth and his fellow brigade commander, Benjamin Poore.[9]

Grammarians would acknowledge that the prepositional phrase at the beginning of the First Army order provides opportunity for mischief. Someone with the requisite verbal agility and a desire to obfuscate *could* use the phrase to misinterpret the order. Apparently Bullard was a wizard at grammatical gymnastics, as his deceitful misinterpretation demonstrates. But there was never cause for confusion. Language appearing later in the

same sentence makes its meaning absolutely clear: the III Corps
is ordered to move "into the section of the hostile second position *within the zone of action of the V Corps*" and to assist in the
capture of "the hostile second position *west of Montfaucon*"—in
other words, on the far side of the butte (emphasis added).[10] The
only way the 4th Division could satisfy these specifications was
by enveloping the rear of Montfaucon. To underscore the importance of the maneuver, the First Army listed the envelopment
first among the five missions of Bullard's III Corps; pushing the
attack toward the Kriemhilde Stellung, the German main line of
resistance, is listed third, to be accomplished once Montfaucon's
hostile observation had been eliminated.[11]

The Two Orders

Original First Army Order to III Corps

D. The III Corps [Including 4th Division on the left]
Mission:
  (a) By promptly penetrating the hostile second position
      it will turn Montfaucon and the section of the hos-
      tile second position within the zone of action of the
      V Corps, thereby assisting the capture of the hostile
      second position west of Montfaucon.

Order Rewritten to Conform to Bullard's Wishes

The 4th Division will push its attack vigorously, regardless of the
advance of the divisions on its right and left . . . The Division will
assist (if necessary) the Division [on] its left by turning MONT-
FAUCON; not by advance into the area of the division on its
left but by steady progression to the front and energetic action
by the left combat liaison group or by reserves, against hostile
detachments on the left flank.[12]

By specifically ordering III Corps to enter the "zone of action of the V Corps," the First Army order eliminates any question about whether the 4th Division was to cross corps boundaries to conduct the turning maneuver. Moreover, V Corps had been warned about the possibility of III Corps troops operating in its front. Shortly after the attack, however, some III Corps officers claimed speciously that AEF tactical doctrine forbade incursions into other units' zones of action. That false impression was specifically put to rest by Pershing's memorandum of October 1, 1918, ordering cooperative maneuvers between units. Moreover, Colonel R. T. Ward of First Army headquarters discussed the issue after the war and stated, "These lines [boundaries] were intended to show the Army conception of the maneuver and were not intended to act as barriers between corps and divisions and thus limit their operations and prevent lateral movement."[13] Regardless of any possible misconception, Bjornstad's testimony demonstrates that Bullard understood the First Army order but deliberately chose to disobey.

The appropriate course of action for commanders encountering ambiguous orders was, of course, to seek clarification. There is no record of any such request from III Corps, and the revised 4th Division orders—rewritten to Bullard's specifications—were forwarded to First Army headquarters. Unfortunately, the officer at headquarters responsible for identifying mistakes—Colonel McCleave or a member of his planning and operations staff—either failed to review the order before the attack or did not notice the discrepancy between the First Army order and that of the 4th Division.

Bullard underscored the import of the rewritten portion of the order in his talk with divisional staffs on the eve of battle. The men of the 4th Division heard sounds of intense combat coming from the 79th's assault on Montfaucon and knew that their comrades were being slaughtered, but because they had been warned to ignore such circumstances by their corps commander, they drove blindly forward in their easy sector. In the words of Bullard biographer Allan Millett, the III Corps advance was little more than a "dangerous hike," with the assault brigade reporting only a single casualty during the entire morning.[14]

As I Corps experienced difficulty in the dense Argonne Forest and V Corps stalled in front of Montfaucon, III Corps rejected the order to turn Little Gibraltar and continued straight forward. The corps commander must have been gratified when he learned of the *New York Times* headline proclaiming "Bullard's Troops Did It."[15] Because of the intense pressure of events and the inevitable confusion that descended on the battlefield after the first cannon was fired, no one from First Army headquarters recognized that III Corps troops had not turned Montfaucon until it was much too late.

The question that hangs over this disastrous episode is Bullard's motivation in purposefully disobeying orders. It might have been prompted by the III Corps commander's experience in the old army, in which there were a few simple tactics: go directly toward the enemy as fast as you can and go with as much force as you can muster. This notion was famously articulated by Civil War general Nathan Bedford Forrest in his advice to get there "the first with the most men," or as some prefer, "the firstest with the mostest."[16] Often cited at West Point, this whimsical adage made perfect sense on the western plains, where mounted Native Americans or Mexican bandits could slip away as quickly as they appeared.

But Bullard extended the dictum a war too far. On the modern battlefields of France, artillery and machine guns destroyed charging attackers before they could reach the enemy. The French—and later the German *Stosstruppen*—had proved that indirection and infiltration around strongpoints were the most successful methods of assaulting fortifications, which could be destroyed more safely by skirting the flanks and attacking the enemy from the rear. These tactics, however, failed to satisfy Bullard's heroic vision of spirited troops marching in waves.

As usual, Bullard personalized the tactical issue. According to Millett, the general complained about "his officers' tendency to plan attacks which put a premium on exotic envelopments and complex coordination. He diagnosed the disease as Leavenworthitis. Army officers, [Bullard] mused, had learned so much tactical theory that they forgot that 'somebody has to take the enemy head on.'"[17]

A "head-on" American attack on the Hindenburg Line would be the perfect opportunity to prove the "textbook warriors" of Leavenworth wrong. By declining to envelop Montfaucon, Bullard would gain freedom of action to move smartly through his weak sector, smash the Kriemhilde Stellung, and demonstrate the ageless validity of old-army tactics. The Leavenworth boys, including Bullard's own chief of staff, would be left holding a useless bag of complex maneuvers, while he captured the distinction of advancing the farthest on the first day of battle.

Although the "Leavenworth clique" was clearly in the back of Bullard's mind, there are strong indications that the general's malice might have had an even finer point. Speculation was rife that Pershing would soon surrender one of his two responsibilities: he was then serving concurrently as commander of the AEF and commander of the First US Army. Every week, more American troops were landing in France; there were already enough divisions to form two armies. Senior officers had begun to speculate about who would win the assignments when Pershing stepped back to devote his full time to being AEF commander. Only two of Pershing's three corps commanders in the Meuse-Argonne Offensive would earn command of a US Army and the coveted three stars accompanying those assignments. Because Commander Hunter Liggett of I Corps had the longest corps experience, he was considered a shoo-in for one spot. That left Bullard and George Cameron, commander of V Corps, contesting for the second slot. Each had just been appointed to corps commands, so the jury was still out as to whom would be selected. The Meuse-Argonne Offensive would decide the matter, and one historian believes that "Pershing may have used the vacancy to prod his corps commanders."[18]

To vault himself into stronger contention, Bullard would have to achieve spectacular success in the Meuse-Argonne, but the battle plan developed by First Army staff had lifted the bar for the corps commander. He had been given a weak sector through which to advance, while Cameron had been given the "honor" of attacking Little Gibraltar of the Western Front. Moreover, the order for Bullard's best division to assist Cameron's troops by turning Montfaucon placed III Corps in a position subordinate to the untrained troops charging up the face of the butte. One of 4th Division's senior officers put the dilemma succinctly: "Well, if we put everything over all right, the 79th will get all the credit. If not, we get all the blame."[19]

On the other hand, if Cameron's V Corps were held up in front of Montfaucon's strong defenses while the III Corps sailed smoothly through its sector, the limelight would shine on Bullard.

A month before the Meuse-Argonne Offensive was launched, the III Corps commander began to focus his attention on the officer whom he considered his prime competitor—much as he had earlier fixed his scrutiny on General William Sibert. As might be expected, he found George Cameron's performance lacking. When the St. Mihiel operation began on September 12, just as the Germans were preparing to withdraw from the salient, First Army had an opportunity to trap retreating enemy troops by closing pincers around the neck of the salient. One of the pincers was V Corps led by Cameron, whose troops did not move swiftly enough to close the gap and bag the retreating Germans. Under pressure from headquarters, he issued several strongly worded messages urging a more vigorous advance. Hawkeyed Bullard, however, discerned that Pershing "himself was the driving power behind this corrective effort; and that he finally ordered the Vth Corps to have one regiment in [the town of] Hattonchattel by dawn" to close the trap's jaws on September 13.[20] Because Cameron did not move quickly enough, an estimated 80 percent of the enemy troops escaped. Paying special attention to this unhappy outcome, Bullard noted that "the Commander-in-Chief, in citations and dispatches, praised Liggett's [I] Corps and Dickman's [IV Corps], but not the Vth [Cameron's corps]."[21]

On September 26, as action shifted from St. Mihiel to the Meuse-Argonne, Bullard began to barrage First Army headquarters with complaints about V Corps' lack of progress. Because Cameron failed to capture the observatory on schedule, the 4th Division's flank was exposed to fierce enemy fire, Bullard carped. Knowing that the best defense against being blamed for a debacle is complaining about someone else, Bullard fired off notes to the First Army, V Corps, and the 79th Division criticizing the slowness of Cameron's assault and the way it was retarding his own corps.[22] By pleading that V Corps' failure to keep pace was hampering III Corps, Bullard was employing exactly the same excuse that he had barred his own divisional commanders from using at their conference on the eve of battle: that an adjacent unit was slowing his advance. The irony of the situation, however, was lost on the pompous general.

Later—after the drive had stalled and Pershing directed corps commanders to undertake cooperative maneuvers—Bullard claimed,

> I had in vain tried to induce the General commanding the Vth Corps to take concerted action with me in order to unite our two flanks. My left flank remained for days in the air, catching a deadly fire from our left front. This fire caused steady losses among my front-line troops in the Bois de Fay, whose southern edge was being swept by a terrible machine-gun fire from the enemy on both the right and the left flank.[23]

There is no record of Bullard's attempt to communicate with Cameron on this matter, but Bullard complained to Pershing about his rival's unresponsiveness. To appear evenhanded, Bullard praised V Corps' 79th and 37th Divisions for "proving their courage and will: where there was fault, it was with the leadership rather than the men."[24]

Bullard's decision to disobey the order to turn Montfaucon was taken not in the heat of battle—when it might have been argued that some exigency had compelled it—but during the planning phase of the offensive, following careful consideration. After the decision was made, news of Bullard's unusual interpretation of the envelopment order circulated broadly through III Corps and the 4th Division; officers immediately grasped the grim implications for their V Corps comrades. Because the intervention of the corps commander was unusual and the incident took place in the calm before the battle, the discussions that changed the order were remembered with clarity by those who participated: Bjornstad, Bach, Booth, Poore, and other senior officers.

After the offensive's first shot was fired, however, confusion reigned on the Meuse-Argonne battlefield. Unanticipated dangers quickly emerged, flurries of new orders flew from headquarters, priorities were shuffled or forgotten, and danger imperiled everyone. The pressure of events frazzled the nerves of those trying to direct troop movement, as they began to work around the clock to oversee assignments. Taken together, these elements generated the notorious psychological fog, a state in which emotions run high, judgment diminishes, memories dull, and nerves are on edge. All these maladies are apparent in the testimony that Booth assembled to determine what happened on the afternoon of the first day of battle. A few letters contradict one another, the timing of events is sometimes confused, and the actions of various individuals are disputed—much as they had been on the day of battle.

Despite the muddled thoughts and strong emotions, one fact was abundantly clear in the late morning of September 26: the 79th Division was stalled in front of Montfaucon. As Ewing Booth led his reserve brigade just east of the 79th, he heard heavy sounds of battle, fierce volleys of artillery fire, and the clattering of countless machine guns to the left. He knew that the "right regiment [the 314th] of the Fifth Corps, which was attacking Montfaucon, was meeting intense resistance."[25] Following Bullard's strict orders, the assault brigade of the 4th Division had already surged beyond the butte and was continuing northward, ignoring the destruction of the 79th and the imperative to take Montfaucon. But to one who had started his career as a rifleman like Booth, the ordeal the 79th was experiencing was unconscionable.

When Booth met with the 4th's commanding officer, General John Hines, in the midafternoon, he proposed an innovative solution: that Hines direct the 8th Brigade to move up abreast and left of the assault brigade and slash westward behind the butte to join the 37th Division to turn the strong enemy position.[26] Hines, who also had learned of Bullard's disheartening decision to forgo the envelopment, knew that he could not undertake such a movement without permission of III Corps headquarters, where it would come under Bullard's review. Hines was properly pessimistic about winning approval, but when he called headquarters, he encountered a stroke of luck: the corps commander had departed on horseback to witness the exciting advance of his troops at the front.[27] Bjornstad was in command.

The circumstances put the chief of staff in a tough situation: He knew that III Corps had disobeyed First Army orders to turn Montfaucon, but Bjornstad was on a short leash for acting behind Bullard's back at Fismette. Approving Hines's suggestion could be fatal to his career. Bjornstad might have considered pleading his case to Bullard based on the exigencies of battle, and he knew that he could also rely on the support of his friends at First Army and AEF headquarters, who would be furious about Bullard's disobedience. Mustering his courage, Bjornstad authorized the move and promised to have the III Corps reserve division—the veteran 3rd—come forward to backstop the operation.[28] The chief of staff told Hines to draft an order for his review, and the 4th Division commander directed Booth "to move out without delay with your brigade."[29]

By approximately 3:30 p.m., Hines received the approved order from III Corps headquarters: "The division on your left is held up by MONTFAUCON. Therefore in order to assist their progression you will send out strong patrols to the west to seize strongpoints in that division's area . . . ."[30] Bjornstad hedged his bet by weakening the order's language, but Hines bravely strengthened the mission in his message to Booth:

> Pursuant to verbal instructions Commanding General III Army Corps, the 8th Infantry Brigade will proceed with all possible speed via HAUCOURT—CUISY—CUNEL and take up a position on the American Army Objective and establish a line of outposts along the general line CUNEL—BATHEVILLE— ROMAGNE, establishing liaison with the 7th Infantry Brigade on the right, the center division of the V Army Corps on the left and the 79th Division in its rear.[31]

Hines's order envisions the strong teamwork among corps and divisions that the "Leavenworth clique" sought to foster in the First Army and the AEF. Working together, the 4th, 79th, and 37th Divisions might have enveloped Montfaucon from the east and the west and swept on to pierce the dreaded Kriemhilde Stellung at Cunel. Had these objectives been attained on September 26 or even early on September 27, they would have realized Pershing's dream: a breakthrough into the open country north of the German main line of resistance. Thanks to the initiative of Booth and Hines, the First Army could have earned the "more glorious victory" that Drum spoke of at Fort Leavenworth.

The odds against success were long. It was already late afternoon, and night assaults are often doomed to failure; Booth's brigade was still south of the point of the planned attack; and many roads were destroyed. Finally, the Germans were beginning to rouse themselves from the shock of the assault; reinforcements were on their way to strengthen the Kriemhilde Stellung. These factors argue that Booth's *belated* turning maneuver likely would have failed. But the sad truth is that the 8th Brigade was not allowed to complete the maneuver.

Someone at III Corps headquarters rescinded the order for an envelopment, but uncertainty remains about the identity of that person. Several historians argue that it was Bjornstad, but that interpretation makes little sense given the circumstances. The chief of staff had previously approved the move *in writing*. Even if he had rescinded the order in hopes of avoiding Bullard's ire, he could not have denied responsibility for issuing the written order. A belated recension would have done little to defuse the commanding officer's anger.

Those who blame Bjornstad for countermanding the order argue that the chief of staff's motivation was his supposed reluctance to cross corps and divisional boundaries. In 1924, however, when Colonel Bach wrote to ask Bjornstad about the Montfaucon debacle, he strongly denied that charge. To bolster his point, Bjornstad cited several instances throughout his career when he willingly crossed lines when necessary, and argued forcefully that such movements were well within his tactical philosophy. In a startling coda to his denial, Bjornstad declared:

> Any act obviously inconsistent with my tactical conceptions might not be properly chargeable to me in person, even though I was the mouth piece. I do not invite the inference that the matter was referred to General Bullard, or the First Army, or the Fifth Corps. I simply do not remember the facts.[32]

Regardless of Bjornstad's poor memory, his insinuation hangs in the air like a rifle pointing directly at Bullard.

Bullard was the only other officer with the authority to countermand the order—and the *only* person with a compelling reason to do so. After returning to headquarters flushed with the success of his surging troops, the commanding general was briefed by his chief of staff. There is no record of their conversation in the testimony collected by Booth, but there is an intriguing comment reported years later by another source: Major Harry Parkin. According to the affidavit inscribed by Parkin in the book by Harbord, Bullard bellowed that he was not going "to help George Cameron win any battle laurels!"[33]

That statement stands as Bullard's malicious benediction on Montfaucon.

In recording the general's outburst, Parkin provided the final testimony needed to solve the mystery of Montfaucon and complete the picture of Robert Bullard's strange psyche. The general interpreted the tactical situation on the evening of September 26 in a typically egoistic manner—that is, in the way it affected his *personal* prospects. By assisting Cameron, Bullard would have reduced his own chances for advancement. The inverse was also true: Cameron's failure would contribute to Bullard's success.

Around midnight, as Booth continued pressing his brigade toward the envelopment, he finally learned that the order had been rescinded. "The leading troops were by this time well en route, although moving slowly as it was a very dark night, the troops were unfamiliar with the country, and all were subjected to hostile artillery and machine gun fire," the 8th Brigade commander reported. "If they had not been stopped the troops would have been in position to attack Nantillois at daybreak and to prevent the escape of the Boche on Montfaucon."[34]

Bullard's defenders argue that a First Army order received late on the afternoon of September 26 obviated Booth's proposed maneuver by commanding all corps to press the attack northward—as though that order would absolve Bullard of disobeying the original attack instructions and excuse him from the responsibility of rescuing American troops in danger. As III Corps troops pressed the attack farther north on the afternoon

of September 26, they ran into reinforced German lines strong
enough to bring Bullard's charge to a quick halt.

With the I Corps tangled in the brush of the Argonne Forest, V Corps slowed by Montfaucon, and III Corps stopped, the
great Meuse-Argonne Offensive stalled. Bolstered by Bullard's
self-serving complaints about V Corps' failure to keep pace, blame
fell heavily on Cameron. The embattled general exacerbated the
damage Bullard had caused by creating a powerful enemy at headquarters: Chief of Staff Hugh Drum, who had immediate access
to Pershing.

The clash began with the fractious telephone call made by
Drum on the night of September 28 demanding that V Corps
accelerate its advance. Unwisely, Major General Cameron pulled
rank on the colonel by replying, "You can't talk to me that way;
only the army commander can do that."[35] The officers' relationship deteriorated further over the next few days as First Army
continued to struggle. Around October 10, the situation broke
down completely, when Cameron began answering nagging calls
with silent contempt. Later, in a letter to his wife, he wrote:

> The Chief of Staff telephoned and asked me how I accounted
> for the failure. I replied that the Boche had not withdrawn as the
> Army expected and the resistance had increased. He then bore
> in and said, "I think this and it seems to me that," etc. I made no
> reply. He yelled "Hello!" And I said "I am listening." He then
> resumed: "Tum de doo doo! Ta la la loo. Hello!" I said: "I am
> still listening."[36]

Frustrated, Drum hung up. The next phone call made it clear
that Cameron was in deep trouble:

> In a few minutes General P. called me up himself and was tre-
> mendously emphatic about pushing the division commanders.
> Now that is not my method. I have never pounded subordinates

and never will. I get results by team work and by leaving individual initiative unhampered.[37]

When the ax finally fell on October 12, Cameron was "not the least bit surprised at my relief."[38] He looked forward to returning to command his old 4th Division, a position that Pershing had proffered, but the assignment was only temporary window dressing. After conferring further with Bullard, Drum, and other senior officers, Pershing dispatched Cameron back to the United States. Distressed by the death of his son, Douglas, who had been serving with the 1st Division, Cameron accepted his fate with equanimity, confiding to only a few friends his misgivings about the growing influence of staff officers.[39] He probably never knew of the influential role Bullard had played in his demotion.

Cameron's demise heralded Bullard's apotheosis. Not only did the ambitious general capture the prized command of the US Second Army and a third star, but he also persuaded Pershing to install his protégé, General Charles P. Summerall, as the new commander of III Corps. Just like his mentor, Summerall had demonstrated his readiness to sacrifice lives to gain battlefield objectives. "He wanted results, no matter how many men were killed," observed the usually soft-spoken Father Francis Duffy—the celebrated chaplain of New York's "Fighting 69th Regiment."[40] The same bloody characteristics that raised Duffy's ire endeared the youthful general to Bullard, who became his sponsor while they served in the 1st Division at Cantigny.

In addition to being promoted, Bullard won a chestful of decorations from the United States, Britain, France, and Belgium, complete with bright sashes and ribbons. He wore them proudly on every possible occasion, as Harry Parkin noted in his affidavit. When the Armistice arrived, Bullard was one of only two men in the AEF to have achieved the rank of lieutenant general; in prominence, he was equivalent to Douglas MacArthur, Omar Bradley, and George Patton in World War II. The southern farm boy had become a national hero.

The secrets surrounding the III Corps' role in the attack on Montfaucon forged a bizarre bond between Bullard and Bjornstad. Earlier, Bullard's knowledge of Bjornstad's insubordination at Fismette had given the general leverage over his chief of staff and soothed his anxiety about Bjornstad's friends at headquarters. Following September 26, Bjornstad's knowledge of Bullard's disobedience in planning the attack on Montfaucon and in rescinding the rescue operation granted the chief of staff offsetting influence over his commander. One word to the "Leavenworth clique" about Bullard's refusal to follow orders would have destroyed the general's reputation.

Dual acts of betrayal forced Bullard and Bjornstad into a wary tango, a guarded embrace they were forced to sustain throughout the remainder of their careers—indeed, for the rest of their lives. Unresolved anger might inspire each man to snipe from time to time, but neither could reveal the truth for fear that his own sins would be exposed.

One of the most bizarre episodes in this macabre dance occurred in 1925, after Bjornstad had been nominated for the permanent rank of brigadier general. The nomination triggered a review of the candidate's career that exploded in a congressional hearing. Seven years before, when Bullard had been promoted to lead the Second Army, Bjornstad was reassigned to command a brigade of the newly arrived 7th Division. There his abrasive personality and abuse of subordinates created enemies with long memories. Following the war, as Bjornstad was reduced to his permanent rank of colonel, he promptly forgot about the dustups, until his nomination for flag rank generated one of the most disruptive episodes in army history.

In an unprecedented event, officers who served under Bjornstad in the 7th Division hired an attorney, drew up charges, and opposed the nomination. The most prominent was a sitting member of the US Senate, Davis Elkins of West Virginia, who had served as Bjornstad's adjutant. He declared that his former commander was "not temperamentally fitted to command troops, and my opinion coincides with the testimony of the officers who have given their testimony heretofore."[41] In addition to Elkins's brutal judgment, the group of former officers accused Bjornstad of falsifying records and failing to fulfill duties.[42]

The hearing also uncovered the fact that following Bullard's move to Second Army, Bjornstad had been relieved by the new III Corps commander, General John Hines, former commander of the 4th Division. By 1925, Hines was US Army chief of staff, and he appeared before the committee personally to hammer a nail into Bjornstad's coffin. Hines revealed that he supervised Bjornstad for only ten days in 1918, when he became disgusted by his subordinate's high-handed attitude: "I got in my car at once and went down to general headquarters—I mean to the headquarters of the army—saw the Chief of Staff, General Drum, and told him that he would have to get a new chief of staff or a new corps commander for that Third Corps, that I was convinced that Colonel Bjornstad and I could not play the game together."[43] Bjornstad was promptly demoted to the 7th Division.

Testimony of this sort from the highest-ranking army officer should have torpedoed the nomination, but a surprise witness rode to Bjornstad's rescue: General Robert Bullard. Admitting that "General Bjornstad's manner was almost invariably irritating to men and officers to whom he had to give orders," Bullard surprised the senators by going on to recommend promotion.[44] On the verge of retiring from active duty, the lieutenant general based his recommendation on Bjornstad's administrative ability: "In the drawing up of orders, he was, especially of attack and defense, excellent. He devised, in the battle of the Meuse-Argonne, a block system of controlling traffic on a single road on which two corps and a good deal of the artillery and the trains of other organizations had to pass. I considered that the best piece of work that I saw in the war."[45]

Bullard went on to testify that Bjornstad had corrected his demeanor since his service in the war, telling the committee a remarkable story:

> About 1920, General Bjornstad said in substance, "General, I have examined my official reports on file in the War Department made by you during the war. One of your reports is so adverse that I have no hope of future advancement unless it is modified." "Well," I said, "did you see why I made those reports and in what respects they were adverse?" He said, "Yes, I have." He said, "Now that I see my fault, I can correct it." "Well," I said, "you correct your faults, and I will correct my reports." I followed up his conduct for something like two years, and I thought I saw sufficient justification to modify my reports against him, and I did accordingly do so especially in the recommendation for his promotion.[46]

Bullard urged Bjornstad's confirmation "because he is a very able man. I would not want General Bjornstad to command troops in the field under me. I would be very glad to have him as a staff officer to propose movements—operations. He is especially fit for it, and for instructions."[47] This is fulsome praise for an officer whom Bullard had described in 1918 "as poor a chief of staff as I have ever seen."[48]

There is little doubt that Bullard's testimony secured his former chief of staff's promotion, a courtesy that Bjornstad soon repaid. As General Booth pressed forward with his investigation of the Montfaucon debacle, he eventually reached a point beyond which he could not progress. Bjornstad's letter regarding the debate about the wording of the original First Army order and the chief of staff's avowal of his willingness to cross corps boundaries to accomplish his mission settled the two most pressing issues about September 26. But Booth decided to take one more shot at uncovering the truth. He sent the entire file to Pershing with a request that he ask Bjornstad who rescinded the order.

Pershing had little interest in pursuing a matter that could re-enflame the controversy, especially given the efforts he had already taken to disguise the matter as a "misinterpretation" of orders. Perhaps it was for that reason that the AEF chief delayed nearly a decade before replying to Booth's query. In the interim, Bjornstad had died and Bullard had retired. But on June 17, 1940, Pershing wrote Booth to report that the late Bjornstad stated that *he* had rescinded the order because of "his rather ironclad practice of not crossing boundaries."[49] By answering in a manner that directly contradicted his earlier statements about his tactical philosophy, Bjornstad protected Bullard's reputation—in reciprocity for the general's testimony at the Senate hearing.

Booth ended his quest for the truth without drawing any final conclusions or writing the report that he had mentioned to General Drum. Instead, he persuaded Pershing to order the file of letters deposited among official AEF records, where it lay misunderstood and neglected for years. In an odd way, Booth seemed to trust that a young Horatio would eventually emerge, discover the file, and tell the story of Montfaucon aright.

Why does all this matter? Why did General Booth spend twenty years collecting evidence to demonstrate what had happened at Montfaucon? Why did Booth persuade Pershing to place the file among official army records? Why did Chief of Staff Hines ask the army inspector general to review the incident and offer to promote Cameron to the rank of *brigadier* general in 1924?[50] Finally, why did Hines's successor and Congress restore Colonel Cameron to the rank of *major* general in 1930?[51]

The answer to these questions is that the officers knew that the initial Meuse-Argonne attack had come within a hairbreadth of achieving the long-sought breakthrough, a prospect summarized in a compelling manner by Thomas Johnson, the correspondent who investigated Montfaucon following the war.

"There is a great unanswered question about our first day in the Meuse-Argonne," writes Johnson. "It is: Could we, in that single day, have reached our goal, immediate breakthrough to the Kriemhilde Heights at Cunel and Romagne, and great German defeat? Was the plan of attack, however ambitious, not utterly impossible of realization? More, did the door to such a victory stand for a brief space just a little ajar, then before we could slip through, slam in our faces? Was there, in short, ever a chance of a miracle? The answer seems to be: Well, possibly—if—

"The great 'if' of the first day of our greatest battle stands out clearly ten years later as 'If we had taken Montfaucon . . .' Had we got it as we planned, early enough in the day, we might have reached the Kriemhilde Line before the Germans reinforced their none-too-strong front and were ready to defend it," concluded Johnson.[52]

There was no miracle at Montfaucon. Booth's file explains why. The distant chance of a miracle, of a dramatic breakthrough to end the war, disappeared as Bullard disobeyed orders, abandoned the 79th Division to the mercy of German artillery and machine guns on Montfaucon, rejected other opportunities to assist them, and led his troops to capture the hollow distinction of the farthest advance on the first day of battle.

What remained for the First Army was a brutal slog through the mud of the Meuse-Argonne, one that ultimately cost 26,277 American lives and the wounding of 95,786 additional doughboys.[53] Many of these must be attributed to the debacle at Montfaucon.

CHAPTER 21

DENKMAL: REMEMBERING THE DOUGHBOYS

Towering 225 feet over the butte, the American Montfaucon Monument is the principal memorial to the American Expeditionary Forces. Designed by the architect of the Jefferson Memorial, the Doric column is the largest American military monument abroad. Dedication ceremonies, shown here, occurred on August 1, 1937, two years before the start of World War II.

★   ★   ★

Denkmal is the German word for "monument." Literally—and more profoundly—it commands, "Think again."

The American military monument at Montfaucon grandly proclaims duty, valor, and victory. Unfortunately, few visitors complete the demanding pilgrimage required to hear that message. Marooned in a green sea of fields and forests in northeast France, the 225-foot Doric column is well north of the sleek motorway and the high-speed rail line that propel travelers from Paris to Metz. Reaching the site requires negotiating a maze of narrow country roads that provides few directional signs and is routinely clogged by herds of sheep and cattle.

Because of the butte's remoteness, Montfaucon is often deserted. Only the blasted foundations of shops, homes, and barns murmur memories of a prosperous town that occupied the site before the Germans arrived in 1914. After four years of warfare, hardly a stone stood on stone atop Little Gibraltar. The French government decided to leave Montfaucon as one of *les villages détruits*—a scattered array of eloquent reminders of the aggressive nation across the Rhine.

Surrounding the American victory monument, tangled vines barricade silent German bunkers that resounded with the rattle of machine guns in 1918; the entrances to tunnels and galleries lie beneath tons of mossy rubble; and a few fractured ribs of the basilica stand as reminders of the peace once offered by the medieval sanctuary. The only congregation is a flock of falcons that centuries ago lent their name to the mount, by leading St. Baldric to found a monastery on the height.

On a typical day, a handful of cars might wander to the site, pausing just long enough for occupants to glance at the monument and to wonder what could have induced the US government to grace such an isolated hill with such a magnificent memorial. Surely, visitors think, the impressive column should have been stationed high on the cliffs above Omaha Beach, in the dark verge of the Ardennes Forest near Bastogne, or perhaps in a Parisian square, where it could be toasted by hordes of American tourists.

Rebuttal lies close at hand. Within sight of the column are buried 14,246 doughboys who died conquering Little Gibraltar and cracking the Hindenburg Line. On the plush slopes of the Meuse-Argonne American Cemetery, the white crosses are always polished; the grass is neatly mowed; sycamores are trimmed in the stark European manner; and on holidays—especially November 11—American flags adorn the graves. Among them rest 855 members of the 79th Division who fell nearby.

It was to honor these men that the nation established the American Battle Monuments Commission in 1923. General Pershing's position as chair of the commission gave him control over what was to be remembered about World War I and the manner in which it would be memorialized. The commission eventually constructed twelve monuments and eight cemeteries stretching along the Western Front from Ypres, Belgium, to Montsec, France. The largest burial site is the Meuse-Argonne, and the most impressive monument is Montfaucon's classic column.

Yet, as is often the case with the relics of World War I, a more troubled history belies the memorial's serene appearance. When the commission began its work, most Americans recognized the names of few battle sites in France. Among Château-Thierry, St. Mihiel, Belleau Wood, and Montfaucon, the name of the butte was best known, probably because of the mystique of the crown prince's observatory, the massive scale of the Meuse-Argonne Offensive, and the hill's pivotal role. For these reasons, Pershing and his fellow ABMC commissioners decided that Montfaucon should host the most impressive AEF monument, one designed to bury a debacle under a striking column of marble.

Influenced by Pershing's dedication to military hierarchy, the commission also adopted a stringent set of rules governing the placement of other American memorials. With rare exceptions, no unit smaller than a division was permitted to place a monument on the battlefield, and the former AEF commander exercised personal control over the site of these memorials and the wording inscribed on them. Over the years, Pershing engaged in several protracted battles with veterans hoping to mark the battlefield where they fought and their friends fell. None of these postwar conflicts was more bitter, however, than the former AEF commander's lengthy dispute with the 79th Division and its regiments: the 313th, 314th, 315th, and 316th.

Before the commission settled on Montfaucon as the site for the AEF monument, 79th veterans proposed placing a divisional monument on the butte. Pershing was dead-set against the proposal. Not even a modest plinth on the slope up which the 313th fought was acceptable, although a small marble plaque on the side of a building was approved grudgingly. The passing years made short work of that marker.

Using a loophole in the commission's regulations, veterans of the 315th Regiment collected funds to help the devastated village of Nantillois build a community center, a charitable act permitted by the commission. On a prominent wall of the building, the veterans engraved, "Erected in memory of the glorious dead of the 315th Infantry, USA." The ABMC—more accurately, Pershing—was apoplectic and wanted to change the wording to "In memory of the high achievements of the American troops who fought in this region."[1] After protests from the regiment, however, the ABMC relented, and the legend remains.

Pershing's harshest treatment, however, was reserved for the 316th Infantry Regiment. When the unit's veterans association proposed a monument on Corn Willy Hill, the ABMC denied the request, stating that the actions of the unit "were not of a more distinguished character than those of the other regiments of the division."[2] Compounding the insult, the commission went on to declare that the 316th was not "of more distinguished character than the average American regiment that served,"[3] a brutal judgment flying in the face of General Kuhn's glowing citation of the 316th's heroism on Hill 378. It is doubtful that the ABMC would have published such a demeaning statement without Pershing's express approval.

These gratuitous judgments stung. To the men of Harry Parkin's regiment who had flung their bodies against the Kriemhilde Stellung and breasted thick machine-gun fire to capture the Borne de Cornouiller, the response was outrageous. Rather than mount a frontal attack on the ABMC, however, the regiment demonstrated its mastery of the tactics of open warfare that Pershing espoused. Using a stealthy turning maneuver, the 316th donated its funds to the hospice of Sivry-sur-Meuse, the town just below Corn Willy. Hospice officials promptly used the money to buy land on Hill 378, erect a twenty-five-foot-tall monument designed by the regiment, and plant a long rank of conifers that leads the gaze of passing motorists to the granite plinth high on the eastern horizon.

Although it had been twelve years since the last shot of World War I had been fired, Pershing promptly declared war on the 316th. In an official protest directed to French premier André Tardieu, the general "bitterly objected" to the monument and "demanded" that the foreign government raze it.[4] To underscore his determination to obliterate the 316th monument, Pershing followed his letter with a personal visit to his French ally, citing his authority as an official US government representative. The fight was joined when the town of Sivry filed a petition with the government protesting Pershing's move. As news of the melee drifted across the Atlantic, the mothers of 316th Regiment soldiers who had been killed in France wrote heart-rending letters to Congress criticizing Pershing's insensitivity to their sons' sac-rifices.[5]

Finally, French officials wrote to Pershing explaining that the monument was on private property over which they lacked jurisdiction. Thereafter, the controversy subsided slowly, but Per-shing retained the last word. The American guidebook to world war battlefields—written under the general's direction—notes that the monument on Corn Willy Hill honors "American troops who fought in the area," a statement inconsistent with the battle facts and the dedication chiseled in stone.[6] By this malicious act, Pershing seemed intent on erasing the memory of the 79th from history, as well as from the battlefield.

It is impossible to determine what stoked Pershing's animus: whether it was the postwar challenge to his authority or still-smoldering anger about the 79th's failure to capture Little Gibraltar on schedule. But the ferocity of Pershing's ire and his determina-tion to deny recognition to the division and its regiments suggest motivation more profound than mere pique over the veterans' insubordination. Given Pershing's documented efforts to obscure the causes of the Montfaucon debacle and his demonstrated anger at George Cameron, Joseph Kuhn, and the 79th, the guidebook's deletion of the division's contribution appears to be an additional element of the AEF commander's lengthy campaign to conceal the facts of the incident that proved so disastrous to the Meuse-Argonne Offensive.

The column on Montfaucon was designated the premier AEF memorial, and the commission focused much of its energy on making it a grand—some might say *grandiose*—reality. The mon-ument was expected to guarantee a permanent position of honor for Little Gibraltar in the growing American pantheon of prom-ontories that were the sites of US military victories. Bunker Hill, Kings Mountain, Missionary Ridge, Little Round Top, and San Juan Hill deserved a companion from World War I; the butte in northeast France stood tall on the historic horizon. To confirm

Little Gibraltar's inclusion in the august list, the magnificence of the Montfaucon monument would disguise the failure of leadership lying just beneath the surface.

To meet these objectives, the commission hired John Russell Pope, the most prominent public architect of his time. Best known for his designs of the Jefferson Memorial, the National Archives, the National Gallery of Art, and other neoclassical structures in Washington, DC, Pope clearly understood the commission's aspirations. To the Doric column at the top of a broad series of granite steps and terraces ascending the butte's southern slope, the architect added a sculpture of Liberty to the top and provided an observation platform offering a more expansive view than the crown prince enjoyed from his famous observatory.

Just as war clouds were again gathering over Europe, the AEF memorial was dedicated on August 1, 1937. President Franklin D. Roosevelt, speaking to a crowd of ten thousand via an unprecedented "trans-Atlantic radio hook-up," offered assurance that both France and the United States "desire to live at peace with all nations."[7] Surrounded by French cuirassiers arrayed in brass helmets, breastplates, and plumes, the aging General Pershing and Marshal Henri Pétain hailed their historic alliance and voiced wishes that the monument would signal the realization of Woodrow Wilson's dream that the Great War was the war to end all wars. Some European nations, however, were deaf to the pleas for peace. Two years later, Germany launched another conflict that obliterated Wilson's dream and obscured Pershing's monument.

Perhaps it was the obscene violence of the Holocaust or maybe the nuclear dawn over Hiroshima that faded memories of the doughboys' sacrifices. Whatever the cause, the name Little Gibraltar of World War I was never inscribed in the American military pantheon, and the available space was readily filled by Monte Cassino, Mount Surabachi, Pork Chop Hill, Khe Sanh, and Tora Bora. Official notification of the disappearance of World

War I from the American consciousness arrived as the annual observance of Armistice Day was subsumed by the amorphous Veterans Day in 1954.

If the Montfaucon monument shouts, Henry Gunther's memorial whispers. Yet its message of sacrifice, loss, and sadness lingers, echoing softly across the final battlefield of the 79th Division.

Located on the east side of the Meuse, approximately fourteen miles from Montfaucon, the Gunther tribute is more difficult to find than the butte. It is some distance from any other American war memorial, and requires winding over high ridges and driving along a meandering creek that the French call the River Thinte. Resting in the saddle of the Côte de Chaumont, the five-foot-tall granite marker would scarcely be noticed were it not for the American flag fluttering high on a pole above the stone. In the tortured topography of the Meuse-Argonne region, the Stars and Stripes is a beacon summoning travelers to determine why the banner waves in such a deserted spot.

"En homage à Henry Gunther," is the stone's simple explanation. The brief story of the last American to die in World War I is related by a small plaque in French and English. The monument was erected not by the French government or the American Battle Monuments Commission, but by villagers of Chaumont-devant-Damvillers, the farming hamlet liberated by Gunther and the 313th minutes before the Armistice. Somehow the simple expression of gratitude from the village is more poignant than the massive monuments lining the roads from Verdun to Sedan. Above all, the stone fulfills the aspiration of every *denkmal*, by compelling visitors to "think again." Inevitably they conclude that Henry's final act was a sacrificial death intended somehow to redeem his earlier mistake—and perhaps even the perceived shortcomings of his regiment and division.

Although Gunther's suicide by combat was the final American death *in* the war, it was far from the final death *of* the war. Contemporary newspapers, magazines, and books are filled with stories of other doughboys who returned from France as "hollow men," once-enthusiastic soldiers who found it impossible to live with the brutal knowledge acquired in the trenches.[8]

Perhaps the most memorable postwar death—as well as the paradigm for others—is that of Major Charles Whittlesey, commander of the famed "Lost Battalion." The unit of the 77th Division was surrounded by Germans for six days deep in the Argonne Forest. After enduring vicious German attacks and shortages of water, food, and ammunition, the battalion emerged with only one-third of its men. The major and other survivors were welcomed triumphantly. After being awarded the Medal of Honor, the Harvard-educated Whittlesey sought amnesia in the quotidian work of a Wall Street law firm. The strategy worked until the letters began to arrive.

"Not a day goes by but I hear from some of my old outfit, usually with some sorrow or misfortune," Whittlesey confessed to a friend. "I cannot bear it much more."[9] The major conscientiously responded to each plea, always with encouraging words and often with a few dollars.

In 1921, Whittlesey served as pallbearer for the Unknown Soldier—an unidentified member of the AEF who symbolized the nation's dead—but he was unusually quiet at the ceremony. Soon thereafter he booked passage on the SS *Toloa* bound for Havana. On the first night at sea, the former major donned his tuxedo, dined with the ship's captain, and announced that he was retiring for the evening. Instead, he walked out onto the deck, climbed the rail, and plunged into the dark water. His absence was not noted until the following morning.

In the 1920s and beyond, veteran suicides were epidemic. An American Legion survey determined that an average of two former AEF members killed themselves each day. That number was thought to be understated because most families obscured the circumstances of their loved ones' deaths.[10] From New York to San Francisco, newspapers ran stories of veterans from all social strati, educational backgrounds, vocations, and economic circumstances who ended their lives to escape memory. A surprising number died clutching medals for bravery earned in France, as if the bright ribbons might explain their invisible wounds.[11]

The veterans of this sad "last parade" died in a variety of ways: hanging, inhaling gas, taking poison or narcotics, leaping from buildings, or diving in front of trains. Many shot themselves, using service revolvers or, ironically, souvenir German Lugers.[12] A few emulated Major Whittlesey in choosing death by water. Nicholas Iverson, a graduate of the US Naval Academy and a flight officer in the Atlantic war, sailed over Niagara Falls in 1926.[13] Eleven years later, AEF member Harold Wobber, who had just been released from a Veterans Bureau hospital for depression, strolled to the center of the Golden Gate Bridge, handed his coat to a companion, and jumped over the rail to become the first suicide from the new span. Wobber's final words echoed the resolution of thousands of his comrades: "This is as far as I go."[14]

Veterans of the 79th Division bore their share of psychic scars, and many endorsed Wobber's declaration. One was Joseph Ferrero, who had gained notoriety in 1917 as the first District of Columbia citizen drafted into the National Army.[15] After training at Camp Meade, he was assigned to the 79th Division's 311th Machine Gun Battalion, which fought with distinction on Corn Willy Hill. When Ferrero returned to Washington in 1919, he inherited a $1.5 million fortune, but his bright prospects could not dispel memory's dark shadows. On the evening of May 27, 1921, he told his sister that he was leaving soon, found his service revolver, and shot himself in the forehead. Ferrero had been "extremely nervous, which his sister later said was due to wounds he received in France."[16]

Most veterans of the 79th avoided suicide, but many grappled with demons. Disgraced corps commander George Cameron found uneasy retirement in Virginia, where his son-in-law was superintendent of Staunton Military Academy. When General Hines wrote offering to restore Cameron's flag rank, the corps commander replied curtly that he had no interest in pursuing the matter.

The only AEF general denied a Distinguished Service Cross, Joseph Kuhn, found his promising career demolished by Montfaucon. The engineer who had once been mentioned prominently as a candidate for US Army chief of staff, read the handwriting on the wall, retired from the service, and spent the rest of his days constructing waste disposal plants on the West Coast.

Rejected by an army that refused to accept the reality of shell shock, Colonel O. J. Charles yearned for an opportunity to prove that he was capable of command. As a new war neared in 1940, Charles wrote his old friend Hugh Drum, pleading for an opportunity to serve. Drum apparently looked into the circumstances of the colonel's psychological collapse north of Montfaucon and never replied.

Surrounded by glorious relics from wars gone by, Major Harry Parkin secluded himself in his study and pondered the pain of his own military experience. He was heartened when his heroism on Corn Willy Hill was recognized by the award of a Distinguished Service Cross and a Silver Star in 1924, and he annually marked the date of the 316th's charge up the ridge by sending a dozen roses to Sergeant Major Robert MacCormack, the aide who had covered Parkin's body after German machine guns stitched four bullets into his legs.[17]

But Harry spent most of his time mentally circling Little Gibraltar, wondering what he could have done differently, pondering the role of Bullard in the debacle, and mourning the loss of soldiers such as Captain Hewit, Lieutenant Kellar, and above all, Major Sinkler Manning. The South Carolinian remained central in Harry's memory of the war, one whose sacrifice he weighed for years. As Parkin grew older, recalled the aging Civil War veterans of his youth, and contemplated what lay ahead, he mused,

> And are we that survived to become old men in time and be set aside and disregarded, our war stories of such men as Sinkler Manning wearied of, are we the fortunate ones or are those who died in the full flush of youth, and in the great moment of their lives, doing something wonderfully fine and heroic, something worthwhile, something utterly unselfish, are they the fortunate ones? Sometimes I wonder, and were it not for those near and dear to us, whom we want to care for and protect, I wonder if I would wonder.[18]

Crippled by missing limbs, disfigured by ghastly wounds, smothered by scar tissue, and terrorized by nightmares, the twenty-eight thousand men of the 79th were quickly forgotten by a nation intent on returning to normalcy. "The business of America is business," proclaimed President Calvin Coolidge, and the postwar boom was on. But a generation of veterans unable to participate in the careless celebration of capitalism their blood had purchased were left sitting on the front porches of America, hacking their lungs out, comforted only by whiskey and cigarettes. Their stories are legion, but most have faded from memory over the last century.

Yet something of the 79th Division did endure: Harry Parkin's affidavit, scribbled hastily in the back of a book in 1936, and the file of letters laboriously compiled by General Ewing Booth, buried for years in the National Archives. After nearly a century, these documents disclosed how the betrayal at Little Gibraltar doomed thousands of doughboys to death and extended the killing of World War I. Ultimately, the documents helped solve the mystery of Montfaucon and restore the reputation of the 79th Division. In this, perhaps, lies at least a small part of the redemption that Harry Parkin, Henry Gunther, Sinkler Manning, and other men of the division sought but never found on the battlefields of France.

Denkmal.

If the Montfaucon memorial shouts, the modest monument to Henry Gunther whispers. Its melancholy message of sacrifice and loss hangs over the final battlefield. The stone was erected by the village that Gunther and his fellow soldiers liberated just before the Armistice.

"SOME COULD, SOME COULD NOT, SHAKE OFF MISERY"

Aboard the USS *Princess Matoika*, troops of the
314th Regiment sighted the Statue of Liberty as they returned
from France in May 1919 following the Armistice.

★   ★   ★

Calm fell. From heaven distilled a clemency;
There was peace on earth, and silence in the sky;
Some could, some could not, shake off misery:
The Sinister Spirit sneered: "It had to be!"
And again the Spirit of Pity whispered, "Why?"

—Thomas Hardy, British poet[1]

The Meuse-Argonne Offensive remains the largest and bloodiest battle in US military history. Although the forty-seven-day campaign never attained its objective of cutting the rail lines between Sedan and Mézières, it involved 1.2 million American troops, of whom 26,277 died and 95,786 were wounded. These totals far surpass those of the World War II battles at Normandy and the Bulge.

The Meuse-Argonne had long-lasting consequences—for both the United States and the individuals who fought in it. The horror that soldiers endured became the touchstone of America's experience with modern warfare, and gave substance and strength to those who argued that the nation should avoid foreign disputes and alliances. Isolationists deftly used soldiers' memories and mothers' tears to undermine support for President Wilson's League of Nations and national security. When World War II began, America was once again unprepared.

For individuals, the effects of the war were similarly disappointing. The best case in point is that of General Pershing, who hoped to be elected president in 1920. He had every reason to expect such a reward because, as Donald Smythe points out, "Up until World War I every major American conflict had catapulted a military hero into the presidency."[2] The voters, however, proved how fleeting popularity is. In Nebraska, a state in which he spent much of his early life, Pershing won only one county and 21 percent of the vote in the primary.[3] Many veterans—both from the Allies and the Central Powers—found that their exploits were soon forgotten as civilians rushed to return to a normal life. As Edward Lengel has pointed out, America in the 1920s seemed to adopt a purposeful forgetting of the horrors of modern warfare.

John N. Bentley (1895–1969)—Jack Bentley returned to the mound following service in France. A left-handed pitcher, he played on the New York Giants' pennant-winning teams of 1923 and 1924. In the fifth game of the '24 World Series, Bentley was the winning pitcher against the Washington Senators' Walter Johnson, but he lost the deciding seventh game to Johnson a few days later. In addition to being excellent on the mound, Bentley was a fine hitter. He sported a .427 batting average in 1923, including five hits—and a home run—in World Series play.[4]

Alfred W. Bjornstad (1874–1934)—Eager for more fighting, the pugnacious Bjornstad sought an opportunity to command a proposed American Volunteer Legion to oppose the Bolsheviks in Poland following the Armistice.[5] Told he would have to resign his commission, Bjornstad stuck with the army. Assigned to Camp Snelling, Minnesota, he continued his contentious ways by becoming embroiled in disputes with local officials about a garbage dump and rifle range.[6] Bjornstad had better luck in love, marrying Pearl Ladd Sabin, the wealthy daughter of the founder of Pacific Telephone and Telegraph.[7]

Maximilian A. W. Boll (1892–1980)—When Sergeant Boll returned home in 1919, his "Philadelphia's Own" Regiment voted not to march in a victory parade down Broad Street. The officers were furious, but the enlisted men had had enough of war. Although he remained patriotic, Boll confessed later, "My own feeling about the First World War is that our entry into it made it a major disaster for the world. I believe that if we had kept out of it, a truce would eventually have been worked out, as it had often happened in the past without any of the countries being completely humiliated and ruined to the point of desperation . . . It made a Second World War inevitable."[8]

Ewing E. Booth (1870–1949)—In depositing his Montfaucon file in official army records, General Booth proudly declared, "Thus there is ended a research of thousands of pages of records, and interviews, both verbal and written, with hundreds of officers, covering a period of approximately twenty years, in an effort to determine definitely who at III Army Corps headquarters gave the orders which prevented the 4th Division from assisting the V Army Corps in taking Montfaucon."[9] Booth's investigation did not damage his career; he retired as a major general.

Robert Lee Bullard (1861–1947)—After retiring from the army, Bullard found that maintaining the posh lifestyle of a general was impossible on his small government pension. In addition to launching a writing career to secure additional income, he was paid to pose in his dress uniform and medals for a magazine advertisement declaring, "An army man must keep fit—reach for a Lucky instead of a sweet."[10] The mercenary endorsement disgusted former colleagues, including General Pershing, who decried "one of our comrades [appearing] in all his glory as an advertisement for Lucky Strike cigarettes."[11]

To earn a regular salary, Bullard became president of the National Security League, a New York group that advocated a stronger US military. As the nation flirted with Fascism in the dark 1930s, he led the organization to demand the deportation of communists, warn that military training camps were targets for subversives, purge internationalist university professors, cite the danger of Mexican radicals, and urge the funding of an armed National Volunteer Security Corps to protect America from invasion.[12] After these ideas had been discredited and the organization had gone bankrupt, Bullard closed the office in 1942. The general is buried in a place of honor at West Point.

James M. Cain (1892–1977)—After returning to civilian life, Cain worked as a journalist at the *New York World*, *American Mercury*, and, briefly, the *New Yorker*. He published his first novel, *The Postman Always Rings Twice*, in 1934, and became well known for "hard-boiled" crime novels such as *Double Indemnity*. Aside from one story on Montfaucon, he never wrote about the war again, shifting his focus from violence on the battlefield to violence in domestic life.

George H. Cameron (1861–1944)—Although Cameron retired at the rank of colonel in 1924, his colleagues recognized that his reputation had been unfairly besmirched and restored him to the rank of brigadier general and, in 1930, major general.

Georges Clemenceau (1841–1929)—For "the Tiger," violence did not end with the Armistice. In 1919 a would-be assassin fired several shots at him, hitting the premier only once. Clemenceau observed wryly that his nation had just won a terrible war, yet "here is a Frenchman who misses his target 6 out of 7 times at point-blank range."[13] The prime minister recovered in time to persuade his fellow statesmen to impose costly reparations against Germany that some historians argue fostered the rise of Fascism.

Crown Prince's Observatory—For several years following the Armistice, the observatory atop Montfaucon was a prime tourist attraction. Visitors could view the periscope's concrete housing and descend into Wilhelm's bunker. Because the roof was partially destroyed, exposure to the elements deteriorated the house to the point that it was demolished in the 1930s. Today, the only trace of the structure is a stone casement gazing north toward the Kriemhilde Stellung. The oculus of the beast—the multistory telescopic periscope—was sent to the West Point Museum, where it symbolized victory over Imperial Germany. In 1941, the device was featured in *Life* magazine, but soon thereafter, it disappeared without a trace.[22] A museum curator speculated that the relic had been sacrificed for scrap metal during World War II.[23]

Ferdinand Foch (1851–1929)—Following the Armistice, the Allied commander in chief demanded that Germany be forever precluded from occupying its former territory on the west bank of the Rhine River, a measure to protect France from invasion. When the Allies gathered at the Paris Peace Conference rejected that request, Foch declared presciently, "This is not peace. It is a 20-year armistice."[14]

Max von Gallwitz (1852–1937)—Gallwitz strongly opposed the German decision to seek an armistice and issued a call for his countrymen to rise up against the Allies. After retiring from the army in 1918, he served as a deputy for the National People's Party in the Reichstag for four years. Gallwitz's son, a general in the World War II German army, was killed during the siege of Sebastopol, Crimea.

Henry N. Gunther (1895–1918)—Rather than having her son's body interred in France, Gunther's mother chose to have it returned to Baltimore. Gunther now rests under the watchful gaze of a marble angel in the Most Holy Redeemer Cemetery. On the anniversary of his death, the German Society of Baltimore holds a memorial service at his grave.

Paul von Hindenburg (1847–1934)—Following his resignation as chief of the General Staff in November 1918, Hindenburg was elected second president of the Weimar Republic. He opposed the rise of the Nazi Party, scorning Hitler as "that Bohemian corporal." To block the future dictator, Hindenburg ran and was reelected in 1932, but due to declining health, he appointed Hitler chancellor of Germany in 1933 and died the following year. Shortly after the Armistice, a group of American correspondents asked Hindenburg about the deciding factor in the conflict. Hindenburg replied, "The American infantry in the Argonne won the war."[15]

Andrew J. Kachik (1895–1975)—After being treated for gas wounds, Private Kachik returned to his family in Bellefonte, Pennsylvania. He went back to work in the coal mines, but his lungs were in such poor condition that he could not stand the strain. The government retrained him as an electrician, a job that enabled him to put three children through college.

Joseph E. Kuhn (1864–1935)—Kuhn retired as a major general in 1925, after forty years of service in the army. He was awarded the Croix de Guerre and the Legion of Honor by the French government, but his leadership was never recognized by the United States.

Joseph Labrum (1896–1964)—After returning from France, Labrum became a sportswriter for several Philadelphia newspapers, before taking the pioneering post of sports publicity director for the University of Pennsylvania in 1924. In 1947 he became the director of publicity for the National Football League, a post he held until 1961.

W. Sinkler Manning (1886–1918)—With Pershing in attendance, Manning was buried at Arlington National Cemetery in 1921; the pallbearers were his brothers, five of whom were AEF veterans. A recipient of the Distinguished Service Cross, Manning was the son of the former governor of South Carolina. In the late 1920s, Harry Parkin wrote Manning's parents describing their son's last hours, and in reply, the governor offered to return Parkin's gold major's leaves then in the possession of Manning's widow. Parkin insisted that he had *given*—not loaned—the insignia to Manning, "but even if I had not done so there was no one in the world I would rather have them than his wife."[16]

George C. Marshall (1880–1959)—Perhaps the most talented soldier and statesman of the twentieth century, Marshall held a succession of army posts before becoming chief of staff on September 1, 1939, the day Hitler invaded Poland to start World War II. He was the principal military architect of victory, who selected top army leaders, including Dwight Eisenhower. Named secretary of state in 1947, Marshall was later awarded the Nobel Peace Prize for his efforts to rebuild Europe.

Frederick Palmer (1873–1958)—After attending the Paris Peace Conference, Lieutenant Colonel Palmer declared, "I am convinced that more wars are already in the making."[17] To warn the United States of what was to come, he wrote *The Folly of Nations*, describing the horror of modern war. When his prediction came true, Palmer answered the trumpet's call and worked for General Douglas MacArthur in the Pacific.

Harry D. Parkin (1880–1946)—In a ceremony at San Francisco's Presidio in 1924, Secretary of War John Weeks awarded the former major the Distinguished Service Cross and the Silver Star for valor.[18] Parkin steadily declined in the 1940s, and never learned of General Booth's investigation of the attack on Montfaucon, although the two lived little more than a mile apart.

John J. Pershing (1860–1948)—Pershing was promoted to the rank of five-star general of the armies and served as chief of staff from 1921 to 1924. After retiring, Pershing chaired the American Battle Monuments Commission until his death in 1948. His grave at Arlington National Cemetery is marked by a standard government-issue tombstone.

Wilfred Puttkammer (1891–1978)—A graduate of Princeton University and the University of Chicago Law School, Puttkammer left a thriving legal practice to enlist in the AEF as a private.

After surviving the dangers of Montfaucon and Hill 378, he was recruited to teach law at Chicago, a pursuit he followed for the next thirty-six years.

Claude B. Sweezey (1868–1939)—The courageous, stuttering colonel of the 313th Regiment was a popular hero on his return from France. After exploring politics, he was appointed warden of Baltimore's prison. Acclaimed by many as an innovator, Sweezey retired in 1925 because of controversy arising from his decision to allow an inmate to run a mail-order business that reduced the cost of running the prison.[19]

US Unknown Soldier—To make sure that the doughboy selected as the nation's Unknown Soldier would remain anonymous, the army took extraordinary steps to conceal his identity. Despite these precautions, the 316th Regiment Association announced in 1937, "It is well known that the body of the Unknown Soldier was taken from the vicinity of Hill 378 in the Argonne sector, where the 316th Infantry suffered its greatest casualties. As yet we have no documentary evidence to prove that the Unknown Soldier was a member of the 316th Infantry, but it is reasonable to believe that he may have been."[20] The association dispatched a delegation to France to determine whether the soldier buried at Arlington National Cemetery was one of its comrades. The search was inconclusive, and the soldier representing the 50,280 US servicemen killed in World War I remains unidentified.[21]

Wilhelm, Crown Prince of Germany (1882–1951)—After abdicating in 1918, Wilhelm fled to Holland. In 1923 he returned to Germany after promising not to engage in politics, a vow he broke by befriending Hitler. The prince hoped that Hitler would restore the monarchy, but when it became clear that the Fuhrer intended to secure power for himself, Wilhelm dropped out of politics. During World War II, diplomats sounded him out about the possibility of replacing Hitler in a coup, an offer the prince wisely declined. The Nazis learned of the matter and placed Wilhelm under Gestapo surveillance. In 1945, the Russians captured his estate, which was used for the postwar Potsdam Conference.

Wilhelm II, Emperor of Germany (1859–1941)—The Treaty of Versailles called for trying the former German emperor for "a supreme offense against international morality," but Queen Wilhelmina refused to extradite him from the Netherlands.[24] He settled in Doorn, writing his memoir, hunting, and sketching grand palaces and massive battleships. Like his son, Wilhelm hoped that Hitler would restore the monarchy, a fantasy he harbored until his death in 1941.

APPENDIX

Organization Chart—American Expeditionary Forces (September 1918)

Unit	Personnel	Sub-Units	CO rank	Commander(s)
AEF	2 million	1 army	General (4-star)	Pershing*
First US Army	1.2 million	3 corps	Lt. General (3-star)[†]	Pershing*
Corps	112,000	4 divisions	Maj. General (2-star)	Liggett (I), Bullard (III), Cameron (V)**
Division	28,000	2 brigades	Maj. General (2-star)	Kuhn (79th)
Brigade	8,134	2 regiments	Brig. General (1-star)	BG Nicholson (157th), BG R. H. Noble (158th)[‡]
Regiment	3,699	3 battalions	Colonel	Col. Sweezey (313th), Col. Oury (314th), Col. Knowles (315th), Col. Charles (316th)[††]
Battalion	1,027	4 companies	Major	Maj. Parkin[‡‡] (1st Batt. of 316th)
Company	255	4 platoons	Captain	Capt. Hewit (F Co. 316th)
Platoon	60	5 squads	Lieutenant	Lt. Goetz
Squad	12		Sergeant	Sgt. Cabla

* During the Meuse-Argonne Offensive, Pershing served concurrently as commanding officer of the AEF and commanding officer of the First US Army.

† Lieutenant General (3-star) would normally command an army.

** Cameron relieved October 12, 1918.

‡ Noble relieved by Knowles and Oury September 27, 1918.

†† Charles relieved by Lieutenant Colonel R. L. Meador September 27, 1918, and by Williams ca. October 15, 1918.

‡‡ Parkin served as CO of the 316th from October 8, 1918, to October 26, 1918.

ACKNOWLEDGMENTS

The destroyed German pillbox at Haucourt memorializes
the French and American soldiers who assaulted the area.

Until I began researching and writing this book, I scoffed at
lengthy acknowledgments. But over the course of the last twenty
years, I have benefited from the support of so many people that
I now fear leaving someone out. My sincere apologies to those I
overlooked.

My principal debt is to Professor Edward Lengel of the
University of Virginia, who lent me his skepticism. I asked the
award-winning World War I historian to review my project with
a critical eye, and for six months he did exactly that. Ed concluded
that my research was sound and my findings accurate. He remains
a valued mentor and friend.

A corps of wonderful friends read my drafts, proofed copy, and provided encouragement. They include Amy and Leigh Allen, Geoff Feiss and Nancy West, Andy and Jean Petkofsky, Jim and Ann Bill, Frank and Jarka Shatz, David Cowan, Mary K. LLewellyn, David Holmes, Carl Strikwerda, Paul Aron, Scott Nelson, Clare Song, Martin Townsend, Joel Hodson, John Shetler, Gretchen Long, Gina and Ned Andrew Solomon, Paul Cora, George Ray, Harvey Edber, Ted Hamady, Von Hardesty, and James Walker, my late uncle who landed on Omaha Beach on June 6, 1944. Other friends provided documents, photographs, and anecdotes, including Peter Parkin; Charlie and Cordie Puttkammer; the late Joseph Labrum Jr. and his son, Kingdon Gould; George Creel; Preston Manning; Ted Anthony; Earle Dunford; and Between the Covers Bookstore (Merchantville, New Jersey), which kindly furnished a copy of Jack Bentley's memoir. The illustrations were prepared by Gretchen Long of Staunton, Virginia.

I salute those in France who have walked the fields of memory with me: David Bedford, superintendent of the Meuse-Argonne American Cemetery; Jean-Paul DeVries, Rob van Zanten, and Maarten Otte, all excellent battlefield guides; Frederick Castier, Republic of France; Peter Folkers; and Ian and Carol Moore, who always provided a warm welcome, interesting conversation, and comfortable bed in Dun-sur-Meuse.

My deep appreciation goes to those who keep the torch burning at the Descendants and Friends of the 314th Regiment, including Nancy Schaff, Joel Rentz, John Shetler, Tony Patti, and Joseph Labrum III.

I owe a vast debt to archivists and librarians: Robin Wagner and Alice Huff at Gettysburg College; Timothy Nenninger, Mitchell Yockelson, and others at the US National Archives in College Park, Maryland; and helpful professionals at the Library of Congress, National World War I Memorial, US Army Center for Military History, College of William & Mary Library, the Hoover Institution, Historical Library of Maryland, Pennsylvania Historical Society, Woodrow Wilson Presidential Library, Mary

Baldwin College Library, and the 79th Division Museum at Fort Meade.

I am deeply grateful to my agent, John Silbersack, of Trident Media Group, who guided the project and secured a wonderful publisher. Colin Harrison, my editor at Scribner, added immeasurably to the final product; I appreciate his confidence, sensitivity, guidance, and friendship, and that of his able assistants, Katrina Diaz and Sarah Goldberg. Charlie Euchner, a superb coach and author of the *Writing Code*, provided critical assistance and encouragement.

Finally, I acknowledge gratefully the inspiration of three family members. Years ago, my grandmother Bessie McGill Walker fostered my love of military history by reading me Old Testament battle stories, with their insights into human motivation. My daughter, Lara W. Kessler, offered encouragement, editorial advice, and, most importantly, motivation by declaring at my retirement, "Your career is over, Dad; now you can relax." That inadvertent nudge, as well as her personal courage and persistence, will forever challenge me.

Ultimately, my greatest debt is to my wife, Jan LLewellyn Walker, who has always believed. She accompanied me on the winding path of an academic career, along the way becoming my indispensable proofreader, battlefield strider, trench jumper, bunker crawler . . . and best friend.

NOTES

The ruins of the Montfaucon church are maintained by the American Battle Monuments Commission as a memorial to the men who died nearby. The west-front pier of the sanctuary was converted by the Germans into an observation post that is open to visitors.

Prologue: Words Tongued with Fire

1. James Harbord, *American Army in France*.
2. T. S. Eliot, "Little Gidding," in *Complete Poems and Plays*, 139.

Chapter 1: "Horrors from the Abyss"

1. Sigfried Sassoon, "To the Warmongers," in Fiona Waters, ed., *A Corner of a Foreign Field*, 160.
2. Interview with H. D. "Pete" Parkin.
3. Harbord, *American Army in France*, 434–35.
4. Harry D. Parkin, marginalia in Harbord, *American Army in France* (located in Musselman Library, Special Collections, Gettysburg College), 435.
5. Ibid., 633.
6. John Pershing, *Experiences in the World War*, vol. 2, 295–96.

7. Interview with H. D. "Pete" Parkin.
8. Harry D. Parkin, marginalia in Harbord, *American Army in France*, 435.
9. Ibid., 633.
10. E. E. Booth, *Observations and Experiences*, 18.
11. Ibid., 218.
12. Hugh A. Drum to John L. Hines, September 12, 1921, Hugh A. Drum Papers, box 3, MHI. Includes the following statements: "General Pershing has ruled against criticism in the Army report," and, "Nothing is gained by criticism."
13. Edward Lengel, *Conquer Hell*, 191.
14. E. E. Booth to H. A. Parker, December 16, 1920, NARA, Adm. Materials Re to AEF Records, box 3, RG 120 located at 290/78/2/7 (hereafter cited as Montfaucon Study).

Chapter 2: Little Gibraltar of the Western Front

1. Crown Prince Wilhelm of Germany, *My War Experiences*, 236.
2. Ibid., 66.
3. Ibid.
4. Ibid.
5. Ibid., 199.
6. John Keegan, *First World War*, 28. David Stevenson, in *Cataclysm: The First World War as Political Tragedy*, argues that the Schlieffen Plan was never refined into an operational plan; and David Fromkin, in *Europe's Last Summer: Who Started the Great War in 1914?*, makes the case that the plan was really the product of Moltke the Younger, who succeeded Schlieffen as chief of the General Staff in 1906.
7. Hew Strachan, *First World War*, 56.
8. Crown Prince Wilhelm, *My War Experiences*, 91.
9. Joseph Persico, *Eleventh Month*, 380.
10. Author's collection of postcards, contemporary German views of Malancourt, Montfaucon, Nantillois, Romagne, and other villages, as well as fortifications in 79th Division's Meuse-Argonne sector.
11. Ibid.
12. Crown Prince Wilhelm, *My War Experiences*, 140.
13. Martin Gilbert, *First World War*, 227.
14. Keegan, *First World War*, 279.
15. Herbert Jager, *German Artillery*, 46.
16. Ibid., 68.
17. Author's collection.
18. J. Frank Barber, *Engineering Regiment*, 300.
19. Ibid., 301; DuPuy, *Machine Gunner's Notes*, 95.
20. Alistair Horne, *Price of Glory*, 123.

21. Crown Prince Wilhelm, *My War Experiences*, 223.
22. Martin Middlebrook, *Kaiser's Battle*, 151.
23. Keegan, *First World War*, 290.
24. Peter Hart, *Somme*, 65.
25. Ibid., 68; for the number of shells, see Youel, *Somme: Then and Now*, 47.
26. Gilbert, *First World War*, 258.
27. Middlebrook, *First Day on the Somme*, 244.
28. Ibid., 243.
29. Keegan, *First World War*, 285.
30. Horne, *Price of Glory*, 327.
31. John Ellis, *Databook*, 272.
32. Spencer Tucker, "Wilhelm, Crown Prince," in *Encyclopedia of World War I*, 1260.
33. Crown Prince Wilhelm, *My War Experiences*, 199, 216.
34. John Cooper, *Woodrow Wilson*, 285.
35. Ibid., 352.
36. Ibid., 286.
37. August Heckscher, *Woodrow Wilson*, 372.
38. According to Cooper, Wilson first used this phrase in a confidential interview with Herbert Brougham of the *New York Times*. Cooper, *Woodrow Wilson*, 276.
39. Gilbert, *First World War*, 306.
40. Keegan, *First World War*, 351.

Chapter 3: "Do You Wish to Take Part in the Battle?"

1. Ferdinand Foch, *Memoirs of Marshall Foch*, 270.
2. All figures from Keegan, *First World War*, 372.
3. Ellis, *Databook*, 247.
4. David Kennedy, *Over Here*, 144.
5. John Eisenhower with Eisenhower, *Yanks*, 27.
6. Pershing, *Experiences*, vol. 1, 18.
7. Ellis, *Databook*, 247.
8. Robert Doughty, *Pyrrhic Victory*, 25.
9. Ibid., 37.
10. Donald Smythe, *Pershing: General of the Armies*, 174.
11. Ibid., 175. In discussing this important conversation, I have drawn on several sources, including Smythe and "Notes on Conversation Between General Pershing and Marshal Foch at Ligny-en-Barrois." US Army Center of Military History, *United States Army in the World War*, vol. 8, 36ff.
12. Pershing, *Experiences*, vol. 2, 244.
13. *United States Army in the World War*, vol. 8, 38.

14. Ibid.
15. Lengel, *Conquer Hell*, 51.
16. Smythe, *Pershing*, 176.
17. Ibid., 177.
18. Robert Ferrell, *America's Deadliest Battle*, 38.
19. Smythe, *Pershing*, 191.
20. Gilbert, *First World War*, 308.
21. B. H. Liddell Hart, *Real War*, 300.
22. Tucker, "Gallwitz, Max von," in *Encyclopedia of World War I*, 464.
23. Barbara Tuchman, *Guns of August*, 195.
24. Holger Herwig, *Marne*, 128.
25. Keegan, *First World War*, 87.
26. Paul Strong and Marble, *Artillery*, 107.
27. See T. J. Mitchell, *Casualties and Medical Statistics*.

Chapter 4: "This Appalling Proposition"

1. Maurice Swetland and Swetland, *"These Men,"* 61.
2. George Marshall, *Memoirs of My Service*, 137.
3. Ibid., 138.
4. Ibid., 139.
5. Lengel, *Conquer Hell*, 71.
6. Pershing, *Experiences*, vol. 2, 255, 285.
7. Marshall, 139.
8. Hunter Liggett, A E F: *Ten Years*, 167–68.
9. Pershing, *Experiences*, vol. 2, 290.
10. Ibid., vol. 2, 293.
11. Frederick Palmer, *John J. Pershing*, 302.
12. Smythe, *Pershing*, 183.
13. Pershing, *Experiences*, vol. 2, 287.
14. B. A. Poore to E. E. Booth, January 8, 1920, Montfaucon Study.
15. Pershing, *Experiences*, vol. 2, 293.
16. Thomas Phillips, *Roots of Strategy*, 404.
17. Hugh Drum, *General Discussion of the Offensive*, 97.
18. Eisenhower with Eisenhower, *Yanks*, 204.
19. *United States Army in the World War*, vol. 9, 84.
20. Ibid.
21. Liggett, *AEF: Ten Years*, 255.
22. Pershing, *Experiences*, vol. 2, 269.
23. Eisenhower with Eisenhower, *Yanks*, 204.
24. Interview with George Creel.
25. Eisenhower with Eisenhower, *Yanks*, 204.

26. Frederick Palmer, *Greatest Battle*, 363.
27. Allan Millett, *The General*, 39.
28. Robert Bullard, *Reminiscences*, 33.
29. Ibid.
30. Ibid.
31. Ibid., 295.
32. Ibid., 298.
33. According to the *U.S. Army History of the Staff College*, only five Leavenworth graduates commanded divisions, but twenty-three Staff College graduates served as chiefs of staff of the twenty-six AEF divisions.
34. Pershing, *Experiences*, vol. 2, 253.

Chapter 5: "Feeling Like Crusaders"

1. Pershing, *Experiences*, vol. 1, 58.
2. Parkin, "Memoirs," vol. 1, 58.
3. Ibid.
4. Ibid.
5. MHI Questionnaire, Fleming, "World War I Service," 3, 315th Infantry Regiment.
6. Ibid.
7. John McKenna, *315th Infantry*, 22.
8. Jared Sparks, *Writings of George Washington*, vol. 4, 114.
9. Susan Carter, *Historical Statistics*, vol. 1,, 602.
10. David Laskin, *Long Way Home*, 134.
11. Ibid., 134.
12. Maximilian Boll, "My First Journey," *i*.
13. John "Jack" N. Bentley, "My Experiences in the Army," 12.
14. David McCullough, *1776*, 293–94.
15. Parkin, "Memoirs," vol. 1, 22.
16. Lester Muller, *313th of the 79th*, 60.
17. Ibid., 61.
18. Corinna Smith, *Interesting People*, 302.
19. "Jack Bentley," Baseball-Reference.com; Bentley won 16 games and lost only 5 in 1924 with the New York Giants; his ERA for that season was 3.78. Bentley's batting average in 1923 was a phenomenal .427, and his on-base average was .446.
20. Bentley, "My Experiences in the Army," 1 (manuscript).
21. Boll, "My First Journey," 39.
22. Ibid., 40.
23. Lengel, *Conquer Hell*, 33.
24. J. Frank Barber, *Seventy-Ninth Division*, 37.

25. Ibid., 37.
26. American Battle Monuments Commission, *79th Division Summary of Operations in the World War* (Washington, DC: US Government Printing Office), 1944, 4, 8; compare with summaries of other divisions.
27. Parkin, "Memoirs," vol. 1, 67.
28. Boll, "My First Journey," 61.
29. Parkin, "Memoirs," vol. 1, 77.
30. Ibid., 81.

Chapter 6: Training for Disaster

1. Quoted in Mark Grotelueschen, *AEF Way*, 44.
2. Parkin, "Memoirs," vol. 1, 91.
3. Arthur Joel, *Lorraine Cross*, 23.
4. Grotelueschen, *AEF Way*, 24.
5. Edward House, *Intimate Papers of Colonel House*, 3, 268–69.
6. Pershing. *Combat Instructions*, 3.
7. Ibid.
8. Parkin, "Memoirs," vol. 1, 89–90.
9. Douglas Johnson, *A Few Squads*, 247.
10. Parkin, "Memoirs," vol. 1, 102.
11. Ibid., 103.
12. Ibid.
13. Ibid., vol. 2, 38.
14. Ibid., 39.
15. MHI Questionnaire, Fleming, "World War I Service," 5, 315th Infantry Regiment.
16 Ibid., 25.
17. "Our Attaché in Peril," *New York Times*, June 28, 1915.
18. "Gen. Kuhn Slated to Succeed Scott," *New York Times*, September 20, 1917.
19. Millett, *The General*, 48–49.
20. MHI Questionnaire, Fleming, "World War I Service," 36, 315th Infantry Regiment.
21. Parkin, "Memoirs," vol. 2, 20.
22. Ibid.
23. Ibid.
24. Ibid., 29.
25. Ibid., 30.
26. Rod Paschall, *Defeat of Imperial Germany*, 180.
27. See Smythe, *Pershing*, 188–89; Paschall, *Defeat of Imperial Germany*, 180–81.
28. Barber, *Seventy-Ninth Division*, 48.
29. Carl Glock, *316th Infantry Regiment*, 29.
30. Parkin, "Memoirs," vol. 2, 62.

31. Bentley, "My Experiences in the Army," 7.

32. Parkin, "Memoirs," vol. 2, 79.

33. Ibid., 71.

34. Ibid., 78.

35. Ibid., 72.

36. Ibid.

37. Ibid., 75.

38. Joseph Labrum, *Company G*, 35.

39. McKenna, *315th Infantry*, 49–50.

Chapter 7: "An Ominous, Dread-Inspiring Place"

1. "Argonne Forest at Midnight, A Sapper's Song from the World War, 1915," Translated by Jeff Curtis on http://roadstothegreatwar-ww1.blogspot.com.

2. Parkin, "Memoirs," vol. 2, 83.

3. Ibid., 81.

4. Barber, *Seventy-Ninth Division*, 61.

5. Bentley, "My Experiences in the Army," 9.

6. Ibid.

7. Boll, "My First Journey," 70.

8. Ibid.,76.

9. Ibid., 73.

10. *United States Army in the World War*, vol. 9, 509.

11. Muller, *313th of the 79th*, 90.

12. Henry Thorn, *"Baltimore's Own,"* 23.

13. Barber, *Seventy-Ninth Division*, 69.

14. McKenna, *315th Infantry*, 48–49.

15. John Kress, *"Rugged Individualists,"* 36.

16. Bentley, "My Experiences in the Army," 9.

17. Parkin, "Memoirs," vol. 2, 95.

18. Ibid., 86.

19. Barber, *Seventy-Ninth Division*, 62.

20. Ibid., 61.

21. Bentley, "My Experiences in the Army," 10.

22. Ibid.

23. Parkin, "Memoirs," vol. 2, 91.

24. Ibid.

25. Barber, *Seventy-Ninth Division*, 72.

26. Bullard, *Reminiscences*, 270.

27. Lengel, *Conquer Hell*, 61.

28. Parkin, "Memoirs," vol. 2, 91.

29. Ibid., 93.

30. Barber, *Engineer Regiment*, 77.

31. MHI Questionnaire, Andrew J. Kachik, Company H, 314th Infantry Regiment.
32. Raymond Tompkins, *Maryland Fighters*, 79.
33. Joel, *Lorraine Cross*, 25.
34. Bentley, "My Experiences in the Army," 11.
35. Ibid., 10.
36. Ibid., 10–11.
37. Lengel, *Conquer Hell*, 60.

Chapter 8: Toward Montfaucon and into a Trap

1. Liddell Hart, *Fog of War*, 341.
2. Edward Rickenbacker, *Fighting the Flying Circus*, 212.
3. Ibid.
4. Parkin, "Memoirs," vol. 2, 99; Bullard, *Reminiscences*, 86.
5. *United States Army in the World War*, vol. 9, 127.
6. John Toland, *1918*, 431.
7. Pershing, *Experiences*, vol. 2, 285n; John Rowe, *Company F*, 52; Lengel, *Conquer Hell*, 62, states that there were 2,775 artillery pieces in the opening barrage; Ferrell (*Deadliest Battle*, 41) uses a higher figure of 3,980 guns.
8. Bentley, "My Experiences in the Army," 12.
9. William Hanson, *I Was There*, 69; Kress, "*Rugged Individualists*," 37.
10. Erich Ludendorff, *General Staff and Its Problems*, 355.
11. George Viereck, ed., *As They Saw Us*, 239.
12. Muller, *313th of the 79th*, 105.
13. James Cain, "Taking of Montfaucon," *American Mercury*, 114–15.
14. Rowe, *Company F*, 53. To spare civilians who would read his account, Rowe adopted the art term *cossakers* as a substitute for an obscene slur the doughboys applied to the Germans.
15. Ibid.
16. Paschall, *Defeat of Imperial Germany*, 186.
17. Palmer, *Greatest Battle*, 66–67.
18. Labrum, *Company G*, 38.
19. *Regimental History of the 316th*, 37.
20. Parkin, "Memoirs," vol. 2, 103.
21. Barber, *Seventy-Ninth Division*, 85.
22. Parkin, "Memoirs," vol. 2, 106.
23. MHI Questionnaire, James E. Meehan, "My Diary," 7, 313th Regiment.
24. McKenna, *315th Infantry*, 54.
25. Barber, *Seventy-Ninth Division*, 434.
26. Parkin, "Memoirs," vol. 2, 109.
27. MHI Questionnaire, Casper W. Swartz, 33, 314th Regiment.
28. Bentley, "My Experiences in the Army," 14.

29. Ibid.
30. Barber, *Seventy-Ninth Division*, 93.
31. Palmer, *Greatest Battle*, 127.
32. Barber, *Seventy-Ninth Division*, 93.
33. Parkin, "Memoirs," vol. 2, 101.
34. John Ellis, *Eye-Deep in Hell*, 21.
35. Palmer, *Greatest Battle*, 215.
36 McKenna, *315th Infantry*, 55.
37. Smythe, *Pershing*, 205.
38. Joel, *Lorraine Cross*, 27.
39. MHI Questionnaire, Casper W. Swartz, 30, 314th Regiment.
40. Ibid., 31.
41. Labrum, *Company G*, 40.
42. Barber, *Seventy-Ninth Division*, 86–87.
43. Winter, *Death's Men*, 126.
44. Lengel, *Conquer Hell*, 100.
45. Barber, *Seventy-Ninth Division*, 87.
46. Victor Keller, "A German Reply to Gen. Pershing's War Story," *New York Times*, May 3, 1931.
47. Muller, *313th of the 79th*, 39; for the attrition rate of tanks, see Ferrell, *Deadliest Battle*, 8.

Chapter 9: "The 79th Is Holding Up the Entire First Army"

1. Thomas Johnson, *Without Censor*, 159.
2. Bentley, "My Experiences in the Army," 109.
3. Ibid.
4. Barber, *Engineer Regiment*, 77.
5. Tompkins, *Maryland Fighters*, 82.
6. Denis Winter, *Death's Men*, 184.
7. Edwin I. James, "Our Prisoners Now 8,000," *New York Times*, September 28, 1918.
8. Tompkins, *Maryland Fighters*, 84.
9. Ferrell, *Deadliest Battle*, 49.
10. Elbridge Colby, "Taking of Montfaucon," *Infantry Journal*, 7–8.
11. Cain, "Taking of Montfaucon," *American Mercury*, 17.
12. Colby, "Taking of Montfaucon," *Infantry Journal*, 8.
13. Barber, *Seventy-Ninth Division*, 100.
14. Reports on the number of French tanks that participated in the attack vary from two to seven.
15. Tompkins, *Maryland Fighters*, 90.
16. Bentley, "My Experiences in the Army," 210.
17. Tompkins, *Maryland Fighters*, 84.

18. Barber, *Seventy-Ninth Division*, 102.
19. Bentley, "My Experiences in the Army," 14.
20. Barber, *Seventy-Ninth Division*, 102.
21. Gordon Johnston to E. E. Booth, December 3, 1933, Montfaucon Study. Johnston's intriguing story and its implications about the battle plan were also reported in a review of B. H. Liddell Hart's book on Foch in the *Chattanooga (Tenn.) News* on February 6, 1932.
22. Eisenhower with Eisenhower, *Yanks*, 221.
23. Edward Coffman, *War to End All Wars*, 309.
24. Christian Bach and Henry Noble Hall, *Fourth Division*, 164.
25. Colby, "Taking of Montfaucon," *Infantry Journal*, 9.
26. Coffman, *War to End All Wars*, 309.
27. Barber, *Seventy-Ninth Division*, 106.
28. Ibid.
29. Interview with Charles Puttkammer.
30. Parkin, "Memoirs," vol. 2, 111.
31. Max von Gallwitz to T. M. Johnson, March 20, 1928, H. A. Drum Papers, box 18, MHI.

Chapter 10: "Bayonet and Rifle Butt, Pistol and Trench Knife"

1. Quoted in Eric Leed, *No Man's Land*, 11.
2. MHI Questionnaire, Kachik, 16, 314th Regiment.
3. Ibid., 16–17.
4. Ibid., 17.
5. Thomas Fleming, *Illusion of Victory*, 71.
6. Ibid., 70–71.
7. Ralph Cole and Howells, *Thirty-Seventh Division*, vol. 2, 244.
8. Ibid., 248. Although the "chateau" captured by the Thirty-Seventh Division resembled the manor house that was the site of the observatory, it was not that important facility. The observatory was located on the east side of the butte, not the west side assaulted by the Thirty-Seventh.
9. Raymond S. Tompkins, "Records Back Seventy-Ninth's Claim to Montfaucon Capture," *Baltimore Sun*, May 3, 1923.
10. Parkin, "Memoirs," vol. 2, 116.
11. Boll, "My First Journey," 87.
12. Parkin, "Memoirs," vol. 2, 120.
13. Ibid., 121.
14. Coffman, *War to End All Wars*, 309.
15. Bentley, "My Experiences in the Army," 14.
16. Tompkins, *Maryland Fighters*, 87.
17. Bentley, "My Experiences in the Army," 15.
18. Tompkins, *Maryland Fighters*, 87–88.

19. Charles DuPuy, *Machine Gunner's Notes*, 86.
20. Ibid.
21. Interview with Earle Dunford, son of Junius Dunford.
22. *Regimental History of the 316th*, 38.
23. Rowe, *Company F*, 55.
24. Labrum, *Company G*, 43.
25. Ibid., 45.
26. Boll, "My First Journey," 87.
27. Bentley, "My Experiences in the Army," 24.
28. Barber, *Seventy-Ninth Division*, 58–59.
29. Ibid., 113.
30. Ibid.
31. Viereck, ed., *As They Saw Us*, 242–43.
32. Bentley, "My Experiences in the Army," 15–16.
33. Tompkins, *Maryland Fighters*, 90.
34. Ibid.
35. Barber, *Seventy-Ninth Division*, 148.
36. Rowe, *Company F.*, 56.
37. MHI Questionnaire, James Meehan, 9, 313th Regiment.
38. Rowe, *Company F*, 62.
39. Parkin, "Memoirs," vol. 2, 123.
40. Viereck, ed., *As They Saw Us*, 243.
41. Parkin, "Memoirs," vol. 2, 127.
42. Ibid., 128.
43. Ibid., "Memoirs," vol. 3, 1–2.

Chapter 11: "All America Is Behind Us"

1. Lengel, *Conquer Hell*, 100.
2. Parkin, "Memoirs," vol. 3, 5.
3. Rowe, *Company F*, 59.
4. Barber, *Seventy-Ninth Division*, 134.
5. Philadelphia War History Committee, *Philadelphia in the World War*, 145.
6. Rowe, *Company F*, 60–61.
7. Ibid., 58.
8. Parkin, "Memoirs," vol. 3, 13.
9. Ibid.
10. Ibid.
11. Barber, *Seventy-Ninth Division*, 135.
12. Ibid.
13. Ibid.
14. MHI Questionnaire, Fleming, "World War I Service," 50, 315th Regiment.
15. Rickenbacker, *Fighting the Flying Circus*, 215.

16. Labrum, *Company G*, 46.
17. Barber, *Seventy-Ninth Division*, 435.
18. McKenna, *315th Infantry*, 69.
19. Parkin, "Memoirs," vol. 3, 17.
20. Ibid., 101.
21. Rowe, *Company F*, 60.
22. Ibid., 60–61.
23. Ibid., 61.
24. Parkin, "Memoirs," vol. 3, 21.
25. Barber, *Seventy-Ninth*, 141–43.
26. Hanson, *I Was There*, 79.
27. Boll, "My First Journey," 92.
28. Parkin, "Memoirs," vol. 3, 18.
29. Rowe, *Company F*, 61.
30. Ibid., 62.

Chapter 12: "Regardless of Cost"

1. James Rainey, "Questionable Training," 100.
2. Pershing Papers, box 3, Pershing Diary, 692, LOC.
3. Ibid., 694.
4. Eisenhower with Eisenhower, *Yanks*, 223.
5. *United States Army in the World War*, vol. 9, 148.
6. Barber, *Seventy-Ninth Division*, 149.
7. Ibid.
8. Parkin, "Memoirs," vol. 3, 25.
9. McKenna, *315th Infantry*, 74.
10. Barber, *Seventy-Ninth Division*, 150.
11. McKenna, *315th Infantry*, 71.
12. Rowe, *Company F*, 63.
13. Parkin, "Memoirs," vol. 3, 32; Barber, *Seventy-Ninth Division*, 153.
14. Parkin, "Memoirs," vol. 3, 31.
15. Rowe, *Company F*, 64.
16. Parkin, "Memoirs," vol. 3, 29–30.
17. Rowe, *Company F*, 64.
18. Parkin, "Memoirs," vol. 3, 34.
19. Muller, *313th of the 79th*, 43.
20. Parkin, "Memoirs," vol. 3, 40.
21. Barber, *Seventy-Ninth Division*, 154.
22. Ibid., 157.
23. McKenna, *315th Infantry*, 254.
24. Barber, *Seventy-Ninth Division*, 154.
25. Ibid., 157.

26. Muller, *313th of the 79th*, 122.
27. Hanson, *I Was There*, 84.
28. Barber, *Seventy-Ninth Division*, 165.
29. Ibid., 166.
30. Ibid., 164.
31. Pershing Papers, box 3, Pershing Diary, 696, LOC.
32. Foch, *Memoirs*, 435.

Chapter 13: The Cost of "Regardless"

1. Maury Maverick, *Maverick American*, 129.
2. Parkin, "Memoirs," vol. 3, 42.
3. Quoted from General Order No. 29, 79th Division, 1919, Paragraph I, in Barber, *Seventy-Ninth Division*, 158.
4. Muller, *313th of the 79th*, 121.
5. Ibid., 122.
6. Bentley, "My Experiences in the Army," 17.
7. Ibid.
8. Ibid.
9. Ibid.
10. Ibid.
11. Parkin, "Memoirs," vol. 3, 48–49.
12. Ibid., 53–54.
13. Ibid., 56.
14. Ibid., 62.
15. Ibid., 63.
16. Ibid., 65.
17. Ibid., 70.
18. Ibid., 71.
19. Barber, *Seventy-Ninth Division*, 461.
20. American Battle Monuments Commission, National Archives, RG 117, 79th Division, box 242.
21. Ibid.
22. Ferrell, *Deadliest Battle*, 49.
23. Parkin, "Memoirs," vol. 3, 66.

Chapter 14: Relief and Disgrace

1. James Hallas, *Doughboy War*, 247.
2. Ibid., 250.
3. Ibid.
4. Bentley, "My Experiences in the Army," 15.

5. Hallas, *Doughboy War*, 252.

6. Parkin, "Memoirs," vol. 3, 76, 87.

7. Eisenhower with Eisenhower, *Yanks*, 251.

8. Palmer, *Greatest Battle*, 194.

9. Quoted in Smythe, *Pershing*, 200.

10. Ibid., 206.

11. Harvey Cushing, *Surgeon's Journal*, 462.

12. Ibid.

13. Parkin, "Memoirs," vol. 3, 108.

14. Ibid., 120.

15. Ibid., 129.

16. Ibid.

17. Ibid., 131.

18. Eisenhower with Eisenhower, *Yanks*, 254.

19. In 1919 the AEF press office issued a series of releases to announce the award of the Distinguished Service Medal to sixteen divisional commanders. Kuhn's name does not appear among them.

20. Quoted in Coffman, *War to End All Wars*, 320.

21. Hallas, *Doughboy War*, 247.

22. Smythe, *Pershing*, 208.

23. Richard O'Connor, *Black Jack Pershing*, 182.

24. Frank Simonds, *They Won the War*, 18.

25. *United States Army in the World War*, vol. 8, 92.

26. Ibid.

27. Ibid.

28. Frank Vandiver, *Black Jack*, vol. 2, 975.

29. John Eisenhower comes close to connecting most of the dots about the situation in his discussion of the incident (Eisenhower with Eisenhower, *Yanks*, 226–27). He fails, however, to examine the letters contained in the NARA Montfaucon Study.

30. H. A. Drum to J. L. Hines, September 12, 1921, H. A. Drum Papers, box 16, MHI.

31. Noel F. Busch, "General Drum: Nation's No. 1 Field Soldier," *Life*, June 16, 1941, 88.

32. Field Order No. 33, October 1, 1918, First U.S. Army, RG 120, box 3382, NARA.

33. Coffman, *War to End All Wars*, 323.

Chapter 15: Into the Cyclone . . . Once Again

1. Alvin York, October 7, 1918, *Diary of Alvin York*, http://acacia.pair.com /Acacia.Vignettes/The.Diary.of.Alvin.York.html.

2. Rowe, *Company F*, 72.
3. *History of the 316th Infantry*, 74.
4. Parkin, "Memoirs," vol. 4, 115.
5. Ibid., 118.
6. Ibid.
7. Ibid., 118–19.
8. Ibid., 119.
9. Ibid., 120.
10. Ibid.
11. John Kress, *Great Adventure*, 43.
12. Ibid.
13. Labrum, *Company G*, 58.
14. Rowe, *Company F*, 72.
15. Parkin, "Memoirs," vol. 4, 58–59.
16. Ibid., 137.
17. Ibid.
18. Kress, *Great Adventure*, 45.
19. Bentley, "My Experiences in the Army," 20.
20. Parkin, "Memoirs," vol. 4, 128.
21. Ibid., 136.
22. Barber, *Seventy-Ninth Division*, 221.
23. MHI Questionnaire, Kachik, 19, 314th Regiment.
24. Ibid.
25. Ibid.
26. Parkin, "Memoirs," vol. 4, 131.
27. Ibid.
28. Ibid., 131–32.
29. Ibid., 125.
30. Ibid., 35.
31. Ibid., 151.
32. Ibid., 121.
33. Ibid., 67.
34. Rowe, *Company F*, 75.
35. Ibid., 76.
36. Barber, *Seventy-Ninth Division*, 225–26.
37. Glock, *316th Infantry Regiment*, 68.

Chapter 16: Redemption on Corn Willy Hill

1. Parkin, "Memoirs," vol. 4, 50.
2. Rowe, *Company F*, 77.
3. *History of the 316th Infantry*, 70.

4. Susan Krouse, *American Indians*, 40.
5. American Battle Monuments Commission, NARA, RG 117, box 243, Parkin's Post Combat Report, 4.
6. Ibid., 5.
7. Ibid.
8. Ibid.
9. Ibid., 6.
10. Ibid., 7.
11. Parkin, "Memoirs," vol. 5, 1.
12. Ibid., 3–4.
13. Ibid., 3.
14. Ibid., 5.
15. *History of the 316th Infantry*, 72.
16. Ibid., 74.
17. Ibid., 75.
18. Krouse, *American Indians*, 41.
19. Ibid., 42.
20. Barber, *Seventy-Ninth Division*, 239.
21. "William Sinkler Manning," *New York Times*, January 5, 1919.
22. Barber, *Seventy-Ninth Division*, 242.
23. Krouse, *American Indians*, 40.
24. *History of the 316th Infantry*, 77.
25. Barber, *Seventy-Ninth Division*, 242.
26. Ibid., 253.
27. Ibid., 243.
28. Ibid., 242.
29. Ibid., 245.
30. *History of the 316th Infantry*, 77.
31. Ibid., 78.
32. Rowe, *Company F*, 79.
33. Barber, *Seventy-Ninth Division*, 254.
34. MHI Questionnaire, Samuel Fleming, "World War I Service," 74, 315th Regiment.
35. Barber, *Seventy-Ninth Division*, 258.

Chapter 17: Making Good . . . at Last

1. Joseph Persico, "Wasted Lives on Armistice Day," MHQ: HistoryNet: http://www.historynet.com/world-war-i-wasted-lives-on-armistice-day.htm. Pershing made the statement on November 5, 1919, in testimony before the US House of Representatives Committee on Military Affairs.
2. "Call 'America' Repugnant," *New York Times*, August 6, 1913.

3. "Flood Town with Anti-Arms Posters," *New York Times*, June 9, 1915.
4. James Richardson, ed., *Messages and Papers of the Presidents*, vol. 16, 8113–14.
5. Fleming, *Illusion of Victory*, 252.
6. "313th Non-Coms Named," *Sun*, October 9, 1917.
7. "Died to Prove Loyalty," *Baltimore Sun*, March 16, 1919.
8. Ernest F. Powell, "The Last American Killed in World War I," *Baltimore Sun*, November 10, 1968.
9. Ibid.
10. "Died to Prove Loyalty," 16.
11. Ibid., 16.
12. Labrum, *Company G*, 61.
13 Parkin, "Memoirs," vol. 5, 25.
14 Ibid., 20.
15 Ibid., 21.
16 Ibid., 30.
17 Ibid., 43.
18 Parkin, "Memoirs," vol. 4, 109.
19. Barber, *Seventy-Ninth Division*, 274.
20. Ibid., 287.
21. Powell, "Last American," *Sun*, November 10, 1968.
22. Barber, *Seventy-Ninth Division*, 310.
23. Ibid., 312.
24. Ibid., 314.
25. Persico, "Wasted Lives," MHQ: HistoryNet.
26. "Died to Prove Loyalty," 16.
27. Ibid.
28. Barber, *Seventy-Ninth Division*, 317.

Chapter 18: Controlling the Narrative

1. Smythe, "John J. Pershing," 22.
2. Ibid.; also cited in Palmer, *John J. Pershing*, 41; Vandiver, *Black Jack*, vol. 1, 195.
3. Ibid., 34.
4. Ibid., 123.
5. Ibid.
6. Emmet Crozier, *American Reporters*, 123.
7. Nathan Haverstock, *Fifty Years at the Front*, 192.
8. Palmer, *With My Own Eyes*, 336.
9. Ibid., 337.
10. Ibid., 339.
11. Crozier, *American Reporters*, 176.
12. Phillip Knightley, *First Casualty*, 2.

13. Palmer, *America in France*, 452.
14. Ibid.
15. Palmer, *Greatest Battle*, 194.
16. Ibid.
17. Ibid., 16.
18. H. A. Drum to J. L. Hines, September 12, 1921, Montfaucon Study, NARA.
19. Bullard, *Reminiscences*, 273.
20. Smythe, *Pershing*, 288.
21. Ibid., 289.
22. Ibid., 290.
23. John J. Pershing, Pershing Papers, box 366, draft of *Experiences*, LOC: chap. LXIII–21.
24. Ibid., chap. LXIV–6.
25. Ibid.
26. Ibid., chap. XLIV–4.
27. Pershing, *Experiences*, vol. 2, 295–96.
28. Smythe, *Pershing*, 293.
29. Johnson, *Without Censor*, x.
30. Ibid., 162.
31. Ibid., 134.
32. Ibid., 162.
33. Ibid., 164.

Chapter 19: Bullard, Bjornstad, and Booth

1. Bullard, *Reminiscences*, 97. The complete King James Version of the verse is, "There is a way that seemeth right unto a man, but the end thereof are the ways of death."
2. Booth, *Observations and Experiences*, 218.
3. Ibid.
4. Ibid.
5. E. E. Booth to H. A. Drum, March 21, 1921, Montfaucon Study, NARA.
6. Millett, *The General*, 387.
7. Bullard, *Reminiscences*, 12.
8. Quoted in Millett, *The General*, 130.
9. Quoted in Millett, *The General*, 178.
10. Bullard, *Reminiscences*, 206.
11. Ibid., 207.
12. Ibid., 45.
13. Ibid., 47.
14. Cooke, *Pershing and His Generals*, 34–35.

15. Millett, *The General*, 387.
16. Bjornstad was appointed chief of staff of III Corps on March 30, 1918 (Millett, *The General*, 378); Bullard was appointed commanding general of III Corps on July 8 (Millett, *The General*, 381).
17. Cooke, *Pershing and His Generals*, 130.
18. Millett, *The General*, 387.
19. Edward Lengel, author of *Thunder and Flames*, believes that Bullard's professed intention to withdraw the men was a fiction he concocted to protect his reputation.
20. Bullard, *Reminiscences*, 235–36.
21. Senate Committee on Military Affairs, *Hearings on the Nomination of Col. Alfred W. Bjornstad, U.S. Army, for Promotion to Be a Brigadier General*, 68th Congress, 2nd session, January 9, 12, 13, and 14, 1925, 85.
22. Millett, *The General*, 388.
23. "How the Gallant 13th Minnesota Came Home from the Isles of Death 25 Years Ago Today," *Minneapolis Journal*, October 12, 1924.
24. Ibid.
25. *Northfield (Minn.) News*, September 26, 1898.
26. Ibid., September 27, 1898.
27. "Gallant 13th Minnesota."
28. Millett, *The General*, 379.
29. Cooke, *Pershing and His Generals*, 129.
30. Millett, *The General*, 379.
31. Ibid.
32. Bullard, *Reminiscences*, 29.
33. Ibid., 27.
34. Ibid., 64.
35. Ibid., 112.
36. Ibid., 92.
37. Ibid., 266.
38. Lengel, *Thunder and Flames*, 328.
39. Alden Brooks, *As I Saw It*, 294.
40. Ibid.
41. Ibid., 294–95.
42. Persico, *Eleventh Month*, 379.
43. Thomas Ricks, *Generals*, 26.
44. Ibid., 26–27.

Chapter 20: Betrayal at Little Gibraltar

1. Henry Canby, *Education by Violence*, 23.
2. C. A. Bach to C. L. Bolte, June, 25, 1922, Montfaucon Study, NARA.

3. F. W. Clark to C. A. Bach, December 5, 1922, Montfaucon Study, NARA; see also T. M. Johnson to E. E. Booth, December 3, 1933, Montfaucon Study, NARA.

4. *United States Army in the World War*, vol. 8, 84.

5. A. W. Bjornstad to C. A. Bach, December 24, 1924, Montfaucon Study, NARA.

6. Ibid.

7. Ibid.

8. C. A. Bach to E. E. Booth, December 14, 1920, Montfaucon Study, NARA.

9. Ibid.

10. *United States Army in the World War*, vol. 9, 84.

11. Ibid.

12. C. A. Bach to E. E. Booth, December 14, 1920, Montfaucon Study, NARA.

13. Colonel R. T. Ward, "Explanation and Execution of Plans of Operation, 1st American Army for Argonne-Meuse Operation to November 11, 1918," G-3, General Staff, First Army, Special Operations Report: Part C: Meuse-Argonne Operations, January 5, 1919, File 110.1, NARA.

14. Millett, *The General*, 402.

15. "Bullard's Troops Did It," *New York Times*, October 5, 1918.

16. "Forrest," *New York Times*, May 28, 1918.

17. Millett, *The General*, 253.

18. Ibid., 417.

19. B. R. Poore to E. E. Booth, January 8, 1920, Montfaucon Study, NARA.

20. Bullard, *American Soldiers*, 90.

21. Ibid.

22. Bullard, *Reminiscences*, 270.

23. Ibid., 273.

24. Bullard, *American Soldiers*, 101.

25. Booth, *Observations and Experiences*, 216.

26. J. L. Hines to E. E. Booth, December 30, 1920, Montfaucon Study, NARA.

27. Ibid. Lieutenant Colonel Parker thought that Hines had discussed the matter with Bullard, but Hines corrects the record in this letter: "Parker is also in error in saying I got my instructions from General Bullard, for I remember that it was from Bjornstad by 'phone.'"

28. Ibid.

29. Ibid.

30. Quoted in Oliver Spaulding to E. E. Booth, February 18, 1921, Montfaucon Study, NARA.

31. Quoted in C. A. Bach to F. W. Clark, November 18, 1922, Montfaucon Study, NARA.

32. A. W. Bjornstad to C. A. Bach, December 24, 1924, Montfaucon Study, NARA.

33. Harry D. Parkin, marginalia in Harbord, *American Army in France* (located in Musselman Library, Special Collections, Gettysburg College), 633.

34. E. E. Booth to C. A. Bach, December 9, 1920, Montfaucon Study, NARA.
35. Ferrell, *Woodrow Wilson and World War I*, 256.
36. George Cameron to wife, October 12, 1918, Cameron Papers.
37. Ibid.
38. Ibid.
39. George Cameron to M. F. Steele, September 22, 1918, Cameron Papers.
40. Charles P. Summerall, *The Way of Duty, Honor, Country*, 4.
41. Senate Committee on Military Affairs, *Hearings . . . to Be a Brigadier General*, 42.
42. Ibid.
43. Ibid., 17.
44. Ibid., 82.
45. Ibid., 84.
46. Ibid., 85.
47. Ibid., 89.
48. Bullard Diary Book 9, October 31, 1918, Bullard Papers, box 2, LOC.
49. J. J. Pershing to E. E. Booth, June 17, 1940, Montfaucon Study, NARA.
50. Cooke, *Pershing and His Generals*, 150.
51. "Retired Officers Get Army War Rank," *New York Times*, August 20, 1930, 37.
52. Johnson, *Without Censor*, 161–62.
53. Lengel, *Conquer Hell*, 4.

Chapter 21: *Denkmal*: Remembering the Doughboys

1. Lisa Budreau, *Bodies of War*, 159.
2. Minutes of 15th Meeting of ABMC, November 4, 1925, RG 117, National Archives; Annual Report of the ABMC, June 1925, 44.
3. Ibid.
4. "Gold Star Mothers Charge 'Desecration,'" *New York Times*, December 14, 1931.
5. "French Group Resists Pershing on Memorial," *New York Times*, August 12, 1930.
6. *Guide to American Battles and Battlefields*, 524.
7. "Speeches at U.S. War Shrine at Montfaucon," *New York Times*, August 2, 1937.
8. Eliot, "The Hollow Men," in *Complete Poems and Plays*, 56.
9. Robert Laplander, *Finding the Lost Battalion*, 556.
10. "Veterans' Suicides Average Two a Day," *New York Times*, June 2, 1922.
11. "War Hero a Suicide; Motive a Mystery," *New York Times*, September 20, 1925; "Wounded Veteran Tries Thrice to Die," *New York Times*, August 14, 1922.
12. "Veteran a Suicide, Tubercular Victim," *New York Time*, August 11, 1921.

13 "Goes over Niagara Falls," *New York Times*, January 29, 1925.

14. George Colt, *November of the Soul*, 340, and "Lethal Beauty," *San Francisco Chronicle*, October 30, 2005.

15. "Wealthy Veteran Puts End to Life," *Washington Post*, May 28, 1921.

16. Ibid.

17. "War Hero Receives His Annual Thanks," *New York Times*, November 6, 1936; see also "World War Hero Gets 25th Yearly Letter from an Ex-Soldier He Saved in 1918," *New York Times*, November 4, 1943.

18. Parkin, "Memoirs," vol. 4, 153.

Epilogue: "Some Could, Some Could Not, Shake Off Misery"

1. Thomas Hardy, "And There Was a Great Calm," in *Complete Poems*, 588.

2. Smythe, *Pershing*, 269.

3. Ibid., 272.

4. "Jack Bentley," Baseball-Reference.com.

5. Janusz Cisek, *Koscicszko, We Are Here!*, 15.

6. "Army Officer Indicted for Performing Duty," *Washington Post*, February 10, 1923.

7. "Society by Lady Teazle," *San Francisco Chronicle*, October 3, 1905.

8. Boll, "My First Journey," 144.

9. Booth comment attached to letter from Pershing to Booth, June 17, 1940, Montfaucon Study, NARA.

10. *Time*, March 25, 1929, 13.

11. Smythe, *Pershing*, 287.

12. "Wants to Deport Countess Karaolyi," *New York Times*, October 27, 1924; "Training Camps Target for Reds," *New York Times*, July 7, 1927; "Otis Officially Out of Security League," *New York Times*, January 22, 1926; "Fights Reds with History," *New York Times*, October 13, 1927; and "Home Defense Plan Is Offered by Group," *New York Times*, May 23, 1940.

13. Margaret Macmillan, *Paris 1919*, 151.

14. Ruth Henig, *Versailles and After*, 52.

15. George Seldes, *Can't Print*, 35.

16. Parkin, "Memoirs," vol. 4, 152.

17. Palmer, *With My Own Eyes*, 380.

18. Parkin, "Memoirs," vol. 5, 103.

19. "Col. Sweezey, Former Head of Pen, Dies," *Baltimore Sun*, September 23, 1939.

20. "Unknown Soldier Sought," *New York Times*, September 26, 1937.

21. Leonard Ayres, *Statistical Summary*, 122; some 205,690 were wounded.

22. *Life* magazine, "Crown Prince's Khothole," November 24, 1941, 123.

23. Walker interview with curator.

24. Macmillan, *Paris 1919*, 164.

BIBLIOGRAPHY

More than 14,200 Yanks are buried in the Meuse-Argonne
Military Cemetery, which lies within view of the Montfaucon monument.

Betrayal at Little Gibraltar is based entirely on fact. All indented
passages and those within quotation marks are verbatim tran-
scripts from cited sources.

In this volume, recollections of the same event by different observers might differ, and in several critical instances, participants
contradict statements they made earlier. In light of the pressure
on soldiers, some discrepancies can be anticipated; other incon-
sistencies raise serious questions about the reliability of witnesses.
In the early years of my study, I deliberately reserved judgment
about the veracity of sources and concentrated on gathering recollections from as many observers as possible. Only after digesting
the views of all witnesses did I begin to draw conclusions based
on my estimation of their trustworthiness, supporting evidence,
and contradictory opinions.

Several of my conclusions challenge previous interpretations of the Meuse-Argonne Offensive and call into question the reputations of senior officers, some of whom are national heroes. As the documentation demonstrates, my deductions are based on fact, and I stand by them unreservedly. So that others can weigh the evidence, I submit the following list of consulted and cited works.

Abbreviations

LOC: Library of Congress
NARA: National Archives, College Park, Maryland.
Montfaucon Study: Materials assembled by E. E. Booth in NARC
MHI: US Army Military History Institute

Unpublished Sources

Library of Congress, Washington, DC

Robert L. Bullard papers
John J. Pershing papers

Military History Institute, Carlisle, Pennsylvania

Hugh A. Drum papers
John L. Hines papers
Andrew J. Kachik questionnaire
Samuel W. Fleming questionnaire and manuscript
James E. Meehan questionnaire and manuscript
Casper W. Swartz questionnaire and manuscript

US National Archives, College Park, Maryland

Record Group 111.11, Records of the Chief Signal Officer, Still Pictures (General), 1860–1982.
Record Group 117, American Battle Monuments Commission.
Record Group 120, Records of the American Expeditionary Forces, Historical Files: Operations Reports, Unit Histories, Messages, 3rd, 4th, 37th, 79th, 80th Divisions; V Corps; III Corps; First Army; and general headquarters.

Montfaucon Study, Adm. Materials Re to AEF Records, box 3, RG 120 located at 290/78/2/7.
Ward, R. T. "Explanation and Execution of Plans of Operation, 1st American Army for Argonne-Meuse Operation to November 11, 1918," G-3, General Staff, First Army, Special Operations Report: Part C: Meuse-Argonne Operations, January 5, 1919, in File 110.1.

George C. Marshall Foundation, Lexington, Virginia

George C. Marshall papers

Woodrow Wilson Presidential Library, Staunton, Virginia

Thomas Woodrow Wilson papers

Internet Sources

BaseballReference.com, http://www.baseball-reference.com/players/b/bentlja01.shtml
HistoryNet: http://www.historynet.com/world-war-i-wasted-lives-on--armistice-day.htm
Roads to the Great War: http://roadstothegreatwar:ww1.blogspot.com

Other Manuscript Sources

Bentley, John N. "Jack," "My Experiences in the Army." Author's collection.
Bjornstad File, Northfield, Minn.: Rolvaag Memorial Library, Special Collections, St. Olaf College.
Boll, Maximilian A. W. "My First Journey, 1917–1919." Stanford, Calif.: Hoover Institution Archives.
Cameron, George H., Letters. Courtesy of George Creel.
Gould, Kingdon, Letters. Courtesy of Kingdon Gould Jr.
Manning, W. Sinkler, Family Papers. Courtesy of Dr. and Mrs. Preston Manning.
Parkin, Harry D., Marginalia in James Harbord's *The American Army in France, 1917–1919*. Gettysburg, Pa.: Musselman Library, Special Collections, Gettysburg College.
Parkin, Harry D., "Memoirs of World War I." Five Volumes. Gettysburg, Pa.: Musselman Library, Special Collections, Gettysburg College.
Puttkammer, Wilfred., Letters, Courtesy of Mr. and Mrs. Charles Puttkammer.

Interviews

My research benefited from interviews conducted with family members of American participants in the Meuse-Argonne Offensive. Among these are George Creel, Earle Dunford, Kingdon Gould Jr., Joseph Labrum Jr. and Joseph Labrum III, Preston Manning, Peter Parkin, and Charles Puttkammer.

Photographs and Maps

In addition to photographs from the US National Archives, this volume features photographs, postcards, maps, and trench maps from the author's collection.

Published Sources

Action! Philadelphia: 310th Machine Gun Battalion, John C. Winston, n.d.

Allen, Henry T. *My Rhineland Journal.* Boston: Riverside Press, 1923.

American Battle Monuments Commission. *37th Division Summary of Operations in the World War.* Washington, DC: US Government Printing Office, 1944.

———. *4th Division Summary of Operations in the World War.* Washington, DC: US Government Printing Office, 1944.

———. *79th Division Summary of Operations in the World War.* Washington, DC: US Government Printing Office, 1944.

———. *American Armies and Battlefields in Europe.* Washington, DC: US Government Printing Office, 1938.

American Troops at the Argonne. Hearings Before the Committee on Military Affairs, US Senate, 65th Congress, 3rd session. Washington, DC: Government Printing Office, 1919.

Asprey, Robert B. *The German High Command at War: Hindenburg and Ludendorff Conduct World War I.* New York: William Morrow, 1991.

Ayres, Leonard P. *The War with Germany, a Statistical Summary.* Washington, DC: Government Printing Office, 1919.

Bach, Christian A., and Henry Noble Hall. *The Fourth Division: Its Services and Achievements in the World War Gathered from the Records of the Division.* Garden City, N.Y.: Christian A. Bach, 1920.

Barber, J. Frank. *The Official History of the Three Hundred and Fourth Engineer Regiment, Seventy-Ninth Division, U.S.A. During the World War.* Philadelphia: 304th Engineering Regiment, 1920.

Barber, J. Frank, chairman. *History of the Seventy-Ninth Division A.E.F. During the World War: 1917–1919.* Lancaster, Pa.: Steinman & Steinman, n.d.

Beatty, Jack. *The Lost History of 1914: Reconsidering the Year the Great War Began.* New York: Walker, 2012.

Booth, Ewing E. *My Observations and Experiences in the United States Army.* Los Angeles: printed privately, 1944.

Bowe, John. *With the 13th Minnesota in the Philippines.* Minneapolis: A. B. Farnham, 1905.

Braim, Paul F. *The Test of Battle: The American Expeditionary Forces in the Meuse-Argonne Campaign.* Newark: University of Delaware Press, 1987.

Brands, H. W. *Woodrow Wilson.* New York: Times Books, 2003.

Brooks, Alden. *As I Saw It.* New York: Alfred A. Knopf, 1930.

Budreau, Lisa M. *Bodies of War: World War I and the Politics of Commemoration in America, 1919–1933.* New York: New York University Press, 2010.

Bull, Stephen. *Trench Warfare.* Havertown, Pa.: Casemate, n.d.

———. *Trench: A History of Trench Warfare on the Western Front.* Oxford, U.K.: Osprey Publishing, 2010.

Bullard, Robert L. *Personalities and Reminiscences of the War.* Garden City, N.Y.: Doubleday, 1925.

Bullard, Robert Lee, and Earl Reeves. *American Soldiers Also Fought.* New York: Maurice H. Lewis, 1939.

Busch, Noel F. "General Drum: Nation's No. 1 Field Soldier Commands Biggest and Handiest of Four New Armies." *Life*, June 16, 1941: 82–96.

Cain, James M. "The Taking of Montfaucon." In *The Baby in the Icebox and Other Short Fiction*, by James M. Cain. Edited by Roy Hoopes. New York: Holt, Rinehart, and Winston, 1981.

Canby, Henry Seidel. *Education by Violence: Essays on the War and the Future.* New York: Macmillan, 1919.

Carter, Susan B. *Historical Statistics of the United States.* Cambridge, UK: Cambridge University Press, 2006.

Cisek, Janusz. *Koscicszko, We Are Here!* Jefferson, N.C.: McFarland, 2002.

Clark, William Bell. *War History of the 79th Division, National Army.* Williamsport, Pa.: printed privately, 1918.

Clemenceau, Georges. *Grandeur and Misery of Victory.* New York: Harcourt, Brace, 1930.

Coffman, Edward M. *The War to End All Wars: The American Military Experience in World War I.* New York: Oxford University Press, 1968.

Cohen, Eliot A. *Supreme Command: Soldiers, Statesmen, and Leadership in Wartime.* New York: Anchor Books, 2003.

Colby, Elbridge. "The Taking of Montfaucon." *Infantry Journal* 47, no. 2 (March/April 1940): 128–40.

Cole, Ralph D., and W. C. Howells. *The Thirty-Seventh Division in the World War, 1917–1918.* Columbus, Ohio: Thirty-Seventh Division Veterans Association, 1929.

Colt, George Howe. *November of the Soul: The Enigma of Suicide*. New York: Touchstone, 1991.

Cooke, James J. *Pershing and His Generals*. Westport, Conn.: Praeger, 1997.

Cooper, John Milton. *Woodrow Wilson: A Biography*. New York: Alfred A. Knopf, 2009.

Crozier, Emmet. *American Reporters on the Western Front, 1914–1918*. New York: Oxford University Press, 1959.

Cushing, Harvey. *From a Surgeon's Journal: 1915–1918*. Boston: Little, Brown, 1936.

Davenport, Matthew J. *First Over There: The Attack on Cantigny, America's First Battle of World War I*. New York: Thomas Dunne Books, 2015.

Doughty, Robert A. *Pyrrhic Victory: French Strategy and Operations in the Great War*. Cambridge, Mass.: Harvard University Press, 2005.

Drum, H. A. *A General Discussion of the Offensive*. Fort Leavenworth, Kans.: General Service Schools Press, 1920.

DuPuy, Charles M. *A Machine Gunner's Notes: France 1918*. Pittsburgh: Reed & Witting, 1920.

Eisenhower, John S. D., with Joanne Thompson Eisenhower. *Yanks: The Epic Story of the American Army in World War I*. New York: Free Press, 2001.

Eliot, T. S. *The Complete Poems and Plays, 1909–1950*. New York: Harcourt, Brace & World, 1962.

Ellis, John. *Eye-Deep in Hell: Trench Warfare in World War I*. Baltimore: Johns Hopkins University Press, 1976.

Ellis, John, and Michael Cox. *The World War I Databook: The Essential Facts and Figures for All the Combatants*. London: Aurum Press, 2001.

Evans, Martin Marix, ed. *American Voices of World War I: Primary Source Documents, 1917–1920*. London: Fitzroy Dearborn, 2001.

Falkenhayn, Erich von. *General Headquarters and Its Critical Decisions, 1914–1916*. London: Hutchinson, n.d.

Faulkner, Richard S. *The School of Hard Knocks: Combat Leadership in the American Expeditionary Forces*. College Station: Texas A&M University Press, 2012.

Ferrell, Robert H. *America's Deadliest Battle: Meuse-Argonne 1918*. Lawrence: University Press of Kansas, 2007.

———. *Woodrow Wilson and World War I, 1917–1921*. New York: Harper & Row, 1985.

Fleming, Thomas. *The Illusion of Victory: America in World War I*. New York: Basic Books, 2003.

Foch, Ferdinand. *The Memoirs of Marshal Foch*. Translated by T. Bentley Mott. Garden City, N.Y.: Doubleday, Doran, 1931.

Fromkin, David. *Europe's Last Summer: Who Started the Great War in 1914?* New York: Vintage Books, 2005.

Gilbert, Martin. *First World War*. London: Weidenfeld and Nicolson, 1994.

Glock, Carl E. *History of the 316th Regiment of Infantry in the World War, 1918*. 2nd printing. Philadelphia: Biddle-Deemer, 1930.

Griffith, Paddy. *Battle Tactics of the Western Front: The British Army's Art of Attack, 1916–1918*. New Haven, Conn.: Yale University Press, 1994.

Grotelueschen, Mark Ethan. *The AEF Way of War: The American Army and Combat in World War I*. Cambridge, UK: Cambridge University Press, 2007.

Hallas, James H. *Doughboy War: The American Expeditionary Force in World War I*. Mechanicsburg, Pa.: Stackpole Books, 2009.

Hanson, Heil. *Unknown Soldiers: The Story of the Missing of the First World War*. New York: Vintage Books, 2007.

Hanson, William L., MD. *World War I: I Was There*. Gerald, Mo.: Patrice Press, 1982.

Harbord, James G. *The American Army in France, 1917–1919*. Boston: Little, Brown, 1936.

Hardy, Thomas. *The Complete Poems of Thomas Hardy*. New York: Macmillan, 1976.

Harries, Meirion, and Susie Harries. *The Last Days of Innocence: America at War, 1917–1918*. New York: Random House, 1997.

Hart, Peter. *The Somme: The Darkest Hour on the Western Front*. New York: Pegasus Books, 2008.

Hastings, Max. *Catastrophe 1914: Europe Goes to War*. New York: Alfred A. Knopf, 2013.

Haverstock, Nathan A. *Fifty Years at the Front: The Life of War Correspondent Frederick Palmer*. Washington, DC: Brassey's, 1996.

Heckscher, August. *Woodrow Wilson: A Biography*. New York: Scribner, 1991.

Henig, Ruth. *Versailles and After, 1919–33*. 2nd ed. New York: Routledge, 1995.

Herwig, Holger. *The Marne*. New York: Random House Trade Paperbacks, 2011.

History of the 7th Infantry Brigade During the World War, 1918. Cologne, Ger.: M. DuMont Schauberg, 1919.

History of the Third Division United States Army in the World War. Andernach-on-the-Rhine, 1919.

Hogg, Ian V. *Machine Guns: 14th Century to Present*. Iola, Wisc.: Krause, 2002.

Hoopes, Roy. *Cain*. New York: Holt, Rinehart and Winston, 1982.

Horne, Alistair. *The Price of Glory: Verdun 1916*. Harmondsworth, U.K.: Penguin Books, 1964.

House, Edward Mandell. *The Intimate Papers of Colonel House*. Edited by Charles Seymour. Boston: Houghton Mifflin, 1928.

Hughes, Russell C. *History of the 311th Machine Gun Battalion, 79th Division, A.E.F.* East Stroudsburg, Pa.: Press Pub. Co., 1919.

Infantry in Battle. Washington, DC: Infantry Journal, 1939.

Jager, Herbert. *German Artillery of World War One*. Ramsbury, U.K.: Crowood Press, 2001.

Joel, Arthur H. *Under the Lorraine Cross: An Account of the Experiences of Infantrymen Who Fought with the Lorraine Cross Division in France during the World War.* Printed privately, 1921.

Johnson, Douglas V. *A Few Squads Left and off to France: Training the American Army in the United States for World War I.* Philadelphia: Temple University, 1992.

Johnson, Hubert C. *Breakthrough! Tactics, Technology, and the Search for Victory on the Western Front in World War I.* Novato, Calif.: Presidio Press, 1994.

Johnson, Ray Neil. *Heaven, Hell, or Hoboken.* Memphis, Tenn: General Books, 2012.

Johnson, Thomas M. *The Lost Battalion.* Lincoln, Neb.: Bison Books, 2000.

———. *Without Censor: New Light on Our Greatest World War Battles.* Indianapolis: Bobbs-Merrill, 1928.

Jones, Simon. *Underground Warfare 1914–1918.* Barnsley, South Yorkshire, U.K.: Pen and Sword Military, 2010.

Junger, Ernst. *On Pain.* Candor, N.Y.: Pelos Press, 2008.

———. *Storm of Steel.* New York: Penguin Classics, 2004.

Keegan, John. *The First World War.* New York: Alfred A. Knopf, 1999.

Kennedy, David. *Over Here: The First World War and American Society.* Oxford, U.K.: Oxford University Press, 2004.

Knightley, Phillip. *The First Casualty: From the Crimea to Vietnam: The War Correspondent as Hero, Propagandist, and Myth Maker.* New York: Harcourt Brace Jovanovich, 1975.

Kramer, Alan. *Dynamics of Destruction: Culture and Mass Killing in the First World War.* New York: Oxford University Press, 2007.

Kress, John W. *One of the Last "Rugged Individualists."* 1972.

———. *The Great Adventure.* Sparta, Wisc. Published privately, 1962.

Krouse, Susan Applegate. *North American Indians in the Great War.* Lincoln, Neb.: University of Nebraska Press, 2009.

Labrum, Joseph T. *History of Company G, 314th Infantry.* Philadelphia, Pa.: Published privately, n.d.

Lanza, Conrad H. "The Battle of Montfaucon, 26 September 1918—An Artilleryman's View." *Field Artillery Journal* 23, no. 3 (May/June 1933): 226–48.

———. "The End of the Battle of Montfaucon." *Field Artillery Journal* 23, no. 4 (July/August 1933): 347–67.

Laplander, Robert. *Finding the Lost Battalion.* Raleigh N.C.: Lulu Press, 2007.

Laskin, David. *The Long Way Home: An American Journey from Ellis Island to the Great War.* New York: HarperCollins, 2010.

Leed, Eric J. *No Man's Land: Combat & Identity in World War I.* Cambridge, UK: Cambridge University Press, 1979.

Lengel, Edward G. *Thunder and Flames: Americans in the Crucible of Combat, 1917–1918.* Lawrence: University Press of Kansas, 2015.

———. *To Conquer Hell: The Meuse-Argonne, 1918*. New York: Henry Holt, 2008.

Lengel, Edward G., ed. *A Companion to the Meuse-Argonne Campaign*. Malden, Mass.: John Wiley & Sons, 2014.

Liddell Hart, B. H. *Through the Fog of War*. New York: Random House, 1938.

———. *Reputations: Ten Years After*. Boston: Little, Brown, 1928.

———. *The Real War, 1914–1918*. Boston: Little, Brown, 1963.

Liggett, Hunter. *A.E.F.: Ten Years Ago in France*. New York: Dodd, Mead, 1928.

———. *Commanding an American Army: Recollections of the World War*. Boston: Houghton Mifflin, 1925.

Linn, Brian McAllister. *The Philippine War 1899–1902*. Lawrence: University Press of Kansas, 2000.

Ludendorff, Erich Friedrich. *The General Staff and Its Problems, The History of the Relations Between the High Command and the German Imperial Government as Revealed by Official Documents*. Vol. 2. New York: E. P. Dutton, n.d.

MacMillan, Margaret. *Paris 1919: Six Months That Changed the World*. New York: Random House, 2002.

———. *The War That Ended Peace: The Road to 1914*. New York: Random House, 2013.

Malcolm, Gilbert, and James M. Cain. *79th Division Headquarters Troop: A Record*. Printed privately, 1919.

Marshall, George C. *Memoirs of My Service in the World War, 1917–1918*. Boston: Houghton Mifflin, 1976.

Marshall, S. L. A. *American Heritage History of World War I*. New York: American Heritage, n.d.

Maverick, Maury. *A Maverick American*. New York: Covici, Friede, 1937.

McCullough, David G. *1776*. New York: Simon & Schuster, 2005.

McKenna, John A. *The Official History of the 315th Infantry U.S.A.: Being a True Record of Its Organization and Training, of Its Operation in the World War, and of Its Activities Following the Signing of the Armistice*. Philadelphia: Historical Board of the 315th Infantry, 1920.

McMeekin, Sean. *July 1914: Countdown to War*. New York: Basic Books, 2013.

———. *The Russian Origins of the First World War*. Cambridge, Mass.: Belknap Press, 2011.

Meyer, G. J. *A World Undone: The Story of the Great War, 1914–1918*. New York: Delacorte Press, 2006.

Middlebrook, Martin. *The First Day on the Somme, 1 July 1916*. New York: W. W. Norton, 1972.

———. *The Kaiser's Battle*. Barnsley, South Yorkshire, U.K.: Pen and Sword Books, 2007.

Millett, Allan R. *The General: Robert L. Bullard and Officership in the United States Army, 1881–1925*. Westport, Conn.: Greenwood Press, 1975.

Mitchell, Paul B. *What Were the Causes of the Delay of the 79th Division Capturing Montfaucon During the Meuse-Argonne Offensive in World War I?* Fort Leavenworth, Kans.: Command and General Staff College, 2011.

Mitchell, T. J. *Casualties and Medical Statistics of the Great War and Surgeon General's Report of 1920.* Washington, DC: US Government Printing Office, 1920.

Mosier, John. *The Myth of the Great War.* New York: HarperCollins, 2001.

———. *Verdun: The Lost History of the Most Important Battle of World War I, 1914–1918.* New York: NAL Caliber Penguin, 2013.

Muller, E. Lester. *The 313th of the 79th in the World War.* Baltimore: Meyer and Thalheimer, 1919.

Neiberg, Michael S. *Dance of the Furies: Europe and the Outbreak of World War I.* Cambridge, Mass.: Belknap Press, 2011.

———. *Foch: Supreme Allied Commander in the Great War.* Potomac, Md.: Potomac Books, 2003.

Nenninger, Timothy K. "Tactical Dysfunction in the AEF, 1917–1918." *Military Affairs* 51, no. 4 (October 1987): 177–81.

O'Connor, Richard. *Black Jack Pershing.* Garden City, N.Y.: Doubleday, 1961.

Odom, William O. *After the Trenches: The Transformation of the U.S. Army 1918–1939.* College Station: Texas A&M University Press, 1999.

Otte, Maarten. *The U.S. 79th Division in Nantillois 1918.* Rosmalen, Neth.: ExpoSure, 2014.

Page, Arthur W. *The Truth About Our 110 Days' Fighting.* Garden City, N.Y.: Doubleday, 1920.

Palmer, Frederick. *America in France.* New York: Dodd, Mead, 1918.

———. *John J. Pershing, General of the Armies: A Biography.* Harrisburg, Pa.: Military Service, 1948.

———. *My Year of the Great War.* Toronto, Can.: McClelland, Goodchild & Stewart, 1915.

———. *Our Greatest Battle (The Meuse-Argonne).* New York: Dodd, Mead, 1919.

———. *With My Own Eyes: A Personal Story of Battle Years.* Indianapolis: Bobbs-Merrill, 1933.

Paschall, Rod. *The Defeat of Imperial Germany, 1917–1918.* Chapel Hill, N.C.: Algonquin Books of Chapel Hill, 1989.

Passingham, Ian. *All the Kaiser's Men: The Life and Death of the German Army on the Western Front 1914–1918.* Thrupp, U.K.: Sutton, 2003.

Pershing, John J. *Combat Instructions.* Chaumont, France: General Headquarters, AEF, 1918.

———. *Final Report of Gen. John J. Pershing, Commander-in-Chief, American Expeditionary Forces.* Washington, DC: US Government Printing Office, 1920.

———. *My Experiences in the World War.* 2 vols. New York: Frederick A. Stokes, 1931.

————. *Report of General John J. Pershing, U.S.A.* Chaumont, Fr.: General Headquarters, A.E.F., 1919.

Persico, Joseph E. *Eleventh Month, Eleventh Day, Eleventh Hour: Armistice Day, 1918—World War I and Its Violent Climax.* New York: Random House, 2005.

Philadelphia War History Committee. *Philadelphia in the World War 1914–1919.* Philadelphia: Wynkoop Hallenbeck Crawford, 1922.

Phillips, Thomas R., ed. *Roots of Strategy: The Five Greatest Military Classics of All Time.* Mechanicsburg, Pa.: Stackpole Books, 1985.

Philpott, William. *Three Armies on the Somme: The First Battle of the Twentieth Century.* New York: Alfred A. Knopf, 2010.

Pogue, Forrest C. *George C. Marshall: Education of a General.* New York: Penguin Books, 1993.

Rainey, James W. "Questionable Training of the AEF in World War I." *Parameters: Journal of the US Army War College* 22 (Winter 1992–93): 100.

Reynolds, David. *The Long Shadow: The Great War and the Twentieth Century.* London: Simon & Schuster U.K., 2013.

Richards, J. Stuart, ed. *Pennsylvania Voices of the Great War: Letters, Stories and Oral Histories of World War I.* Jefferson, N.C.: McFarland, 2002.

Richardson, James D., ed. *A Compilation of the Messages and Papers of the Presidents.* New York: Bureau of National Literature, 1929.

Rickenbacker, Eddie B. *Fighting the Flying Circus: The Greatest True Air Adventure to Come out of World War I.* New York: Doubleday, 2001.

Ricks, Thomas E. *The Generals: American Military Command from World War II to Today.* New York: Penguin Press, 2012.

Rowe, John A. *History of Company F, 316th Infantry, Seventy-Ninth Division, A.E.F. in the World War, 1917–18–19.* Philadelphia: Company F Association of the 316th Infantry, 1930.

Rubin, Richard. *The Last of the Doughboys: The Forgotten Generation and Their Forgotten World War.* New York: Mariner Books, 2014.

Seldes, George. *You Can't Print That! The Truth Behind the News, 1918–1928.* Garden City, N.Y.: Payson & Clarke, 1929.

Senior, Ian. *Home Before the Leaves Fall: A New History of the German Invasion of 1914.* Oxford, U.K.: Osprey, 2012.

Simonds, Frank H. *They Won the War.* Freeport, N.Y.: Books for Libraries Press, 1931.

Smith, Corinna L. *Interesting People: Eighty Years with the Great and the Near-Great.* Norman: University of Oklahoma Press, 1962.

Smythe, Donald. "John J. Pershing in the Spanish-American War." *Military Affairs* 30 (Spring 1966).

————. *Pershing: General of the Armies.* Bloomington: Indiana University Press, 1986.

Sparks, Jared. *The Writings of George Washington Being His Correspondence, Addresses, Messages, and Other Papers, Official and Private,* n.d.

Stallings, Lawrence. *The Doughboys: The Story of the AEF, 1917–1918*. New York: Harper & Row, 1963.

Stephenson, Michael. *The Last Full Measure: How Soldiers Die in Battle*. New York: Crown, 2012.

Stevenson, David. *Cataclysm: The First World War as Political Tragedy*. New York: Basic Books, 2004.

———. *With Our Backs to the Wall: Victory and Defeat in 1918*. Cambridge, Mass.: Belknap Press, 2011.

Strachan, Hew. *The First World War*. New York: Penguin Books, 2003.

Strong, Paul, and Sanders Marble. *Artillery in the Great War*. Barnsley, U.K.: Pen and Sword Books, 2011.

Summerall, Charles Pelot. *The Way of Duty, Honor, Country: The Memoir of General Charles Pelot Summerall*. Edited by Timothy K. Nenninger. Lexington: University Press of Kentucky, 2010.

Swetland, Maurice J., and Lilli Swetland. *These Men*. Harrisburg, Pa.: Military Service Pub. Co., 1940.

Thorn, Henry C., Jr. *History of the 313th Infantry, "Baltimore's Own."* New York: Wynkoop Hallenbeck Crawford, 1920.

Toland, John. *No Man's Land: 1918—The Last Year of the Great War*. New York: Doubleday, 1980.

Tompkins, Raymond S. *Maryland Fighters in the Great War*. Baltimore: Thomas & Evans, 1919.

Tuchman, Barbara W. *The Guns of August*. New York: Random House, 1962.

Tucker, Spencer C. "Gallwitz, Max von." In *The Encyclopedia of World War I: A Political, Social, and Military History*, 464. Edited by Spencer C. Tucker. 5 vols. Santa Barbara, Calif.: ABC-CLIO, 2005.

———. "Wilhelm, Crown Prince." In *The Encyclopedia of World War I: A Political, Social, and Military History*, 1260. Edited by Spencer C. Tucker. 5 vols. Santa Barbara, Calif.: ABC-CLIO, 2005.

Tupper, Joseph L. *Study of the Operations of the Fourth Division in the First Phase of the Meuse-Argonne Offensive: 26 September to 2 October, 1918*. Fort Leavenworth, Kans.: Command and General Staff School, n.d.

United States Army Center of Military History. *United States Army in the World War 1917–1918: Military Operations of the American Expeditionary Forces*. Vol. 8. Washington, D.C.: US Government Printing Office, 1990.

———. *United States Army in the World War, 1917–1919: Military Operations of the American Expeditionary Forces*. Vol. 9. Washington, DC: US Government Printing Office, 1990.

U.S. Senate Committee on Military Affairs. *Hearings on the Nomination of Col. Alfred W. Bjornstad, U.S. Army, for Promotion to Be a Brigadier General*. 68th Congress, 2nd session, January 9, 12, 13, and 14, 1925.

Vandiver, Frank E. *Black Jack: The Life and Times of John J. Pershing*. 2 vols. College Station: Texas A&M University Press, 1977.

Viereck, George Sylvester. ed. *As They Saw Us—Foch, Lundendorff and Other Leaders Write Our War History*. Garden City, N.Y.: Doubleday, Doran, 1929.

Walker, William T. "The Chance of a Miracle at Montfaucon." In *A Companion to the Meuse-Argonne Campaign*. Edited by Edward Lengel. Malden, Mass.: John Wiley & Sons, Inc., 2014.

Waters, Fiona, ed. *A Corner of a Foreign Field: The Illustrated Poetry of the First World War*. Hertfordshire, UK: Transatlantic Press, 2007.

Wilhelm, Crown Prince. *Memoirs of the Crown Prince of Germany*. Uckfield, U.K.: Naval & Military Press, 2005.

———. *My War Experiences*. New York: Robert M. McBride, 1923.

Willmott, H. P. *World War I*. New York: DK Publishing, 2006.

Winter, Denis. *Death's Men: Soldiers of the Great War*. New York: Penguin History, 1985.

Yockelson, Mitchell A. *Borrowed Soldiers: Americans Under British Command, 1918*. Norman: University of Oklahoma Press, 2008.

Newspapers

Baltimore Sun
New York Times
Washington Post
San Francisco Chronicle
Minneapolis Journal
Northfield (MN) News

PHOTOGRAPH CREDITS

INDEX

Page numbers in *italics* refer to illustrations.

African Americans, 70–71, 84, 307

Alberich operation, 50–51

Allen, Henry, 237–38

Allen, Hervey, 89

Allies, 5, 25, 32, 35, 36, 42, 43, 44, 46,
47–48, 50, 54, 91, 102, 111, 112, 237,
238, 239, 244, 292, 384
   amalgamation plans of, 41
   barrages against Germans by, 130–32,
147, 193
   bunkers of, 111–12
   casualties of, 5, 33, 143–44, 145, 155, 177,
197, 209, 218, 220, 226, 227, 230, 231,
259–60, 367, 369, 387
   equipment hidden by, 102–3
   fighter planes of, 116, 206
   frontline advancement of, 133–34
   German commission to negotiate Armistice with, 286, 292
   offensive role assumed by, 24
   Somme Offensive of, 32–33, 35–36
   supply lines of, 47
   tanks of, 145–46, 148, 153, 154–55, 168,
169, 192, 193–94, 196, 218
   United States implored to enter war by, 34
   veterans of, 380
   weapons preparations by, 115
   see also specific Allied armies

Alston, Harold, 262

America in France (Palmer), 313, 314

American Army in France, 1917–1919, The
(Harbord), xi, 5, 6, 10

American Battle Monuments Commission
(ABMC), 318, 367, 368–69, 370–71,
372, 386, *395*

American Expeditionary Forces (AEF), 5,
6–7, 10, 14, 41, 47, *66*, 79, 85–86, *89*,
97–98, 100, 117, 295–96, 324, 335, *389*
   aircraft of, 130–31, 192, 280
   ambiguous orders of, 348

   army hospitals of, 211, 212, 234
   artillery of, 122–23, 131, 169, 188, 189,
192, 194, 210, 212, *215*, 224, 231, 298
   artillery staff of, 123, 217
   assessments of Meuse-Argonne Offensive
failures of, 231–34, 239
   attacks by, 42, 43
   barrages of, 130–32, 138, 139, *147*, 180,
181, 193, 205, 206, 223–24, 263
   black troops in, 70–71
   camaraderie among, 257
   casualties in, 5, 143–44, 145, 155, 177,
197, 209, 218, 220, 226, 227, 230, 231,
367, 369, 387
   combat training of, 41, 86, 90–91, 93–94
   communication within, 150–54, 160,
174–75, 189, 191–92, 195, 204,
223–24, 225, 226–27, 232, 291, 319,
352–53
   competition within, 336, 350–51
   desire to "make good" and, 83, 286, 290,
297
   as divided into two operations, 48–49
   divisions of, under foreign command, 237
   foreigners in, 281
   France training for, 86, 90–91, 93–94,
337
   friendly fire within, 154, 224
   frontline advancement of, 133–34
   generals' struggles to enhance reputations of, 210
   German ambush of, 142–46
   German Americans in, 289
   German prisoners taken by, 136–37, 138,
157, 172, 190, 252, 262, 279
   German "suicide squads" and, *37*, 135–37
   headquarters of, 152, 353, 354, 360, 361
   immigrant troops in, 80–81
   improvised tactics of, 138
   inadequate medical support in, 197–98

American Expeditionary Forces (*cont.*)
  inexperienced divisions and troops of, 41,
    55, 60–61, 62–63, 68, 72, 74–76, 100,
    232, 233; *see also* 79th Division, US
  inexperienced staff and generals of, 232
  intelligence gathered by, 171
  lack of commitment of, feared by Foch,
    44
  lack of cooperation in, 341–42, 351, 352,
    355
  lack of support to 79th Division by, 192,
    194, 206, 208, 210, 222, 224
  last-minute attacks by, 340–41
  leadership in, 75–76, *89*, 95, 371
  "Leavenworth clique" of, 332, 341, 350,
    355, 360
  malicious officers in, 93–95
  medical staff of, 233
  military censorship and, 311, 312
  Montfaucon attack of, *see* Montfaucon
    assault
  monuments to, *365*, 366–77, *395*
  mop-up regiments of, 136
  mutual arrangements among Germans
    and, *256–57*
  new warfare tactics for, 92, 310
  observatory salvaged by, 180
  outdated warfare tactics of, 91–92, 93,
    119, 138–39, 144, 145, 260, 327,
    349–50
  Pershing as commander of, *see* Pershing,
    John J.
  poor road conditions encountered by,
    150
  press operations in France of, 307,
    309–13, 321
  pressure on commanders from headquar-
    ters of, 204
  psychic scars of, 373–75
  as replacing French troops, 109
  revenge and savagery inflicted on Ger-
    mans by, 171, 173–74
  rolling barrage of, 267
  rumors of impending Armistice and, 295,
    299, 300
  runners in, 151
  sense of dread and unease felt by, 115–16,
    117, 123–25, 167
  shortage of leaders in, 258
  shortages of weapons and equipment in,
    85, 93, 312
  success of, 201
  316th Infantry unsupported by, 225

  untrained troops of, 49, 60–61, 85–86, 93
  veteran divisions of, 60, 63, 232, 233
  veterans of, 380
  veteran suicides and, 373–75
  war diary of, 313
  see also First Army, US; Meuse-Argonne
    Offensive; St. Mihiel operation; Sec-
    ond Army, US; *specific corps, divisions,
    and regiments*
American Montfaucon Monument, *365*,
    366–68
Ardennes, 46, 61, 312
Argonne Forest, 21, 27, 28, 50, 60, 67, 100,
    101, 107, 168, 176, 185, 205, 223, 234,
    241, 349, 358, 373
Arlington National Cemetery, 385, 386, 387
Armistice, 8, 9, 12, 171, 236, *285*, 299, 301,
    324, 339, 340, 341, *343*, 359, 372, *377*,
    379, 381, 383, 384, 387
Armstrong, Bob, 124
Army, US, 12, 13
  cuts in, *324–25*
  lack of troops in, 39
  see also American Expeditionary Forces
    (AEF); *specific divisions*
Army Staff College, US, 6, 12, 64, 71, 98,
    240, 324–25, 341
Army War College, US, 67, 97, 236
Atwood, Baird, 183–84, 188, 189, 194, 260
Avocourt, France, 113, 121, 124, 150, 198,
    212, 290, *305*
Ayres, Lawrence, 277
Azannes, France, 299, 300

Bach, C. A., 326, 344, 345, 346, 353, 356
Bair, Howard A., 195, 224, 260
Baker, Newton D., 39–40, 238, 307
Baltimore, Md., *xiii*, 80, 85, 286–89, 291,
    300, 387
"Baltimore's Own" Regiment (313th), *ix*,
    17, 82, 84, 85, 102, 113, 114, 118, 119,
    121, 122, 124, 126, 132, 133, 135, 139,
    144, 146, 148–49, 151, 153, 154, 155,
    159, 160, 167–69, 173, 174, 180, 181,
    183, 184, 194, 216, 217, 220, 235, 282,
    290–91, 297, 299, 300, 368, 372, 387
  in assault on Madeleine Farm, 221–22
  casualties suffered by, 218
  in Montfaucon assault, 291
  and orders to cease hostilities, 299
  Second Battalion of, 280
Barber, Frank, 116–17, 120, 123, 144–45,
    150

Bar-le-Duc, France, 31, 102
Belgium, 20, 22, 50, 52–53, 161
Belleau Wood, 246, 367
Belleau Wood, battle of, 42, 67
Belleu Wood, 246, 247
Bentley, John N. "Jack," 83, 84–85, 102,
  111–12, 115, 124–25, 132, 148, 154, 169,
  171, 173–74, 178, 218–20, 230, 252, 381
  assigned to cut wires, 118, 122, 125–26
Berlin, Germany, 36, 270, 286
Bjornstad, Alfred W., 73, 98, 322, 329–30,
  341, 342, 344–46, 348, 353, 354–55,
  356, 361–63
  abrasive and malicious personality of,
    332, 333, 335–36, 360–61, 381
  background of, 327
  Bullard's relationship with, 327–28,
    330–32, 360, 361–62, 363
  as disliked by subordinates, 333–35
  leadership style of, 333–34
  orders disobeyed by, 327–28, 329–30
  successes and promotions of, 335–36
  unapproved orders issued by, 330
"Black Tom" explosion, 288
Bliss, Tasker, 37
Bois 250, 193, 206, 207, 210, 216, 217, 218,
  220
Bois 268, 193, 194, 195–96, 204, 206, 207,
  216, 217
Bois de Beuge, 178, 180–82, 185, 188–91,
  193, 194, 195, 211, 217, 223, 231, 235
Bois de Cuisy, 30, 140, 148, 160, 167
Bois de Cunel, 178, 205, 209, 217, 221, 224,
  226, 227, 235, 247
Bois de la Tuilerie, 157, 173, 175, 182, 211,
  212
Bois de Montfaucon, 21, 30, 117, 120, 146,
  148, 149, 153, 168
Bois des Ogons, 178, 193, 196, 199, 205,
  206, 209, 210, 217, 224, 235
Boll, Maximilian A. W., 83–84, 87, 112, 122,
  173, 198, 289, 381–82
Bolles, Frank, 158
Bolsheviks, 41, 42, 381
Booth, Ewing E., 11–14, 158, 321, 324–27,
  346, 353, 355–56, 357, 382
  Montfaucon controversy investigation of,
    11, 13–14, 323, 326–27, 341, 353–54,
    362–63, 364, 376, 382, 386
Borah, William, 312
Brabant, 246, 247, 248
Bradley, Omar, 359
Brest, France, 74–75, 76, 86, 87, 101

Brewer, Bill, 104–5
Brewster, André W., 233–34
Brieulles, 175, 244
Brooks, Alden, 340–41
Broun, Heywood, 312
Browning, Val, 123
Browning machine guns, 122–23, 145, 193,
  215, 274, 277, 279, 300, 301
Bruchmüller, Georg, 53
Bryan, William Jennings, 35
Bulge, Battle of the, 61, 380
Bullard, Robert Lee, xi, 7, 8–9, 10, 12, 13,
  17, 42, 69–72, 73, 97, 119, 131, 156,
  157, 158, 173, 185, 231, 241, 306, 314,
  317, 318, 322, 323, 327, 330, 337–39,
  342, 344, 345–46, 354, 356–58, 361,
  382, 389
  accusations against 79th Division by,
    209–10, 352
  Bjornstad's relationship with, 327–28,
    330–32, 360, 361–62, 363
  callous disregard for troops by, 340–41
  Cameron's rivalry with, 8, 10, 351–53,
    357
  in cigarette advertisement, 382
  and drive to get ahead, 350–51, 357, 359
  ego of, 57, 327, 329, 343, 357
  failure of, to assist in Montfaucon attack,
    xi, xii, 8
  hospitalizations of, 332
  last-minute attacks ordered by, 340
  leadership style of, 328, 340
  malicious personality of, 332, 336,
    339–40, 350
  Montfaucon controversy and, 375
  Montfaucon orders as interpreted by,
    345–48, 353
  orders disobeyed by, 57, 320, 327–29,
    331, 348, 349, 350, 353, 354, 357, 360,
    364
  orders issued by, 120–21
  outdated war tactics used by, 327, 349–50
  Pershing's relationship with, 338–39
  promotion of, 339, 359–60
  rewritten orders for III Corps by, 347–48
  xenophobic and racial attitudes of, 70–71
  see also III Army Corps, US
Burroughs, Edgar Rice, 76

Cabla, Joseph, 137–38, 389
Cain, James M., 152–53, 159, 180, 291, 300,
  383
Cameron, Douglas, 359

Cameron, George H., 8, 9, 12, 13, 17,
    68–69, 117, 119–21, 152, 156, 159,
    160, 185, 204, 205, 315, 317, 339, 350,
    351, 358, 363, 370, 375, 383, *389*
  Bullard's rivalry with, 8, 10, 351–53, 357
  Pershing's dismissal of, *229*, 236, 359,
    383
  see also 79th Division, US; V Army Corps,
    US
Camp Meade, 79, 85, 86, 88, 226, 281, 288,
    289, 374
Canby, Henry Seidel, 343
Cantigny, Battle of, 42, 67, 69, 340, 359
carrier pigeons, 151, 174, 278
Carroll, William M., 192, 277
censorship, 311, 312, 320–21
Chamberlain, Joshua, 269
Champagne, France, 237, 259
Charles, Oscar J., 74, 75, 145, 160, 167, 168,
    183, 189, 191, 195, 205, 217, 224, 225,
    226, *389*
  carelessness of, 223–24
  hospitalization of, 234
  as indecisive, 195–96
  leadership style of, 74, 75, 82, 95
  questionable character of, 93–94
  as relieved from duty, 234
  shell shock suffered by, 226, 375
Château-Thierry, 42, 230, 367
Chaumont-devant-Damvillers, 297–98,
    299, 372
"Christmas Truce" (1914), 256
Civil War, US, 14, 34, 60, 76, 131, 269, 306,
    308, 349, 376
Claudel, Henri, 245, 263, 297
Clemenceau, Georges, 91, 144, 212–13,
    216, 229, 232, 236–37, 238, 383
Cockey, Joshua, III, 171
Coffman, Edward, 241
Colaizzi, Adam, 279
Combat Instructions (pamphlet), 92
Congress, US, 12, 36, 40, 78, 83, 287, 288,
    315, 336, 370
Conway, Bill, 124
Cooke, James J., 329–30, 335
Coolidge, Calvin, 376
Corn Willy Hill, 179, 244, 245, 255–56,
    260, 261, 263, 266, *268*, 286, 292, 296,
    387
  AEF barrages on, 263
  American observation platform on, 255
  American reinforcements sent to, 262,
    263, 266

  capture of, 282–83
  German defenses at, 258, 260, 279
  German divisions at, 259
  German fortifications on, 253
  German observation posts on, 244–45,
    248, 251, 259, 265, 279, 283
  proposed monument for, 368–70
  as strongest remaining German bastion,
    246
Corn Willy Hill assault, 263–64, *265*,
    266–83, 374, 375, 386, 387
  American barrages during, 276–77, 278
  American casualties in, *265*
  American relief troops for, 281
  attack by German planes during, 280
  Civil War tactics used during, 269–70
  German barrages in, 251, 253, 262–63,
    266, 267, 271, 278, 280
  German resistance and counterattacks in,
    245, 262, *265*, 266–67, 269, 271, 273,
    274, 279
  German retreat and withdrawal from, 282
  Manning's attack during, 275–77, 279
  plans for, 260–61
  79th Division's orders for, 258–64
  316th Regiment soldiers taken prisoner
    by Germans in, 271–73
Corps of Engineers, 96, 336
Côte 304, 31–32, 104, 108, 114, 291
Côte Dame Marie, 51, 61
Côte de Chaumont, 296, 297–98, 372
Côte de Romagne, 296, 297, 298, 299, 300
Creel, George, 307
Cuba, 38, 40, 63, 67, 71
Cunel, France, 51, 175, 178, 203, 209, 227,
    244, 355
Cunel Wood, 220, 221, 258, 281, 291
Cushing, Harvey, 233–34

Davitt, Major, 278
Dawes, Charles, *73*
D-day (term), 117
Death Valley, 247, 250
defensive warfare, 306
Degoutte, Jean, 331–32
denkmal, 365, 372, 377
Dewey, George, 308–9
Dijon, France, 86, 88
Doric column, *365*, 366, 367, 370, 371
Double Indemnity (Cain), 383
Drum, Hugh A., 12, 50, 58, 59–60, 64, 65,
    239–41, 242, 245, 321, 324, 325–26,
    355, 358, 359, 361, 363, 375

Duffy, Francis, 359
Duncan, George, 230, 330
Dunford, Junius, 171–72
DuPuy, Charles, 171

Eastern Front, 28, 33, 42, 54, 97
80th Division, US, 69, 319
Eisenhower, Dwight D., 318, 319, 386
Eisenhower, John, 64, 68, 69, 156, 203, 231
Elkins, Davis, 361
Esnes, France, 115, 212
Etzel-Giselher Stellung, 50, 51, 160, 176

Falkenhayn, Erich von, 26, 31, 33–34, 49
Fascism, 382, 383
Ferdinand, Franz, 20
Ferrell, Robert, 49, 227
Ferrero, Joseph, 374
Field Order No. 6, 117
Field Order No. 33, 240–41
Field Order No. 46, 204, 295
Field Service Regulations, 1914, 91
V Army Corps, US, 9, 12, 13, 14, 60, 68,
    117, 152, 157, 159, 185, 204, *229,* 231,
    233, 236, 315, 317, 325, 339, 344–45,
    347, 348, 349, 350, 351, 352, 353, 354,
    358
    III Corps assigned to assist, 64–65, 69,
        119–20, 146, 156, 345, 347, 351, 360,
        382
    see also 79th Division, US
15th French Colonial Division, 260, 263
First Army, US, 38, 42, 45, 47, 50, 58, 62,
    64, 65, *66,* 67, 68, 119, 121, 126, 138,
    146, 149, 152, 159, 160, 176, 185, 202,
    203–4, 213, 225, 226–27, 231–33,
    238–41, 244, 245, 275–76, 282, 283,
    297, 298, 314, 319, 321, 324, 326–27,
    342, 344–49, 350, 351, 352, 354–56,
    357, 358, 362, 364
    see also American Expeditionary Forces
        (AEF); *specific corps, divisions, and
        regiments*
First Army Field Order No. 20, 64, 65, 119
First Battalion, 267, 275
I Corps, 60, 67, 185, 231, 241, 349, 350, 352
1st Division, US, 233, 336, 337, 338, 359
First Prussian Guards Division, 113–14
Fismette, France, 331, 340, 344, 354, 360
flamethrowers, 30, 144, 187, 331
Flanders, Belgium, 256, 259
Fleming, Samuel W., Jr., 77–78, 95–96, 166,
    192, 282

Foch, Ferdinand, *xiv–xv,* 41, 42–49, 58,
    61–62, 118, 213, 236, 238–39, 297,
    299, 384
Folly of Nations, The (Palmer), 386
Forges Brook, 29, 109–11, 126, 136
Forrest, Nathan Bedford, 349
Fort Leavenworth, Kans., 6, 64, 71, 98, 240,
    324, 327, 329, 330, 332, 335, 341, 345,
    350, 355
Fort Niagara, N.Y., 78, 172
4th Division, US, 7, 11, 13, 17, 62, 63,
    64–65, 68, 69, 121, 139, 149, 166, 173,
    183, 198, 204, 209–10, 236, 315, 324,
    326, 353, 354–55, 359, 361
    assault brigade of, 354
    assigned to assist 79th Division, 64–65, 69,
        119–20, 146, 156, 346, 347, 351, 360, 382
    complaints about unclear orders in, 321–22
    in contingency plan, 65
    8th Brigade, 158, 324, 354, 356, 357
    "galloping for glory" tactic of, 156–57
    and lack of support to 79th Division,
        8–13, 17, 156, 161
    and opportunities to capture Montfaucon,
        157–59, 175, 241–42, 319, 321, 355
    order to turn/envelop Montfaucon and,
        64–65, 152, 158, 175, 239, 241, 314,
        317, 318–19, 321, 325, 344–45, 346,
        347–48, 351, 353
    79th Division unsupported by, 120–21,
        185, 321, 325, 327, 348–49, 354
    39th Infantry Regiment of, 157
    turning maneuver of, 119, 120, 314,
        325–26, 327
    turning order rejected by, 152, 239, 241,
        318–19, 321, 345–48, 349, 350, 354
    see also III Army Corps, US
"fragging," 334
Fraley, Harry, 146
Fraley, William, 146
France, French, xi–xiii, *xiii,* 5, 23, 42, *89,* 91,
    176, 186, 251, 259, 267
    AEF supplied by, 42
    African colonial troops of, 20
    attack on Montfaucon in, *see* Montfaucon
        assault
    casualties of, 33
    combat training in, 86, 90–91, 93–94,
        95, 105
    counterattacks in Verdun by, 54
    German invasion and occupation of,
        20–23, 24, 60, *107*
    surveillance planes of, 112

France, French (*cont.*)
   tanks of, 145–46, 148, 153, 154–55, 168,
      192, 193–94, 196
   temporary withdrawal tactics used by, 329
   warfare tactics of, 118–19
   Western Front in, *see* Western Front
Freya Stellung, 50, 51
Funston, Frederick, 39, 240

Gabriel, Harry, 260
Gallwitz, Max von, 51–53, 54–55, 61, 100,
     112–13, 114, 132, 146, 149, 161, 175,
     183, 185, 202, 241, 245, 273, 279,
     384
gas alert, 104–5, 116
gas masks, 255
gas warfare, 169, 189, 206, 253, 255–56,
     261, 266, 278, 385
German Americans, 35, 286, 287–89
German army, 39, 42, 96–97
German Fifth Army, 20, 23, 26, 54, 112,
     183, 202
German General Staff, 22, 296, 384
Germania Club, 288
German Imperial Army, 163
German Imperial General Staff, 26
German MG08s, 145
Germany, Germans, *ix*, 20–21, 39, 41
   aircraft of, 116, 280
   ambush by, 142–46, 148
   Americans' entering in war feared by, 25
   American soldier captured by, 114, 126
   Armistice sought by, 286, 292, 384
   artillery of, 6, 17, 26–27, 30–31, 50,
     52–54, 55, 61, 114, *127*, 130, 144, 168,
     178, 179, 181, 184, 185, 205, 207, 218,
     220, 233, 244–45, 253, 261, 331
   attack planes of, 298
   attempts by, to capture Paris, 22–23, 42
   attempt to destroy observatory by, 180
   barrages by, 115–16, 176, 177, 179–80,
     182–83, 189, 192, 193–94, 195,
     244–45, 262–63, 266, 271, 278, 280,
     331–32
   British blockade and, 36
   casualties of, 33, *265*
   Côte 304 attack of, 31–32
   "defense-in-depth" strategy of, 139–40
   defense strategy of, 149
   first-aid stations attacked by, 211–12
   fortifications of, *ix*, 24, 28–30, 50–51, 55,
     61, 92, *107*, 109, 123, 131, 139–40, 149,
     177, 178, 179, 186, 213, *243*, *303*, 353

France invaded and occupied by, 20–23,
   24, 60, *107*
gas warfare used by, 169, 189, 206, 253,
   261, 266
hole in Kriemhilde Stellung defenses of,
   222–23, 226–27
intelligence gathered by, 112–13, 126
Kriemhilde Stellung assault and, *see*
   Kriemhilde Stellung assault
machine-gun units of, 37, 135–36, 137–
   38, 140, 142, 145, 154, 155, 164–65,
   167, 168, 169, 171, 173, 178, 181, 182,
   190, 205, 230, *243*, 246, 261, 262, 266,
   267, 269, 270, 331
Meuse-Argonne Offensive and, *see*
   Meuse-Argonne Offensive
military cohesion of, 25–26
Montfaucon assault and, *see* Montfaucon
   assault
Montfaucon captured and occupied by,
   20–22, 24–25, 27, 366
Montfaucon observatory of, xi, *1*, 6, 8,
   19, 27–29, 30, 54, 55, 61, 63, *127*, 130,
   149, 169, 175, 179, 180, *187*, 233, 244,
   303, 344, 352, 367, 371, 383–84
move of troops from Eastern to Western
   Front by, 42
mutual arrangements among AEF and,
   256–57
observation balloons of, 112, 130, 192,
   193, 206, 280
observation planes of, 112, 191–92, 271,
   280
occupation of, 171
offensive designed to capture Verdun
   (*Wirkung Gericht*), 26–27, 33
prisoners treated kindly by, 272, 292–94
reinforcements from, 13, 14, 26, 61, 101,
   123, 157, 161, 173, 175, 185, 203, 205,
   222, 355–56
resistance by, 168–69, 174, 182, 183, 186,
   203, 207–8, 209–10, 216, 218, 220,
   221, 245, *265*, 266–67, 269, 271, 273,
   274, 279, 354
revolt in, 296–97
snipers of, 135–36, 137, 138, 143, 155,
   255, 279
Somme Offensive and, 32–33, 35–36
spring offensives (1918) of, 7, 43, 44, 68,
   328, 330
submarine warfare by, 25, 34, 35, 36, 97
supply lines of, 46
surrendering by, 259

term "Boche" and, 23, 137, 154, 171
treacherous tactics used by, 137, 171, 211–12
trench raids by, 113–14
in two-front war, 42
Verdun attacked by, 30–31, 33, 35–36, 50–51
in war with Russia, 22, 25, 42
Germany, Imperial, 316, 383
Gestapo, 388
Gettysburg, Battle of, 306, 329
  Little Round Top in, 269
Glock, Carl, 101, 253, 273, 274, 275, 276
Goetz, Mowry, 223, 224, 225, 258, *389*
Golfe de Malancourt, 144–45
Gould, Jay, 253
Gould, Kingdon, 253–55
Grant, Ulysses S., 60
Great Britain, 24, 32, 34, 44, 91, 186, 237, 256, 259
  blockade by, 36, 288
  Easter 1916 uprising in Dublin and, 35
  German submarine warfare against, 36
  Somme Offensive and, 32–33
Greco-Turkish War (1897), 308
Greimann, Emil, 190
Groener, Wilhelm, 296
Grotelueschen, Mark, 91
Gruebl, Olga, 289
Gunther, Henry N., 122, 286–87, 289–90, 291–92, 297–98, 299, 300–301, 372–73, 377, *377*, 384

Haedicke, George, 273, 275, 276, 278
Haig, Douglas, 32, 33, 41
Hanson, William, 132, 197
Harbord, James G., xi, 5, 6–7, 10, 335
Harding, Warren, 322
Hardy, Thomas, 379
Harlem Hellfighters (369th Regiment), 70
Hart, B. H. Liddell, 129
Harvard University, 9, 10, 77
Hassan (Moro leader), 328
Haucourt, France, 21, 34, 109, 117, 121, 136, *391*
Heights of the Meuse, 176, 179, 295
Hewit, Benjamin, 133, 172, 180–82, 194, 195, 199, 206, 207, 208, 260, 375, *389*
  leadership style of, 188–89, 199
Hilken, Paul, 288
Hill 274 (Suicide Hill), 196, 197, 198, 206, 210, 217

Hill 282, 140
Hill 304, 152, 165–66, 176, 198, *305*, 313
Hill 319, 297, 298, 299, 300
Hill 328, 297–98
Hill 370, 263, 267
Hill 378, *see* Corn Willy Hill
Hindenburg, Paul von, 33, 50, 139, 140, 296, 384–85
Hindenburg Line, xii, 50–51, 61, 86, 92, 111, 120, 123, 135, 186, 196, 203, 222, 237, 245–46, 342, 350, 367
Hines, John L., 158, 239, 317, 354–55, 361, 363, 375
Hitler, Adolf, 384, 386, 387–88
Holloway, Slim, 133
Holocaust, 371
Holtzendorff, Henning von, 36
House, Edward, 35, 310, 313
Hughes, Charles Evans, 35

Indian Wars, 38, 67, 68, 75
Ingersoll, Harry, 146
Ireland, 34, 35
Irish Americans, 35
Islamic Moros, 39, 328
Iverson, Nicholas, 374

Jacks, Gene, 133
Jacks, L. V., 231
Jackson, Thomas "Stonewall," 342
James, Edwin, 151
Japan, 67, 96
Jefferson Memorial, *365*, 371
Joel, Arthur, 142, 169
Joffre, Joseph, 23
Johnson, Douglas, 93
Johnson, Francis, 260, 261, 267
Johnson, E. M., 263, 273, 279–80
Johnson, Hiram W., 312
Johnson, Thomas M., 147, 320–22, 364
Johnson, Walter, 381
Johnston, Gordon, 156
Jordan, Jimmy, 261
Jünger, Ernst, 163

Kachik, Andrew J., 124, 164–65, 166, 192, 255–56, 385
Keegan, John, 22, 36, 53
Kellar, Dan, 204–5, 208, 225, 260, 375
Keller, Victor, 145
Kelly, Hugh, 184
Kennedy, David, 39
Kevitch, Isaac, 173

Kilroy, Joseph, 277
Knack, Louis, 194, 270
Knowles, Alden, 166, *389*
Knowlton, Lauriston, 194
Koenig, Paul, 288
Kress, John, 115, 122, 132, 250, 252
Kriemhilde Stellung, 50, 51, 55, 114, 121, 146, 149, 157, 158, 160, 161, 175, 177, 178, 185, 193, 196, 204, *219*, 221–22, 227, 231, 233, 283, 347, 350, 355, 356, 364, 369, 383
Kriemhilde Stellung assault, 199, 203–10, 216–27, *219*, 241
Kuhn, Joseph, 69, 85, 94, 96–98, 117, 120, 121, 150, 151–53, 159, 160, 165–66, 174, 180, 185, 191, 198, 204, 205, 210, 217, 224, 226, 233, 234, 236, 247, 258, 263, 275, 278–79, 281–83, 295, 298, 299, 316, 369, 370, 375, 385, *389*

Labrum, Joseph, 104, 134, 143–44, 172, 192, 250–51, 292, 385
Lady, Ira, 260, 261, 262
Langley, Jesse, 144
Langres, France, 98, 335
Lautenbacher, Ivan, 204–5
League of Nations, 380
Lee, Robert E., 60, 306, 329
Lengel, Edward G., 126, 187, 340, 381
Lenin, Nikolai, 42
Liggett, Hunter, 60, 67–68, 185, 241, 306, 350, 352, *389*
Ligny-en-Barrois, France, 38, 41, 43, 44–45, 58, 67
Lind, John, 334
Little Gibraltar, *see* Montfaucon, France
Livelsberger, George, 190
Longstreet, James, 306
Lorraine, France, 22, 100
Los Angeles, Calif., 4–5, 9, 11, 14
Lost Cause, 306
Ludendorff, Erich, 132, 259
Lusitania, 34

MacArthur, Douglas, 335, 359, 386
McCawley, John A., 142
McCleave, Robert P., 59–60, 61, 62, 63, 64, 65, 240, 345, 348
MacCormack, Robert, 271, 272, 375
machine guns, 135–36, 137–38, 142, 171, 176, 181, 189, 349
    Browning, 122–23, 145, 193, *215*, 274, 277, 279, 300, 301

machine-gun units, German, *37*, 135–36, 140, 142, 145, 154, 155, 164–65, 167, 168, 169, 171, 173, 178, 181, 182, 190, 205, 230, *243*, 246, 261, 262, 266, 267, 269, 270, 331
McKenna, John, 211
McKim, Anthony, 113
McKinley, William, 334
Madeleine Farm, 178, 196, 210, 218, 221–22
Malancourt, France, 21, 29, 109, 117, 121, 138, 140, 142, 143, 150, 155, 164, 166, 169, 174, 198, 205, 212, 230, 296
Manning, W. Sinkler, 131, 234, 247–49, 250, 260, 263, 267, 273, 274, 275, 282, 375–76, 377, 385
    death of, 277, 278, 283
    Parkin's friendship with, 225, 247, 249, 257, 276, 385
    promotion of, 257–58
March, Peyton, 320
Marines, US, 39, 246
Marne-Rhine Canal, 58–59
Marne River, 91
Marshall, George C., 58–59, 67, 131, 318, 342, 386
Mati, battle of, 308
Matlawski, Adam, 181–82
Maverick, Maury, 215
Max, Prince of Baden, 296
Meador, R. L., *389*
Metz Corps, 20
Meuse-Argonne American Cemetery, 367–68
Meuse-Argonne Offensive, *ix*, xi, 5, 7–13, 24, 45–46, 47, 49, 51, 57, 58, 72, 86, 93, 96, 98, 101, 118, 237, 297, 313, 324, 350–51
    aircraft in, 130–31
    Allied barrages during, 130–32, 193
    Allied equipment hidden for, 102–3
    American casualties in, *ix*, 5, 13, 182, 191, 197–98, 227, 230, 233, 259–60, 315, 364, 380, 387
    American soldier captured by Germans during, 126
    assessments of AEF failures in, 231–34, 239
    communication difficulties during, 150–54, 160
    element of surprise as important to, 61, 101, 126, 132
    failures of, 233–34

gas warfare in, 169, 189, 206
German ambush in, 142–46, 148
German barrages in, 115–16, 176, 177,
    179–80, 182–83, 189, 192, 193–94,
    195, 331–32
German fortifications in, 186
German intelligence gathered about,
    112–13
German reinforcements in, 61, 157, 173,
    175, 185, 203, 205
German resistance in, 203, 209–10, 218
German retreat and withdrawal in, 297
Germans' capture of American soldier
    during, 114
impending Armistice and, 291, 292, 294,
    295, 299, 300
inexperienced troops in, xiii, 6, 7, 62–63,
    117
Montfaucon attack of, see Montfaucon
    assault
Montfaucon controversy and, see Mont-
    faucon controversy
Pershing's concerns about, 202–3
plans and orders for, 60, 67, 72, 117–19,
    123–24, 149, 185–86, 197, 344–48,
    351, 353
poor road conditions and, 150, 197, 198,
    212, 232
rolling barrage in, 119, 123, 134, 135,
    138, 143
second phase of, 233
signing of Armistice and, 299, 301
speed as essential to, 203, 231
stalling of, 358
tanks in, 145–46, 148, 153, 168, 169, 192,
    193–94, 196
316th Infantry's advanced position in,
    222–23, 226, 231
transportation plan for, 58, 59
see also specific attacks
Meuse-Argonne region, 51, 59, 61, 64, 68,
    107, 196
    burial site in, 367
    as dread-inspiring, 108
    fortifications of, 50–51, 72, 107, 177, 178,
        179, 186
    fractured landscape of, 134, 148–49, 175
    tortured topography of, 50, 54, 60, 72,
        108, 111, 213, 238, 245–46, 372
    war artifacts left in, 178–79
Meuse River, 20, 28, 30, 31, 47, 50, 53,
    60, 69, 101, 112, 168, 185, 205, 206,
    244–49, 251, 259, 265, 282, 297, 372

Meuse River Valley, 22, 100, 166, 273
Mexico, 38, 40, 64
Mézières, France, 46, 380
Middlebrook, Martin, 32–33
Miller, Nellie, 287–88
Millett, Allan, 97, 328, 332, 349, 350
Minello, Pasquale, 280–81
minenwerfers, 24, 155, 161, 189, 246, 262
Mitchell, Jack, 136
Molleville Farm, 246, 247, 251, 263, 265,
    273
Montfaucon, France, xiii, 3, 4, 13, 17, 51,
    55, 61, 105, 109–11, 114–15, 117, 129,
    138, 140, 157, 201, 205, 211, 212–13,
    236, 255, 263, 296
    as dread-inspiring, 108
    French desultory barrages on, 27
    German artillery in, 6, 17, 30, 61, 130,
        168
    German capture and occupation of,
        20–22, 24–25, 27, 366
    German comforts in, 25, 29
    German fortifications at, 6, 23–24, 28–30,
        55, 61, 303
    German observatory at, xi, 1, 6, 8, 19,
        27–29, 30, 54, 55, 61, 63, 127, 130,
        149, 169, 175, 179, 180, 187, 233, 244,
        303, 344, 352, 367, 371, 383–84
    Germany's Russian prisoners of war in,
        28–29
    monument at, 365, 366–68, 370–71, 372,
        377
    photographs/postcards of Germans in,
        24–25
    as preserved in devastated state, 305,
        366, 395
    remoteness of, 366
    ruins of, 1, 163, 303, 395
    vantage points from, 20, 23, 27, 28
    Wilhelm's interest in, 20, 22, 23
Montfaucon assault, xi–xiii, xiii, 1, 6–10,
    12, 13, 61, 66, 147, 153–61, 164, 222,
    230–31, 244, 263, 281, 283, 290–91,
    296, 313, 325, 383, 386
    American barrages in, 138
    American casualties in, xi, 17, 155, 169,
        177
    contingency plan for, 65
    crack in German defenses during, 157–58
    early capture as essential in, 63, 160
    first-day failure of, xii, 8, 9, 13, 14,
        153–61, 185, 229, 233–34, 318–19,
        322, 339, 352, 370

Montfaucon assault (*cont.*)
   4th Division's opportunities during,
      157–59
   German barrages against, 180
   German counterattack in, 181
   German messages of concern during, 157
   German reinforcements sent during, 157,
      160, 161, 173, 175, 355–56
   German resistance during, 168–69, 186,
      354
   in Montfaucon cemetery, 171
   ordered turn/envelopment of, 64–65,
      152, 158, 175, 239, 241, 314, 317,
      318–19, 321, 325, 344–45, 346, 347–48
   Parkin's battlefield memories of, 4, 5, 8
   plans and orders for, 6–7, 13, 61–63,
      64–67, 117–18, 120–21, 123–24,
      149, 175, 238–39, 314–15, 318, 325,
      344–45, 351, 356, 362
   rescinded turning maneuver order of,
      356–57, 363
   37th Division's attack in, 166–67
   79th Division assigned to, xi, 6, 7, 62–63,
      64, 65, 117, 119–20, 121–22, 153, 291,
      351
   79th Division as unsupported in, xi, xii,
      8–13, 17, 120–21, 156, 161, 185, 321,
      325, 327, 342, 348–49, 353–54, 382
   79th Division in advancement on,
      134–46, *141*, 148–49
   79th Division night attacks in, 154–56,
      159–60, 355
   79th Division's capture of, 17, 174–75,
      176–77
   79th Division's difficulties in, 155–56,
      158
   79th Division's second-day attack in,
      164–66, 167–75, *170*
   turning maneuver in, 63–65, 239–40,
      241, 314, 344–45, 356
Montfaucon controversy, 314–22, 324, 357,
   362–64, 375
   Booth's investigation of, 11, 13–14, *323*,
      326–27, 341, 353–54, 362–63, 364,
      376, 382, 386
   Johnson's investigation of, 364
   "misinterpretation" of orders in, 353, 363
   Parkin's investigation of, xi, 5, 9–11, 13,
      15–16, 17, 376
   Pershing and, 12–13, *229*, 315–26, 363,
      370
Mordacq, Jean-Henri, 232, 239
Moro Insurrection, 156, 335

Mort Homme, Le (Dead Man), 22, 23, 24,
   27, 31, 32, 34
Muller, Lester, 133, 208
mustard gas, 189, 206
My Experiences in the World War (Pershing),
   xii, 11, 63, 317–20

Namur, Belgium, German attacks on, 52–53
Nantillois, France, 25, 149, 157, 159, 175,
   177–78, 182, 183, 191–93, 196, 211,
   223, 231, 244, 247, 277, 319, 357
Napoléon I, Emperor of France, 63, 76
National Archives, 62, 371, 376
National Army, US, 78–79
   see also American Expeditionary Forces
      (AEF)
National Guard, US, 39, 111, 146
   26th Division of, 245
   29th Division of, 245, 246, 247, 248, 252,
      256
   33rd Division of, 245
   volunteer troops of, 78–79
Naylor, Raymond, 261
Nazi Party, Nazis, 384, 388
New York Times, xiii, 97, 151, 276–77, 322,
   349
Nicholas II, czar of Russia, 41
Nicholson, William J., 118, 119, 121,
   153–54, 159–60, 209, 216–17, 234–36,
   297–98, 299, *389*
91st Division, US, 68, 117, 315
Noble, Robert H., 94–95, 118–19, 121, 153,
   159, 160, 165–66, 234, *389*
Normandy, battle of, 380
Norris, George, 312

observation balloons, 112, 130, 192, 193,
   206
Oeuvre du Demon ("Work of the Demon"),
   29, 30, 51, 109, 140–46, 148, 161, 164,
   172, 314
Officers Training School, 6, 83–84, 195,
   258, 289
157th Infantry Brigade, 114, 119, 121, 297
158th Infantry Brigade, 121, 263
Ortega, Aniseto, 269, 274–75, 277–78
Our Greatest Battle (Palmer), 313, 314–15
Oury, William, 155, 156, 191–92, 210, *389*
Owens, John, 277

Palmer, Frederick, 307–14, 315–16, 386
Paris, France, 42, 52, 73, 202, 294
   Germany's attempts to capture, 22–23, 42

Paris Peace Conference, 384, 386
Parkin, Alice, 5, 78
Parkin, Harry, Jr., 78
Parkin, Harry D., xi–xii, 3, 6–11, 74–75,
    79, 83, 85, 87, 90, 93–94, 96,
    99–100, 102, 103–4, 108–9, 111,
    113, 116, 122, 132, 134–35, 136,
    145, 160, 167, 168, 172, 174, 180–81,
    182, 183–85, 188, 189, 190–91,
    192–94, 195–96, 199, 204–5, 206–9,
    210, 216, 217, 220–26, 227, 231,
    234, 247–48, 250, 251, 252, 253,
    256, 260, 263–64, 265, 266, 267–74,
    280, 282, 295, 321, 357, 359, 369,
    375–76, 377, 386, 389
  anger and black moods of, 4–5, 6, 10, 13,
    135, 225–26, 235
  background of, 76–78
  battlefield memories of, 4, 5, 8, 103, 135,
    139, 160, 188, 191, 207, 209, 225,
    248–49, 252, 271–72
  leadership style of, 74, 75–76, 81–82, 88,
    95, 168, 269
  Manning's friendship with, 225, 247, 249,
    257, 276, 385
  military training program attended by,
    77–78
  misconceptions about Germans of, 294
  Montfaucon controversy investigation by,
    xi, 5, 9–11, 13, 15–16, 17, 376
  on nature of military leadership, 98–99
  negative sentiments of, about World
    War I, 294–95
  1935 regimental reunion attended by,
    5, 7–8
  outdated warfare tactics taught by,
    92–93
  79th's assignment and, 121–22
  as taken prisoner by Germans, 271–72,
    283, 292–94
  316th Infantry Regiment lead by, see
    316th Infantry Regiment
  weapons studied by, 98
  World War I enlistment of, 78
  wounded legs of, 270–71, 272, 283, 293,
    294
Patterson, Francis, 144
Patton, George, 360
Pegler, Westbrook, 312
Pennsylvania, xi, 62, 85, 172, 385
Pepper, Benjamin Franklin, 144
Percy-le-Grand, 88, 95, 98, 99
Pershing, Frances, 40

Pershing, John J., xi–xii, 1, 5, 9, 10, 38,
    40–41, 42, 43–49, 54–55, 57, 57, 58,
    59, 61–62, 63–64, 65, 67–68, 70, 71,
    72, 73, 79, 83, 86, 91, 98, 100–101,
    114, 117, 119, 123, 126, 132, 138, 146,
    150, 152, 156, 159, 160, 185, 202–4,
    212, 213, 222, 226, 229, 231, 232,
    233, 236–39, 240, 242, 245, 247, 259,
    260, 263, 285, 297, 298, 305, 306,
    307, 309–11, 313, 324, 325, 330, 332,
    335, 337–38, 343, 345, 348, 350–51,
    352–53, 355, 358–59, 363, 371, 380,
    382, 385, 386, 389
  after-action reports of, 316–17
  army of, see American Expeditionary
    Forces (AEF)
  Bullard's relationship with, 338–39
  Cameron's relationship with, 68
  continued push for aggressive action by,
    295–99
  criticisms of, 236–37
  divided staff of, 49
  Foch's relationship with, 44–45, 48
  illogical decisions and sacrifices made by,
    49, 62–63, 315, 321–22
  last-minute attacks ordered by, 340, 341
  memoir of, xii, 11, 63, 317–20
  Montfaucon controversy and, 12–13,
    229, 315–16, 317–21, 363, 370
  placement of monuments and, 367–70
  press and, 307, 309–10, 312
  promotion of, 386
  79th Division disliked by, 368–70
  strict adherence to orders by, 329
  316th Corn Willy Hill monument and,
    369–70
  unclear orders given by, 321–22
  as worn out, 237
Pétain, Henri Philippe, 30, 33, 72, 176, 203,
    371
"Philadelphia's Own" 315th Regiment, 381
Philippines, 38–39, 40, 64, 67, 68, 156, 328,
    333–34, 335
phosgene gas, 169, 206
Pietruszka, Waclaw, 182
pigeon carriers, 151, 174, 278
Plattsburgh, N.Y., military training program
    in, 77–78
poilu, 31, 38, 44, 91
Poore, Benjamin A., 62–63, 326, 346, 353
Pope, John Russell, 371
Postman Always Rings Twice, The (Cain), 152,
    383

Potsdam Conference, 388
Powell, Ernest, 290, 291, 297, 299, 300, 301
press, 307–13, 320–21
    AEF and, 307, 309–13
    censorship in, 311, 312
    European correspondents and, 311
    propaganda in, 311
Pritts, Brian, 136
Prodoehl, Paul, 287
propaganda, 311, 321
Prussia, 22, 52
Prussian Guards, 113–14, 182
Putnam, Israel, 154, 155
Puttkammer, Wilfred, 159, 180, 255, 386–87

Quekemeyer, John, 237

racism, 70–71, 84
Rainey, James W., 201
Ravine de Moyemont, 251, 260, 261, 263,
    266, 272–73
Rawlinson, Henry, 237
Redoute du Golfe, 30, 51, 139–46, 148, 161,
    314
Regular Army, US, 39–40, 78–79, 95–96,
    336
Repp, Bernard, 135
Rhine River, 101, 133, 366, 384
Rickard, Paul, 256–57
Rickenbacker, Edward V. "Eddie," 130–31,
    192, 206
Ricks, Thomas, 342
Rivel, Thomas, 180
rolling barrages, 119, 123, 134, 135, 138,
    143, 263, 267
Romagne, France, 193, 203, 211, 222, 227,
    244
Roosevelt, Franklin D., 77, 371
Roosevelt, Theodore, 35, 336
Ross, Tenny J., 165–66
Runkle, Paul, 181
runners, 151, 152–53, 159, 255, 269, 281,
    291–92
Russia, 41, 96, 388
    German prisoners of war from, 28–29
    revolution in, 34
    in war with Germany, 22, 25, 42
Russo-Japanese War, 309

Sabin, Pearl Ladd, 381
St. Mihiel operation, 38, 42, 44, 45, 46–47,
    49, 58, 62, 67, 68, 100–101, 113, 146,
    197, 246, 259, 332, 351–52, 367

St. Mihiel region, France, 59, 100, 230, 231
St. Olaf College, 327, 334
Sassoon, Siegfried, 3
Schlieffen, Alfred von, 22–23
Schlieffen Plan, 22
Scott, Hugh, 39, 97
Second Army, US, 9, 47, 340, 359, 360, 361
Sedan, France, 46, 47, 51, 55, 61, 64, 176,
    238, 241, 245, 321, 341, 380
Seiders, Clifford M., 138
Seidewitz, Edwin, 288–89
7th Division, US, 360–61
77th Division, US, 67, 80, 373
79th Division, US, xiii, 5–9, 10, 13, 17, 69,
    78, 80–81, 83, 84–85, 89, 96, 97–98,
    101–2, 109, 110, 113, 114–15, 122,
    132, 136, 139, 158, 175, 178, 182, 199,
    204, 229, 236, 241, 249, 253, 254,
    263, 282, 286, 289–90, 292, 296, 301,
    313–14, 315, 323, 345, 353, 355, 368,
    372, 376–77
    in advancement on Montfaucon, 134–46,
        141, 148–49
    AEF's lack of support for, 189–90, 192,
        194, 206, 208, 210, 222, 224
    arrival in France of, 74–75, 86
    artillery staff of, 123, 285
    blame and accusations for AEF failures
        aimed at, 233, 234–36, 242, 317
    in Bois de Beuge, 180–82, 185, 188–91, 194
    casualties of, 5, 143–44, 145, 155, 177,
        197, 209, 218, 220, 230, 231, 367
    combat training in France of, 86, 90–91,
        93–94, 95, 105
    communications in, 160
    Corn Willy Hill mission of, 251–64
    demoralized troops of, 216, 218, 220
    difficulties of, in Montfaucon attack,
        155–56, 158
    diverted munitions for, 198
    equipment shortages in, 93
    farthest advance in Meuse-Argonne
        Offensive made by, 222–23
    fear and unease felt by, 104–5, 115–16,
        123–25, 207, 222
    fierce fighting by, 231
    first air raid escaped by, 103–4
    first-day failure in taking Montfaucon of,
        xii, 8, 9, 13, 153–61, 185, 229, 233–34,
        318–19, 339, 352, 370
    4th Division assigned to assist, 64–65,
        69, 119–20, 146, 156, 346, 347, 351,
        360, 382

frontline trenches manned by, 112
German body recovered by, 113–14
German machine gunner and sniper
  strikes on, 135–36, 137, 155
impeachment of, 235
as inexperienced and undertrained, *xiii*,
  6, 7, 62–63, 68, 79–80, 86, 90–91, 93,
  103, 105, 190, 315
in journey to Western Front, 86–87,
  101–2, 117
Kriemhilde Stellung assault by, *see*
  Kriemhilde Stellung assault
lack of food and water for, 167, 198, 199
medical staff of, 197
Montfaucon attack assigned to, xi, *xiii*, 6,
  7, 62–63, 64, 65, 68, 119–20, 121–22,
  153, 291, 351
Montfaucon captured by, 17, 174–75,
  176–77
Montfaucon monument proposed by, 368
Montfaucon night attacks of, 154–56,
  159–60, 355
Nantillois captured by, 183
outdated war tactics taught to, 92–94,
  144, 190, 260
"pioneer platoon" of, 85
poor communication between headquarters and, 150–52
psychic scars of, 374–75
redemption for, 283
as relieved from duty, 226, 230, 231, 234,
  246–47
second-day attack on Montfaucon of,
  164–75, *170*
shortage of replacements for, 247
slow progress of, 149–50, 152–53, 155,
  156, 204, 352
29th Division relieved by, 251
as unsupported in Montfaucon attack, xi,
  xii, 8–13, 17, 120–21, 156, 161, 185,
  321, 325, 327, 342, 348–49, 353–54,
  382
veterans of, 374–76
see also V Army Corps, US; *specific regiments*
Shafter, William R., 306–7
Sheckart, Grover C., 136, 137, 190–91
Sherff, Warren, 133
Sheridan, Lieutenant, 99–100
Sherman, William Tecumseh, 63, 77
Sibert, William L., 336–38, 339, 351
Sivry-sur-Meuse, 245, 369
Smith, Harrison, 278–79

Smythe, Donald, 49, 62, 233, 237, 380
snipers, 135–36, 137, 138, 143, 155, 255,
  279
Somers, John, 209, 210
Somme Offensive, 32–33, 35–36, 45, 90,
  132, 309, 313
Sommer, Bill, 133
Somme River, 32–33, 237
Souilly, France, 202, 204
Spanish-American War, 12, 38, 75, 306–7,
  333
"Star-Spangled Banner, The" (song), 287
Statue of Liberty, *379*
Stevens, Frank, 260
stollen, 24, 29, 50
Stosstruppen, 7, 271–72, 331, 349
Stuart, Jeb, 329, 342
Suicide Hill (Hill 274), 196, 197, 198, 206,
  210, 217
suicides, of veterans, 373–75
suicide squads, *37*, 135, 136–37, 165
Summerall, Charles P., 359
Swartz, Casper, 137, 142–43
Sweezey, Claude B., 82, 118, 125, 132, 144,
  145, 149, 151, 153–54, 155, 156, 160,
  167–68, 174, 177, 180–81, 182, 183,
  216–17, 218, 220, 221, 235, 387, *389*

tanks, 54, 145–46, 148, 153, 154–55, 168,
  169, 192, 193–94, 196, *215*, 218
Tardieu, André, 369
III Army Corps, US, 7, 9, 12, 14, 60, 63,
  71, 157, 158, 185, 204, 231, 239–40,
  241–42, 317, 318, 319, 320, 325,
  326–27, 328, 330, 332, 335, 344, 353,
  354–55, 356, 357–58, 359, 361, 382
assault brigade of, 349
assigned to assist V Corps, 64–65, 69,
  119–20, 146, 156, 345, 347, 351, 360,
  382
Bullard's rewritten orders for, 347–48
changes to orders made by, *57*, 326–27
complaints about unclear orders by,
  321–22
turning order rejected by, 345–48, 349,
  350
see also 4th Division, US
Third Battalion, 260, 267, 275, 276, 277
3rd Division, US, 226, 230–31, 240, 354
13th Minnesota Volunteer Infantry, 333–34
37th Division, US, 65, 68, 117, 120, 139,
  146, 149, 156, 166–67, 235, 314, 315,
  353, 354, 355

39th Regiment, 157, 318
Thomas, John, 190, 262
Thorn, Henry, 114
304th Engineering Regiment, 116, 150
311th Machine Gun Battalion, 145, 374
313th Infantry Regiment, *see* "Baltimore's
    Own" Regiment (313th)
314th Infantry Regiment, 104, 115, 119,
    121, 124, 131, 134, 136, 137, 138, 140,
    142–43, 148, 149, 153, 155, 156, 159,
    164, 166, 169, 173, 175, 182, 192, 245,
    255, 296, 298, 354, 368, *379*
314th Machine Gun Company, 115, 122, 250
315th Infantry Regiment, "Philadelphia's
    Own," 95, 105, 121, 136, 144, 159,
    166, 173, 192, 196–97, 198, 205, 206,
    209, 210, 211, 221, 251, 264, 275, 276,
    277, 280, 282, 368
316th Infantry Regiment, 17, 74, 88, 93,
    95, 99, 101, 104, 118, 121, 133, 136,
    153, 159–60, 172, 173, 180–81, 183,
    184–85, 190, 192–93, 195, 196, 199,
    205, 206–7, 209, 216, 217, 220–21,
    247, 251, 256–57, 258, 273–76, 277,
    278, 279, 281, 368, 375
    AEF barrage over, 223–24, 235
    casualties of, 226, 227, 369, 387
    Civil War tactics used by, 269–70
    Corn Willy Hill assault and, 279–80
    as designated to Corn Willy assault,
        263–64
    hole in Kriemhilde Stellung defense
        exploited by, 222–23, 226
    inexperienced reinforcements given to, 258
    Kuhn's tribute to, 283
    lack of food and water for, 223, 280
    low spirits of, 258
    Meuse-Argonne Offensive advanced
        position of, 222–23, 226, 231
    open warfare tactics used by, 369
    proposed Corn Willy Hill monument
        for, 368–70
    reconnaissance on Corn Willy Hill of,
        260–63
    survivors of, as relieved from duty, 280
    taken prisoner by Germans, 271–73
    unjust rumors about, 235
    as unsupported by AEF, 222, 224, 225
    weakness of, 258
    in withdrawal from Bois de Cunel, 224,
        227, 235
trench warfare, 25, 92, 203
Trier, Germany, 272, 293

Turn, Raymond, 136
turning maneuvers, 63–65, 119, 120, 239–
    40, 241, 314, 325–26, 327, 344–45,
    347–48, 355, 356
29th US National Guard Division, 245,
    246, 247, 248, 251, 252, 256

United States:
    anti-German sentiment in, 84, 287–89
    declaration of war by, *xiii*, 36, 39, 78, 80,
        85, 172, 288, 309, 381
    entry into World War I of, 25, 34–35,
        36, 75
    entry into World World II of, 38
    Germans submarine warfare and, 25, 34, 36
    immigration to, 80
    national conscription in, 39
    neutrality of, 35
    use of black troops in combat by, 70–71
US Military Commission, 96–97

Verdun, France, 20–22, 27, 38, 46, 72, 102, 113,
    132, 134, 156, 202, 245, 247, 248, 295
    casualties at, 31, 33
    fortifications in, 22
    French counterattacks in, 54
    French reinforcements sent to, 32
    German attacks on, *19*, 30–31, 33–34, 35,
        42–43, 50–51
    German offensive to capture (*Wirkung
        Gericht*), 26–27, 33
    siege of 1916 in, 202
Versailles, Treaty of, 388
veteran suicides, 373–75
Villa, Pancho, 38
von Frienburg, Frederich, 113–14
von Knobelsdorf, Schmidt, 21

Wagner, Richard, 50
Walker, William, xi–xiii
Ward, R. T., 348
War of 1870, 22, 52
Warren, Francis E., 40
Washington, George, 79, 81
Watkins, Eugene, 255
Wavrille, France, 295–96
Weeks, John, *3*, 386
Weimar Republic, 384
Welling, Hank, 181, 199
Western Front, xii, 20, 23–24, 26, 32, 34, 38,
    39, 43, 45, 47, 49–50, 54, 85, 101, 105,
    213, 259, 286, 287
    Allied bunkers in, 111–12

casualties in, 5, 24, 31, 33, 34, 143–44,
145, 155, 177, 191, 197, 209, 218, 220,
226, 227, 230, 231, *265*, 367, 369, 387
combined-arms technique in, 119
defensive weapons in, 24
fortifications in, *ix*, 24–25, 28–30, 50–51,
55, 61, 92, *107*, 109, 123, 131, 139–40,
149, 177, 178, 179, 186, 213, *243*, *303*,
353
German Eastern Front troops moved
to, 42
Little Gibraltar of, *see* Montfaucon,
France
map of, *xiv–xv*
Meuse-Argonne Offensive along, *see*
Meuse-Argonne Offensive
Meuse-Argonne region and, *see*
Meuse-Argonne region
as modern battlefield, 349
monuments in, 367–71
Somme Offensive and, *see* Somme
Offensive
stalemates on, 24, 25, 34, 36, 41
US in, 38
West Point (military academy), 9, 11, 63–64,
67, 68–69, 82, 96, 237, 239, 307, 327,
336, 349, 382
Whittlesey, Charles, 373, 374
"whizz-bangs," *129*, 189
Wilhelm, Prince of Germany, 19, 20–22, 23,
25–26, 49, 51, 54, 167, 387–88
attack on Verdun and, *19*, 30–31, 33–34, 42
Fifth Army of, *see* German Fifth Army
French resurgence and, 23
interest in Montfaucon of, 20, 22, 23
Montfaucon captured by, 25
Montfaucon observatory post ordered by,
19, 27–29, 30, 180, *187*, 367, 371, 383–84
Wilhelm II, Emperor of Germany, 7, 21,
42, 46, 50, 54, 80, 112, 114, 132, 140,
160, 169, 225, 246, 270, 272, 286, 296,
297, 388

Wilhelmina, Queen of Netherlands, 388
Williams, George, 263, 273, 275
Wilson, Edith Bolling, 85
Wilson, Woodrow, *xiii*, 34–35, 39, 40, 41,
44, 85, 229, 237, 287, 288, 307, 309,
313, 371, 380
criticism of, 35
war declared by, *xiii*, 36, 39
Winter, Denis, 150
Winton, Roy, 158
wire cutters, 118, 122, 125–26
Wirkung Gericht, 26–27, 33
Without Censor (Johnson), 321–22
Wobber, Harold, 374
Wood, Leonard, 40, 77
World War I, xi, 5, 12, 13, 20, 52, 294–95,
306, 367
casualties in, 5, 24, 31, 33, 34, 143–44,
145, 155, 177, 191, 197, 209, 218,
220, 226, 227, 230, 231, 237, *265*,
369, 387
cautionary tales from Civil War and,
306
defensive weapons in, 25
end of, 301
as first mechanized conflict, *215*
lectures on, 325
Meuse-Argonne Offensive in, *see*
Meuse-Argonne Offensive
US declaration of war and, *xiii*, 36, 39,
78, 80, 85, 172, 288, 309, 381
US entry into, 25, 34–35, 36, 75
US national conscription in, 39
warfare tactics in, 91–92
see also specific attacks
World War II, 38, 342, 360, *365*, 371, 375,
380, 382, 384, 386, 388
Wright, Samuel O., 7–8, 9, 10–11, 17

York, Alvin, 243

Zimmermann, Arthur, 36

ABOUT THE AUTHOR

An educator and a writer with a lifelong fascination for military history, **William Walker** grew up in Knoxville, Tennessee, exploring Civil War forts surrounding the city and interviewing veterans of foreign wars. After a forty-year career in college teaching and administration, he returned to his first love to investigate a pivotal event in America's longest and bloodiest battle—World War I's Meuse-Argonne Offensive.

After completing a BA with high honors and an MA in English at the University of Virginia, Walker undertook further graduate studies at Tulane University. He taught at the University of New Orleans and Lamar University in Beaumont, Texas. Moving from the classroom to academic administration, he served as associate vice president for public affairs at Virginia Tech, Gettysburg College, and the College of William and Mary in Williamsburg, Virginia.

The author lectures on World War I, leads battlefield tours, and teaches a course on the conflict as part of the lifelong learning program of the University of Virginia. Walker and his wife, Jan, live in Staunton, Virginia.

To examine additional photographs and maps, visit the website betrayalww1.com.